Christianities in th ⸻,
1500–1800

Series Editors

Professor Crawford Gribben,
Queen's University Belfast, UK

Dr R. Scott Spurlock,
University of Glasgow, UK

Building upon the recent recovery of interest in religion in the early modern trans-Atlantic world, this series offers fresh, lively and interdisciplinary perspectives on the broad view of its subject. Books in the series will work strategically and systematically to address major but understudied or overly simplified themes in the religious and cultural history of the early modern trans-Atlantic.

More information about this series at
http://www.springer.com/series/14892

Lady Mico's almshouses near St Dunstan's church, Stepney (nineteenth-century watercolour by an unknown artist); reproduced by courtesy of the Mercers' Company.

Ariel Hessayon
Editor

Jane Lead and her Transnational Legacy

palgrave
macmillan

Editor
Ariel Hessayon
Department of History
Goldsmiths, University of London
London, United Kingdom

Christianities in the Trans-Atlantic World, 1500–1800
ISBN 978-1-137-39613-6 (hardcover)   ISBN 978-1-137-39614-3   (eBook)
ISBN 978-1-349-67943-0 (softcover)
DOI 10.1057/978-1-137-39614-3

Library of Congress Control Number: 2016944988

This Palgrave Macmillan imprint is published by Springer Nature
The registered company is Macmillan Publishers Ltd. London

To the Panacea Charitable Trust

ACKNOWLEDGEMENTS

This volume emerged from the conference 'Blessed Virago: The International Mysticism of Jane Lead' held at the Hoxton Hotel, London on 8 September 2012. I am grateful to the trustees of the Panacea Charitable Trust for their generous financial support in hosting this event. Additional gratitude is due to the Panacea Charitable Trust, which has very generously supported my larger research project on the prophetic thought and legacies of Jacob Boehme. Thanks also to Jade Moulds and the rest of the staff at Palgrave Macmillan for their courtesy, kindness and efficiency. Finally, of course, thank you to the contributors for their unstinting cooperation and unfailing patience.

CONTENTS

7 The Restitution of 'Adam's Angelical and Paradisiacal
Body': Jane Lead's Metaphor of Rebirth and Mystical
Marriage   143
Stefania Salvadori

8 Mystical Divinity in the Manuscript Writings of Jane
Lead and Anne Bathurst   167
Sarah Apetrei

9 'God's Strange Providence': Jane Lead in
the Correspondence of Johann Georg Gichtel   187
Lucinda Martin

10 Philadelphia Resurrected: Celebrating the Union
Act (1707) from Irenic to Scatological Eschatology   213
Lionel Laborie

11 Jane Lead's Prophetic Afterlife in the Nineteenth-Century
English Atlantic   241
Philip Lockley

12 'A Prophecy Out of the Past': Contrasting
Treatments of Jane Lead Among Two North American
Twentieth-Century Millenarian Movements: Mary's
City of David and the Latter Rain   267
Bridget M. Jacobs

General Index   291

Index of Places   301

NOTES ON THE CONTRIBUTORS

Sarah Apetrei is Departmental Lecturer in Ecclesiastical History at the University of Oxford. She is the author of *Women, Feminism and Religion in Early Enlightenment England* (2010), and has co-edited collections of essays on prophecy and mysticism in seventeenth-century England, and on the reception of Jacob Boehme. She is currently working on a book dealing with the place of mystical theology in seventeenth-century British religion.

Amanda L. Capern is a Senior Lecturer in History at the University of Hull. She is a specialist on early-modern English women's history, publishing widely in this area including *The Historical Study of Women: England 1500–1700* (Palgrave, 2008; 2010). She is co-editor of Palgrave's *Gender and History* book series and was sub-editor on the Chawton House Library edition of Mary Hays' *Female Biography* (2013–14).

Ariel Hessayon is a Senior Lecturer in the Department of History at Goldsmiths, University of London. He is the author of *'Gold tried in the fire'. The prophet Theaurau John Tany and the English Revolution* (2007) and has co-edited several collections of essays. He has also written extensively on a variety of early modern topics: antiscripturism, book burning, communism, environmentalism, esotericism, extra-canonical texts, heresy, crypto-Jews, Judaizing, millenarianism, mysticism, prophecy and religious radicalism.

Bridget M. Jacobs is a PhD candidate in English literature at the University of Louisiana at Lafayette whose research interests focus on blending print culture and reader-response approaches to early modern religious literature. Jacobs was a 2012 winner of the Andrew W. Mellon Foundation funded Central New York Humanities Corridor grant for her North American archival work on Jane Lead.

Warren Johnston is an Associate Professor in the Department of History and Philosophy at Algoma University in Ontario, Canada. He has published a number of peer-reviewed articles and chapters on early modern English apocalyptic ideas. His book *Revelation Restored: The Apocalypse in Later Seventeenth-Century England* explains the importance of apocalyptic belief to political thought and culture during the Restoration. His current research project examines *National Thanksgivings and Identity in Britain* from the late seventeenth century to the end of the Napoleonic wars.

Lionel Laborie is a visiting researcher at Goldsmiths, University of London. His work concentrates on religious toleration and dissent in early modern Europe, with a particular interest in the Camisard rebellion (1702–1710) and its international legacy in the Protestant world. He is the author of *Enlightening Enthusiasm: Prophecy and Religious Experience in Early Eighteenth-Century England* (2015).

Philip Lockley wrote his chapter in this volume while British Academy Postdoctoral Fellow in the Faculty of Theology and Religion, University of Oxford. He is the author of *Visionary Religion and Radicalism in Early Industrial England: from Southcott to Socialism* (2013) and editor of *Protestant Communalism in the Trans-Atlantic World, 1650–1850* (Palgrave Macmillan, 2016). He is now an ordinand in the Church of England at Cranmer Hall, Durham University.

Lucinda Martin holds a position at the Gotha Research Centre of the University of Erfurt, Germany, where she is the principal investigator for a project funded by the German Research Council on the 'Philadelphians'. Her publications have concentrated on religion as an agent for change in the Early Modern era.

Stefania Salvadori is a Research Fellow at the Herzog August Bibliothek—Wolfenbüttel, where she is working on the inventory of the correspondence of Johann Valentin Andreae. Her publications include a monograph on Sebastian Castellio and the history of tolerance (2009), editions of works of Erasmus (2011), of pietistic theological treatises (2014), and of Melanchthon's *Loci* (forthcoming, 2016), as well as essays on religious and political dissent in early modern Europe.

LIST OF ABBREVIATIONS

BL	British Library, London
Bodl.	Bodleian Library, Oxford
Chetham's	Chetham's Library, Manchester
CJ	*Journals of the House of Commons* (34 vols, 1742–92)
CSPD	*Calendar of State Papers, Domestic*
CUL	Cambridge University Library
DWL	Dr Williams's Library, London
FbG	Forschungsbibliothek Gotha
FHL	Friends House Library, London
G & C	Gonville & Caius College, Cambridge
GL	Guildhall Library, London
LJ	*Journals of the House of Lords* (64 vols., 1767–1830)
LMA	London Metropolitan Archives
LPL	Lambeth Palace Library, London
Norfolk R.O.	Norfolk Record Office, Norwich
ODNB	*Oxford Dictionary of National Biography*
Thune, *Behmenists*	Nils Thune, *The Behmenists and the Philadelphians: A Contribution to the Study of English Mysticism in the 17th and 18th Centuries*, trans. G.E. Björk (Uppsala: Almquist and Wiksells, 1948)
TNA: PRO	The National Archives: Public Record Office
Walton, *Notes*	Christopher Walton, *Notes and Materials for an adequate Biography of the celebrated divine and theosopher, William Law* (London: privately printed, 1854)

TABLES

CHAPTER 1

Introduction: Jane Lead's Legacy in Perspective

Ariel Hessayon

Jane Lead (pronounced Leed or Leeds by contemporaries) and sometimes written with a final 'e' (especially in printed German translations of her works) was among the most prolific published female authors of the long eighteenth century.[1] More than a dozen different printed titles bearing Lead's name, with one consisting of multiple volumes, were originally issued in English between 1681 and 1702.[2] Her final work 'The Resurrection of Life' (1703) was issued posthumously in German translation and has recently been re-translated into English.[3] Moreover, during Lead's lifetime four of her works appeared in a second edition, while from 1694 several writings were also published in translation at Amsterdam—primarily in German, with two rendered into Dutch as well.[4] In addition to these languages one tract was translated into Swedish, most likely from the German version, although this remained in manuscript.[5] Besides being the author of extensive spiritual diaries, theological treatises, epistles and some verse, during the last decade of her 80-year life Lead became the centre of an extensive correspondence network stretching from Pennsylvania to the Electorate of Saxony. Yet as her son-in-law and amanuensis Francis Lee conceded, outside a small community of believers Lead's writings were largely ignored in her own country. Instead they enjoyed a widespread if

A. Hessayon (✉)
Department of History, Goldsmiths,
University of London, London, UK

© The Editor(s) (if applicable) and The Author(s) 2016
A. Hessayon (ed.), *Jane Lead and her Transnational Legacy*,
DOI 10.1057/978-1-137-39614-3_1

1

mixed continental reception among an audience of assorted Spiritualists, Behmenists and Pietists—not to mention occasional curious readers, such as Gottfried Wilhelm Leibniz.[6]

Although the devotional writer William Law (1686–1761) initially claimed to know little of Lead, within a few years he was recounting the Philadelphians' thirst for 'visions, openings and revelations &c.' in private correspondence. Since Law later transcribed many of Francis Lee's manuscripts he doubtless learned much there concerning Lead.[7] Other eighteenth-century figures familiar with Lead's name are largely identifiable through ownership inscriptions in printed English editions of her writings. These included a Mr. Portales, most likely Charles Portales (1676–1763), an early supporter of the French Prophets, and the Methodist preacher and writer Cornelius Cayley (1727–1779).[8] The latter may have been drawn to Lead because of an interest in the doctrine of the universal restoration of all humanity. Indeed, Cayley's reading extended to Richard Coppin (*fl.*1646–*fl.*1659), who like Lead was incorporated within a catalogue of authors advocating the possibility of universal redemption.[9] Other owners of works by both Lead and Coppin included the publisher Henri Lion,[10] the bookseller John Denis the elder (*c.*1735–1785),[11] and the Alsatian artist Philippe Jacques de Loutherbourg (1740–1812).[12] It should be noted that after obtaining his copy of one of Lead's books Denis published the third edition of *The Restoration of All Things* (1779), a defence of universal salvation by the nonconformist minister Jeremiah White, to which Denis added a preface. Furthermore, in partnership with his son and namesake Denis sold several volumes in English and French by the polymath and mystic Emanuel Swedenborg. Significantly, several people attracted to Swedenborg's teachings were also readers of Lead. These included de Loutherbourg, an elected member of the Royal Academy, who dated two of the five known copies of Lead's works in his possession '1796'; de Loutherbourg's associate and self-described 'Lover of the Lamb of God', Mary Pratt; the former vegetarian turned Methodist Ralph Mather (1750?–1803); the clergyman John Clowes (1743–1831); the Huguenot surgeon and pharmacist Benedict Chastanier (*c.*1739–*c.*1818); and the surgeon and apothecary Henry Peckitt (1734?–1808), who possessed a manuscript account of Lead's last hours.[13] Some owners, however, have proved more difficult to trace: A. Bremner (Strand, 1782), Thomas Kane (9 June 1772), and an Alexander Leslie of Aberdeen (no date).[14]

From 1771 to 1782 some of Lead's works had been advertised for sale in book catalogues issued by George Wagstaff.[15] But as the nineteenth century progressed they seem to have become rarer, prompting a handful of reprints: one perhaps marking the centenary of her death, another issued with the approval of Zion Ward and his Southcottian followers.[16] Hence rather than purchasing books between 1825 and 1834 a certain John Phillips transcribed extracts from Lead's printed English writings together with an English re-translation of a German account of her last hours. In addition, Phillips made excerpts from books held in the British Museum by the Behmenists John Pordage and Quirinus Kuhlmann. Phillips's interest in Lead was shared by a Miss Peacock and Samuel Jackson, the English translator of Johann Heinrich Jung [Heinrich Stilling].[17] Eventually Phillips's transcripts were acquired by the jeweller and goldsmith Christopher Walton (1809–1877), an undeservedly neglected figure who contributed substantially to the demise of his own legacy through an unfortunate mix of humourlessness, appalling inter-personal skills and inability to adequately organise his immensely rich manuscript and rare book collections.[18] By about 1871 Walton owned copies of several printed titles by Lead together with important manuscript accounts.[19] Yet Walton, himself a Methodist, judged Lead harshly, remarking:

> It would not, perhaps, be difficult to dissect Mrs. Lead's character, and demonstrate the philosophy of her prophetic assumptions, from a consideration of the constitution of her mind, the character of the piety of the Cromwell-Muggletonian-fanatic days in which she lived, her intricate study of Behmen's works ... and the popular spiritual topics of her age.

Acknowledging that she was a woman of 'great piety' and not wishing to ridicule her writings, a disappointed Walton still complained that Lead, the 'chief heroine' of the Philadelphian Society, had buried her profound spiritual experiences in 'a huge mass of parabolicalism and idiocratic deformity'.[20]

A few nineteenth-century commentators were more charitable. One reckoned Lead a woman of 'elevated and enthusiastic piety' while others suggested that the visions and spiritual experiences of this 'most singular' if then lesser-known English disciple of Boehme had influenced Swedenborg's theological system.[21] Nonetheless, Lead's prophetic pretensions and obscure style were derided as a 'lamentable example of bad English' and 'confusion of thought', amounting to nothing more than a 'wonderful concatenation of folly' and 'strange farrago of nonsense'.[22] This unflattering verdict, pronounced by Walton's correspondent the clergyman and translator Robert Charles Jenkins (1816–1896), brings to mind the Quaker historian Rufus Jones (1863–1948) who felt Lead was too emotional, criticising her 'ungrammatical' language and 'involved style', which was 'full of overwrought and fanciful imagination'.[23] Similarly, the peace activist Stephen Hobhouse (1881–1961) dismissed Pordage and Lead as 'Christians of a dangerously psychic type' whose 'visionary eccentricities and speculations' resulted in 'confused writings'.[24] Even the Anglo-Catholic writer Evelyn Underhill (1875–1941) thought Lead and the Philadelphians exhibited mysticism 'in its least balanced aspect mingled with mediumistic phenomena, wild symbolic visions, and apocalyptic prophecies'.[25]

Such criticism was not new. It went back to an early eighteenth-century life of Lead in Latin by Johann Wolfgang Jaeger, a German professor of theology hostile to mysticism and chiliasm.[26] Jaeger was doubtless responding to the popularity of Philadelphian texts within radical Pietist circles and the legacy of that appeal saw greater interest in Lead's writings among German rather than English speakers—at least until the mid-1970s. Most notable in this regard were studies by C.W.H. Hochhuth and especially the Swedish scholar Nils Thune, whose work remains valuable despite its then fashionable preoccupation with applying psychology to the study of religion.[27] Also noteworthy was the Viennese psychoanalyst Herbert Silberer's pioneering *Probleme der Mystik und ihrer Symbolik* (1914) which inspired Carl Jung's *Psychology and Alchemy* (1944).[28]

Although Lead was discussed during the 1960s within the context of monographs focusing on the reception of Boehme's thought and the doctrine of universal salvation,[29] it was only with a second-wave of feminism that she began to be studied in her own right by North American scholars such as Catherine Smith and Joanne Sperle. Indeed, Smith's earlier work drew attention to supposed similarities between feminist theory and mystic philosophy, positioning Lead within a tradition stretching from the Eleusinian mysteries through the Protestant Reformation to present-day feminism.[30] In the wake of Second Wave Feminism it is unsurprising that within the last 20 years Lead's reputation has undergone a remarkable ascent from the depths of disdain to the peaks of veneration. So much so, that she is now lauded as an example of 'female genius' and regarded by her most recent biographer, Julie Hirst, as the most important female religious leader in late seventeenth-century England.[31]

* * *

Including this brief survey of Lead's legacy there are 12 chapters in this volume. The next focuses on the period of Lead's life before she became a widow in 1670 and suggests that Lead was far more radical than has been supposed. Making use of a great many archival discoveries it provides mainly circumstantial but nonetheless cumulatively overwhelming evidence that Lead's relatively well-known autobiography (printed in German in 1696) conceals almost as much as it reveals. Constructed to reassure its intended audience of continental Spiritualists, Behmenists and Pietists of Lead's upright character, respectable social status and divinely bestowed gifts this so-called 'Life of the Author' adopted a similar strategy to that observable in a number of Philadelphian publications which masked private heterodox beliefs and rituals with public professions of irenic conformity. Accordingly key names, activities and teachings were omitted from Lead's German biography because in the political, military and religious contexts of the mid-1690s detailing past associations would have damaged Lead's reputation among her heterogeneous readership.

Chapter three covers the period from 1670 to 1695—that is from the beginning of Lead's widowhood until she went blind. Here the focus is as much on extensive and overlapping domestic and continental networks of assorted millenarians, prophets, theosophists and devotees of mystic and spiritualist authors generally as on Lead herself. It also traces an evolution of Lead's thought as she came under successive influences and began to develop her own distinctive beliefs. This was a religious journey with staging posts: an initial Calvinist obsession with sin and predestination wedded to a conventional Protestant understanding of the coming apocalypse; then the introduction of Jacob Boehme's teachings and accompanying visions of a female personification of divine wisdom; finally, the adoption, albeit with inconsistencies, of the doctrine of the universal restoration of all humanity. It was the last, together with Lead's apparent dependence upon visions and revelations, that repulsed certain former admirers of her writings, turning them into some of Lead's most vehement critics. The fourth chapter covers the period from 1696 to 1704, that is from Lead's first published message to the Philadelphian Society until her death and burial. It outlines how Lead's little band of supporters intended to warn and prepare prospective believers of the coming Philadelphian age through a flurry of publications. Yet this coordinated publicity campaign abruptly fractured the Philadelphians' precursor society, which hitherto had negotiated a path between secrecy and openness. Consequently, only the minority who favoured a public testimony owned the Philadelphian name. Wanting to expose her visions and teachings to public view Lead was given the opportunity to do so through a succession of mainly male patrons and amanuenses. Accordingly, she became synonymous with the Philadelphian Society. At the same time Lead's principle supporters set about fashioning an image of irenic conformity and social standing for the Philadelphians at large. Hostile observers, however, readily compared Philadelphians with Quakers. Some even incorporated them within a catalogue of innumerable sects or else grouped them with foreign Quietists and Pietists. More damaging still was the allegation that Lead envisaged herself as the woman clothed with the sun (Revelation 12:1), indeed as the grandmother of a new Christ.

In chapter five, 'Jane Lead and the Tradition of Puritan Pastoral Theology', Amanda Capern argues that Lead and the Philadelphians were part of a continuous, evolutionary tradition of transatlantic radical Calvinist Protestantism. Lead's works are compared with those of Eleanor Davies to suggest that the pastoral imperative of puritan and dissenting Protestant nonconformity led to emphasis on the ideas of John the Baptist, the Noahic covenant and the operation of the Holy Spirit in salvation. Lead's household worship and feminine spirituality took millenarian thinking towards a new spatial and sensate imagining of the last days. Lead's eschatology also moved beyond Behmenism to foreshadow ideas about the invisible church later seen in Jane Wardley, Ann Lee and the Shakers. In Capern's view, Lead was thus crucial in the shift from a logocentric to an experiential Calvinist puritanism. Chapter six by Warren Johnston examines Lead's apocalyptic thought, analysing her application of scriptural prophecies, her own prophesying on the coming of the millennial kingdom, and her belief in her privileged place alongside biblical prophets and visionaries. It describes how Lead's understanding of the Book of Revelation concentrated on a mystical interpretation that saw the fulfilment of apocalyptic prophecies playing out within individual believers. Though focusing largely on Lead's thought in its own right, the chapter also compares her ideas to more standard and widely accepted historicist interpretations of apocalyptic prophecies that had developed in England throughout the early modern period and into the Restoration. This demonstrates how her thought diverged from prevailing English apocalyptic ideas of the late seventeenth century.

The seventh chapter by Stefania Salvadori examines Lead's teaching of twofold corporality, arguing that it was a major influence on German radical Pietism. Focusing on Lead's interpretation of Boehme's work and reading of the Genesis story, this chapter discusses her teaching concerning the four-stage process of spiritual growth that leads to both physical and spiritual transfiguration. As well as describing the mystical death and resurrection of the new Adam in believers' souls, Salvadori explores the role of the heavenly Wisdom and of the Bridegroom Christ in preparing and completing the restitution of the paradisiacal perfect body, showing how Lead tried to combine spiritual regeneration and gradual refinement of the new magical body with the corporal earthly life. Chapter eight, 'Mystical Divinity in the Manuscript Writings of Jane Lead and Anne Bathurst' by Sarah Apetrei brings to light two previously unknown manuscripts, situating them within the broader difficulties that printing mystical works could cause female prophets and visionaries. Positioning her discussion within recent work on scribal publication as an alternative to print publication, and in particular the challenges that female authors faced, Apetrei locates Lead's and Bathurst's manuscript writings within a context extending to works by, among others, the nun Gertrude More, the prophetess Grace Cary and the visionary Antoinette Bourignon. Apetrei also provides transcriptions of her manuscript discoveries in two appendices that will be helpful to future researchers.

In chapter nine Lucinda Martin offers a corrective to previous discussions of the way in which Lead's writings reached German Pietist circles. Most accounts of Lead's reception on the continent begin with one of her manuscripts falling into the hands of the radical Pietists Johanna Eleonora and Johann Wilhelm Petersen in 1695. Yet Martin demonstrates not only that Johann Georg Gichtel distributed Lead's texts in manuscript before the Petersens, but also that Gichtel's correspondence contributed to Lead's thought and the production of certain texts. She argues that Lead's influence began much earlier and was more multilayered than has been assumed, since her thought was transformed by a series of mediators, including Gichtel, the Petersens and others. In addition, Martin explores the nature of international correspondence networks among nonconformists and millenarians, showing how shared tenets were debated and developed in the discursive space of these epistolary networks. Finally, the chapter traces the evolution of the key Philadelphian doctrine of universal salvation to discussions within such networks, disputing the notion of a one-way knowledge transfer from England to Germany.

Chapter ten by Lionel Laborie is entitled 'Philadelphia Resurrected: Celebrating the Union Act from Irenic to Scatological Eschatology'. This chapter examines the state of the Philadelphian Society in the aftermath of Lead's death in 1704. It challenges the centrality of her matriarchal authority and portrays her instead as a controversial, divisive figure among the Philadelphians, whose Society had already collapsed by the time of her death. Laborie shows how the arrival of the Camisards in London in 1706 gave the Philadelphian Society a second life, as both movements merged into the 'French Prophets' the following year in celebration of the Union Act. Yet if the Prophets became notorious for their spiritual performances, he argues that this owed more to the Philadelphians' influence among them than to their actual French followers. Overall, he concludes that the Philadelphians proved far more radical than hitherto acknowledged and that Lead's English legacy was almost non-existent.

In chapter eleven Philip Lockley looks at Lead's prophetic afterlife among several transatlantic traditions of millennial religion in the nineteenth century, most notably Shakers, Mormons and Southcottians (the followers of Joanna Southcott). He shows that Shaker and Mormon interest in Lead was later than previously assumed, while Southcottians were more consistently linked to the transatlantic influence of Lead's prophetic writings. Sifting printed records and scattered sources, this chapter traces how Lead's prophecies were compared to Southcott's writings before 1814, and later used by Southcottian followers of Zion Ward and James Jezreel. Southcottian links are also shown to lie behind notice of Lead within Transcendentalist literary circles on either side of the Atlantic. The twelfth and last chapter by Bridget Jacobs examines contrasting treatments of Lead among two North American twentieth-century millenarian movements. Jacobs notes that throughout the nineteenth and into the early twentieth century Lead had faded into near-obscurity in the English-speaking world. However, several waves of Lead reprints still circulated within millenarian circles. Two notable North American groups encountered these texts and incorporated them into their own theologies and writings. Mary's City of David, an American Southcottian communal group, acquired and read closely most of Lead's extant works, eventually embedding them into their print canon. The Latter Rain movement, a mid-twentieth century offshoot of Pentecostalism, instead constructed a masculinised version of Lead whose anonymous 'prophecy out of the past' was reworked into a voice purportedly coming directly from God that proclaimed the imminent reign of the Latter Rain over earth.

NOTES

1. Mercers' Company (London), Acts of Court, 1700–1707, fol. 101r; TNA: PRO, Prob 11/357 fol. 122r; LPL, MS 1048a, fol. 150; Bodl., MS Rawlinson D 832 fol. 47v; Bodl., MS Rawlinson D 833 fols. 66r, 89r; DWL, MS 186.18 (1), p. 15.
2. A. Hessayon, 'A census of Jane Lead's writings' (forthcoming).
3. Bodl., MS Rawlinson D 833 fol. 87r; Jane Lead, *Die Auferstehung des Lebens* (Amsterdam: Wetstein, 1705); http://www.passtheword.org/jane-lead/resurrection.htm.
4. János Bruckner, *A Bibliographical catalogue of Seventeenth-Century German books published in Holland* (The Hague and Paris: Mouton, 1971), pp. 508, 509–10, 511–14, 515–17, 518–19, 523–24; Edgar Mckenzie, *A Catalog of British Devotional and Religious Books in German Translation from the Reformation to 1750* (Berlin: W. de Gruyter, 1997), pp. 280–86; Cornelius Schoneveld, *Intertraffic of the Mind: studies in seventeenth-century Anglo-Dutch translation with a checklist of books translated from English into Dutch, 1600–1700* (Leiden: E.J. Brill, 1983), p. 213.
5. Thune, *Behmenists*, pp. 150–51.
6. *Gottfried Wilhelm Leibniz sämtliche schriften und briefe. Erste Reihe. Allgemeiner Politischer und Historischer Briefwechsel*, vol. 17 (2001), pp. 287, 313, 476, 570–71; vol. 18 (2005), p. 271; vol. 21 (2012), p. 32.
7. Joseph Trapp, *A reply to Mr. Law's Earnest and Serious Answer* (London: L. Gilliver, 1741), p. 121; William Law, *The Works of the Reverend William Law, M.A.* (1762; reprinted, 9 vols., London: G. Moreton, 1893), vol. 6, p. 201; Walton, *Notes*, pp. 45–46 n.; Isabel Rivers, 'Law, William (1686–1761)', *ODNB*.
8. DWL, C.4.29; BL, 4375.de.11(2); William Andrews Clark Memorial Library, BV 5091.R4 L4*.
9. Cayley contributed the preface to a reprint of Richard Coppin's *The advancement of all things in Christ* (London: Henry Fenwick [1763]); see also, Thomas Whittemore, *The Modern History of Universalism, from the era of the Reformation to the present time* (Boston, 1830), pp. 112–14.
10. DWL, C.4.29; University of Illinois Library, X 252 C79S1763.
11. *Denis's catalogue of ancient and modern books, for 1787* (1787), p. 38 no. 930, p. 96 nos. 2748, 2749, p. 114 no. 3276, p. 241 no. 7574; BL, 4412.I.25; Bodl., Antiq.e.E 34(2).
12. BL, 4139.bbb.52(1); BL, 4105.de.2(1); BL, 4378.a.32; BL, 4412.I.25; BL, 3185.I.22(1); BL, 4409.de.32.
13. E.P. Thompson, *Witness against the beast: William Blake and the Moral Law* (Cambridge: CUP, 1994), pp. 43–44; A. Hessayon, 'Jacob Boehme, Emanuel Swedenborg and their readers', in Stephen McNeilly (ed.),

Philosophy, literature, mysticism. An anthology of essays on the thought and influence of Emanuel Swedenborg (London: The Swedenborg Society, 2013), pp. 337–84.

14. BL, 3186.bb.50; BL, Cup.403.s.27(1).
15. *Wagstaff's new catalogue of rare old books* (1771), p. 15 nos. 479, 480, p. 16 no. 534, p. 17 no. 552; *Wagstaff's winter catalogue of rare old books* (1774), p. 19 nos. 446, 447, p. 21 no. 523; *Wagstaff's new catalogue of rare old books* (1782), p. 9 no. 269.
16. John Denley, *A catalogue of a miscellaneous collection of books* (London: E. & J. Thomas, [1834?]), p. 6; Philip Lockley, 'Jane Lead's prophetic afterlife in the nineteenth-century English Atlantic' (this volume).
17. DWL, B.6.1 (6, 7, 8, 9); DWL, MS 186.18 (1), pp. 77–91.
18. David L. Wykes, 'Walton, Christopher (1809–1877)', *ODNB*.
19. DWL, C.4.29; DWL, C.5.28; DWL, C.5.29; DWL, MS 186.18 (1, 2, 3).
20. Walton, *Notes*, pp. 141, 148.
21. C. Barry, 'The English Mystics: Jane Lead', *Notes & Queries*, 2nd series, 1 (1856), p. 93; A. Roffe, 'Jane Lead and Swedenborg', *Notes & Queries*, 2nd series, 2 (1856), pp. 470–71; 'The Philadelphian Society—Mrs. Jane Lead', *The Dawn* (1 December 1862), pp. 236–42; 'Spiritualism in Biography:- John Pordage: Jane Lead: the Countess of Asseburgh', *The Spiritual Magazine*, 4:5 (May, 1863), pp. 199–204.
22. [R.C. Jenkins], 'Miracles, Visions, and Revelations, Mediaeval and Modern', *British Quarterly Review*, 58 (1873), p. 183.
23. Rufus Jones, *Spiritual Reformers in the 16th and 17th Centuries* (1914; reprinted, Gloucester, MA: Peter Smith, 1971), p. 230. Jones was echoing Charlotte Fell Smith's entry on Lead in the *Dictionary of National Biography* published in 1892.
24. S. Hobhouse, 'Fides et Ratio. The book which introduced Jacob Boehme to William Law', *Journal of Theological Studies*, 36 (1936), pp. 357–58.
25. Evelyn Underhill, *Mysticism. The Nature and Development of Spiritual Consciousness* (1911; 12th edn., 1930, reprinted, Oxford: Oneworld, 1993), p. 470; cf. C.E. Whiting, *Studies in English Puritanism from the Restoration to the Revolution, 1660–1688* (London: Macmillan Company, 1931), pp. 298–308.
26. Johann Wolfgang Jaeger, *Dissertatio historico-theologica, de Johannæ Leadæ Anglo-Britan. Vita* (Tübingen, 1712).
27. C.W.H. Hochhuth, 'Geschichte und Entwicklung der philadelphischen Gemeinden, I: Jane Leade und die philadelphische Gemeinde in England', *Zeitschrift für die historische Theologie*, 35 (1865), pp. 171–290; Thune, *Behmenists*; see also, Joseph Ennemoser, *The History of Magic*, trans. William Howitt (2 vols., London: Henry Bohn, 1854), vol. 2, p. 224; Wilhelm Struck, *Der Einfluss Jakob Boehmes auf die Englische Literatur des 17. Jahrhunderts* (Berlin, 1936), pp. 127–42.

28. Herbert Silberer, *Problems of Mysticism and its Symbolism*, trans. Smith Ely Jelliffe (1917; reprinted New York, 1970), pp. 379–407; cf. Carl Jung, *The Practice of Psychotherapy*, trans. R.F.C. Hull in *Collected Works of C.G. Jung: The First Complete Edition*, eds. Sir Herbert Read, Michael Fordham and Gerhard Adler (20 vols., London & New York: Routledge, 2014), vol. 16, pp. 296–302 [506–18].

29. Serge Hutin, *Les Disciples Anglais de Jacob Boehme aux XVIIe et XVIIIe siècles* (Paris, 1960), pp. 89–91, 96, 105–19; Desirée Hirst, *Hidden Riches: Traditional Symbolism from the Renaissance to Blake* (New York: Eyre & Spottiswoode, 1964), pp. 107–08, 171–72; Daniel Walker, *The Decline of Hell. Seventeenth-Century Discussions of Eternal Torment* (London: Routledge & Kegan Paul, 1964), pp. 218–30.

30. C.F. Smith, 'Mysticism and Feminism: Jacob Boehme and Jane Lead', in Dana Hiller and Robin Ann Sheets (eds.), *Women and Men: The Consequences of Power* (University of Cincinnati, 1977), pp. 398–408; C.F. Smith, 'Jane Lead: Mysticism and the Woman Cloathed with the Sun', in Sandra Gilbert and Susan Gubar (eds.), *Shakespeare's Sisters: Feminist Essays on Woman Poets* (Bloomington, IN, 1979), pp. 3–18 (at p. 17); C.F. Smith, 'Jane Lead: The Feminist Mind and Art of a Seventeenth Century Protestant Mystic', in Rosemary Ruether and Eleanor McLaughlin (eds.), *Women of Spirit: Female Leadership in Jewish and Christian Traditions* (New York: Simon and Schuster, 1979), pp. 184–203; C.F. Smith, 'A Note on Jane Lead with selections from her writings', *Studia Mystica*, 3:4 (1980), pp. 79–82; C.F. Smith, 'Jane Lead's Wisdom: Women and Prophecy in Seventeenth-Century England', in Jan Wojcik and Raymond-Jean Frontain (eds.), *Poetic Prophecy in Western Literature* (Cranbury, NJ, 1984), pp. 55–63; Joanne Sperle, 'God's healing angel: A biography of Jane Ward Lead', unpublished Kent State University Ph.D., 1985.

31. E. Keizer, 'Jane Lead and the Philadelphian Society: connections with Anne Conway and the Quakers', *Guilford Review*, 23 (1986), pp. 71–89; Brian Gibbons, *Gender in Mystical and Occult Thought: Behmenism and its Development in England* (Cambridge: CUP, 1996), pp. 143–52; Paula McDowell, *The Women of Grub Street: Press, Politics, and Gender in the London Literary Marketplace 1678–1730* (Oxford: OUP, 1998), pp. 167–79; Arthur Versluis, *Wisdom's Children: A Christian Esoteric Tradition* (Albany, NY: SUNY, 1999), pp. 57–77; B.S. Travitsky, 'Juxtaposing genders: Jane Lead and John Milton', in Susanne Woods and Margaret Hannay (eds.), *Teaching Tudor and Stuart Women Writers* (New York: MLA, 2000), pp. 243–47; C.F. Smith, 'Remembering the Rhetorics of Women. The Case of Jane Lead', in Laura Gray-Rosendale and Sibylle Gruber (eds.), *Alternative Rhetorics: Challenges to the Rhetorical Tradition* (Albany, NY: SUNY, 2001), pp. 17–32; P. McDowell, 'Enlightenment Enthusiasms

and the Spectacular Failure of the Philadelphian Society', *Eighteenth-Century Studies*, 35:4 (2002), pp. 515–33; Sylvia Bowerbank, *Speaking for Nature: Women and Ecologies of Early Modern England* (Baltimore, MD: John Hopkins University Press, 2004), pp. 106–32; A. Kouffman, 'Reflections on the Sacred: The mystical diaries of Jane Lead and Ann Bathurst', in Kristina Groover (ed.), *Things of the Spirit: Women Writers Constructing Spirituality* (Notre Dame, IN, 2004), pp. 90–107; D.F. Durnbaugh, 'Jane Ward Leade (1624–1704) and the Philadelphians', in Carter Lindberg (ed.), *The Pietist Theologians. An Introduction to Theology in the Seventeenth and Eighteenth Centuries* (Oxford: Blackwell, 2005), pp. 128–46; T. Kemp, '"Here must a beheading go before": The Antirational Androgynist Theosophy of Jane Lead's *Revelation of Revelations*', *Clio*, 34:3 (2005), pp. 251–75; Julie Hirst, *Jane Leade: Biography of a Seventeenth-Century Mystic* (Aldershot: Ashgate, 2005); A. Scott-Douglass, 'Self-Crowned Laureatesses: The examples of Margaret Cavendish and Jane Lead', in Pilar Cuder-Domínguez and Zenón Luis-Martínez (eds.), *The Female Wits: Women and Gender in Restoration Literature and Culture* (Huelva, 2006), pp. 65–78; Sarah Apetrei, *Women, Feminism and Religion in Early Enlightenment England* (Cambridge: CUP, 2010), pp. 187–98, 200–04, 225–29, 231–34, 240–41, 246, 248–49, 270–71; A. Jasper, 'Female Genius: Jane Leade (1624–1704)', in Heather Walton (ed.), *Literature and Theology: New Interdisciplinary Spaces* (Aldershot: Ashgate, 2011), pp. 81–97; N. Smith, 'Pregnant Dreams in Early Modern Europe: The Philadelphian Example', in Johanna Harris and Elizabeth Scott-Baumann (eds.), *The Intellectual Culture of Puritan Women, 1558–1680* (Winchester: Palgrave Macmillan, 2011), pp. 190–201.

CHAPTER 2

Lead's Life and Times (Part One): Before Widowhood

Ariel Hessayon

There have been several secondary accounts of Lead's life. The earliest was published eight years after her death in Latin as *Dissertatio historico-theologica, de Johanna Leada Anglo-Britan* by Johann Wolfgang Jaeger (1647–1720), chancellor of Tübingen University. This was subsequently twice reprinted, first with an appended discussion of Lead's contemporary the French mystic Madame Guyon (1648–1717), then as a section of the second volume of Jaeger's monumental *Ecclesiastical History* where he reviewed the profusion of new-spawned sects as part of a broader attack on mysticism and chiliasm.[1] Although Jaeger drew on an unnamed learned informant for some aspects of his discussion of Lead's life, visions and doctrines, his narrative of Lead's childhood, adolescence and marriage was based primarily on her recollections and spiritual diaries. While the diaries had been issued in three volumes as *A Fountain of Gardens* (1696–1701), Lead's autobiography was most likely dictated after she went blind to her

I am deeply grateful to the Panacea Society for generously funding my research. I have profited from the advice of Lorenza Gianfrancesco, Crawford Gribben and Lionel Laborie but remain responsible for any mistakes or shortcomings. Place of publication, where known and unless otherwise stated, is London.

A. Hessayon (✉)
Department of History, Goldsmiths,
University of London, London, UK

13

son-in-law and amanuensis Francis Lee. Edited and then issued in German translation—probably by Loth Fischer of Utrecht—these reminiscences appeared as 'Lebenslauff Der AVTORIN' towards the end of a collection of six of Lead's 'priceless' works (Amsterdam, 1696).[2] Elements were thereafter reworked into the publisher's preface to Lead's *The Wars of David* (London, 1700).[3] Like Jaeger, subsequent biographers have naturally relied on both sources, particularly 'The Life of the Author'. For the period before Lead's widowhood these have since been supplemented with a handful of scattered references, nearly all printed, notably heralds' visitations for London and Norfolk.

What has not been noticed is that the 'The Life of the Author' was constructed to reassure its intended audience of continental Spiritualists, Behmenists, Pietists and other assorted 'lovers of her writings' of Lead's upright character, respectable social status and 'God-given high-talents'.[4] Accordingly it conceals almost as much as it reveals. Indeed, in chapter 4 we shall see that a similar strategy is observable in a number of Philadelphian publications, which masked private heterodox beliefs and rituals with public professions of irenic conformity. Thus key names have been omitted from 'The Life of the Author', while the activities and teachings of others have been passed over silently or treated superficially. Doubtless this was because some of these individuals, including one of Lead's older brothers and several relations by marriage, had been Parliamentarian stalwarts and functionaries during the English Civil Wars. This suggests that in the aftermath of the revocation of the Edict of Nantes (1685), the Glorious Revolution (1688–89), William III's campaign in Ireland, Jacobite risings in Scotland, and a resurgence of apocalyptic exegesis more generally, the spectre of revolutionary radicalism still engendered fear within the British Isles and continental Europe at a moment when the Nine Years' War (1688–97) had yet to be concluded. Consequently, detailing past associations would have damaged Lead's reputation among her heterogeneous readership.

My challenging reading of what is quite familiar published evidence has been made possible through a great many archival discoveries. These constitute the cornerstone of what has been a painstaking reconstruction. Moreover, since most of what follows is substantially new in the sense that it was previously unknown, I have tended to disregard the secondary literature dealing with this period of Lead's life. Unfortunately, much is superficial at best, ill-informed and incorrect at worst. It should be added that because of the nature and paucity of the extant evidence Lead is intermittently absent from the ensuing account. Instead I have chosen to focus on the wider contexts, particularly the intricate and extensive networks of kin, friends and neighbours that were an integral aspect in the formation of early modern English identities. Although mainly circumstantial, cumulatively the evidence is overwhelming. It suggests that Lead was far more radical than has been supposed. Indeed, her religious beliefs were largely moulded by a militant puritanism that she may have shared with an elder brother but which conflicted with her parents' more moderate attitude, reflected in their outward adherence to the Church of England.

I

Jane was baptized on 9 March 1624 in the parish of Letheringsett, Norfolk.[5] She was a younger daughter of Hamond Ward (c.1577–1651), and his wife Mary (1582–1657). Jane's father was the son of Richard Ward (d.1579?) of Clentigate in Redenhall, Norfolk and Elizabeth, daughter of Hamond Claxton of Chediston, Suffolk. Her mother was the daughter of Sir James Calthorpe (1558–1615) of Cockthorpe, Norfolk and Barbara (c.1553–1639), daughter of John Bacon of Hessett, Suffolk.[6] Altogether, Lead's parents had 16 children: 12 sons and 4 daughters.[7] Only 11, however, are named in the herald's visitation of London of 1633, indicating that five doubtless died young (four sons, including one named Francis, and a daughter called Ann).[8] The eight surviving sons were James Ward (d.1678) who about 1626 married Sarah, daughter of Thomas Wright of Kilverston, Norfolk[9]; Hamond Ward the younger (c.1605–fl.1661), a London merchant; John Ward (baptized 1 November 1608, but not named in the 1664 visitation of Norfolk); Richard Ward (baptized 6 August 1610); Charles Ward (1612–1664), who became rector of Acle, Norfolk; William Ward (baptized 7 February 1614); Edward Ward (baptized 18 January 1616), sometime of Lisbon; and Philip Ward (fl.1650), sometime of Massachusetts.[10] The three surviving daughters were Jane the elder, who married William Reade of Walpole, Suffolk; Susanna (1620–1678), who married Henry Ferrour (d.1686) of St Nicholas, King's Lynn[11]; and Jane the younger (1624–1704), who as we shall see married William Lead (1620–1670) of St Margaret's, King's Lynn.

Jane stressed that her father was 'called the squire Ward', and Hamond the elder certainly displayed the outward signs of gentility.[12] He was styled a gentleman and bore the coat of arms *azure, a stag statant and an orle flory, counter flory or*. He also possessed land in Redenhall and nearby Topcroft, where by 1606 he was living in a building known locally as the Hall.[13] Moreover, his property transactions helped cement his relationship with both his wife's family and with his eldest son and heir's landowning father-in-law.[14] In addition, through various land transfers and co-appraising the estate of a deceased baronet Hamond often dealt with prominent members of the county community, including a Norwich alderman.[15] About 1623 he purchased the manor of Laviles in Letheringsett together with the Hall, which had been built around 1600.[16] It was here in the parish church dedicated to St. Andrew that Jane was baptized, and it was in the chancel of this same church that Hamond would be laid to rest following his death on 20 March 1651.[17]

According to Jane, her parents were 'esteemed in their honesty around the Norfolk countryside', leading 'honourable and modest lives' and adhering to the customs and doctrines of the Church of England. This depiction of a conformist religious background is matched by a corresponding silence in the ecclesiastical records. Furthermore, the burial of one of Hamond's sons at Bedingham rather than neighbouring Topcroft in September 1621 was doubtless not because of a dispute with Topcroft's rector Robert Cook, but rather in accordance with local custom since Topcroft Hall was under the jurisdiction of the vicar of Bedingham.[18] Jane added that her father had her 'educated in all good outward manners and morals befitting the dignity and class of his house'.[19] Although nothing more is known of the education she received (presumably from a tutor at home),[20] it is noteworthy that her elder brother Charles attended the free school in nearby Holt where he was taught by master Thomas Tallis for six years before going up to Gonville and Caius College, Cambridge in April 1630.[21]

Jane dated her spiritual awakening to her sixteenth year when 'some inner promptings' began growing within her, as a result of which she 'became convinced of the vanity of youth'. Then on Christmas Day 1640 she remembered receiving a divine gift manifested 'by means of a beam of Godly light' which burst into her 'mind and faculties' during the Yuletide feast. As was customary, the gentry assembled at her father's house at Letheringsett Hall were celebrating the feast of Christ's nativity by happily 'indulging in music and dancing'. Jane, however, was 'overcome by a feeling of sadness' and rather than continue dancing ceased on the instruction of a 'strange' yet gentle inward voice that promised to lead her in 'another dance' away from vanity.[22] In this she not only anticipated early

Quaker opposition to music and dancing,[23] but was also in accord with those among the godly who believed the celebration of Christmas to be a superstitious relic of popery (observance of the feast was to be abolished by Parliamentary ordinance in June 1647).[24] So she withdrew from the party to her father's study, where she confided the nature of her religious experience to a preacher 'who was chaplain to a certain knight that dined regularly with my father'. He advised that Jane remain steadfast, with the assurance that God had 'something good and great in store' for her.[25]

John Cliffe has pointed out that 'many Puritan gentry kept chaplains',[26] and although neither knight nor chaplain were named in Jane's narrative it is possible that the former was Sir Valentine Pell (1587–1658) and the latter William Gurnall (1616–1679).[27] Pell is certainly alluded to later in 'The Life of the Author' and will be discussed shortly. As for Gurnall, he was born and baptized in the parish of St Margaret's, King's Lynn the eldest son by his second wife of Gregory Gurnall (c.1582–1631), linen draper and future mayor of the borough. His mother was Katherine, the widow of John Cressy (d.1615) locksmith, and a sister of John Lead— making William Gurnall a cousin by marriage of William Lead, Jane's future husband.[28] Gurnall was admitted at Emmanuel College, Cambridge in March 1632 and was thus a contemporary of several future Cambridge Platonists including Peter Sterry and John Sadler. He graduated with the degree of Bachelor of Arts in 1635 and proceeded Master of Arts in 1639. Gurnall's whereabouts in 1640 are unknown so he may have served as a chaplain while awaiting ecclesiastical preferment.[29] In 1644 he was presented to the rectory of Lavenham, Suffolk by his patron the diarist, antiquary and Parliamentarian Sir Simonds D'Ewes. Afterwards Gurnall found fame through the publication of a three-part work of 'spiritual consolation and exhortation', *The Christian in Compleat Armour* (1655–62).[30]

Another possible influence on Jane's spiritual development may have been her elder brother Charles, who had graduated BA in 1634 and MA in 1637. Having entered holy orders and been ordained a deacon (Peterborough, 12 June 1636) and a priest (Norwich, 4 September 1637), he officiated in the cures of Fakenham and Letheringsett. In April 1641 a certificate supplied by the rector of Syderstone and Thomas Lougher (d.1645?), rector of Letheringsett, attested that Charles had 'demeaned himself soberly' and was 'in all things conformable to the doctrine and discipline of the Church of England'.[31] Lougher's testimonial suggests more than a cursory relationship with the Ward family, although it should be noted that he had been presented to the living in 1629 not by Hamond but by John Jermy (*d.*1630/31), who held the advowson.[32] At any rate, Jane's parents 'spared no effort' in attempting to free their daughter from what they regarded as her unhealthy preoccupation with sin, not to mention Jane's 'melancholy fantasies' that her soul would suffer eternal damnation for having '*persisted in a falsehood*' about a trifling matter.[33]

In August 1642 Civil War broke out in England between Charles I and Parliament. Significantly, 'The Life of the Author' is silent about the conflict. Instead Jane recounted that she remained in a lingering state of 'spiritual perplexity' and despondency for 'three whole years'. Then, by her own account, at the age of 19 (but actually 18) she went to London in search of spiritual comfort for the 'malady' she had been stricken with. Even so, Jane only went with her father's approval, having implored a 'recently married' brother with whom she had been secretly corresponding to politely intercede on her behalf.[34] He was described as a merchant and hence can very probably be identified as Hamond Ward the younger.

Hamond the younger had married Sarah Skottow by licence on 22 April 1632 at St Giles Cripplegate, London. She was the daughter of John Skottow (*d.*1625/26) a wealthy merchant of Norwich who had bequeathed her 1,000 marks (just over £666) as her dowry. This was with the proviso, however, that Sarah wed with the consent of her mother and four uncles.[35] One of these uncles was Augustine Skottow (*d.*1636), a Norwich alderman whose will bore the formulaic scribal preamble characteristic of orthodox Calvinist doctrine. In addition, Augustine Skottow made bequests to seven ministers including William Bridge, lecturer at St George Tombland, Norwich who suffered deprivation for nonconformity in 1636; George Cocke, rector of Barsham, Suffolk; William Stynnet, rector of St John Maddermarket, Norwich; and John Ward, rector of St Michael-at-Plea, Norwich who was suspended in 1636.[36] Another of Sarah's uncles was Timothy Skottow (*d.*1645), a Norwich goldsmith who in 1642 was appointed to receive and weigh plate donated or loaned to supply revenue for the Parliamentary cause.[37]

Hamond the younger's links with Norwich extended in 1634 to trading yarn supplied by the city's worsted weavers. His business partner in this venture was Edmund Trench, a puritan merchant.[38] Besides wool Hamond had also imported tobacco.[39] He had been living in London since at least 1633, first in the parish of St Stephen Walbrook and then from summer 1634 in St Clement's Eastcheap—although he may have held property elsewhere in the City since he was also assessed in neighbouring St. Edmund the King, Lombard Street in 1638.[40] With his wife

Sarah, Hamond had four children though only one survived infancy. Sarah too succumbed and was buried at St Clement's Eastcheap on 26 December 1638.[41] Nearly 16 months later Hamond married Elizabeth, daughter of Robert Tichborne (*d*.1644/45), skinner of St Michael-le-Querne, by licence.[42] They would have seven children. Three survived infancy, the eldest son taking his father's name.[43] Thereafter Hamond served two terms as a churchwarden at St Clement's Eastcheap, from Easter 1641 to Easter 1643.[44] In March 1642 Hamond purchased property in St Olave, Southwark from his brother-in-law Robert Tichborne as part of the latter's marriage contract with the daughter of a Norfolk gentleman.[45] The following month he was named an ensign and Tichborne a captain in the third regiment of London's militia, a force under the command of Philip Skippon recruited to defend Parliament and the City.[46] Then in October that year he brought the sum of £71-14*s*.-8*d*. to Goldsmiths' Hall in support of the Parliamentary war effort.[47] The following month he added to this by loaning £10 to Parliament.[48]

Jane recalled spending the first six months after her arrival in London tirelessly attending both public religious services and conventicles. Yet her soul remained unmoved. Then through supposed divine guidance she stumbled upon a congregation that introduced her to the 'richness and breadth' of God's 'love and grace'. Foremost 'marshal' on this path was Dr Tobias Crisp (1600–1643), whose sermon on the new covenant touched her in 'a most wonderful way'.[49] According to the antiquary Anthony Wood, the 'puritanically affected' Crisp had left his rectory at Brinkworth, Wiltshire for London in August 1642 so as to avoid the insolence of Cavalier soldiers. Crisp died of smallpox on 27 February 1643 and was buried in the family vault at St Mildred, Bread Street, the parish of his birth, with his sermon on 'The New Covenant of Free Grace' taken from Isaiah 42:6–7 published posthumously as part of *Christ Alone Exalted* (1643).[50] The preface to this collection contained a defence of libertinism as '*the preaching of the free Grace in Christ*' while in his explication of Romans 6:14 Crisp himself maintained that 'when we come under grace by Christ, the dominion of the Law, or rather the dominion of sin ... is captivated and subjected by Christ' so that 'we are discharged from the fault and guilt' of sin.[51] Consequently, several contemporaries considered him an Antinomian.[52] Yet like another of Crisp's hearers, the future Ranter Lawrence Clarkson,[53] Jane joyfully departed from his sermon and thereafter committed herself along the spiritual path outlined by Crisp. It was at this moment that she had a conversion experience, when '*the Light of the Divine Countenance*' shone upon her and brought her soul out of its '*State of Obscurity and Darkness, and out of the Pains of Hell*'. Jane beheld a vision in her mind's eye of something akin to a legal document, namely a pardon with a seal upon it, signifying that her past transgressions had been absolved and blotted out. Henceforth she was comforted and assured of God's love.[54]

That Jane identified 'Dr Crisp' as a spiritual mentor in the context of the mid-1690s is significant. For in January 1690—just months after the Toleration Act—Crisp's son Samuel had republished 42 of his father's sermons, adding to them transcriptions of 10 more from manuscript notes. This precipitated further controversy, especially among nonconformist ministers, and in J.F. Maclear's judgement both 'heightened mistrust between Presbyterians and Independents' and 'foreshadowed the great division of eighteenth-century Nonconformity between "high Calvinism" and the moderate puritan tradition'.[55] Perhaps the mention of Crisp's name signalled a staging post in Jane's religious journey since by then she had rejected predestination in favour of the doctrine of the universal restoration of all humanity.

Equally noteworthy were Tobias Crisp's mercantile family ties. For his father had been a London alderman while Tobias himself had married Mary, daughter of merchant Rowland Wilson the elder. His brother-in-law was Rowland Wilson, a freeman of the East India Company who was involved in the Spanish wine trade and whom Keith Lindley has identified as 'a leading City parliamentarian' during the Civil War. Moreover, Tobias's widow would marry the Massachusetts Bay Company investor, Virginia tobacco trader and regicide Owen Rowe.[56] All of which suggests that Jane's merchant brother may have had dealings with this powerful commercial network.

Jane remained in London for a further six months; that is until roughly autumn 1643 when—with the war turning in the King's favour and Jane freed from her 'sadness'—her worried family wished that she return home to Norfolk. Suspecting their daughter had been 'led astray' and 'poisoned by errors' they were apprehensive lest she accept a marriage proposal 'without permission' from a co-religionist. They had reason to be anxious for Jane had been tempted to marry a man who had chosen the same 'spiritual path' had not her brother—the head of the household where she lodged—intervened. Accordingly, she 'acquiesced' to her parents' request 'out of an indebted obedience'.[57]

II

In March 1643 Hamond the younger, then serving as one of the churchwardens at St Clement's Eastcheap, was named by the House of Lords as one of eight parishioners empowered to sequester the minister for 'Popish Doctrine, Drunkenness, Tavern-haunting' and other scandalous activity.[58] In April 1644, however, he himself was brought into custody by order of the Committee for Advance of Money for failing to pay substantial arrears on his assessment. The charge was eventually dropped in May 1647,[59] by which time his finances were sufficiently healthy to enable him to act as a joint creditor with a London grocer whose estate was valued at almost £50,000.[60] Assessments and tithe payments indicate that Hamond was then living in the northern part of St Clement's Eastcheap, within the jurisdiction of Langborne ward, occupying a house in Three Kings Court.[61] By this time he had also become a citizen of London, purchasing his freedom from the Mercers' Company on 17 May 1644. Over the next 14 years he would take on 10 apprentices, the first being a nephew.[62]

Chancery cases and notarial documents indicate that besides loaning money and binding apprentices Hamond the younger had trans-Atlantic commercial interests. One suit concerned the purchase of oil and iron hoops in the Canary Islands from a sea captain who subsequently perished in a shipwreck. Additional merchandise included Canary wine valued at £980.[63] Another related to the acquisition of goods from Lisbon where along with John Mules, a Portuguese-speaking merchant described as Hamond's 'great acquaintance', his brother Edward acted as a factor. Indeed, the siblings were said to correspond frequently concerning 'matters of trade and merchants affaires'.[64] Another brother, Philip, was based at Massachusetts where he facilitated Hamond's corn trading.[65] Significantly, in April 1649 Hamond was one of 19 men appointed as commissioners for the sale of prize goods.[66] Other appointees included Owen Rowe (husband of Tobias Crisp's widow), the tobacco and slave trader Maurice Thomson and Robert Tichborne, a political Independent and member of George Cockayn's gathered congregation (Cockayn had provided a commendatory epistle to Crisp's posthumously published sermons). Tichborne was a signatory to Charles I's death warrant and, as we have seen, also Hamond's brother-in-law through his second marriage to Elizabeth.[67] That Jane omitted to mention her elder brother's links to a regicide is unsurprising.

Over in Norfolk, Hamond the elder was named in several Parliamentary ordinances issued between February 1645 and November 1650. Together with just over 65 colleagues he was responsible for maintaining the Parliamentary war machine in England and Ireland by recruiting troops in the county and levying taxes.[68] In addition, he served as a Justice of the Peace at quarter sessions held at Fakenham and Little Walsingham in 1650.[69] While his eldest son James had some goods distrained for neglecting to pay his share for the repair of the bridge at Twyford,[70] one of his younger sons, Charles, was presented to the rectory of Acle in December 1645. This was achieved through the patronage of James Calthorpe, a nephew of Hamond the elder's wife, afterwards knighted during the Protectorate and High Sheriff for Suffolk in 1656.[71]

Meanwhile, Jane had rejected a suitor. Although he was someone of whom her parents 'well approved', she felt he placed more value on 'outward things' than 'indwelling' matters. So she dedicated herself instead to Christ 'as his Bride'. Thereafter she rejected 'all candidates and comers' until her twenty-first year; i.e., about 1644. For it was at this moment in her life that Jane was introduced to her future husband, a 'god-fearing' and devout merchant named William Lead. She had made William's acquaintance 'on account of the fact that he was the son of the brother of a certain knight who had married my mother's sister'. Moreover, this knight had been 'entrusted with the care of his dead brother's son, in addition to the goods and chattels bequeathed him'.[72] These circuitous allusions were doubtless to avoid naming the man who had helped broker her marriage. And Jane succeeded, since scholars were hitherto unaware of his identity. Yet it has been a straightforward task to unmask him as Sir Valentine Pell.

Valentine was one of the children of Jeffrey Pell (*d*.1615) merchant of St Margaret's, King's Lynn and himself the son of a mayor of the borough.[73] Baptised at St Margaret's on 5 March 1587, he had matriculated at Peterhouse, Cambridge in 1604 where he took notes on several treatises by Aristotle. Afterwards he attended Gray's Inn to train as a lawyer.[74] His sister Mary (1588–1633) had married John Lead at St Margaret's on 9 December 1613 making him an uncle by marriage of William Lead. In addition, Valentine Pell, along with his brother John, was named as a supervisor of his brother-in-law John Lead's will.[75] For his own part, Valentine married Barbara Calthorpe (1592–1667) at St Luke's, Norwich on 2 March 1617. His wife was a younger sister of Mary, Jane's mother.[76] He was knighted on 2 July 1641. The following year Valentine's loyalty to the Parliamentary cause resulted in his appointment as captain of a troop of horse, a command he entrusted to a surrogate.[77] During the Civil War he played a prominent administrative role in Norfolk through overseeing the collection of assessments, including those imposed on delinquent Royalists. Indeed, he served as High Sheriff for Norfolk in 1645.[78] Afterwards Sir Valentine Pell was a member of the Committee for Norfolk during the Commonwealth.[79] Besides introducing Jane to her future husband Valentine was in regular communication with both his nephew Hamond the younger and his brother-in-law Hamond the elder. The former provided news from London and acted as an agent to transfer money, while the latter requested favours through the reduction of taxes levied on certain friends.[80] Valentine Pell, moreover, had been one of the guardians of his nephew James Calthorpe who, as mentioned above, held the advowson of Acle.[81] Little wonder that Jane did not reveal the name of this Parliamentary official that was so intimately connected with her family.

III

William Lead's father John was the son of John Lead (*d.*1595), cordwainer of St Margaret's, King's Lynn.[82] John Lead the elder had purchased his freedom in 1541–42, afterwards taking on six shoemaker apprentices. He had been elected to the Common Council in 1560 but was never selected as an alderman, despite 35 years' service. He had married Margaret Houghton at St Margaret's on 8 August 1575 and had six or more children. At least four survived infancy and adolescence: Katherine (1576–*fl.*1648), Margaret (1577–*fl.*1608), John (1578–1639) and Edmund (1583–1608).[83] Edmund Lead died a bachelor. He was a merchant of modest wealth who possessed three tenements and a coal yard in King's Lynn. Besides bequeathing some household goods (featherbed, bolster, pillow, rug, blankets, little trunk, old cloak and gold ring), he had shares in a flyboat called the 'Joanne of Lynn'.[84] Margaret married Thomas Dixe (*d.*1649), merchant and common councilman.[85] Katherine married twice. As we have seen, her first husband was John Cressy (*d.*1615) locksmith. Besides having a house in Checker Street, Cressy also possessed property on Stone Bridge and in Dampgate, the latter acquired as Katherine's dowry. In addition, he had a lease from Edmund Lead for property near Baxter's Bridge as well as land and houses in Aylsham, Norfolk.[86] Her second husband was Gregory Gurnall (*c.*1582–1631), linen draper, common councilman (from 1607), alderman (from 1618), and mayor of King's Lynn in 1624. Among their children was the preacher William Gurnall.

Katherine survived both her partners and was bequeathed land and properties together with £130 from the sale of her house in Dampgate.[87]

John Lead, father of William Lead, was apprenticed to John Bassett (*d.*1611), merchant and alderman, and made a freeman of the borough in 1603–04.[88] About April 1605 John Lead and some other English merchants docked at Lisbon with a cargo of 600 quarters of wheat (equivalent to 4,800 bushels), which they valued at £1,469-12*s.*-6*d.* Unable to speak Portuguese and ignorant of the local customs they employed John Rolls, a resident Englishman, to maximise their profits. Afterwards Lead journeyed to southern Spain remaining there roughly two years and all the while maintaining correspondence with Rolls.[89] Unfortunately for Lead a cargo of wheat belonging to him and other merchants, including Thomas Carrow of King's Lynn, was seized by the purveyor of the King of Spain's galleys in October 1605 at El Puerto de Santa María. Although Lead and Carrow eventually received financial compensation after appealing to the Spanish court Lead was subsequently imprisoned, probably at Seville, and the money seized.[90] Following his release, possibly on the intercession of the Earl of Salisbury, he gave evidence in December 1608 during Star Chamber proceedings against Thomas Baker, an alderman and former mayor of King's Lynn. Among other charges, Baker was accused of sexually assaulting two Dutch ship-boys, thrusting his hand into a young man's britches, and having his bare buttocks whipped with a birch rod.[91]

During the 1610s Lead was among the leading Lynn merchants trading with the Netherlands. From Amsterdam he imported a variety of goods—mainly to Lynn but also to Boston—including rye, raisins, brown paper, cork, broad cloth and sheep's leather. In addition, he sent out leather and cloth to Amsterdam as well as exporting wheat to Toulon.[92] As we have seen, John Lead married Mary daughter of Jeffrey Pell on 9 December 1613. Though the full value of Mary's dowry is unknown it included the sum of £50.[93] The couple had eight or more children, with at least three surviving infancy: William (1620–1670), Mary (1632–*fl.*1654), and Margaret (*fl.*1639).[94] Between Easter 1630 and Easter 1633 Lead served as one of the two churchwardens at St Margaret's.[95] He was also elected to the Common Council on 6 July 1632 but like his father never became an alderman.[96] His wife was buried at St Margaret's on 4 July 1633 and after a short but expensively treated illness he followed her to the grave on 4 February 1639.[97]

John Lead made provision for his children William, Mary and Margaret. Besides bequeathing to his daughters money and household goods (bedsteads, featherbeds, bolsters, valences, blankets, sheets, pillows, childbed linen, curtains, chairs, stools, embroidered cushions, rugs, needlework, and rings of ruby and gold), he also left them property. This was an inn called 'The Boar's Head' in Dampgate purchased from his brother-in-law Gregory Gurnall and which had originally formed part of his sister Katherine's dowry. In addition, he passed on rents from properties in Wiggenhall St Mary Magdalen together with his house in Bridgegate Street. William was named his father's executor with John and Valentine Pell nominated supervisors of his will. From Valentine Pell's papers it is clear that between John Lead's death and William Lead's agreement to a financial settlement on 11 June 1642 at least part of the property in Bridgegate Street was rented annually for £8-10s.-0d. Additional sums amounting to just over £420 were collected through bonds and obligations, while borrowed money was repaid. Several debtors and a creditor were fellow common councilmen. Moreover, John Lead had invested in an eighth share of two ships, the 'Bonadventure' and the 'Edward and John'. The 'Bonadventure' usually sailed from London or Gravesend and according to the historian G.A. Metters 'was involved very heavily in the coal trade from Newcastle' in 1639. Although domestic returns were small but steady bringing in £19-13s.-0d., riskier voyages to Bordeaux, Spain and Portugal proved more profitable returning about £120 altogether. The 'Edward and John' in Metters' opinion was 'probably a smaller vessel … employed almost exclusively in the coastal coal trade'. Frequent repairs, however, meant that profits, while fairly regular, tended to be moderate.[98]

By 20 May 1639, just months after his father's death, William Lead was living at 'The Three Golden Lions' in Lombard Street, London. He remained in the capital during the early part of the Civil War before occasionally staying with Sir Valentine Pell at Dersingham in the 'Norfolk countryside'.[99] His absence from King's Lynn coincided with the take-over of this strategic port at the mouth of the River Great Ouse by a Royalist faction, not to mention the subsequent siege of the borough in August 1643 by Parliamentary forces commanded by the Earl of Manchester. Following a brutal bombardment which damaged St Margaret's church as well as the market place and a number of houses, the town was stormed by land and sea. The defenders surrendered on 16 September and shortly afterwards Oliver Cromwell's brother-in-law Valentine Walton was appointed governor.[100]

As for William and Jane, they were married between 15 June and 14 July 1644, possibly at Letheringsett or Dersingham.[101] It was evidently a happy union; Jane remarked that they 'lived together in love and unity for twenty-seven years'.[102] Her marriage portion appears to have been £230.[103] Interestingly, during her widowhood she would use the imagery of worldly transactions to describe the spiritual marriage between the virgin soul and Christ her bridegroom. Hence she wrote of 'a Stock of Spiritual Goods', a 'great and large' dowry, 'jointured ... Lands and Possessions', and 'Eternal Revenues' belonging to the Lamb's wife.[104]

It is usually—but wrongly—assumed that William and Jane Lead settled in London. In fact, they dwelled at King's Lynn between at least 1647 and 1657. Thus William was made a freeman of the borough by birth in 1646–47. Thereafter he was elected to the Common Council on 21 May 1649 and became an alderman on 20 August 1655.[105] The man he replaced on the aldermanic bench was John Bassett, the eldest son of his father's former master and one of the people with whom he had the witnessed the will of a King's Lynn gentleman in October 1652.[106] Jane remarked that together with William she had raised four daughters. Two would eventually marry, but 'two died in childhood'. While two babies may have been christened at Letheringsett or Dersingham before 1647, two were certainly baptized at St Margaret's: Mary on 18 January 1649 and Barbary on 24 February 1653. Evidently there was no opposition within this godly household to infant baptism.[107] The minister John Almond (c.1608–1653), it should be added, was a Royalist who took the unusual step of recording in St Margaret's parish register the burial on 30 January 1649 of 'King Charles king of Great Brittaine'.[108] As for the church where Jane and her husband may have worshipped, its 'offensive' stained glass windows had been broken in 1643—probably by Parliamentarian soldiers—and then taken away by parishioners to be replaced with white glass, with many brass plates also removed from gravestones.[109]

In December 1656 William Lead occupied a property leased from an alderman and former mayor of the borough. This was a brewery situated near Lady's Bridge which was described as a messuage with two acres of pasture adjoining and which contained an assortment of brewing utensils including copper coolers and water pipes.[110] Merchant William may still have been, yet this suggests diversification of business interests, an impression confirmed by a complicated Chancery case concerning the estate of Robert Morris a King's Lynn inn-holder. The defendants were William and Jane Lead together with their brother-in-law Philip Read sometime of Watlington, Norfolk (he had married William's sister Mary). Morris's goods had been inventoried and appraised in March 1653 and William claimed that he had subsequently purchased some of them for £100-2s.-11d. at a sale conducted by the undersherriff of Norfolk. In his defence Jane said 'she beleiveth the answere of her said husband to be true & knoweth nothing to the contrary she having not beene in any co[u]'te privy to any transacc[i]ons'. Proceedings in the case spanned from June 1659 to November 1660, with William and Jane giving evidence at Poole, Dorset on 26 April 1660.[111] It is likely that they had left King's Lynn by this date since William had been discharged at his own request from the aldermanic bench on 16 November 1657.[112]

IV

Meanwhile, Hamond the younger's growing prosperity enabled him to purchase the manor of Bedwellhay Grange in the Isle of Ely for £618-19s.-2d. on 9 March 1649.[113] Thereafter he also bought a former possession of the dean chapter of Ely cathedral, namely the manor of Sutton, for £2,048-8s.-2d.[114] Between June 1657 and March 1660 Hamond was one of several notable personages in the Isle of Ely named in Parliamentary ordinances concerning the collection of assessments and the upkeep of the militia.[115] For much of the Commonwealth and Protectorate, however, he was mainly at St Clement's Eastcheap or else a few miles away at Tottenham High Cross, where at an unknown date he acquired a mansion.[116] When residing at St Clement's Eastcheap Hamond was active in vestry affairs until February 1658, even having a room assigned for his maid at a nominal rent.[117] More importantly he maintained his commercial connections with the Iberian Peninsula and the Canary Islands. Thus in February 1653 along with some other London merchants he petitioned the Council of State for protection for a ship bound for the Canaries.[118] Two years later he and other merchants petitioned the Protector bemoaning losses and damages sustained in trading with Portugal, probably as a consequence of Royalist piracy. Further petitions concerned the sale of Spanish wines and the redemption of captives held at Algiers.[119]

Some of Hamond's wealth was used to subsidise scholarship and he was one of the many London merchants who acted as patrons of Thomas Fuller's *Church History of Britain* (1655), an ambitious work that has been called 'the first comprehensive English protestant account of Christianity in the island from the earliest times'.[120] Yet all the while he was embroiled in litigation in the court of Chancery—sometimes as defendant, sometimes as complainant—in cases over money and property that tended to join him with siblings and kinsmen against contending parties.[121] Following the death of his and Jane's mother, Mary Ward, and her burial at Letheringsett on 30 March 1657 he transferred land and property in Letheringsett to his older brother James and James's son and heir.[122] Another transfer in November 1661 was of £600 of East India Company stock to John Bathurst.[123] Presumably this was the East India Company committee member, fishmonger and London alderman of that name.[124] But whether this was the same John Bathurst who in 1676 would entertain the Behmenist prophet Quirinus Kuhlmann and whom we shall encounter shortly is difficult to say.

As for William and Jane Lead, nothing is known of their life together after the Restoration of the Stuart monarchy in May 1660. William died on 5 February 1670 and was buried the next day at St Botolph without Bishopsgate, London.[125] The anniversary of his passing became a day of spiritual reflection and commemoration for Jane.[126] William died intestate and administration of his estate was granted in the Prerogative court of Canterbury on 2 March. According to Jane, the loss of 'such a magnificent husband' was immediately the cause of 'great suffering' and 'worldly sorrows' because she and her two surviving daughters, Barbary and R., were defrauded of 'what was rightfully theirs'. Apparently her husband had unwisely 'invested and risked a large part of his possessions' with an agent overseas. Following William's death this factor received everything and 'relinquished nothing'. Jane was therefore left 'mired in a manifold, deep and most desperate poverty'.[127]

*   *   *

When Jane Lead became a widow both her parents, Hamond and Mary Ward (neé Calthorpe), were dead. So too were her father- and mother-in-law John and Mary Lead (neé Pell). As were her uncle and aunt, Sir Valentine and Dame Barbara Pell (neé Calthorpe), her cousin James Calthorpe, her brother-in-law William Reade, her sister-in-law Sarah Ward (neé Skottow), not to mention at least six siblings (including Ann, Francis and Charles Ward), and a number of nephews and nieces. Moreover, the fate of seven more siblings is uncertain (Hamond, John, Richard, William, Edward, Philip and Jane the elder), as is what befell her brother- and sister in-law Philip and Mary Read (neé Lead). Among Jane's living relatives were Jane's eldest brother James Ward (d.1678) of Twyford, Norfolk together with his eldest son James and his grandchildren Hamond, Elizabeth and Katherine; Jane's sister Susanna (*d*.1678) together with her husband Henry Ferrour (*d*.1686) of St Nicholas, King's Lynn and their children William, Elizabeth and Barbara; Jane's sister-in-law Elizabeth Ward (neé Tichborne) together with her surviving children Hammond, Robert and Elizabeth; Jane's brother-in-law the regicide Robert Tichborne (*d*.1682); and Jane's cousin the preacher William Gurnall (*d*.1679).[128] In a society where kinship— along with social status, neighbourliness, church membership, mutual economic interests, patronage and friendship—was an integral element of social networks, the religious beliefs and political views of Jane's extended family may well have shaped her identity and influenced her behaviour as a single then married woman to a considerable degree.

Had Lead predeceased her husband, for example as a victim of the Great Plague of 1665, too little would have been known of this woman's spiritual development to merit detailed investigation. Indeed, prior to widowhood Jane's only known words were taken down by a clerk in Chancery. At best her piety might have been memorialised through an account of her godly life and character. This was how Tobias Crisp's daughter Mary Carleton (*d*.1670) was remembered.[129] Alternatively, her virtues and sufferings might have been honoured through a funeral sermon similar to that preached by William Gurnall for Lady Mary Vere.[130] But Jane outlived William Lead. And it was during her 34 years of widowhood and the concomitant loosening of patriarchal constraints that she was afforded the opportunity of relating her spiritual experiences and having them recorded and disseminated. Accordingly, it is to this fundamental chapter of her long life that we now turn.

NOTES

1. Johann Wolfgang Jaeger, *Dissertatio historico-theologica, de Johannæ Leadæ Anglo-Britan. Vita* (Tübingen, 1712); Johann Wolfgang Jaeger, *Historia Ecclesiastica* (2 vols., Hamburg, 1709–17), vol. 2, part ii, pp. 90–117.

2. Jane Lead, 'Lebenslauff der Autorin', in *Sechs Unschätzbare Durch Göttliche Offenbarung und Befehl ans Liecht gebrachte Mystische Tractätlein* (Amsterdam, 1696), pp. 413–23. I am grateful to Leigh Penman for his translation of this document.

3. Jane Lead, *The Wars of David* (1700), sigs. A2^{r-2}–A2^{r-3}.

4. 'Lebenslauff', p. 413.

5. Norfolk R.O., PD 547.

6. E.E.G. Bulwer (ed.), *The Visitation of Norfolk in the year 1563* (2 vols., Norwich, 1878–95), vol. 2, pp. 448–49, 460, 463; Walter Metcalfe (ed.), *The Visitations of Suffolk … 1561, … 1577, and … 1612* (Exeter, 1882), pp. 14–15; Sheffield Archives, BFM/1228, BFM/1229, BFM/1219; Joseph Jackson Howard and Joseph Lemuel Chester (eds.), *The Visitation of London anno domini 1633, 1634, and 1635*, Harleian Society 15, 17 (2 vols., 1880–83), vol. 1, p. 167, vol. 2, p. 322; A.W. Hughes Clarke and Arthur Campling (eds.), *The Visitation of Norfolk Anno Domini 1664*, Harleian Society 85–86 (2 vols., 1933–34), vol. 1, pp. 233–34.

7. Francis Blomefield, *An Essay towards a Topographical History of the county of Norfolk* (11 vols., 1805–10), vol. 9, p. 413.

8. Norfolk R.O., PD 389, Topcroft parish register, baptism of 'Ann Ward yᶜ daughᵗʳ of Hamond Ward generosus dwellinge at yᶜ halle place' on 23 December 1606; Norfolk R.O., PD 443, Bedingham parish register, burial of 'Francys the sonn of Hamon Warde gentleman' (15 September 1621), printed in *The East Anglian*, 4 (1869), p. 273.

9. Sheffield Archives, BFM/1141.

10. Norfolk R.O., PD 389.

11. Norfolk R.O., PD 389; Edmund Farrer, *The Church heraldry of Norfolk* (3 vols., Norwich, 1887–93), vol. 3, p. 155; TNA: PRO, Prob 11/386 fol. 39r-v.

12. 'Lebenslauff', p. 414.

13. Topcroft Hall is a grade II listed building that retains some original features including a first floor hall probably dated to the early sixteenth century, see; http://www.britishlistedbuildings.co.uk/en-227421-topcroft-hall-topcroft-norfolk.

14. Sheffield Archives, BFM/987, BFM/1139, BFM/1140, BFM/1141, BFM/1209, BFM/1212, BFM/1218; Norfolk R.O., PD 389; TNA: PRO, Prob 11/225 fols. 109r–11v.

15. Sheffield Archives, BFM/987; TNA: PRO, Prob 11/165 fols. 148r–49v; Sheffield Archives, BFM/1210; *Norfolk Archaeology*, 23 (1929), p. 321; CUL, Ch(H), Pell papers, 5 no. 71; Norfolk R.O., WLS XI/3, 409X2; Norfolk R.O., WLS X/6, 409X1.

16. B. Cozens-Hardy, 'Some Norfolk Halls', *Norfolk Archaeology*, 32 (1961), p. 192; Norfolk Heritage Explorer, http://www.heritage.norfolk.gov.uk/record-details?MNF13448. Because of reconstruction undertaken in 1870 little of the original exterior remains. Today Letheringsett Hall serves as a nursing home.

17. Blomefield, *Norfolk*, vol. 9, p. 413.

18. Blomefield, *Norfolk*, vol. 10, pp. 188, 189. Two other sons, William and Edward, had been baptized at Topcroft by licence from the vicar of Bedingham.

19. 'Lebenslauff', pp. 413–14; cf. Lead, *Wars of David*, sig. A2^{r-2}.
20. Cf. Lucy Hutchinson, *Memoirs of the Life of Colonel Hutchinson*, ed. N.H. Keeble (2000), pp. 14–15.
21. John Venn, *Biographical History of Gonville and Caius College 1349–1897* (3 vols., Cambridge, 1897 1901), vol. 1, p. 294; John Venn and J. Venn (eds.), *Alumni Cantabrigienses from the earliest times to 1751* (4 vols., Cambridge, 1922–27), vol. 4, p. 330; Norfolk R.O., DN/INV 46/80, probate inventory of Thomas Tallis, master of the free school at Holt, Norfolk (1640–41).
22. 'Lebenslauff', pp. 413–14; Lead, *Wars of David*, sigs. A2^{r-2}–A2^{r-3}.
23. John Nickalls (ed.), *Journal of George Fox* (Cambridge, 1952; reprinted, 1986), p. 38; Rosemary Moore, *The Light in their Consciences. The early Quakers in Britain 1646–1666* (Pennsylvania State University, 2000), pp. 120–21.
24. C. Durston, 'The Puritan War on Christmas', *History Today*, 35:12 (1985), http://www.historytoday.com/chris-durston/puritan-war-christmas.
25. 'Lebenslauff', pp. 414–15; Lead, *Wars of David*, sig. A2^{r-3}.
26. John Cliffe, *The World of the Country House in Seventeenth-Century England* (1999), p. 133.
27. J. M. Blatchly, 'Gurnall, William (*bap.* 1616, *d.* 1679)', *ODNB*.
28. TNA: PRO, Prob 11/160 fols. 422v–23r; Benjamin Mackerell, *The History and Antiquities Of the Flourishing Corporation of King's-Lynn in the County of Norfolk* (1738), p. 52. *ODNB* here erroneously follows H. McKeon, *An Inquiry into the birth-place, parentage, life, and writings, of the Reverend William Gurnall* (Woodbridge, 1830), p. 1, in identifying Gurnall's mother as Catherine Dressyt. This is based on a mistranscription of the parish register, see; Norfolk R.O., PD 39/2, Lynn St Margaret parish register, marriage of 'Gregorye Gurnall wth Katheryne Cressye wid' on 31 December 1615.
29. McKeon, *Inquiry into … William Gurnall*, p. 5.
30. Blatchly, 'Gurnall, William (*bap.* 1616, *d.* 1679)', *ODNB*.
31. Clergy of the Church of England Database http://theclergydatabase. org.uk/; *CSPD 1640–41*, p. 531.
32. Blomefield, *Norfolk*, vol. 9, p. 414; TNA: PRO, Prob 11/159 fols. 341v–42r.
33. 'Lebenslauff', pp. 415–16; Lead, *Wars of David*, sig. A2^{r-3}.
34. 'Lebenslauff', pp. 415–16.
35. Clarke and Campling (eds.), *Visitation of Norfolk 1664*, vol. 2, pp. 199–200; TNA: PRO, Prob 11/148 fols. 134r–35r.
36. TNA: PRO, Prob 11/171 fols. 322v–25r; Farrer, *Church heraldry of Norfolk*, vol. 3, p. 126; Richard L. Greaves, 'Bridge, William (1600/01–1671)', *ODNB*; Clergy of the Church of England Database.

37. Bodl., MS Tanner 64 fols. 98, 99, 105; TNA: PRO, Prob 11/193 fols. 374v–75r; Blomefield, *Norfolk*, vol. 3, p. 383; R.W. Ketton-Cremer, *Norfolk in the Civil War* (1969), p. 152.

38. William Sachse (ed.), *Minutes of the Norwich Court of Mayoralty 1632–1635*, Norfolk Record Society (1967), p. 177; TNA: PRO, Prob 11/282 fols. 297v–98v; Edmund Trench, *Some Remarkable Passages in the Holy Life and Death Of ... Mr Edmund Trench* (1693), pp. 4–5.

39. TNA: PRO, E 190/35/4, fol. 26r.

40. Howard and Chester (eds.), *Visitation of London 1633, 1634, and 1635*, vol. 2, p. 322; T.C. Dale, *Inhabitants of London in 1638* (1931), pp. 53–54.

41. W.B. Bannerman and W.B. Bannerman (eds.), *The Registers of St. Stephen's, Walbrook, and of St. Benet Sherehog, London*, Harleian Society, 49–50 (1919), pp. 20, 93; A.W. Hughes Clarke (ed.), *The Register of St. Clement, Eastcheap, and St. Martin Orgar, London*, Harleian Society, 67–68 (1937–38), pp. 25, 26, 180, 181. Hamond and Sarah's children were Hamond junior (baptized 1 July 1633, buried 10 July 1633), Barbary (baptized 19 August 1634, buried 6 October 1634), Joseph (baptized 28 September 1635, buried 29 September 1635), and James (baptized 12 September 1637).

42. Reginald Glencross (ed.), *A Calendar of Marriage Licence Allegations in the Registry of the Bishop of London, vol.1, 1597 to 1648*, British Record Society 62 (1937), p. 201; LMA, formerly GL, MS 10,091/22, p. 66; Howard and Chester (eds.), *Visitation of London 1633, 1634, and 1635*, vol. 2, p. 289; TNA: PRO, Prob 11/192 fols. 185r–86r.

43. Hughes Clarke (ed.), *Register of St. Clement, Eastcheap*, pp. 28, 29, 31, 182, 185, 186; TNA: PRO, Prob 11/421 fols. 396v–99r. Hamond and Elizabeth's children were a chrisom (buried 16 February 1641), Barbara (baptized 6 April 1643, buried 28 January 1651), Hammond (baptized 30 January 1645), Robert I (baptized 6 September 1649, buried 27 October 1649), Robert II (born 13 February 1651), Elizabeth (baptized 10 April 1652), and a stillborn (buried 5 February 1654).

44. LMA, formerly GL MS 977/1, no foliation.

45. TNA: PRO, C 6/197/94; Clarke and Campling (eds.), *Visitation of Norfolk 1664*, vol. 1, p. 112.

46. *The names, dignities and places of all the Collonells ... and Ensignes of the City of London* (1642), brs.; Keith Lindley, *Popular Politics and Religion in Civil War London* (Aldershot, 1997), pp. 207–08.

47. TNA: PRO, SP 19/95, p. 24; Mary Anne Everett (ed.), *Calendar of the Committee for Advance of Money, part 1. 1642–45* (1888), p. 374.

48. LMA, formerly GL, MS 978/1, p. 8.

49. 'Lebenslauff', p. 416.

50. Anthony Wood, *Athenae Oxonienses* (1692), vol. 2, pp. 12–13; Roger Pooley, 'Crisp, Tobias (1600–1643)', *ODNB*. The London bookseller George Thomason dated his copy of *Christ Alone Exalted* 22 July 1643.

51. Tobias Crisp, *Christ Alone Exalted* (1643), preface, p. 19.

52. C. Hill, 'Dr Tobias Crisp, 1600–43', in *The Collected Essays of Christopher Hill. Volume Two* (Brighton, 1986), pp. 141–61; D. Parnham, 'The humbling of "High Presumption": Tobias Crisp dismantles the puritan *Ordo Salutis*', *Journal of Ecclesiastical History*, 56 (2005), pp. 50–74; D. Parnham, 'The Covenantal Quietism of Tobias Crisp', *Church History*, 75 (2006), pp. 511–43.

53. Lawrence Clarkson, *The Lost sheep Found* (1660), p. 9.

54. 'Lebenslauff', pp. 416–17; Lead, *Wars of David*, sig. A2^{r-3}. Elsewhere, Jane recalled being about 18 when she had her transformative religious experience. This is accurate since she did not turn 19 until within 10 days of Crisp's death, see; Jane Lead, *A Fountain of Gardens* (1697), vol. 2, sig. a^v.

55. J.F. Maclear, 'Crisp, Tobias (1600–1643)', in Richard Greaves and Robert Zaller (eds.), *Biographical Dictionary of British Radicals in the Seventeenth Century* (3 vols., Brighton, 1982–84), vol. 1, p. 192.

56. Frederick Arthur Crisp, *Collections relating to the family of Crispe* (1882), vol. 1, pp. 13–15, 19; Henry Waters (ed.), *Genealogical Gleanings in England* (2 vols., Boston, 1901), vol. 1, pp. 831–34, vol. 2, pp. 1362–63; Keith Lindley, 'Wilson, Rowland (*bap.* 1613, *d.* 1650)', *ODNB*; Michael J. Jarvis, 'Rowe, Owen (1592/3–1661)', *ODNB*.

57. 'Lebenslauff', pp. 417–18.

58. LMA, formerly GL, MS 978/1, p. 11; *LJ*, v, 663.

59. TNA: PRO, SP 19/3, p. 84, SP 19/5, p. 258, SP 19/95, p. 24; Everett (ed.), *Calendar Committee Advance of Money, part 1*, p. 374.

60. Parliamentary Archives, HL/PO/JO/10/1/232; TNA: PRO, Prob 11/233 fols. 273r–76v.

61. TNA: PRO, E 179/252/15; LMA, formerly GL, MS 978/1, no pagination. John Strype would note that Three Kings Court was inhabited by wholesale dealers.

62. Records of London's Livery Companies Online, http://www.londonroll.org/search.

63. TNA: PRO, C 6/154/186; TNA: PRO, C 6/39/295.

64. TNA: PRO, C 6/106/11; Thomas Birch (ed.), *A Collection of State Papers of John Thurloe* (7 vols., 1742), vol. 5, p. 56, vol. 6, p. 399. According to Anthony Wood, Sir John Mules was a Portuguese ambassador, see; Andrew Clark (ed.), *The Life and Times of Anthony Wood, antiquary, of Oxford, 1632–1695*, Oxford Historical Society 19, 21, 26, 30, 40 (5 vols., Oxford, 1891–1900), vol. 2, p. 289.

65. John Hassam *et al.* (eds.), *A Volume relating to the early History of Boston containing the Aspinwall Notarial Records from 1644 to 1651* (Boston, 1903), p. 360.
66. Charles Firth and R.S. Rait (eds.), *Acts and Ordinances of the Interregnum, 1642–1660* (3 vols., 1911), vol. 2, pp. 75–78.
67. Valerie Pearl, 'Thomson, Maurice (1604–1676)', rev. *ODNB*; Keith Lindley, 'Tichborne, Robert, appointed Lord Tichburne under the protectorate (1610/11–1682)', *ODNB*; Tai Liu, 'Cokayn, George (*bap.* 1620, *d.* 1691)', *ODNB*; C.B. Cockett, 'George Cokayn', *Transactions of the Congregational Historical Society*, 12 (1933–36), pp. 225–35.
68. Firth and Rait (eds.), *Acts and Ordinances*, vol. 1, pp. 614–26, 958–84, 1072–105; vol. 2, pp. 24–57, 456–90; *LJ*, vii, 201–09, 219–30; *LJ*, x, 46–62.
69. D.E. Howell James (ed.), *Norfolk Quarter Sessions Order Book 1650–1657*, Norfolk Record Society 26 (1955), pp. 21, 25, 27, 28, 30.
70. Howell James (ed.), *Norfolk Quarter Sessions*, pp. 59, 60.
71. LPL, COMM/12B/2; TNA: PRO, Prob 11/308 fols. 66r–70v; Blomefield, *Norfolk*, vol. 7, p. 56, vol. 11, p. 94; *Gentleman's Magazine*, 101, part ii (1831), pp. 406–07.
72. 'Lebenslauff', pp. 418–19.
73. *A Calendar of the freemen of Lynn, 1292–1836*, Norfolk Archaeological Society (1913), p. 114; Norfolk R.O., PD 39/2; TNA: PRO, Prob 11/125 fols. 450v–51r; Clarke and Campling (eds.), *Visitation of Norfolk 1664*, vol. 2, pp. 163–64; G.A. Metters, 'The rulers of King's Lynn in the early seventeenth century', unpublished University of East Anglia Ph.D. thesis, 1982, pp. 58, 329.
74. Norfolk R.O., PD 39/1; Venn and Venn (eds.), *Alumni Cantabrigienses*, vol. 3, p. 337; Joseph Foster (ed.), *The Register of Admissions to Gray's Inn, 1521–1889* (1889), p. 115; CUL, Ch(H), Pell papers, 6, 7.
75. Norfolk R.O., PD 39; TNA: PRO, Prob 11/180 fols. 46v–47r.
76. Bulwer (ed.), *Visitation of Norfolk 1563*, vol. 2, p. 449; TNA: PRO, Prob 11/289 fol. 132r–v; Blomefield, *Norfolk*, vol. 4, pp. 514, 518.
77. Bodl., MS Tanner 64 fol. 106; Ketton-Cremer, *Norfolk in Civil War*, p. 154.
78. CUL, Ch(H), Pell papers, correspondence; Norfolk R.O., BL/F 1/12, BL/F 1/14, BL/F 1/15, BL/F 1/16, BL/F 3/12; *Norfolk lists from the Reformation to the present time* (Norwich, 1837), p. 16.
79. CUL, Ch(H), Pell papers, 3.
80. CUL, Ch(H), Pell papers, 2 nos. 11, 15; Pell papers, 5 nos. 16, 21, 71; Pell papers, correspondence nos. 57, 87, 93.
81. CUL, Ch(H), Pell papers, 2.
82. Norfolk R.O., PD 39/2; Norfolk R.O., ANW 22/1, will register, Glover, fol. 268.

83. *Calendar of freemen of Lynn*, pp. 92, 96, 100, 107, 111, 114, 117; Norfolk R.O., PD 39/1, 2; Metters, 'Rulers of King's Lynn', pp. 32, 321, 333, 357, 422. John Lead the elder's children were Katherine (baptized 1 November 1576), Margaret (baptized 29 September 1577), John (baptized 7 December 1578, buried 4 February 1639), Robert (baptized 4 February 1582), Edmund (baptized 20 September 1583, buried 14 June 1608), and Susan (baptized 28 January 1587, buried 9 December 1591). The Margaret Lead, daughter of John, buried on 11 December 1591 may have been a second daughter of that name.

84. Norfolk R.O., PD 39/2; TNA: PRO, Prob 11/112 fols. 10v–11r.

85. Norfolk R.O., PD 39/2; TNA: PRO, Prob 11/209 fol. 33r–v; Metters, 'Rulers of King's Lynn', p. 415.

86. Norfolk R.O., PD 39/2; TNA: PRO, Prob 11/126 fol. 94r–v; Norfolk R.O. (King's Lynn), KL/C 51/71; Metters, 'Rulers of King's Lynn', p. 359.

87. Norfolk R.O., PD 39/2; TNA: PRO, Prob 11/160 fols. 422v–23r; TNA: PRO, Prob 11/164 fol. 22r; Metters, 'Rulers of King's Lynn', p. 419.

88. *Calendar of freemen of Lynn*, p. 131; TNA: PRO, Prob 11/118 fols. 215r–16r; Metters, 'Rulers of King's Lynn', p. 410.

89. TNA: PRO, C 2/JasI/R6/39, 44.

90. M.S. Giuseppi and D. McN. Lockie (eds.), *Calendar of the Cecil Papers in Hatfield House. Volume 19, 1607* (1965), pp. 9, 493; G. Dyfnallt Owen (ed.), *Calendar of the Cecil Papers in Hatfield House. Volume 24, Addenda, 1605–1668* (1976), p. 106; Metters, 'Rulers of King's Lynn', pp. 305, 358.

91. TNA: PRO, STAC 8/59/6; Metters, 'Rulers of King's Lynn', pp. 44–48, 358.

92. G.A. Metters (ed.), *The King's Lynn Port Books 1610–1614*, Norfolk Record Society, 73 (2009), pp. 67, 164, 165, 170, 171, 191, 201; R.W.K. Hinton (ed.), *The Port Books of Boston, 1601–40*, Lincoln Record Society, 50 (1956), pp. 64–65; Metters, 'Rulers of King's Lynn', pp. 146, 147, 179, 184, 234, 244, 246, 261, 275, 280, 283, 287, 307, 333, 358.

93. TNA: PRO, Prob 11/125 fol. 450v.

94. Norfolk R.O., PD 39/1, 2. John and Mary Lead's children were John I (baptized 3 March 1615, buried 21 May 1615), Katherine (baptized 26 January 1617, buried 5 February 1617), Barbary (baptized 26 March 1618), William (baptized 11 October 1620, buried 6 February 1670), Mary I (baptized 30 November 1622, buried 1 December 1622), John II (baptized 8 July 1630, buried 22 July 1630), Mary II (baptized 13 February 1632), and Margaret (date of baptism unknown).

95. Norfolk R.O., PD 39/1, 2.

96. Metters, 'Rulers of King's Lynn', pp. 358, 422.

97. CUL, Ch(H), Pell papers, 1 no. 8; Norfolk R.O., PD 39/2.

98. TNA: PRO, Prob 11/138 fol. 282r; TNA: PRO, Prob 11/180 fols. 46v–47r; CUL, Ch(H), Pell papers, 1; Pell papers, 8 nos. 107, 115; Metters, 'Rulers of King's Lynn', pp. 359–62.

99. CUL, Ch(H), Pell papers, 5 no. 16; Pell papers, correspondence nos. 51a, 57a, 97, 81, 159; 'Lebenslauff', pp. 418–19.

100. Anon., *A briefe and true Relation of the Seige and Surrendering of Kings Lyn to the Earle of Manchester* (1643); Mackerell, *Antiquities of King's-Lynn*, pp. 235–36; Henry Hillen, *History of the Borough of King's Lynn* (Norwich, 1907), vol. 1, pp. 347–62.

101. CUL, Ch(H), Pell papers, 8 no. 117; Pell papers, correspondence no. 66.

102. 'Lebenslauff', p. 419; cf. Lead, *Fountain of Gardens*, vol. 2, sig. a2ᵛ, where she recalled being '*the Wife of a Pious Husband*' for about 25 years.

103. CUL, Ch(H), Pell papers, 8 no. 117; Norfolk R.O., NCC, will register, Battelle, 81, will of Hamond Ward of Letheringsett (probate 28 March 1651).

104. Jane Lead, *The Enochian Walks with God* (1694), p. 30; Jane Lead, *A Fountain of Gardens* (1697), vol. 1, p. 69.

105. *Calendar of freemen of Lynn*, p. 131; Metters, 'Rulers of King's Lynn', pp. 375 n. 74, 410.

106. TNA: PRO, Prob 11/225 fol. 131r.

107. 'Lebenslauff', p. 419; Norfolk R.O., PD 39/1.

108. Norfolk R.O., PD 39/2; Mackerell, *Antiquities of King's-Lynn*, pp. 25–26; Hillen, *History of King's Lynn*, vol. 1, p. 375.

109. Mackerell, *Antiquities of King's-Lynn*, pp. 9, 236; Hillen, *History of King's Lynn*, vol. 1, pp. 365–66.

110. TNA: PRO, Prob 11/266 fol. 49v; Mackerell, *Antiquities of King's-Lynn*, pp. 42, 278; Metters, 'Rulers of King's Lynn', p. 428. Perhaps this was the same site later used by Elijah Eyre & Co who operated the Lady Bridge Brewery from about 1820 to 1896, see; Lesley Richmond and Alison Turton (eds.), *The Brewing Industry: A Guide to Historical Records* (Manchester, 1990), p. 139.

111. TNA: PRO, C 5/395/151; TNA: PRO, C 5/41/70; TNA: PRO, C 5/150/Pt2/16; TNA: PRO, Prob 11/238 fol. 154v; Clarke and Campling (eds.), *Visitation of Norfolk 1664*, vol. 2, p. 183.

112. Metters, 'Rulers of King's Lynn', p. 375 n. 74.

113. Edmund Carter, *The History of the county of Cambridge* (1819), p. 79; *Collectanea Topographica et Genealogica*, 1 (1834), p. 127.

114. TNA: PRO, C 54/3624, no. 13; TNA: PRO, C 111/188, packet 23.

115. Firth and Rait (eds.), *Acts and Ordinances*, vol. 2, pp. 1320–42, 1355–1403, 1425–55.

116. LMA, parish register of All Hallows, Tottenham, 'Robert Warde the sonn of Hamond Warde gent and by Elizabeth his wife was baptised Thursday

the vi^th of September 1649'; apprenticeship of Robert Ward II, son of Hamon Ward, gentleman of Tottenham High Cross, to Benjamin Hinton, goldsmith on 19 February 1668 in Records of London's Livery Companies Online, http://www.londonroll.org/search; LMA, ACC/0564/052.

117. LMA, formerly GL, MS 978/1, no pagination.

118. TNA: PRO, SP 18/33, fol. 54; *CSPD 1652–53*, p. 150.

119. Thomas Birch (ed.), *A Collection of the State Papers of John Thurloe* (7 vols., 1742), vol. 3, p. 200, vol. 4, pp. 396–97; TNA: PRO, SP 18/153, fol. 240; *CSPD 1656–57*, p. 280.

120. Thomas Fuller, *The Church History of Britain* (1655), p. 189, section vii; W.B. Patterson, 'Fuller, Thomas (1607/8–1661)', *ODNB*.

121. TNA: PRO, C 5/378/115; TNA: PRO, C 6/124/14; TNA: PRO, C 7/379/81; TNA: PRO, C 7/401/79; TNA: PRO, C 7/420/5; TNA: PRO, C 7/442/82.

122. Norfolk R.O., PD 547/1; Norfolk R.O. MC 632/8/1-16, 797x4.

123. Ethel Bruce Sainsbury (ed.), *A Calendar of the Court Minutes of the East India Company, 1660–1663* (Oxford, 1922), p. 372.

124. Alfred Beaven, *The Aldermen of the City of London* (1908), pp. 75–119 http://www.british-history.ac.uk/no-series/london-aldermen/hen3-1912.

125. A.W. Cornelius Hallen (ed.), *The Registers of St. Botolph, Bishopsgate, London* (3 vols., 1889–93), vol. 2, p. 181.

126. Lead, *Fountain of Gardens*, vol. 2, sig. a2^v; Jane Lead, *A Fountain of Gardens. Vol. III. Part I.* (1700), pp. 61–62; Jane Lead, *A Fountain of Gardens. Vol. III. Part II.* (1701), pp. 20–21, 304–05; cf. Lead, *Wars of David*, sig. A2^{r-2}, which inaccurately dates her widowhood to 1671.

127. TNA: PRO, Prob 6/45 fol. 42v; 'Lebenslauff', p. 419.

128. TNA: PRO, Prob 11/357 fol. 122r-v; TNA: PRO, Prob 11/386 fol. 39r-v; TNA: PRO, Prob 11/421 fols. 396v–99r; TNA: PRO, Prob 11/502 fols. 338r–40r.

129. Bodl., MS Rawlinson D 106.

130. William Gurnall, *The Christians Labour and Reward* (1672).

CHAPTER 3

Lead's Life and Times (Part Two): The Woman in the Wilderness

Ariel Hessayon

This part of Lead's life and times covers the period from 1670 to 1695; that is from the beginning of her widowhood until she went blind. Because of her extensive spiritual diaries it is much better documented than the preceding chapter. Even so, Lead's memory began to deteriorate with age with the result that her recollection of certain dates is not always reliable. Added to this are some stylistic interventions introduced by Lead's first amanuensis to his manuscript transcripts of her earliest writings not to mention subsequent minor editorial intervention on their publication. All of which means that when reading Lead's printed works we should not assume that every sentence is an exact copy of the original, even if we can be confident that the text accurately conveys her sense.

In the following discussion I have supplemented familiar published evidence with more discoveries. The suggestion that Lead was more radical than has been supposed is here reinforced. My argument again

I am grateful to Olaf Simmons and Andrew Weeks for their help with the German; to Jane Ruddell, archivist of the Mercers' Company; and to Guido Naschert and Mirjam de Baar for information concerning Friedrich Breckling and Tanneke Denijs respectively. I have also profited from the advice of Lorenza Gianfrancesco and Lionel Laborie but remain responsible for any mistakes or shortcomings.

A. Hessayon (✉)
Department of History, Goldsmiths,
University of London, London, UK

© The Editor(s) (if applicable) and The Author(s) 2016
A. Hessayon (ed.), *Jane Lead and her Transnational Legacy*,
DOI 10.1057/978-1-137-39614-3_3

relies somewhat on association, with the focus as much on extensive and overlapping domestic and continental networks of assorted millenarians, prophets, theosophists and devotees of mystic and spiritualist authors generally as on Lead herself. What we see in this part is an evolution of Lead's thought as she came under successive influences and began to develop her own distinctive beliefs. It was a religious journey with staging posts: an initial Calvinist obsession with sin and predestination wedded to a conventional Protestant understanding of the coming apocalypse; then the introduction of Jacob Boehme's teachings and accompanying visions of a female personification of divine wisdom; finally, the adoption, albeit with inconsistencies, of the doctrine of the universal restoration of all humanity. It was the last together with Lead's apparent dependence upon visions and revelations that repulsed certain former admirers of her writings, turning them into some of Lead's most vehement critics.

I

In 'The Life of the Author' Lead recalled being 'visited once again with a vision from God'. This vision was of an unprecedented intensity in which she was 'given to understand' that:

> the loss of outward things, and all impediments and various sufferings served only to prepare the path by which the heavenly powers and gifts could descend into our souls unhindered, and make us forget and abandon all that perpetually distracts and opposes the outward person.

Thereafter Lead was daily inspired by 'new revelations' which broke forth with such frequency that she was initially incapable of finding someone who might 'accept and understand' what had been made manifest within her. This sequence of events was said to have begun in 1668—about two years before her husband's death. In *A Fountain of Gardens*, however, Lead's '*First Vision*' was dated April 1670; some two months after she became a widow. It is difficult to reconcile the chronology here unless, as seems likely, the supposedly earlier vision of 1668 was misdated: in Jane's narrative its message of spiritual fortitude in the face of worldly sorrows is placed after God withdrew William Lead from the earth and 'transferred him to the upper regions'. Moreover, elsewhere Jane maintained that the 'Spirit of Prophecy' had been declared unto her 'since 1670'.[1]

At any rate, in April 1670 Lead visited an unnamed female friend in the countryside. While walking in isolated woods and contemplating the 'Paradisical World' she saw a vision of an 'overshadowing bright Cloud'. In its midst was a woman 'most richly adorned with transparent Gold, her Hair hanging down, and her Face as the terrible Crystal for brightness, but her Countenance was sweet and mild'. Immediately Jane heard a voice informing her that the figure she beheld was God's 'Eternal Virgin-Wisdom' come to unseal the 'Treasures of God's deep Wisdom'. This female personification of divine wisdom, whose face shone like the sun, would be like a 'true Natural Mother' for Jane, serving as a womb for Jane's spiritual rebirth. Three days later while sitting under a tree the same figure reappeared in 'greater Lustre and Glory' with a majestic crown upon her head, saying; 'Behold me as thy Mother, and know thou art to enter into Covenant, to obey the New Creation-Laws, that shall be revealed unto thee'. Then she held out a golden book with three seals upon it. Hidden within this sealed book were the 'deep Mysteries of the Divine Wisdom' which only the eternal virgin's offspring could break open. Accordingly, Jane bowed and prostrated herself at the virgin's feet. Having returned home to London and encouraged to wait by a 'highly illuminated' man somewhat acquainted with these matters, she received another vision six days later. Now the Virgin Queen was accompanied with an innumerable train of virgin spirits and an immense army of angels. Jane agreed to join the virgin's company and was immediately surrounded by this heavenly host and made a spirit of light.[2]

It is tempting but, as we shall see, problematic to identify the 'highly illuminated' man in Jane's account with Dr John Pordage (1607–1681), whose spiritual meditations and journal from 21 June to 12 July 1675 was entitled 'Sophia: that is the lovely eternal virgin of the godly wisdom'.[3] Pordage had formerly been rector of Bradfield, Berkshire where, together with his wife Mary (d.1668)—whom he had married for 'ye Ex[c] ellent Gift of God he found in her'—and a woman named Mary Pocock (fl.1649–fl.1691), he had established a spiritual community before September 1650. Members adopted biblical names; thus Pordage was 'Father *Abraham*', his wife Mary, '*Deborah*', while Pocock was '*Rahab*'. Afterwards they were joined by Thomas Bromley (1630–1691) and Edmund Brice (fl.1648–fl.1696), two members of Oxford University, who heard Pordage preach a sermon 'in Great Power' at St Mary's, the University church. Another who became convinced of the 'Extraordinary Power & operation of y⁰ Spirit' and joined himself and waited with them was Philip Herbert (1619–1669), fifth Earl of Pembroke. So too did Joseph Sabberton, a former Parliamentarian army officer who became Pembroke's steward after the Restoration.[4] Yet they were repeatedly denounced by the minister Richard Baxter, who considered Pordage and his 'family' to be the principle English followers of the German Lutheran mystic Jacob Boehme (c.1575–1624). Baxter claimed that they 'pretend to hold visible and sensible Communion with Angels', distinguishing between good and evil spirits by sight and smell. Although he maintained that they also espoused community of goods, Baxter conceded that their tenets did not extend to polygamy (community of women). Indeed, these Behmenists were said to abhor sexual relations and, advocating chastity as an alternative, apparently objected to the lawfulness of marriage; Bromley for example died unwed and childless.[5]

Pordage, Bromley and Sabberton are all referred to as highly illuminated men in 'The Life of the Author'; as leaders of a society 'gripped and moved' by the 'self-same spiritual benediction' whom Lead encountered after 'diligent searching and enquiry'. Indeed, there was mutual rejoicing when they finally 'found each other' and came together to await God.[6] In her preface to two posthumously published treatises by Pordage issued together under the title *Theologia Mystica, or The Mystic Divinitie Of the Æternal Invisibles* (1683), Lead called him a 'holy Man of God' possessed of profound spiritual insight; 'not only a *Seeker*, but a successful *Finder* of that rich Pearl of the Gospel'. Yet there has been much confusion as to when Lead first became acquainted with the man whose 'great and spiritual Advantages' enabled him to satisfy her enquiring mind with answers concerning some 'deep and weighty' points of divinity. For although Lead affirmed that this was in 1663, her recollection is contradicted by all other evidence.[7] Thus in one version of Richard Roach's early eighteenth-century retrospective and self-serving history of the Philadelphian Society, Lead was said to have joined in the work after the death of Pordage's wife Mary, who had been buried at Bradfield on 25 August 1668.[8] Moreover, writing in her spiritual diary on 1 January 1682—just three weeks after Pordage's burial—Lead recorded that her friend had stood with her 'in pursuance of the great Things of the Kingdom' for 10 years; i.e., since the end of 1671.[9] To complicate matters further, Lead's future son-in-law Francis Lee reckoned that her 'familiar friendship' with Pordage began in either August 1673 or 1674.[10] So perhaps Lead's printed testimony may have been incorrectly transcribed: instead of 1663 she meant 1673, by which date both she and Pordage had suffered the loss of their spouse.

According to Lead, the society she joined 'grew mightily in size' eventually numbering more than 100 adherents. Foremost among their 'much reputed elders' was Dr Pordage, who became 'a special instrument to encourage, impel and assist' Lead in strengthening the dispensation of divine grace.[11] Pordage had an equally high regard of Lead's spiritual abilities, prizing her 'Extraordinary gift' of revelation. Therefore, they agreed 'to wait together in prayer and pure dedication' in expectation of God's coming.[12] So that they could be united in their 'secret devotion' Pordage welcomed Jane into his house where they 'lived together in great spiritual happiness for around six years' until his demise; that is from roughly 1676 to 1681.[13] Most likely this was in the London suburb of St Andrew's, Holborn where at the time of his death Pordage occupied a property at Red Lion fields.[14]

From 13 March 1676 Pordage is mentioned or alluded to frequently in Lead's *Fountain of Gardens,* even providing—along with Bromley—a posthumously published testimony of his 'fellow traveller' appended to the first volume of these spiritual diaries.[15] Doubtless because Lead held Pordage in great esteem, indeed she 'never knew anyone who possessed such a high and splendid recognition of God's deepest secrets', he was entrusted with joyfully recording her 'new heavenly revelations'.[16] Lead's reliance upon Pordage as her amanuensis is evident to the modern reader: with the exception of her first vision of April 1670 all subsequent entries in *A Fountain of Gardens* appear to date from August 1673 when, as we have seen, Lead's 'familiar friendship' with Pordage may have begun. This dependence was also recognised by contemporaries. Thus gaps in her published spiritual diaries were commonly attributed to missing passages in Pordage's manuscript copy. As the editor's introduction preceding the final instalment indicated, the death of Lead's 'Intimate Friend, who diligently transcribed all her Spiritual Papers, has prevented us from seeing many Things, that would Doubtless have been preserved by him'.[17] Consequently it is unsurprising that in an echo of another authorship controversy, namely that Jacob Boehme did not write Boehme, the patristic scholar Henry Dodwell (1641–1711) alleged in a letter to Francis Lee that Jane Lead did not write Lead:

> I know not how your Mother in law is qualifyed to write the style in which her Books are penned. But this I have observed, that there are many things ingredient in that style, which are quite out of the way of the education, or conversation, or even reading of women. It consists of many Latine terms,

of terms of Art, of the old Platonick Mystical Divinity, of all the modern Enthusiasts, of Jacob Behm, of the Judicial Astrologers, of the Magic Oracles, of the Alchymists, of which too many are in English, but not ordinarily to be met with. I very much doubt whether she would be able to give an account of the terms used in the writings which go under her name, if she were critically examined concerning them. But I think I have discovered the footsteps of another and a more likely Author of them. I mean D^r. Pordage. I find she has been intimate with him ever since the time that she has set up for Prophetick visions ... These things make it very suspicious to me, that the words and style of all her Books are that D^rs, and none of hers.[18]

Dodwell, like Lee, was a nonjuror and he initiated their correspondence in October 1697, shortly after the public emergence of the Philadelphian Society. Aghast that Lee seemed to be promoting schism from the Church of England, Dodwell drew upon his extensive knowledge of early Christianity—specifically the second century Montanist controversy and the example of Tertullian—to warn repeatedly against both the transitory attractions offered by the 'Spirit of Enthusiasm' and the beguiling utterances of charismatic female prophets.[19] Besides these precedents, Dodwell's attack on Lead can be situated more broadly within the context of contemporary fears of heterodox women of the type outlined by Lucinda Martin in her contribution to this volume. Lee, who would write *The History of Montanism*, responded at great length. Explaining that until she went blind in late 1695 his mother-in-law regularly recorded her 'experiences and discoveries', he acknowledged that Pordage 'contributed much to the preservation of the greatest part'. Comparing what Lead wrote on loose slips of paper to the Sibylline leaves—the Sibyls were pagan prophetesses, one of whom supposedly predicted the coming of Christ—Lee declared that having compared the originals with Pordage's transcripts he could find no interpolations designed to improve Lead's style or sense, except for minor adjustments to punctuation and occasional transposition of the verb. Furthermore, Lee attested that he had 'daily undoubted proofs' of Lead's ability to write in such a style on a wide variety of subjects. In short, Lead was the author of the works published under her name.[20]

Although Dodwell may have overstated the case for stylistic intervention, he was surely closer to the mark with regard to content. This is contrary to the view of Lead's modern biographer Joanne Sperle, who has asserted that Lead had a 'profound influence' on Pordage not only as a nurse tending his ailing body but also as a spiritual companion and conversation partner.[21] While Lead and Pordage may have been mutual mentors his influence on her was transformative. As we saw in chapter 2, Lead's religious beliefs were largely moulded by a militant puritanism that conflicted with her parents' moderate Anglicanism. Indeed, her youthful preoccupation with sin and subsequent embrace of what was considered antinomian doctrine left an imprint that could not be erased by mysticism: Calvinist covenant theology and predestination. The residue of these teachings informed Lead's *The Heavenly Cloud Now Breaking* (1681) issued some six months before Pordage's death and, as Lee stressed, 'never transcribed by him nor ... revised as to the prose'.[22] Nonetheless, it was presumably Pordage who introduced Lead to Boehme and perhaps also alchemical terminology.

Among the heterodox views developed by Boehme was his understanding of the Trinity, which he had been accused of denying through his introduction of a fourth person, Sophia (symbolizing the Noble Virgin of Divine Wisdom). Although Lead never went so far as to proclaim belief in a Quaternity, or the four-fold nature of God, her adoption of Boehme's teachings on Sophia invited Dodwell's charge that by calling her Virgin Wisdom a goddess she was reiterating an ancient Gnostic heresy, even making this figure the 'Mother of the Son of God as to his eternal generation'.[23] While Lead's reverence for Virgin Wisdom derived from Boehme, either directly or else mediated by Pordage, her independent-minded elaboration of this figure was also shaped by her Calvinist heritage as well as by idiosyncratic apocalyptic exegesis.

Thus in a vision dated 11 May 1676 concerning the fulfilment of prophecies, Lead felt the stirrings of a new everlasting body growing within her that would bring forth that 'Perfect Life, without the stain of Sin'. Perfect life, however, would only be granted to those predestined to it by God the Father, who would bring forth this 'New Creation' through Wisdom.[24] Elsewhere she anticipated the 'bright *Star*' of Virgin Wisdom's day, describing how the 'Eternal Virgin Wisdom' who had 'brought forth the Son of God before all Time' would soon give birth to a 'new Generation of Virgin Spirits'. As heirs to eternity 'Wisdom's Off-spring' would constitute the glory of God's spouse, the New Jerusalem (Revelation 21:2).[25] But as Warren Johnston shows, besides referring 'again and again' to the New Jerusalem, Lead conflated Virgin Wisdom with the woman clothed with the sun (Revelation 12:1). Hence just as the child brought forth by the pregnant woman of the Apocalypse signified for Lead the introduction of sin and sorrow into the world through the failings of the first woman, Eve, so from Eternal Virgin Wisdom would a new birth spring forth in which there would be 'nothing but Joy, Life, Blessing and Eternal Power and Dominion'. This 'glorious Son of Might' was the man-child that would rule the nations (Revelation 12:5).[26] Modern commentators have invariably understood Lead's ambiguous prophecy in a spiritual sense. As we shall see in chapter 4, however, certain contemporaries were to allege something altogether more dramatic; which brings us to someone whose martyrdom at Moscow Lead was to recall some dozen years after the event, namely the 'Coolman' who perished by fire.

*   *   *

In October 1676 the 'learned' poet and prophet Quirinus Kuhlmann (1651–1689) of Breslau was in London, 'city of miraculous delight', defending the published writings of the 'most highly Illuminated' Jacob Boehme.[27] Whether or not Kuhlmann subsequently returned to the continent is unclear but between 10 March 1677 and 3 March 1678 he can be placed intermittently at Bromley-by-Bow near London.[28] From what Kuhlmann called the '*Rose-lilly*' at Bromley—the lily-rose was an emblem for the sprouting of Boehme's new spirit—he then embarked on a journey for Constantinople ('Eastern Rome'), intending to present Sultan Mehmed IV with a copy of Jan Amos Comenius's *Lux e tenebris* (1665). This book incorporated miscellaneous contemporary prophecies generally focused upon the imminent destruction of the Papacy and the Habsburg Empire.[29] While at Bromley-by-Bow, Kuhlmann had stayed with John Bathurst (*d*.1694?), a blind merchant. In 1697 the Lutheran spiritualist Friedrich Breckling (1629–1711), who had spoken several times with Bathurst at Amsterdam, recalled that Bathurst had bemoaned Kuhlmann's excesses and ingratitude.[30]

To finance Kuhlmann's mission to the Ottoman Empire Bathurst reportedly gave him an enormous amount of money, variously reckoned at more than 30,000 florins or 36,000 guilders. Accompanied by his wife Magdalena von Lindaw (a widow almost twice his age), together with her three children, Kuhlmann journeyed through Calais, Paris, Marseille, Malta and Smyrna before arriving at Constantinople. It was a wasted effort.[31] Upon his return Kuhlmann abandoned Magdalena at Amsterdam in spring 1679 before travelling to London again and then temporarily settling in Paris, 'the lily city'. From there he wrote several epistles between mid-December 1679 to March 1681 including to his former partner the

Dutch prophetess Tanneke Denijs; to his former wife Magdalena; to the elderly visionary Antoinette Bourignon; to Bathurst (then at Jamaica)[32]; and to his 'much esteemed friend' Breckling at Amsterdam.[33] Shortly thereafter Kuhlmann was back in London writing to the Jesuit scholar Athanasius Kircher and to Louis XIV 'king of the lilies'.[34] From late May to mid-June 1681 Kuhlmann was at Islington, probably staying with Bathurst who had settled there on returning from the West Indies.[35]

Kuhlmann clearly had messianic pretensions, believing that he was a new Christ and 'a partaker both of the celestial & terrestrial nature'. With a reportedly pious lady who conjured spirits he hoped to generate a child that would be the grandson of God. She was the daughter-in-law of Bathurst's wife and can probably be identified as either Mary Gould (Maria Anglicana) or Esther Michaelis de Paew. Their unborn offspring was to be a new Solomon, the instrument through whom the Philosopher's stone would be produced. Perhaps Kuhlmann regarded Solomon as the male personification of Divine Wisdom, a counterpart to Sophia. At any rate, his claim was confirmed by that 'doctor of the devil' Dr Hollgraffen. But Mrs Bathurst's daughter-in-law conceived a daughter who was born and buried at Amsterdam.[36]

In his three-part epic apocalyptic poem *Der Kühlpsalter* (Amsterdam, 1684–86), Kuhlmann named a number of people whom he regarded as forerunners, kindred spirits and acquaintances. Among them were Injur ('Injurien') and Lead.[37] The former was Anne Jurien or Jewrin, sometime of St Sepulchre's, London. Suggestively, her extensive but unpublished spiritual diaries recorded that on 23 June 1678 a year of jubilee was proclaimed and prophesied to her by an angel in a dream.[38] After being widowed she married the similarly widowed Bathurst by licence on 9 October 1681.[39] As Anne Bathurst she became a leading light among the Philadelphians.[40] Then there was the prophetess Tanneke Denijs (*d*.1702?) who visited London in 1679 and who would travel from Holland to England and back, probably in 1690, to facilitate the dissemination of pre-Philadelphian writings in the Dutch Republic.[41] Another figure mentioned by Kuhlmann, albeit disapprovingly, was the apostate Baptist prophetess Anne Wentworth.[42] The author of four published pamphlets and some letters, Wentworth was a 'familiar Acquaintance' of Kuhlmann's and knew Lead too. Lead thought her a sincere if 'very Precipitate' woman prone to melancholic delusions, alluding to one of Wentworth's prophecies in an entry dated 29 December 1677. Upon consideration Lead was advised that the spiritual community of which she was a member should have 'no part' with Wentworth, neither as divine avenging agents, nor 'in desiring

Plagues and Vials of Wrath to come so immediately upon the Formal Churches' (Revelation 161:1).[43] Evidently Lead was not a woman alone in the wilderness. Indeed, we shall see that the story concerning Kuhlmann and the grandson of God was to be circulated in the context of Lead allegedly envisaging herself as the grandmother of a new Christ.

*   *   *

All the while Lead's family were anxious about her welfare, and perhaps also the company she was keeping. Thus on 30 August 1676, about six months after she had moved in with Pordage, Lead was visited by her daughter R. who informed her mother that an opportunity had opened for Lead's 'Redemption out of all Straits and Cares'. Urged to forsake her current arrangement Lead was invited to leave London and instead live with her brother, who would provide for her for the remainder of his life. She recalled that he dwelled some hundred miles from the capital which makes it almost certain that this sibling was Jane's eldest brother James Ward of Twyford, Norfolk.[44] Indeed when James composed his will on 26 April 1678 he bequeathed Jane £5 and appointed her one of his executors.[45] Nonetheless, acting upon a 'Divine Impulse' Jane had drawn up a 'Spiritual Contract' with Pordage and resisting temptation refused to break her covenant with her 'elect' friend.[46] Lead remained loyal to Pordage until the end. A few days before his death and in some agony he called for her. And when Pordage drew up his will on 28 November 1681 Lead was one of four witnesses along with Pordage's daughter Sarah Stisted, Elizabeth Douglas and Elizabeth Blagrave.[47]

II

With the passing of her spiritual mate and with both surviving daughters possibly now married—R. died at an unknown date having given birth to a daughter while Barbary married one Walton—Lead seems to have become financially dependent on another man.[48] This was Dr Edward Hooker (c.1614–c.1705) a licentiate of the College of Physicians. Hooker has been undeservedly neglected. Lead called him Pordage's '*true hearted and right worthy Friend*'. It was Hooker who acted as Pordage's literary executor issuing—thanks to the generosity of William Burman physician of Wilmington in Kent—two of Pordage's treatises posthumously as *Theologia Mystica* (1683). Hooker also provided a prolix 100-page prefatory epistle to this collection which was preceded by Lead's briefer address to the 'impartial and well-disposed' reader.[49] Besides his passion for theosophy Hooker was by this date the author of some devotional works entitled *A Notion for the Ocean* and *Divine breathings* (now respectively lost or misattributed). In addition, he owned a substantial library—although shortly before his death its impressive holdings in Hebrew, Greek, Latin, English and various foreign languages had been successively depleted by the Great Fire of 1666, robbery and pilfering. Pride of place in Hooker's collection undoubtedly went to 'all the works of Jacob Behme and his life ... and Edward Taylors compendium of Jacob Behmes works in the inside of the cover of which ... are some verses'.[50]

Hooker may have financed Lead's first publication *The Heavenly Cloud Now Breaking*, which was printed for the author in June 1681.[51] While the verses incorporated within this text were Lead's own compositions, Hooker appended a verse postscript to Lead's second publication *The Revelation of Revelations*.[52] The printing of this book was finished on 8 December 1682 and undertaken by Andrew Sowle, whose main business was printing for the Quakers. The title-page indicates that the work was sold by Sowle at 'the Crooked Billet' in Shoreditch as well as by Lead from what may have been her new residence 'at the Carpenters' in Bartholomew Close (St Bartholomew the Great). This part of London was said to be 'a creditable Place to live in' and was situated near the thriving second-hand book trade in Little Britain. Interestingly one of the places where Lead and some of her fellow Philadelphians would meet was also in the proximity of Bartholomew Close, namely Westmoreland House.[53] *Revelation of Revelations* was Lead's first book intended for the public, with *Heavenly Cloud* issued beforehand as an introduction. While Pordage saw the former work, which was based on what the author had 'seen, heard, tasted and felt' since October 1679, Hooker may have again financed publication.[54]

Lead's association with Hooker appears to have lapsed at an undetermined date. She is not named in Hooker's unpublished writings of 1688 and 1690, while his verse postscript was omitted from the second edition of *Revelation of Revelations* (1701).[55] Moreover, when Francis Lee wrote to Hooker concerning *Theologia Mystica*—probably in the late 1690s—the two had not met.[56] Perhaps Hooker was one of several people who in the years following Pordage's death gradually fell away from Lead's spiritual community leaving their society 'much scattered and distracted'.[57] Lead's fortunes revived, however, when a wealthy widow was so taken with the message of *Revelation of Revelations* that she invited Lead to her home outside London. Meetings then took place at this residence until the widow's death, which seems to have been before the Glorious Revolution of 1688–89.[58] Perhaps this woman was the 'Honourable and Pious Lady' to whom Lead lent a now lost autograph manuscript.[59] All the same, during the 1680s Lead was part of a dwindling and ineffectual circle. Their number had declined still further by the beginning of the 1690s. But it would be a mistake to think that Lead persevered almost alone.[60] For besides an unnamed 'distressed Christian' whom she recorded visiting on 20 September 1684, Lead wrote of her 'fellow Waiters and Believers' who walked with her in 'unity of Love and Life'.[61] Regrettably most have received little or no attention in modern scholarship.

Foremost of these unheralded figures was Joseph Sabberton. Probably the son of a Norwich tanner,[62] Sabberton was a cornet in the Maiden troop mustered at Norwich in August 1643. Having served initially in Oliver Cromwell's cavalry regiment, he rose to the rank of Captain under the command of General Edward Whalley.[63] During the Commonwealth he purchased property, notably the manor of Terrington, Norfolk.[64] But Sabberton lost these estates at the Restoration and with them an annual income of about £300 to £400. A Royalist agent characterised him as a witty, active, discontented person 'above ordinances',[65] while another unsympathetic source considered him an authority among the Philadelphians' precursor society. This is confirmed by the published accounts of both Lead and Richard Roach, the latter recalling an eminent assembly in London headed by Captain Sabberton.[66] Joseph Sabberton was most likely also the man of that name who in 1680 publicised a medicine containing scurvy grass that was available from him at the Norwich coffee house near Aldersgate, London. Suggestively, this supposed elixir was advertised in a sheet printed by John Gain, the same man who printed works for Kuhlmann. Moreover, Pordage's second son and namesake was another manufacturer of medicine concocted from scurvy grass.[67] So too was the physician Charles Blagrave.[68] He was the son of Elizabeth Blagrave, one of the women who along with Lead witnessed the elder Pordage's will.

Elizabeth Blagrave (*d*.1693) had deposed on Pordage's behalf when he was charged with blasphemy in 1654. She was, moreover, the widow of the regicide and former MP for the borough of Reading, Daniel Blagrave.[69] Elizabeth was the recipient of a letter dated 12 June 1687 which mentioned several people associated with the precursor society including Thomas Bromley as well as some obscure women: Mrs Cawton, Mrs Deboray, Mrs Melson and Mrs Pocock. The writer hoped that

Mrs Blagrave could interpret his strange dream and also referred to the preface of one of Boehme's works. He was J.B., i.e. probably John Bathurst.[70] Together with his wife Anne, Bathurst reportedly remained among the Philadelphians' forerunner society, who were said to gather each week to share their 'dreams, visions and revelations'.[71] Significantly, two of four witnesses of John Bathurst's will (3 November 1692) were witnesses of Elizabeth Blagrave's will (3 April 1693): Samuel Sankey and John Coughen.[72] Samuel Sankey (*fl.*1706) was the nephew of Francis Pordage, John's younger brother, and had sold Charles Blagrave's remedy from 'the Three Brushes' in Southwark. He may also have been the Mr Sanchy or Sancky who corresponded with Thomas Bromley.[73] John Coughen (*c*.1638–1717?) was then an extra-licentiate of the College of Physicians. His role in the foundation of the Philadelphian Society was far greater than has been appreciated—as Richard Roach would eventually acknowledge.[74]

Coughen was the Dutch-born son of an English merchant resident at Amsterdam who had corresponded with the Independent minister Joshua Sprigg about the Jewish pseudo-messiah Sabbatai Sevi.[75] Although educated at Cambridge and then ordained at Ely, Coughen converted to Quakerism in 1663 becoming 'fam[e]d and renown[e]d' among them. After conversing with an English minister at Haarlem named Edward Richardson, however, he was persuaded to return to the Church of England. Thereafter Coughen studied medicine at Rotterdam and Leiden before returning to England.[76] It should be added that Richardson (*d*.1678), who had fled England after being implicated in the Yorkshire plot of 1663, was influenced by the prophecies of the Dutch Fifth Monarchist Johannes Rothe and was also a friend of Kuhlmann's.[77]

Another noteworthy member of Lead's spiritual community was Helen Pight (1611–*fl.*1692). She was twice married and had 13 children, but only one surviving son. Helen was the widow of Richard Pight, formerly surveyor of the melting houses at the Mint in the Tower of London and 'a wilfull man, who brought much trouble upon them'. After becoming bed-ridden she experienced a series of visions between December 1680 and October 1682, followed by a final revelation in October 1692. These were transcribed by a Mr Stephens, possibly Samuel Stephens, who married Anne Bathurst's daughter Elizabeth; the identification is suggested by the presence of Bathurst's hymns and visions in the same manuscript.[78] Pight was very likely the widow Elner or Elianor Pight who received bequests from Elizabeth Blagrave and Francis Pordage (1622–1692?).[79]

Like his elder brother John, Francis Pordage had been educated at Cambridge University with his maintenance supported by a London livery company.[80] Although never ordained he was presented to the rectory of Stanford Dingley, Berkshire about 1651 but was ejected at the Restoration.[81] By March 1670 Francis's wife Katherine had become acquainted with the Quaker Isaac Penington and over the next five years Penington sent several letters containing spiritual counsel to the couple.[82] Thereafter Francis and Katherine Pordage became pillars of the Philadelphians' precursor society, holding meetings at a rented house in London.[83] Katherine predeceased her husband, who drew up his will on 20 August 1691 while residing at St Mary's, Whitechapel. Besides bequests to his family, including some of John Pordage's children and grandchildren, Francis also left gifts to certain friends. Among them were Mary Pocock (a spinster whose association with the Pordage family spanned more than 40 years), Elianor Pight, Mrs Leaton, Mrs Wells, Jabez Wood of Westminster (who witnessed Elizabeth Blagrave's will), Jane Lead and her widowed daughter Mrs Barbary Walton. Lead was then living at Francis's house on Lambert Street in Goodman's Fields, Whitechapel since she was given the curtains around her bed as well as an armchair and a little table. In addition, Lead received a tenement on Church Street in Coverly Fields, Stepney that she was entitled to hold for the remainder of her life once ground rent had been paid and covenants performed.[84]

Within three years of Francis Pordage's demise a number of people connected with Lead's society were either dead or most likely dead: John Bathurst, Elizabeth Blagrave, Thomas Bromley, Helen Pight and Mary Pocock. Yet just as Lead was negotiating the transition from insignificance to obscurity, her star unexpectedly began to rise. As we shall see, this was largely because one of Kuhlmann's former partners circulated Lead's writings within the Dutch Republic. Indeed, it was to be claimed that while John Pordage and Thomas Bromley were alive their spiritual community was still respected, whereas when Lead became their 'oracle' the Philadelphians accepted the 'regiment of women' and were little better than Papists, idolising individual religious experiences and revelations.[85]

III

On 18 March 1692 the court of assistants of the Mercers' Company held a vote. They had been petitioned by 20 widows who wanted to be admitted as almswomen to one of the ten recently built Lady Mico's almshouses.

Eight were elected by show of hands. Among them was Jane Lead, whose brother Hamond Ward had been a Mercer. Shortly after Easter, on Monday 4 April 1692 Lead entered her new home. These properties had been erected at a cost of £780-5s.-9d. on a 3-acre field managed by the Mercers situated near the churchyard of St Dunstan's, Stepney. Their construction fulfilled the wishes of Dame Jane Mico (d.1670), who had bequeathed the Mercers £1,500 to build an almoner's house for 10 poor widows aged 50 or upward. Court minutes, contemporary plans and an early nineteenth-century watercolour indicate that the almshouse was a single-storey brick structure with a sloping roof subdivided into ten apartments. Each had slit wooden shutters covering windows at the front together with a cellar which gave access—through a bolted door—into a 12 foot wide backyard. The front yard was 16 foot wide. Lady Mico's almshouses were rebuilt in 1856 and then again in 1976.[86]

Lead was still living at 'the Lady *Mico's* Colledge, right against *Stepney Church*' some two years later when her next publication appeared. Entitled *The Enochian Walks with God*, it contained further revelations dated from 16 July 1693 to 15 July 1694 which Lead felt impelled to issue before she died (she was now 70). Crucially, this work marked her public rejection of a fundamental Calvinist tenet—predestination—and adoption of the doctrine of the '*Universal* Restoration of all *Mankind*, with the *fallen Angels*'. She was to claim that although she had heard of this teaching she had received it neither from the 'Wisdom of men' nor 'according to Tradition' but rather by divine revelation in 1693. Having initially been averse to the notion of 'general Redemption', Lead was eventually encouraged by a 'very Worthy' woman with whom she walked in 'fellowship' to publish this doctrine as a 'foundational Truth'.[87] And while Lead may have largely formulated her conception of universal redemption independently over several years it should be noted that she had forebears. Thus besides a congregation of 'Universalists' active at King's Lynn in 1669,[88] various ideas concerning the possibility of universal redemption had been espoused during the English Revolution by among others Gerrard Winstanley, Theaurau John Tany, Richard Coppin and William Erbery. Indeed, from the early eighteenth century together with these figures Lead would be incorporated within a Universalist tradition that stretched back to Origen, Clement of Alexandria and Gregory of Nyssa.[89]

But because Boehme's writings seemed to contradict the notion that ultimately all the fallen angels would be saved, Lead would become entangled in a damaging controversy with certain 'highly illuminated' followers of the Teutonic Philosopher. A forewarning of these 'zealous angry Flames' was provided in her answer to a question that had been put privately: if God was pure, holy and good then why was there evil and sin in the world? This appeared as a postscript to *Enochian Walks*, which was licensed on 24 July 1694.[90] The book was printed and sold by David Edwards in Nevil's Alley, Fetter Lane (St Andrew's, Holborn). It was also available both from Lead and her daughter Barbary Walton, then lodging at a Mr Mileman's in New Street, at the end of Dean Street, right against the '3 Tuns' (St Andrew's, Holborn).[91] As an impoverished widow subsisting on a charitable allowance of £8 per annum paid in twelve monthly instalments of 13*s*. 4*d*. Lead would have been unable to afford printing costs.[92] Perhaps publication was financed by the same person responsible for the posthumous second edition of Thomas Bromley's *The Way to the Sabbath of Rest* (1692). If so, this person was doubtless one of Bromley's many English friends and acquaintances.[93] Alternatively, a German translation of Bromley's work printed at Amsterdam in 1685 suggests a continental readership for mystical and visionary texts produced by members of Lead's society. The possibility of money coming from abroad matches the view of Lead's editor in 1695 that like Jesus she was a prophet not without honour, save in her own country (Matthew 13:57).[94] So it is to the reception of Lead's writings among Dutch- and German-speakers that we now turn.

* * *

According to Friedrich Breckling in 1690 Tanneke Denijs journeyed to England with two companions. Breckling was well informed since on Tanneke's return he began living with her at The Hague. Either Breckling or an associate added that the purpose of Tanneke's visit had been to disseminate pre-Philadelphian writings in the Dutch Republic. Apparently certain Dutch-based readers of Boehme had become tired of the Teutonic Philosopher and, longing for fresh inspiration, 'fell blindly' for Lead's works. These were received like 'a gospel' and quickly circulated within the Dutch Republic and German-speaking territories.[95] Significantly, another person acquainted with Breckling in 1690 was Loth Fischer (*d.*1709), who had left his native Nuremberg for the comparative religious toleration of the Dutch Republic in the 1680s. As Lucinda Martin outlines in her chapter, Fischer had been in communication with his fellow German exile and Boehme devotee Johann Georg Gichtel (1638–1710) since 1683.

Fischer, moreover, would correspond with Lead and translate many of her works into German from 1694—the year that Breckling mentioned Lead in his autobiography.[96]

Recalling these events Francis Lee would write of how Lead, 'an ancient devoted matron', had retreated from the world and 'retired to end her days in a private cell' (i.e. Lady Mico's almshouses). Suddenly she found herself much noticed abroad. Lee stated that a couple of Lead's books were 'sent over into a neighbouring land' by 'a merchant to his correspondent and friend there'.[97] This fits the evidence discussed above and suggests that the merchant was John Bathurst; his correspondent Friedrich Breckling; the courier Tanneke Denijs; the year 1690. Lee continued, relating that 'first one book, then another' was translated 'without delay into the languages of two considerable nations' to be 'greedily devoured by abundance of pious souls'.[98] Elsewhere, in his editorial preface to Lead's *The Wonders of God's Creation Manifested, In the Variety of Eight Worlds* (1695), Lee considered it a providential blessing that German translations of Lead's two earliest books *The Heavenly Cloud Now Breaking* and *Revelation of Revelations* were being so well received.[99] These had appeared respectively as *Die Nun brechende und sich zertheilende Himmlische Wolcke* (Amsterdam, 1694) and *Offenbahrung der Offenbahrungen* (Amsterdam: Hendrick Wetstein, 1695). The translator of both works was Loth Fischer and it likely that his German versions initially circulated within spiritualist and Behmenist circles consisting of Breckling, Denijs, Gichtel and others. Thus on 14/24 September 1694 Gichtel sent a recently printed copy of Lead's *Himmlische Wolcke* to the Pietists Johann Wilhelm Petersen and his wife Johanna.[100] Moreover, after Gichtel diverged from Lead and Fischer on key points of doctrine, he would censure Fischer for extolling Lead's two 'little books', adding that manuscript passages from Fischer's German translation of *Revelation of Revelations* were discussed daily within Gichtel's spiritual community; a celibate household of so-called 'Angelic Brethren'.[101]

The question remains, however, as to who financed this venture? Lead recalled that about 1694 she suddenly received a letter from a man living in a German-speaking territory. He asked her to clarify some of the ideas advanced in *Heavenly Cloud* (whether the English original or German version is unclear). Thereafter they began corresponding and when the unnamed German learned that Lead had written a number of things he generously offered to publish her works—not just in German translation but also in English.[102] From other sources we know that this person was Baron Dodo von Knyphausen (1641–1698), a privy councillor at the Brandenburg-Prussia court in Berlin who had invested in the trade of African commodities.[103] Indeed, Gichtel claimed that Fischer 'would have gotten stuck with his translation' of Lead had not B[aron] von K[nyphausen] given him an annual pension of 400 guilder.[104] Knyphausen had met Breckling as early as 1679 and temporarily provided shelter to Antoinette Bourignon (1616–1680) at his Lütetsburg estate in East Frisia until she fled following an accusation of witchcraft.[105] This 'distinguished gentleman' was also a patron of the Petersens to whom in 1695 he sent a manuscript copy of Lead's tract dealing with 'the Return of all Creatures', identified as Lead's *Eight Worlds*.[106] It was later issued with a 'further manifestation' that had been prompted by Lead's vigil on 17 October 1695 for a deceased female friend, together with an answer to a question posed by a 'Noble and Worthy Inquirer'.[107] Presumably this was von Knyphausen, who was most likely also the author of '*Entretiens sur la Restitution Universelle de la Creation*; or *A Conference upon the Universal Restitution of the Creation*'. This '*ingenious*' manuscript treatise was advertised in a 1697 publication by Lead and written in vindication of her position by an 'Illustrious Person' against the protests of a certain learned physician. It was subsequently attributed to '*a Noble Eminent Lord and Minister*' at the court of the Prussian king.[108]

As we have seen, the Petersens received Lead's works from Gichtel as well as von Knyphausen. In addition to *Himmlische Wolcke* Gichtel sent them three more books on 20/30 May 1695. One was doubtless *Offenbahrung der Offenbahrungen* because Gichtel referred to their discussion of this text in a letter dated 11/21 June 1695.[109] A further letter from Gichtel of 6/16 August 1695 outlined Lead's biography.[110] About now the Petersens probably made contact with Lead using von Knyphausen as an intermediary, and Johann Petersen would maintain his correspondence with Lead until shortly before her death.[111] While this burgeoning epistolary network enabled Lead to disseminate her writings within German-speaking circles possessed of what she considered to be a greater spiritual understanding than many of her compatriots, it also facilitated the reception of their writings in England.[112] Although it must be stressed that the balance of books circulating within these spiritual communities was weighted more towards the export of English authors—notably Lead, Pordage and Bromley—than the import of their continental counterparts, there were nevertheless signs of mutual influence. Thus among the writings originating abroad discussed by Lead and her circle would be texts concerning universal salvation, apparitions and the appearance of a new Christ.[113] An early example was a little book by the 'Celebrated Dr. Petersen' containing a 'Narrative of some strange Transactions and Revelations' experienced by Rosemunda Juliana von Asseburg over about a dozen years. Published in English translation as *A Letter to some Divines* with a preface by Francis Lee, it occasioned some objections by a learned physician to whom Lee responded on 9 September 1695.[114]

Another of Lead's correspondents was Loth Fischer. He can be placed at Utrecht from November 1693 and would maintain his association with Lead until her death. About autumn 1694—and certainly before the end of May 1695—Fischer began writing to Lead, imploring her to send him more of her manuscripts since he had heard that she 'had written much'. Hard pressed to satisfy the demands of an impatient readership, Fischer promised at the conclusion of *Offenbahrung der Offenbahrungen* that while awaiting further manuscripts from Lead he would begin translating Pordage's *Theologia Mystica*. After Lead acceded to Fischer's request further German translations of her works would be issued at Amsterdam in 1696.[115] But in the meantime a key actor had entered the scene: Francis Lee (1661–1719).

* * *

Born at Cobham, Surrey the younger son of a minor family with connections to the aristocracy, Francis Lee was a solitary child profoundly affected by his mother's premature death.[116] On 11 September 1675 he entered Merchant Taylors' school, London. He was then admitted a probationer fellow at St John's College, Oxford in June 1679 from where he graduated BA on 9 May 1683, proceeding MA on 19 March 1687.[117] Lee quickly gained a reputation for the 'indefatigable' industry with which he pursued the study of Oriental languages, especially Hebrew. Consequently he was dubbed 'Rabbi Lee' at Merchant Taylors', a nickname he retained throughout his life. A memorandum of 1685 indicates that Lee divided his time at university between prayer and learning, focusing upon the Hebrew Bible, the Greek New Testament, Latin, Italian, French, Arabic, mathematics, philosophy, history and poetry. So excessive was his devotion to God and scholarship that he soon 'impair'd his eyes'. In later life Lee developed a cataract in his left eye, prompting him to warn against reading by candlelight. Yet Lee was not a dull man, claiming that had he been able to write the 'Real & Secret History of his own Life' it would not be believed. Judging from Thomas Haywood's self-censored unpublished 1722 biography, which drew on Lee's private papers, friends' recollections and personal knowledge, this was true.[118]

Lee was an 'Original, Genuine, unprevaricating' nonjuror. Deeply loyal to James II he had considered taking up arms during the Duke of Monmouth's rebellion (1685) to help quell the ill-fated rising. After the Glorious Revolution his eyes were said to sparkle with an irregular fire when speaking of the deposed king and Lee later admitted that he would have 'gladly laid down his life' to serve James's son the Old Pretender, James Stuart.[119] Following the Revolution in both 'Church & State' Lee felt obliged to leave Oxford, quitting the university in December 1688. Taking advantage of a College statute which enabled fellows to travel abroad for five years he went initially to Ghent, Bruges, Ostend and Brussels about July 1690 and then towards the end of 1691 on what amounted to a Grand Tour.[120] Lee journeyed first to Holland, entering Leiden University on 11 June 1692 to study medicine.[121] He then passed through German-speaking territories en route to the Italian peninsula. Having viewed the 'Libraries and Curiosities' of Rome, Florence, Naples and Milan he reached Padua where on 1 September 1692 Lee was admitted as a medical student at the university. He did not take a degree, however, and eventually moved to Venice. There with an unnamed friend Lee hired a house.[122]

At Venice Lee began practising medicine, apparently with 'most uncommon Success'.[123] Since June 1691 Lee had also been supported by an annuity of £100 per annum granted by John Stawell, baron of Somerton; one of three students who had been under his care at Oxford.[124] But the young Lord Stawell died about January 1693 leaving huge debts. The management of Stawell's estate together with the claims of various creditors was discussed in both houses of Parliament, with the issue of Lee's annuity pleaded on his behalf by his elder brother William. During these proceedings, which spanned from mid-March to early April 1694, it was alleged that Francis Lee had gone abroad to serve as tutor to James II's son at the French royal château of Saint-Germain-en-Laye. Although the accusation was false, Lee was nevertheless deprived of his annuity. Uncharacteristically he was still angry about it several years later.[125] Lacking funds he was forced to return home in late 1694. Lee's itinerary on this eventful journey included Vienna, Prague, Dresden, Leipzig, Halle, Berlin, Hanover and Leiden.[126] As we shall see, certain connections he made during these travels prepared the way for the subsequent spread of Philadelphian principles.

On reaching Leiden and in the process of making preparations to sail to England, Lee met with some learned men 'at different stages' during the remainder of his time in the Dutch Republic.[127] They were keen to read Lead's writings. Two were 'perfect strangers': Dr William Scott or Schott physician to George William, Duke of Zell,[128] and a Dr B. at The Hague.[129] A third man was Benjamin Furly (1636–1714), Quaker merchant of Rotterdam, who had a considerable reputation 'both for learning and prudence'.[130] Furly would be mentioned in Philadelphian correspondence and when his library was auctioned in 1714 it contained two works by Lead in German translation—one of which was *Himmlische Wolcke*.[131] Furly, moreover, was acquainted with the physician and future Philadelphian John Coughen, who had deposited an almanac containing a prophecy of Charles II's death by poison at Furly's house.[132] Eager to receive a transcript of Lead's writings, Furly recommended that on arriving in England Lee visit Lead. Perhaps because he had seen a copy of *Enochian Walks*, which supplied Lead's address, Furly knew where she lived and so gave Lee directions. Accordingly, soon after returning home Lee made an appointment to see Lead at Lady Mico's almshouses.[133] He was accompanied by two young foreign students of divinity, for whom the multi-lingual Lee acted as interpreter. One was almost certainly Heinrich Johann Deichmann of Hanover, a future secretary of the Philadelphian Society; the other quite likely a Mr Scheller.[134]

Thereafter Lee began visiting Lead regularly and as their friendship grew so he was permitted to view her writings. For the most part these consisted of 'loose papers, like the Sibylline leaves', supplemented with Pordage's transcripts. Some Lee edited as a 'little book'—probably *The Laws of Paradise*—which was afterwards translated into German by Dionysius Andreas Freher (1649–1728), an immigrant from Nuremberg.[135] Disseminated by Loth Fischer the work had a mixed reception, with certain readers 'edified' but others critical of what they perceived as Lead's tendency towards advocating 'a monastical or eremetical faith'. Further objections were soon raised against Lead's books generally: they savoured of 'popish enthusiasm' and were 'contrary to the spirit of the Reformation'. As a nonjuror and devotee of Catholic mystics, notably his namesake St Francis de Sales, Lee was equally suspect. The upshot was that, as Lead's editor, Lee became inextricably linked with her. With an increasing number of letters to deal with (forwarded from abroad by Fischer), Lead also came to depend upon Lee as her secretary and when she went blind towards the end of 1695 he became her amanuensis.[136]

All the while Lee declined to fulfil the residency requirements of his Oxford fellowship. Consequently it was declared void about August 1695 and his place at St John's filled the following June. Although an 'unkind' rumour spread that Lee had been expelled 'either for Schism, or Heterodox opinions', the real reason was his refusal to take priest's orders according to the founder's statutes, and consequently the oath of allegiance to William III. Deprived of his fellowship on a matter of conscience and with meagre financial resources, this became a 'Remarkable Time of Trial' for Lee. He was, however, now free to marry. Having resisted a tempting proposal from a certain Lord's daughter, Lee settled on someone 'much inferior … in respect of Person, Birth & Fortune'. This 'serious, sober, virtuous Gentlewoman' was Lead's long-suffering widowed daughter Mrs Barbary Walton. Friends were surprised that so 'Thoughtful, Contemplative, & Abstracted a scholar' should ever wed. But having developed a spiritual friendship with Barbary, in whom he saw 'a simplicity that was without guile', Lead assured him that their union would be blessed. Nonetheless Lee remained uncertain how to proceed in what was for him a 'great affair', and so decided to await divine guidance.[137]

In the meantime, through von Knyphausen's generosity Lead had vacated her 'cell' at Lady Mico's almshouses and by the beginning of October 1695 had begun renting a 'little house' close to Lee's lodging. Since Lee was probably then living with his brother William, a silk dyer in New George Street near Spitalfields, the property that Lead occupied was doubtless at Hoxton Square in Shoreditch, where she can be placed from mid-July 1697 until her death. The annual rent was £16 and she also paid scot and lot, a rate that would have entitled Lead to vote in Parliamentary elections had she been a male householder.[138] At this house Jane, Barbary and Francis started 'waiting upon God', giving themselves up to 'instant prayer and holy watchfulness' for 40 days in the hope that they would be joined by fellow believers. Despite the misgivings of Lee's friends and the opposition of his brother, who left 'no stone unturned to break asunder this knot', the 40-day wait continued. It culminated in Francis's marriage to Barbary in the presence of their 'spiritual friends' on 12 November 1695.[139]

The devotions of Lead's family at Hoxton evolved into daily private meetings at about 11 o'clock with a celebration of Christ's resurrection every Sunday.[140] Yet with the exception of Richard Roach (1662–1730) almost no one joined them. Like Lee, Roach was educated at Merchant Taylors' and subsequently St John's, Oxford where he graduated BA and was elected to a fellowship before proceeding MA in 1689 and BD in 1695.[141] Unlike Lee, however, Roach remained at Oxford after the Glorious Revolution and evidently took the oath of allegiance since he retained his fellowship. He also subscribed to the Thirty-Nine Articles on being presented to the rectory of St Augustine, Hackney in March 1690.[142] By July 1695 Roach was in communication with his former colleague Lee, as well as with Lead, Bathurst and Deichmann.[143] Then after the 40-day wait and with her eyesight failing Lead dictated a letter to Roach. Claiming that she had received visions from the Virgin Wisdom, whom she regarded as a divine oracle, Lead related how a stream of light emanating from the Virgin had entered Roach and that he was anointed to be a priest in the Virgin's orb. Lead, moreover, had been commanded to escort Roach's spirit to the 'High court of the Princely Majesty' where his commission was confirmed with a new name: Onesimus. She concluded by referring to her two most recent treatises, *Laws of Paradise* and *Eight Worlds*, adding that in 1696 further proof would be given of the coming Virgin Wisdom's day.[144]

Lead's 1695 publications benefited from the lapse of the Licensing Act on 3 May (which marked the end of pre-publication press censorship), and may have been financed by von Knyphausen. They were printed and sold by Tace Sowle from an address near the Quaker meeting house in White-Hart-Court in Gracechurch Street. Like her father Andrew, who had printed Lead's *Revelation of Revelations*, Tace specialised in printing for the Quakers and usually charged about £25 for 100 copies of a book.[145] Significantly, another work printed by Sowle that year was *Unpremeditated thoughts of the knowledge of God*. Written by a woman under the pseudonym Irena who styled herself a 'Lover of Truth and Peace', it can be confidently attributed to Rebecca Critchlow. She became a correspondent of Richard Roach and would hold Philadelphian meetings at her house in Baldwin's Gardens (St Andrew's, Holborn).[146] One additional work by a future Philadelphian needs to be mentioned here. This was *A New Years-Gift, or a Token of Love* (1693) by Mary Sterrell, which dealt with the theme of a year of jubilee in a manner reminiscent of Anne Bathurst. Intriguingly the pair may have shared a common Huguenot background.[147]

*   *   *

In March 1707 the correspondent of an Oxford antiquary wrote concerning Francis Lee's anonymous translation of four books commonly ascribed to Thomas à Kempis which had recently appeared as the second volume of *The Christian Pattern: or, the Imitation of Jesus Christ* (1707). The letter-writer recalled that Lee had married the daughter of Jane Lead, 'famous for her pretended visions and revelations, and one of the first beginners of the enthusiastic sect of the Philadelphians'. But he hoped that Lee had long since given up those 'extravagant religious whimsies and fooleries'.[148] Lee himself became extremely reticent about this episode in his life, refusing to fully answer his biographer's questions on the subject. Instead he made an enigmatic remark: 'There is a secret Idolatry in spiritual Friendship'. As we shall see, considering some of the allegations that were levelled against the Philadelphians dignified silence was perhaps Lee's best recourse. All the same, it is noteworthy that Lee was said to have retained particular Philadelphian beliefs until the very end, notably some derived from Boehme and especially Origen—presumably on the doctrine of universal salvation.[149]

NOTES

1. 'Lebenslauff', pp. 419–20; Jane Lead, *The Tree of Faith* (1696), pp. 2–3.
2. Jane Lead, *A Fountain of Gardens* (1697), vol. 1, pp. 17–21; Jane Lead, *The Laws of Paradise* (1695), preface.
3. Cf. Thune, *Behmenists*, p. 175.
4. Bodl., MS Rawlinson D 833, fols. 63r–64r; Richard Roach, *The Great Crisis* (1725), pp. 98–99; Ariel Hessayon, 'Pordage, John (*bap.* 1607, *d.* 1681)', *ODNB*; Ariel Hessayon, 'Bromley, Thomas (*bap.* 1630, *d.* 1691)', *ODNB*; Ariel Hessayon, 'Brice, Edmund (*fl.* 1648–1696)', *ODNB*; Ariel Hessayon, *'Gold Tried in the Fire'. The Prophet TheaurauJohn Tany and the English Revolution* (Aldershot, 2007), pp. 194–200, 317–23.
5. DWL, MS Baxter, Treatises III 67, fol. 302v; Richard Baxter, *The Vnreasonableness of Infidelity* (1655), part iii, p. 156; Richard Baxter, *A Key for Catholics* (1659), p. 331; Richard Baxter, *Reliquiæ Baxterianæ*, ed. Matthew Sylvester (1696), book 1, pp. 77–78.
6. 'Lebenslauff', p. 420.
7. J[ane] L[ead], prefatory epistle to John Pordage, *Theologia Mystica* (1683), p. 2.
8. Bodl., MS Rawlinson D 833, fol. 64v; Berkshire Record Office, D/P/22/1/1.
9. Jane Lead, *A Fountain of Gardens. Vol. III. Part II.* (1701), pp. 300–01.
10. DWL, MS 24.109, printed in Walton, *Notes*, p. 203.
11. 'Lebenslauff', pp. 420–21.

12. Bodl., MS Rawlinson D 833, fol. 64v; Walton, *Notes*, p. 203.
13. 'Lebenslauff', p. 421.
14. TNA: PRO, Prob 11/369 fol. 59r-v; LMA, formerly GL, MS 6673/5.
15. Lead, *Fountain of Gardens*, vol. 1, pp. 143–49, 151, 156, 181–82, 198, 255, 332, 385, 419–20, 421, 427, 477–78, 506–09; vol. 2, pp. 86–87, 137–38, 205, 246, 247, 260, 400; vol. 3, part one, p. 55; vol. 3, part two, pp. 300–01.
16. 'Lebenslauff', p. 421.
17. Lead, *Fountain of Gardens*, vol. 1, pp. 4, 57, 255, 257; vol. 3, part two, sig. A2r.
18. DWL, MS 24.109 (9), a-b, printed, except the postscript, in Walton, *Notes*, pp. 191–94.
19. Bodl., MS Cherry 22, fols. 48–50, 51–55; DWL, MS 24.109 (7), MS 24.109 (8), a-b, partly printed in Walton, *Notes*, pp. 188, 190–91.
20. Walton, *Notes*, pp. 202–03.
21. Joanne Sperle, 'God's healing angel: A biography of Jane Ward Lead', unpublished Kent State University Ph.D., 1985, pp. 88–89.
22. A. Capern, 'Jane Lead and the Tradition of Puritan Pastoral Theology' (this volume); Walton, *Notes*, p. 203.
23. DWL, MS 24.109 (9), a-b, printed in Walton, *Notes*, p. 193.
24. Lead, *Fountain of Gardens*, vol. 1, pp. 219–20.
25. Jane Lead, *The Wonders of God's Creation Manifested* (London: T. Sowle, [1695]), pp. 29–33; cf. Jane Lead, *The Revelation of Revelations* (1683), pp. 46–53.
26. Lead, *Fountain of Gardens*, vol. 1, pp. 468–71, vol. 2, pp. 125–30; Lead, *Revelation* (1683), p. 38; W. Johnston, 'Jane Lead and English apocalyptic thought in the late seventeenth century' (this volume).
27. E. Bernstein, 'Letters of Hilary Prach and John G. Matern', *Journal of the Friends Historical Society*, 16 (1919), p. 5; Quirinus Kuhlmann, *A. Z! Quirin Kuhlman a Christian Jesuelit his Quinary of slingstones* (1683), pp. 12–13, 22; Hessayon, *'Gold'*, p. 293.
28. Quirinus Kuhlmann, *A.Z. Der Kühlpsalter Oder Di Funffzehngesaenge* (Amsterdam, 1684–86), part 1, sig. A3, pp. 22, 25, 26, 32, 33; Quirinus Kuhlmann, *A.Z. The General London Epistle* (1679), p. 64.
29. Kuhlmann, *Christian Jesuelit*, title-page; Kuhlmann, *General London Epistle*, errata; Arlene Miller, 'Jacob Boehme: from Orthodoxy to Enlightenment', unpublished Stanford University Ph.D., 1971, pp. 300–02.
30. S.J. Baumgarten, *Nachrichten von mertwürdigen Büchern* (Halle, 1756), pp. 324–25; LPL, MS 1048a, fols. 146–49; cf. FbG, Chart A 306, pp. 232–36.
31. Quirinus Kuhlmann, *The Earle of Holland, chief of adepts* (1684), p. 40; Miller, 'Jacob Boehme', pp. 299, 302.

32. Kuhlmann, *Kühlpsalter*, part 1, p. 149; Quirinus Kuhlmann, *Des Christen Des Jesuelitens, Lutetier- Oder Pariser-schreiben* (1681), pp. 22–65.

33. Kuhlmann, *Christen Des Jesuelitens*, pp. 1–15, with partial contemporary English translation at Bodl., MS Rawlinson D 396, fols. 123r–24v.

34. Quirinus Kuhlmann, *A.Z. Quirini Kuhlmanni Kircheriana … ad Ludovicum XIV, regem liligerum* (1681).

35. Kuhlmann, *Christen Des Jesuelitens*, pp. 117, 118.

36. LPL, MS 1048a, fols. 146–49; FbG, Chart A 306, pp. 232–36; Baumgarten, *Nachrichten*, pp. 324–25.

37. Kuhlmann, *Kühlpsalter*, part 3, p. 23 line 6473, p. 40, lines 7829, 7840.

38. Chetham's, Mun. A.7.64, pp. 6, 29–30.

39. Chetham's, Mun. A.7.64, pp. 195–97; LPL, F/B/1-1680-83, printed in R.L. Beare, 'Quirinus Kuhlmann: where and when?', *Modern Language Notes*, 77 (1962), p. 381.

40. Bodl., MS Rawlinson D 833, fols. 57v, 65r, 65v, 82v, 87r.

41. Friedrich Breckling, *Autobiographie. Ein frühneuzeitliches Ego-Dokument im Spannungsfeld von Spiritualismus, radikalem Pietismus und Theosophie*, ed. Johann Anselm Steiger (Tübingen, 2005), pp. 48, 65, 92; Quirinus Kuhlmann, *Pariserschreiben an … Frau Tanneke von Schwindern* (Amsterdam, 1680); Kuhlmann, *Kühlpsalter*, part 1, pp. 151, 203, part 2, p. 35, part 3, pp. 24, 31, 39, 42; FbG, Chart A 306, p. 235; Miller, 'Jacob Boehme', p. 611.

42. Quirinus Kuhlmann, *The Parisian-Epistle of Quirinus Kuhlmann To Albertus Otho Faber* (1683), no. 14, quoted in Miller, 'Jacob Boehme', pp. 315–16 n. 58; Kuhlmann, *Kühlpsalter*, part 1, preface (no. 18), part 2, pp. 41, 54, part 3, pp. 23, 42.

43. Lead, *Fountain of Gardens*, vol. 2, pp. 520–21; Jane Lead, *The Revelation of Revelations* (2nd edn., 1701), pp. 175–76; W. Johnston, 'Prophecy, Patriarchy, and Violence in the Early Modern Household: The Revelations of Anne Wentworth', *Journal of Family History*, 34:4 (2009), pp. 344–68.

44. Lead, *Fountain of Gardens*, vol. 1, pp. 327–28; Lead, *Revelation* (1701 edn.), pp. 170–71.

45. TNA: PRO, Prob 11/357 fol. 122r-v.

46. Lead, *Revelation of Revelations* (1701 edn.), p. 170.

47. J[ane] L[ead], in Pordage, *Theologia Mystica*, p. 3; TNA: PRO, Prob 11/369 fol. 59r-v.

48. 'Lebenslauff', p. 420.

49. Pordage, *Theologia Mystica*, pp. 1, 3–4, 5, 7, 61; Richard Baxter, *The Certainty of the Worlds of Spirits* (London: T. Parkhurst and J. Salusbury, 1691), p. 176; 'William Burman or Boreman', in Early Modern Practitioners http://practitioners.exeter.ac.uk/sample-data/.

50. TNA: PRO, Prob 11/498 fols. 218v–21r.

51. Lead, *Fountain of Gardens*, vol. 3, part two, pp. 256, 260, 267.

52. DWL, MS 186.18 (1), p. 1; Lead, *Revelation* (1683), [p. 131], copy held at Union Theological Seminary Library (New York), Burke Library, 1683 L43; Jane Lead, *Offenbahrung der Offenbahrungen* (Amsterdam, 1695), pp. 263–64.

53. Lead, *Fountain of Gardens*, vol. 3, part two, p. 312; John Strype, *A Survey of the Cities of London and Westminster* (1720), book 3 chapter 12, at http://www.hrionline.ac.uk/strype/index.jsp; Paula McDowell, 'Sowle, Andrew (1628–1695)', *ODNB*.

54. Lead, *Revelation* (1701), sigs. A2v, b; Walton, *Notes*, p. 203.

55. Bodl., MS Rawlinson C 548.

56. Walton, *Notes*, pp. 240–41.

57. 'Lebenslauff', p. 421.

58. FbG, Chart A 297, p. 15; Thune, *Behmenists*, p. 80.

59. Lead, *Fountain of Gardens*, vol. 3, part two, sig. A2r.

60. Cf. Thune, *Behmenists*, pp. 80–81; Brian Gibbons, *Gender in Mystical and Occult Thought: Behmenism and its development in England* (Cambridge, 1996), p. 144.

61. Lead, *Fountain of Gardens*, vol. 3, part two, preface.

62. Percy Millican, *The Register of the Freemen of Norwich 1548–1713* (Norwich, 1934), pp. 144, 145; TNA: PRO, Prob 11/213 fols. 87r–88r.

63. TNA: PRO, E 121/2/5 no. 35, p. 16; C.H. Firth, 'The raising of the Ironsides', *Transactions of the Royal Historical Society*, new series, 13 (1899), p. 32.

64. TNA: PRO, C 54/3781/35; TNA: PRO, E 121/3/6; F.M., 'Account of the sale of Bishops' lands between the years 1647 and 1651', *Collectanea Topographica et Genealogica*, 1 (1834), p. 288; G. Jaggar, 'Colonel Edward Whalley', *Norfolk Archaeology*, 36 (1977), pp. 160–61.

65. TNA: PRO, SP 9/26; TNA: PRO, SP 29/67 no. 120, printed in 'Williamson's Spy Book', *Transactions of the Congregational History Society*, 5 (1911–12), pp. 254, 308.

66. FbG, Chart A 306, p. 235; 'Lebenslauff', p. 420; Roach, *Great Crisis*, p. 99.

67. Joseph Sabberton, *To make the true compound Elixir of scurvy-grass* (1680); John Pordage, *The true Spirit of Scurvy-Grass* (no date); TNA: PRO, Prob 11/393 fol. 71r–v.

68. Charles Blagrave, *Directions for the Golden Purging Spirit of Scurvey-Grass* (no date); Charles Blagrave, *Doctor Blagrave's Excellent and highly Approved Spirits of Scurvey-Grass* (no date).

69. John Pordage, *Innocencie Appearing* (1655), pp. 80–81; T.C. Wales and C.P. Hartley (eds.), *The Visitation of London begun in 1687*, Harleian Society, new series 16–17 (2004), part 1, pp. 38–39.

70. Bodl., MS Rawlinson D 832 fols. 3r–4r.

71. FbG, Chart A 306, p. 234.

72. TNA: PRO, Prob 11/419 fols. 13v–14v; TNA: PRO, Prob 11/414 fols. 227v–28.
73. TNA: PRO, Prob 11/498 fol. 124r-v; Thomas Bromley, *XCIV. Evangelisch-Christlich-Practicale Send-Schreiben Abgelassen an einige des Authoris gute freunde* (1719), pp. 87, 100, 103, 112, 119, 192.
74. Royal College of Physicians (London), Annals, vol. IV, fol. 103v; Staatsbibliothek Preussischer Kulturbesitz Handschriftenabteilung (Berlin), Nachlaß A.H. Francke, Kapsel 30—England betreffend, fol. 300.
75. BL, Add. MS 4292 fols. 134r–35r, partly printed in M. McKeon, 'Sabbatai Sevi in England', *Association for Jewish Studies review*, 2 (1977), pp. 157–58.
76. Gerard Croese, *The General History of the Quakers* (1696), book II, pp. 27–28, 30; 'The convincement of John Coughen', *Journal of Friends Historical Society*, 19 (1922), pp. 22–24; William Hull, *Benjamin Furly and Quakerism in Rotterdam* (1941), pp. 20–26; Charlotte Fell Smith (ed.), *Steven Crisp and his correspondents, 1657–1692* (1892), pp. 59, 61.
77. Breckling, *Autobiographie*, pp. 42, 48; Kuhlmann, *Christen Des Jesuelitens*, pp. 37, 60; Miller, 'Jacob Boehme', pp. 300, 304; Keith Sprunger, *Dutch Puritanism* (Leiden, 1982), pp. 160–61, 414.
78. National Archives of Scotland (Edinburgh), CH 12/20/9; TNA: PRO, Prob 11/476 fols. 281r–82v.
79. TNA: PRO, Prob 11/414 fol. 228r; TNA: PRO, Prob 11/412 fol. 274r.
80. GL, MS 30,708/3 fol. 223r; GL, MS 30,708/4 fol. 10r; Venn and Venn (eds.), *Alumni Cantabrigienses*, vol. 3, p. 381.
81. Pordage, *Innocencie Appearing*, pp. 37, 49, 89; Bodl., MS J. Walker e.5, fol. 156v; Edmund Calamy, *An Abridgment of Mr. Baxter's History of his life and tmes* (2nd edn., 2 vols., 1713), vol. 2, p. 104.
82. FHL, MS vol. 342, John Penington MSS, vol. 2, fols. 227–42, 310, 317, partly printed in John Barclay (ed.), *Letters of Isaac Penington* (2nd edn., Philadelphia, 1828), pp. 31–34, 136, 212–16, 257–61.
83. FbG, Chart A 297, p. 15; Thune, *Behmenists*, p. 81.
84. TNA: PRO, Prob 11/412 fols. 273r–74r.
85. FbG, Chart A 306, p. 235.
86. TNA: PRO, Prob 11/334 fol. 323r; Mercers' Company (London), Acts of Court, 1675–1681, fols. 132r–33r, 134v, 136r, 137r; Acts of Court, 1681–1687, fol. 14r-v; Acts of Court, 1687–1693, fols. 158r, 162v, 163r, 164r, 165r–66r, 178v–79r, 199r, 209r; MC/1/62/D/2; MC/1/62/D/3; *City of London Livery Companies Commission. Report, Volume 4* (1884), pp. 44–52; London Gardens Online, http://www.londongardensonline.org.uk/gardens-online-record.asp?ID=THM025#.
87. Jane Lead, *The Enochian Walks with God* (1694), pp. 17, 18, 21, 36, 37; Jane Lead, *A Revelation of the Everlasting Gospel-Message* (1697), pp. 1, 5, 15.

88. C.B. Jewson, 'Return of Conventicles in Norwich Diocese 1669—Lambeth MS no. 639', *Norfolk Archaeology*, 33 (1965), p. 17; LPL, MS 930 no. 56.

89. [Richard Roach], 'Preface' to [Jeremiah White], *The Restoration of All Things* (1712), no pagination; John Denis, 'Preface' to Jeremiah White, *The Restoration of All Things* (3rd edn., 1779), xxxiii–xxxiv; Thomas Whittemore, *The Modern History of Universalism* (Boston, 1830), pp. 112–14; Sarah Apetrei, *Women, Feminism and Religion in Early Enlightenment England* (Cambridge, 2010), pp. 191–92.

90. Lead, *Everlasting Gospel-Message*, pp. 15, 25; Lead, *Enochian Walks*, pp. 35–37; Jane Lead, *The Enochian Walks with God* (2nd edn., 1702), 'Advertisement'; Thune, *Behmenists*, pp. 72–76; Daniel Walker, *The Decline of Hell. Seventeenth-Century Discussions of Eternal Torment* (1964), pp. 219, 222–23.

91. Lead, *Enochian Walks*, title-page, p. 38; M. Treadwell, 'London printers and printing houses in 1705', *Publishing History*, 7 (1980), p. 22.

92. Mercers' Company, Acts of Court, 1687–1693, fol. 179r; MC/1/62/A/15.

93. Thomas Bromley, *The Way to the Sabbath of Rest* (1692), 'Publisher to the Reader'.

94. Lead, *Wonders of God's Creation*, sig. A2v.

95. Breckling, *Autobiographie*, p. 65; FbG, Chart A 306, p. 235.

96. Breckling, *Autobiographie*, pp. 65, 74; Johann Georg Gichtel, *Theosophia Practica*, ed. J.W. Ueberfeld (3rd edn., Leiden, 1722), vol. 1, pp. 125–26, 414.

97. Walton, *Notes*, p. 508.

98. Walton, *Notes*, p. 508.

99. Lead, *Wonders of God's Creation*, sig. A2v.

100. Johann Georg Gichtel, *Erbauliche Theosophische Send-Schreiben* ('Bethulia', 1710), vol. 3, pp. 132–33; L. Martin, 'Jane Lead in the correspondence of Johann Georg Gichtel' (this volume).

101. Gichtel, *Theosophia Practica*, vol. 5, pp. 3540–41, vol. 7, pp. 326–27; Thune, *Behmenists*, p. 111; Martin (this volume).

102. FbG, Chart A 297, p. 16; Thune, *Behmenists*, p. 81.

103. LPL, MS 1048a, fols. 138, 159; Bodl., MS Rawlinson D 832 fol. 53r-v.

104. Gichtel, *Theosophia Practica*, vol. 5, pp. 3741–42, vol. 7, p. 328; Thune, *Behmenists*, p. 81 n. 8; Martin (this volume).

105. Breckling, *Autobiographie*, p. 49.

106. Johann Wilhelm Petersen, *Lebens-Beschreibung Johannis Wilhelmi Petersen* (1719), pp. 297, 299; *The Life of Lady Johanna Eleonora Petersen Written by Herself*, ed. Barbara Becker-Cantarino (Chicago, 2005), pp. 15–17, 22; Thune, *Behmenists*, pp. 108–10, 113–14; Martin (this volume).

107. Lead, *Wonders of God's Creation*, pp. 67–89.

108. Lead, *Everlasting Gospel-Message*, p. 39; Lead, *Enochian Walks* (1702), 'Advertisement'; [Roach], 'Preface' to [White], *Restoration*, no pagination.

109. Gichtel, *Theosophische Send-Schreiben*, vol. 2, pp. 111–20, 126–33; Martin (this volume).
110. Gichtel, *Theosophische Send-Schreiben*, vol. 2, pp. 136–43; Martin (this volume).
111. J.W. Petersen, *Lebens-Beschreibung*, p. 297; Bodl., MS Rawlinson D 832 fol. 67r; FbG, Chart A 297, pp. 90–91, 123–29.
112. FbG, Chart A 297, p. 16; Thune, *Behmenists*, p. 81.
113. Francis Lee (ed.), *Theosophical Transactions by the Philadelphian Society* (5 vols., 1697), vol. 1, pp. 43–45, 46–52, vol. 3, pp. 142–51; LPL, MS 1048a, fols. 142, 150–52.
114. J[ohann] W[ilhelm] P[etersen], *A Letter to some Divines* (1695); Lead, *Fountain of Gardens*, vol. 1, pp. 493–502; Lead, *Revelation* (1701), pp. 171–72; Bodl., MS Rawlinson D 832 fol. 46r.
115. Walton, *Notes*, p. 508; Lead, *Offenbahrung*, pp. 284–85; Thune, *Behmenists*, p. 100.
116. TNA: PRO, Prob 11/537 fols. 73v–74v; G & C, MS 725/752, [Thomas Haywood], 'An Essay towards the Life or rather some account of the late Learned and pious Francis Lee, M.D.' (1722), no foliation; Francis Lee, *Apoleipomena. Or, Dissertations* (2 vols., 1752), vol. 1, pp. v–vi.
117. Harry Bristow Wilson, *History of Merchant Taylors' School* (1814), part ii, pp. 880–81 n.; Joseph Foster (ed.) *Alumni Oxonienses: The Members of the University of Oxford, 1500–1714* (4 vols., Oxford, 1891–92), vol. 3, p. 893; G & C, MS 725/752; Lee, *Apoleipomena*, vol. 1, p. vi.
118. G & C, MS 725/752; cf. Lee, *Apoleipomena*, vol. 1, pp. xxvii–xxviii.
119. G & C, MS 725/752.
120. G & C, MS 725/752; Anthony Wood, *Athenae Oxonienses*, ed. Philip Bliss (4 vols., 1813–20), vol. 4, col. 713; Walton, *Notes*, p. 509.
121. Bodl., MS Smith 47, fol. 106; R.W. Innes Smith, *English-Speaking Students of Medicine at the University of Leyden* (Edinburgh, 1932), p. 59.
122. G & C, MS 725/752; Lee, *Apoleipomena*, vol. 1, p. xvi; 'Alphabetical list of British medical students at Padua University, 1618–1771', https://members.rcpe.ac.uk/students/list/index.php.
123. G & C, MS 725/752; Lee, *Apoleipomena*, vol. 1, p. xvi.
124. G & C, MS 725/752; Lee, *Apoleipomena*, vol. 1, pp. vi–xvi.
125. G & C, MS 725/752; TNA: PRO, Prob 11/412 fol. 143v; *LJ*, xv, 179, 206, 226–27, 409, 410; *CJ*, xi, 128, 141–42, 150; Walton, *Notes*, p. 509.
126. G & C, MS 725/752; Lee, *Apoleipomena*, vol. 1, p. xvi.
127. Walton, *Notes*, p. 508; G & C, MS 725/752.
128. Bodl., MS Rawlinson D 832 fol. 67r; LPL, MS 1048a, fols. 119, 127, 146–47; FbG, Chart A 297, p. 5; FbG, Chart A 306, pp. 231–32; Thune, *Behmenists*, p. 125.

129. Friedrich Breckling was then at The Hague but he was not a doctor. Nor does he mention Lee in his autobiography.

130. Cf. Walton, *Notes*, p. 508, whose reading of 'Mr Finley at Rotterdam' has lead several modern researchers astray.

131. FbG, Chart A 297, pp. 107, 424; *Bibliotheca Furliana* (Rotterdam, 1714), p. 135, nos. 623, 624.

132. Hull, *Benjamin Furly*, pp. 22–23.

133. Walton, *Notes*, p. 508; Bodl., MS Rawlinson D 833 fol. 65r-v.

134. Breckling, *Autobiographie*, p. 74; Bodl., MS Rawlinson D 832 fols. 13r, 14r, 15r–16r, 17r-18r, 18r–19v; LPL, MS 1048a, fol. 103. Passes were issued for Shilgram Scheller, Salomon Scheller and Sigfred Scheller to go to Holland respectively on 1 October 1690, 1 December 1695 and 5 December 1696. Deichmann's, associate, however, departed on 1 August 1695.

135. Walton, *Notes*, p. 508; Bodl., MS Rawlinson D 833 fols. 16r, 18r, 20v.

136. Walton, *Notes*, pp. 508–09; G & C, MS 725/752.

137. Walton, *Notes*, pp. 509, 226–27; G & C, MS 725/752.

138. Walton, *Notes*, pp. 226–27; Mercers' Company, Acts of Court, 1700–07, fol. 101r.

139. Walton, *Notes*, p. 227; FbG, Chart A 297, pp. 16–17; Thune, *Behmenists*, pp. 82, 85–86.

140. Bodl., MS Rawlinson D 833 fol. 65v; FbG, Chart A 297, p. 178; Thune, *Behmenists*, p. 201.

141. Wilson, *History of Merchant Taylors'*, p. 1000; Foster (ed.) *Alumni Oxonienses*, vol. 3, p. 1261.

142. Bodl., MS Rawlinson D 832 fol. 1r.

143. FbG, Chart A 297, p. 17; Bodl., MS Rawlinson D 832 fols. 8r, 9r, 10r, 11v–12r, 13r, 15r–16r; Bodl., MS Rawlinson D 833 fols. 65v, 82v.

144. Bodl., MS Rawlinson D 832 fol. 51r–v.

145. FHL, Minutes for the Meetings for Sufferings, vol. 10, part i, p. 222, part ii, pp. 26, 48, 279; FHL, Morning Meeting book, vol. 2, pp. 247, 264.

146. Bodl., MS Rawlinson D 832 fol. 37r; Bodl., MS Rawlinson D 833 fols. 25r, 87r; LMA, MJ/SP/1707/07/074; W.J. Hardy (ed.), *Middlesex county records. Calendar of Sessions Books, 1689–1709* (1905), p. 320; Samuel Keimer, *Brand Pluck'd from the Burning* (1718), p. 64.

147. [Mary Sterrell], *A New Years-Gift, or a Token of Love* (1693), pp. 3–4; Francis Lee, *The State of the Philadelphian Society* (1697), p. 32; Bodl., MS Rawlinson D 832 fols. 6r, 95r; Bodl., MS Rawlinson D 833 fol. 92r; Keimer, *Brand Pluck'd*, p. 60.

148. Bodl., MS Smith 127, fol. 173; Bodl., MS Rawl. letters 37, fol. 119; G & C, MS 725/752.

149. G & C, MS 725/752.

CHAPTER 4

Lead's Life and Times (Part Three): The Philadelphian Society

Ariel Hessayon

I

At an unknown date Lead claimed she heard a voice emanating from 'out of the Throne of the Majesty on High'. It was subsequently published as *A Message to the Philadelphian Society, whithersoever dispersed over the whole Earth* (1696). This appeared together with 'A Further Manifestation Concerning this Virgin Philadelphian Church', which had been received on 1 January 1696, and some clarification a few days later as to when 'such a prefect Virgin-Church should be consummated in the Earth'.[1] Philadelphia, meaning brotherly love in the original Greek, was the sixth of the seven churches in Asia Minor to whom John sent a book containing his revelation (Revelation 1:11, 3:7–13). These seven historical churches were understood by Lead as types. Thus the first and eldest church was a prefiguration of the Church of England; the second foreshadowed a 'more refined Order', Presbyterianism; the third Independency; the fourth Anabaptism; the fifth, the Fifth Monarchists; and the sixth most likely the Quakers. Each of these churches had in turn been 'refused', 'excluded', 'dismissed', 'passed away' and 'disowned'. Consequently, they were now to be superseded by a visible church in which God himself would be manifest. Moreover, just as Christ had been born of a virgin mother, so another

A. Hessayon (✉)
Department of History, Goldsmiths,
University of London, London, UK

© The Editor(s) (if applicable) and The Author(s) 2016   71
A. Hessayon (ed.), *Jane Lead and her Transnational Legacy*,
DOI 10.1057/978-1-137-39614-3_4

virgin—identified as the woman clothed with the sun (Revelation 12:1)—would with her 'pure Spirit' and 'bright Sun-like' body 'all impregnated with the Holy Ghost' bring forth her first-born: the Philadelphian church. Although this 'Real Mount *Sion*' church was presently hidden, perhaps in the womb of the 'Morning Sun', the last 'Half Time' during which the 'Virgin-Spirit' must remain concealed in the wilderness was drawing to a close (Revelation 12:14).[2]

Lead's *Message to the Philadelphian Society* was printed and sold by John Bradford from an address in Jewen Street near Crowder's Well Alley (Cripplegate ward). Bradford had been freed by Lead's former printer Andrew Sowle and then married Sowle's eldest daughter, making him the brother-in-law of another of Lead's former printers, Tace Sowle. He was also a Quaker.[3] Later that year Bradford printed another work by Lead: *The Tree of Faith*. Lead's authorial reputation, however, had been damaged by an impostor 'scandalously' issuing things under her name. So to protect it notices were adjoined to these texts cataloguing her published works. These advertisements indicate that before 1697 Lead's books were issued in quarto, octavo and duodecimo, with prices ranging from 6*d.* to 1*s.*[4] Baron Dodo von Knyphausen may have again financed publication. In addition, Dutch versions of Lead's *Heavenly Cloud* and *Revelation of Revelations* were issued at Amsterdam in 1696, as was a German translation of six collected works supplemented with Lead's autobiography.

Clearly this flurry of publications served a purpose. Within England the intention was to warn and prepare prospective believers so as to become 'true members of the Glorious Church of Philadelphia'. Or to quote from Richard Roach's poem 'Solomon's Porch', which heralded the 'Philadelphian Age':

When the fair Virgin Pilgrims Stage is done,
Her travails ended, and her Garland won;
A Temple-Glory of Living Stones to rise;
Whose Base shall fill the Earth; whose Head the Skies.[5]

This suggests a coordinated publicity campaign by Lead's little band of supporters, who regarded her as especially favoured with a timely and 'most Wonderfull series of Manifestation & Revelation'. Hitherto the Philadelphians' precursor society had negotiated a path between secrecy and openness, combining private prayer meetings and selective circulation of members' spiritual diaries through scribal publication with public preaching and print publication. But when in 1697 those clustered around Lead openly 'Engaged in y^c Publick Testimony' for the 'Glorious Kingdom & Reign of Christ wth his Saints in ye Restoration of ye Universal Church & ye Great Sabbath of ye World' the precursor society fractured. The minority, who were 'Animated to bear a Publick Testimony to ye World', called themselves the Philadelphian Society. The majority, however, disowned the Philadelphian name, with some clandestine 'waiters for ye kingdom' even accusing the Philadelphians of schism. Roach would deny the charge by portraying the Philadelphians' 'separation from ye Body of their Brethren' as amicable.[6]

Yet this rupture within the precursor society may explain why Anne Bathurst's spiritual diaries remained in manuscript whereas every scrap that could be found by Lead was printed. Contrary to Roach's claim that Bathurst's writings were too 'highly tinctur'd in the *Seraphick Love* for this Rougher Age to bear' she may have sought privacy. Indeed, as Sarah Apetrei points out in this volume, Bathurst felt compelled 'to attend to my Inward Teachings, and not to Look out after National Concerns, or the publick affairs of the world'.[7] Lead on the other hand wanted to expose her visions and teachings to public view—and was given the opportunity to do so through a succession of mainly male patrons and amanuenses. Consequently when the first instalment of Lead's spiritual diaries appeared as *A Fountain of Gardens* together with Francis Lee's lengthy editorial preface dated 1 January 1697 Lead became synonymous with the Philadelphian Society. Lee and Roach, on the other hand, remained guarded: their printed contributions appeared anonymously or pseudonymously under the names Timotheus and Onesimus respectively.[8]

According to the various versions of Roach's unpublished history of this small religious community, the Philadelphians were not a 'peculiar sect' or party. Rather, while the term was a particularly appropriate description of certain 'Spiritual People' in England, indeed of a blameless, weak community treated with contempt even by their fellow Christians, it signified more generally a belief in 'y^c Coming of Christ to his Glorious Kingdom'.[9] Besides this strong millenarian aspect, Philadelphian teaching emphasised the fulfilment of prophecies and full completion of divine promises—including the conversion of the Jews (usually regarded as 'Antecedent to the coming of Christ'), as well as the 'call of the *Turks* and other Infidels';[10] the 'deeply Mystical Work of the *Regeneration* and *Ascension* of Souls';[11] primitive Christianity as practised by the Apostles;[12] peace, love and Protestant church unity;[13] the Reformation of Manners;[14]

charity;[15] and the 'absolute necessity' of private and public revelation, which superseded insufficient human learning, and on which subject Lee had written a very large but unfinished manuscript treatise.[16]

Comparing them with the Essenes who were best prepared among the Jews to receive Christ's message because they were more conversant with the mysteries of religion, Roach traced the Philadelphians' origin to the spiritual community centred around John Pordage and his wife Mary at Bradfield, Berkshire (mentioned in Chap. 3).[17] We have seen that from autumn 1695 a private week-day prayer meeting was initiated at Lead's rented property in Hoxton Square. It is unclear if the Hoxton gathering pre-dated what Roach called the 'long Rooted & Mother meeting' of the Philadelphians at Baldwin's Gardens in St Andrew's, Holborn. All the same, he indicated that the Baldwin's Gardens meeting was held at Mrs Bathurst's on Sundays for the 'General resort of those who were of this way'.[18] At some point Mrs Bathurst combined with Mrs Joanna Oxenbridge (*fl.*1687–*fl.*1704). She was the widow of Clement Oxenbridge, who had managed the Post Office during the Protectorate and had also been an associate of the conspirator John Wildman. Since Mrs Oxenbridge's husband had impoverished himself by investing over £5,000 in an attempt to improve the Post Office she was compelled to petition the Treasury for an annual pension of £60 to provide for her five children. To this would be added a £20 bequest from Mrs Bathurst.[19] Both women were said to have received 'great & wonderful experiences' and Roach considered them two of the 'principle persons in carrying on ye Spiritual work'.[20]

About the end of March 1697 there appeared the first volume of *Theosophical Transactions by the Philadelphian Society*. Edited by Lee and Roach, this short-lived journal consisted of 'conferences, letters, dissertations, inquiries' and the like for the advancement of 'Piety & Divine Philosophy'.[21] While its title partly recalled the Royal Society's *Philosophical Transactions*, the sub-title 'Acta Philadelphica' suggests a parallel with the Acts of the Apostles.[22] Yet its publication caused a stir resulting in the Baldwin's Gardens meeting becoming overcrowded as 'so many flocked' there.[23] This necessitated moving to a larger place, namely Hungerford Market. Situated near Charing Cross between the Strand and the Thames, this was also the site of a French church.[24] Their first meeting was held there on Sunday, 18 July 1697. It was attended by Lead and her family as well as by Caleb Gilman (1670–*fl.*1708), who noted the fact in the fly-leaf to his copy of Boehme's *Aurora*.[25] Evidently the Philadelphians hoped to attract a large gathering to the Hungerford meeting since they publicised it through the circulation of an announcement. Among the variety of curiosity seekers and scoffers who attended was the former Baptist turned Quaker Richard Claridge, who recorded his impressions of a meeting held on Sunday afternoon, 15 August 1697. Claridge noted that when he entered the men's hats were off and that an unnamed man was preaching in a 'very careless and lazy posture'. This preacher declared on several occasions that:

> God had in this latter day committed to and entrusted them with a more peculiar dispensation of the Spirit, though a small remnant of poor despised people, than any professors of Christianity had been, or were under, since the apostles' days.

Another speaker was a woman called Cresilla, who to Claridge's annoyance was fashionably dressed. She talked much of 'the spiritual flesh and blood of Christ, pretending it was a great mystery'. Moreover, Claridge observed that:

> they held universal redemption, pretended to a special dispensation of the Spirit, were against water-baptism, and outward breaking of bread; but were for justification by Christ's imputed righteousness; and that though the guilt of sin was taken away in believers, and the power and dominion of sin much subdued, yet corruptions and imperfections remained during life.[26]

The Hungerford meeting endured about six months subjected to on the one hand 'great Opposition' and violence from the 'rude multitude', and on the other increasing internal divisions that eventually tore it apart. Beforehand, however, Lead and her family had absented themselves on the pretext that it was 'inconvenient' to travel such a 'great distance' from Hoxton.[27] Instead they obtained licence to gather at Westmoreland House, near Bartholomew Close (St Bartholomew the Great); a site formerly occupied by a Presbyterian congregation. One Sunday, probably 29 August 1697, a 'very great concourse of people' came. Among them were some boys and 'rude fellows' who caused trouble, yet there was also a 'sober sort of company very attentive and inquisitive'. They outnumbered the Philadelphians, who could be counted on one hand: Lead, Francis and Barbary Lee, a woman using the pseudonym Hephzibah (possibly Mary Sterrell), and 'the good honest man' (perhaps Heinrich Johann Deichmann).[28] Although the audience at Westmoreland House was said to have been 'more favourable & civilized' the volume of disturbances gradually increased. So Lead's group was driven to relocate, firstly to Twisters Alley near Bunhill Fields (St Giles-without-Cripplegate); then after a 'considerable time' to Loriners' Hall (which stood on the corner of Aldermanbury Postern and London Wall, facing the north end of Basinghall Street), and finally—sometime after Easter Sunday 1699—back to Hoxton.[29] Again, it is noteworthy that Loriners' Hall was an established venue for nonconformist preaching. It was used, for example, by a Particular Baptist congregation in 1699 and subsequently by an Independent congregation in 1704.[30]

To recap, the Philadelphian Society emerged openly at a particular moment: after the revocation of the Edict of Nantes (1685), the Glorious Revolution (1688–89), the Toleration Act (1689), and the lapse of the Licensing Act (1695). The Protestant Prince of Orange become William III of England had defeated the Catholic James II in Ireland and suppressed Jacobite risings in Scotland, while the Nine Years' War (1688–97), which pitted a coalition lead by William known as the Grand Alliance against the territorial ambitions of Louis XIV, was shortly to be concluded with the Treaty of Rijswijk. More broadly, this period has been viewed by some scholars as the beginning of an English Enlightenment, a so-called 'Age of Reason' brought into being by certain interconnected factors. Among them was the formal creation of a Royal Society, a body populated by experimental scientists who attempted to achieve public respectability through their apparent scepticism, empiricism, affected disinterest and use of non-sectarian language. Isaac Newton's *Principia Mathematica* had been published in 1687 forcing open-minded readers capable of understanding its contents to reconsider their views of the universe. Added to this was the contribution of Baruch Spinoza and his followers who, if Jonathan Israel is to be believed, provided the intellectual backbone of the European Radical Enlightenment. Another disputed strand of Enlightenment rationalism was anti-Trinitarian thought, which arguably contributed to the gradual development of an alternative reasonable form of Protestantism through its hostility to Papal authority, Catholic dogma and superstition against a backdrop of growing anticlericalism and interest in the historical Jesus. Stripped of its mystery this naked Christianity meshed with an acceptance of the cessation of miracles while dismissing the pretensions of those tarnished with the brush of enthusiasm.

At first glance the Philadelphians do not fit comfortably within this framework. Indeed, their belief in the continued communication of higher knowledge through visions and revelations, apocalyptic expectations, privileging of individual religious experiences, engagement with prophecy, theosophy and mysticism, not to mention their reverence for female figures and secret heterodox rituals (of which more shortly), collectively positions them as an alternative to some scholarly conceptions of the Enlightenment. Yet it simultaneously situates them at the heart of what Clarke Garret dubbed the Mystical Enlightenment.[31] This is not a paradox given how elastic and comprehensive our understanding of the Enlightenment has become.

Another context was the proliferation of religious societies. Roach's associate the educator Charles Bridges estimated that there were about 50 in London. These were mainly concerned with eradicating 'vice and debauchery', with some also instrumental in founding free schools for poor children. Significantly, the establishment of these Charity Schools fostered links with likeminded Pietists at Halle—a university Lee had visited on his travels. Indeed, Lee would anonymously translate and probably provide the preface to the English version of *Pietas Hallensis* (1705), an account of an orphanage and other charitable institutions in Saxony by the educator and social reformer August Hermann Francke (1663–1727).[32] Accordingly the Philadelphian Society was preceded by the Society for the Reformation of Manners (1690), but anticipated the Societies for Promoting Christian Knowledge (1698) and for Propagation of the Gospel in Foreign Parts (1701). At least one Philadelphian had also been inspired by the religious society for young men initiated by the Palatinate-born Church of England clergyman Anthony Horneck (1641–1697), who had drawn up strict rules for their conduct.[33] This was John Coughen (encountered in Chap. 3), who had been close to Horneck and actively perpetuated his legacy—as Roach later reported when recounting the Philadelphians' origins to Francke.[34]

Then there is 1697. The year had been carefully selected since it was based on the extensive apocalyptic exegesis of two biblical commentators that can be connected with the Philadelphians—Thomas Beverley (*d.*1702) and Edward Waple (1647–1712). An Independent minister and prolific author, Beverley had predicted that, in Warren Johnston's words, 'the fall of the beast, the resurrection of the two witnesses, and the advent of Christ's millennial kingdom on earth would all begin in 1697'.[35] Specifically, Beverley envisaged Philadelphia as partly arising out of a combination of Protestant sufferings in France, and an undefiled remnant of Protestant churches. This would lead to a settlement 'upon the pure Laws and Ordinances of Christ': the '*Philadelphian state*'.[36] The appointed time of 'Christ's coming to judge the world' was Monday, 23 August 1697 and it is no coincidence that on that very day the Philadelphian Society finalised their constitutions at Westmoreland House.[37] Although Beverley was forced to issue a public apology when his prophecy failed, Roach recalled that Beverley had sought out and conferred with the Society when they openly declared and warned the world of the coming '*Kingdom of Christ*'.[38] And while it is difficult to determine the extent of this collaboration, it should be noted that through their network of international correspondents the Philadelphians facilitated the publication of several of Beverley's treatises in German translation at Frankfurt.[39]

Similarly, in his annotations on each chapter of Revelation, Waple predicted that about 1697 there would be 'some more than ordinary appearance' of the '*Philadelphian* State'. He too incorporated recent events such as the revocation of the Edict of Nantes and the capture of Savoy by a Waldensian force in 1690 within his apocalyptic chronology, reckoning that 1697 would mark both the end of '*the Beasts Months*' and the '*Days of the Witnesses*' (Revelation 11:3).[40] Waple was Archdeacon of Taunton and vicar of St Sepulchre's, a church standing at the eastern end of Snow Hill, London. Like his friend Lee, he had been educated at Merchant Taylor's school and St John's, Oxford. Lee considered him an expert on ancient Christianity possessed of 'a very slow & examining genius' who shunned the limelight.[41] Waple would name Lee in his will together with the engraver Dionysius Andreas Freher, to whom Waple bequeathed the care of his manuscripts and his 'Annotations on the Revelations'.[42] Waple and Freher also shared an ardent interest in mystical theology, particularly Boehme.[43] Freher for his part would serve as one of the conduits between the English and German Philadelphians.[44]

II

Just as Lead's autobiography of 1696 had been crafted to reassure readers of her respectability, so Lee and Roach were the principle movers in fashioning an image of irenic conformity and social standing for the Philadelphians at large. Thus Roach portrayed a meeting of the Philadelphians' precursor society headed by Joseph Sabberton (noted in Chap. 3) as an 'Eminent' assembly frequented by 'Gentry and Persons of *Quality*', including a number of women.[45] Similarly, just as Pordage had written 'against the errors of the Quakers'—notably their refusal to accept the sacrament of baptism, receive communion and be married in church—so Philadelphians likewise stressed how they differed from Quakers.[46] Denying that they were a new sect or faction, they did not challenge the authenticity of the Bible and outwardly conformed by hearing the word preached in Protestant churches. In addition, they acknowledged the authority of civil government and did not have a reputation for disturbing church services. They were 'not for *turning the World upside down*' as some had misrepresented them. Nor were they 'so silly as to place Religion in *Thouing* and *Theeing*, in keeping on their Hats'.[47]

Hostile observers, however, readily compared Philadelphians with Quakers. One thought them derived from the '*same Enthusiastical Stock*' and so alike as to be almost indistinguishable, noting that some Quakers attended Philadelphian meetings. Another complained that the Philadelphians were but:

> a young Sprout from the *Quakers*, as very much resembling them in many Particulars; for they have no Ministers, no Sacraments, no Rule of Faith. Men and Women Preach indifferently, and rave extravagantly, being very ignorant, and accordingly uttering whatsoever occurs next to their Enthusiastick Imaginations.[48]

A Huguenot traveller and subsequent supporter of the French Prophets was more sympathetic, observing that this lately sprung sect of 'Mystical Theologists' were popularly classed as Quakers, and 'not without Reason', although their recently published and 'very obscure' writings suggested a different conclusion.[49] Nonetheless, this was a minority view. More commonly the comparison was extended as in an attack on the 'delusions and errors' of Antoinette Bourignon and 'all other Enthusiastical Impostures', whose author insisted that English Quakers and Philadelphians were 'of the same kidney' as foreign Quietists and Pietists, with all standing 'upon the same foundation'.[50] Indeed, some polemicists even incorporated the Philadelphians within a catalogue of 'Innumerable Sects' reminiscent of Thomas Edwards's *Gangraena*: Socinians, Anabaptists, Quakers, Muggletonians, Antinomians, Seekers and Familists.[51]

While the 'little Company' that made up the Philadelphian Society was understandably concerned with how contemporaries perceived them—particularly through the circulation of printed statements portraying them as a peaceable, reputable non-sectarian body—their public identity conceals some affinity with the Quakers.[52] Although Lead intimated and Roach stated that the Philadelphians had superseded the Quakers, they used the same printers.[53] Moreover, Lee was a nonjuror (Quakers did not swear oaths) and he openly acknowledged that while Philadelphians differed from Quakers 'as to their external Habits, or Customs', they agreed with them as to the '*Internal Principle of a Light within*'—at least when this 'Divine Principle' was correctly explained. Nor in a spirit of accommodation did he assert the validity of baptism in general or of infants in particular. As for communion, Lee hinted that the Philadelphians had a great deal to say about spiritually eating Christ's flesh and drinking his blood which could not be declared to non-initiates.[54] He had every reason to be evasive.

Unbeknownst to the Philadelphians, their extensive transnational correspondence was being intercepted, transcribed and—when necessary—translated by the Archbishop of Canterbury's agents from at least June 1697. Among other things, these letters reveal the existence of a heterodox ritual known as the Love Feast. There were different ways of celebrating this feast, but essentially it was a variation of communion using a mixture of bread and wine. The practise appears to have originated with Dr Johann Salomon Hattenbach (1650–1699), a physician who held conventicles at his home in Lübeck and who had introduced the ceremony to certain Pietists.[55] Besides being a correspondent of August Hermann Francke, Hattenbach was referred to as a 'high Elder of ye Love', an appellation which brings to mind the Family of Love. This Nicodemite religious group was represented by polemicists as a mystical sect who believed in an immanent Christ and perfectibility on earth. The Philadelphians were occasionally confused with them.[56] And perhaps not without reason for like the Familists and Pordage's community, the Philadelphians adopted new spiritual names including Archippus, Barak, Cyrus, Epenetus, Eulychus, Gideon (Loth Fischer), Hephzibah (Mary Sterrell?), Jael, Lydia (Barbary Lee neé Lead), Matthias, Onesimus (Richard Roach), Silas, Timotheus (Francis Lee), and Tychius (one Weinich). Doubtless secrecy was also important. As Lee warned Roach in August 1697; 'Pray be exceeding cautious in your conversation, for I am to suspect that something may have come to the Archbishops ears from some friends not fully establish'd with you. The spies are many, and of serious kinds'.[57]

Additional correspondence indicates that the Philadelphians associated with some notorious figures. Among them was the well-travelled Dr Kortholt or Karthold, possibly the 'K' referred to by Johann Georg Gichtel and discussed in Lucinda Martin's chapter. This 'instrument of Belial' reportedly stabbed the son of Quirinus Kuhlmann's associate

Dr Hollgraffen before fleeing to Lübeck. Besides acquaintanceship with the Duke of Zell's physician Dr William Schott and attempting to manufacture an alchemical medicine for the prolongation of life, Kortholt was allegedly inclined to debauchery and polygamy. Yet he seems never to have progressed beyond bigamy. The woman he took up with was an alchemist who claimed to be Charles II's illegitimate daughter. As for Lead, Kortholt declared in a letter probably addressed to Dodo von Knyphausen that he thought her 'simple'. Indeed, having spoken to her in London, Kortholt judged Lead's pronouncements to be 'but words', adding that most of what was published under Lead's name was 'set down by others'. For good measure Kortholt claimed some of his own things were 'intermixed' in the Philadelphians' *Theosophical Transactions*.[58]

Then there was the most damaging of all allegations namely that like Kuhlmann before her, Lead envisaged herself as the grandparent of a new Christ. Spread by Friedrich Breckling it caught the attention of a Behmenist named Dr Schmidberger who about August 1697 wrote from The Hague to Gichtel at Amsterdam:

> I must communicate to you, that besides that Sect, which according to the Pretension or rather Pretence of Dr Schotten [William Schott], does wait upon the Incarnation of the Father, yet another in England under the Direction of Jane Lead breaks out which have published their acta Philadelphensia ... wherein the son-in-law of Jane Lead, Ly [Francis Lee], & an English man, as also some Dutch men, do collabour, as a studiosus Deuchman [Heinrich Johann Deichmann], and one Frecher [Dionysius Andreas Freher], which besides & above that they, according to their pretence, Jane Lead do beleive to be the apocalyptical woman apoc. 12 as is to be seen in the last Tractax of her, called the Fountain of Gardens or Diarium, yet doe averre that among them/: from out the Daughter of Lead :/shall be brought forth a new Christus, who is to be a Partaker both of the celestial & terrestrial nature even as Quirin Kuhlman, because he did converse with these men and women, did appropriate upon him before this time, that he, as Christ was the son of the Father, so he Christi, of the Son, & of his Kingdom should be, & sit down between the Father.[59]

The 'apocalyptical woman' was the woman clothed with the sun (Revelation 12:1). Moreover, Breckling noted that the Philadelphians had excitedly published an account in the first number of their *Theosophical Transactions* (March 1697) concerning the birth of a new Christ to humble parents living at Guttenberg, a town near Bayreuth in northern

Bavaria.[60] But just as Mrs Bathurst's daughter-in-law had conceived a daughter (see Chap. 3), so Lead's daughter Barbary gave birth to a daughter on Whitsunday, 23 May 1697 who was baptized Deborah Jemima on Trinity Sunday.[61]

Although space precludes further discussion of Philadelphian networks and beliefs it should be emphasised that while they were maligned as enthusiasts they were not the victims of religious persecution. On the contrary, having offered a public apology for his involvement with the Philadelphian Society to the Archbishop of Canterbury, bishops and clergymen of the Church of England on 23 August 1697 Roach was merely required to respond to five written queries. Among them was the question whether the 'Revelation to which Mrs Jane Lead pretends in her first & second Volume of ye Fountain of Gardens be true?' In addition, Roach was asked how he could minister publicly to his congregation at St Augustine, Hackney while simultaneously ministering privately with women preachers.[62] Roach responded at length in November 1697 and though he was subsequently expelled from his fellowship at St John's, Oxford in March 1698—ostensibly for non-residence but more likely for frequenting conventicles—he remained rector of Hackney until his death.[63]

* * *

The Philadelphians remained in public view for six years. On Sunday, 13 June 1703 they issued a protestation at Hoxton against the:

> Degeneracy & Apostacy of yᵉ Christian Churches from their first Love, ag[ains]t yᵗ Spirit of Faction & Party, ag[ains]t yᵉ Formality supineness & deadness of this Sardian Age & Spirit in wᶜʰ yᵉ outward Churches stand.

Sardis was the fifth of the seven churches enumerated in Revelation 1:11 and the 'Deadness and Coldness' of the Sardian age was believed to precede the Philadelphian. Having fulfilled the '*Days* of their *Testimony* in *Ashes*' and having long endured the '*Contradiction of Sinners*' the Philadelphian Society thus retreated from the world. Likening each of the six years of their open existence to a day of the Lord they accordingly welcomed their seventh year as a Sabbath of rest. Following the conclusion of their '*First Ministration and Testimony*' the Philadelphians consoled themselves with scriptural precedents.[64] But consolation was offset by knowledge of their failure: there had been few living stones, no temple of wisdom, no angelic trumpet heralding the everlasting gospel, no universal jubilee, no blessed millennium when 'Divine SOPHIA' would sing the praise of 'Great and Powerful CYRUS'.[65] Quite the opposite, and almost immediately satirists exulted:

> Good *English* Folk, come shake both Sides and Head;
> For after all her Vaunt Poor *Philly's* Dead.
> Who in this Nation made such a fearful riot,
> Folks could not eat and drink their common Dyet,
> Nor play, nor fight, nor go to Church at quiet.
> Whose notions soard above the starry Sky-Balls,
> Beyond the reach of dim, and clearer Eye-Balls.
> *Icarus* like she flew to near the flame,
> Melted her waxen wings, and down she came.[66]

III

Jane Lead died at Hoxton between 5 and 6 o'clock on Tuesday, 8 August 1704 aged 80, possibly of stomach cancer. She was interred three days later on 11 August in the nonconformist burial ground at Bunhill Fields, the site chosen at her own request so that she might be laid to rest near several of her spiritual friends. Richard Roach, who attempted to succeed her as leader of the Philadelphians, preached the funeral sermon between 9 and 10 o'clock in the evening, taking 2 Corinthians 5:1–10 as his text. Evidently the notion of the tabernacle of Lead's earthly body dissolving while her soul ascended to occupy a divinely built house in the heavens was an appealing one. This motif was reaffirmed in Lead's tombstone, which consisted of a cross on top flanked by an alpha and an omega, with a skull below adorned with a crown of glory (1 Peter 5:4). Her epitaph read, '1704. Exuvias Carnis hic deposuit Venerabilis Ancilla Domini JANE LEAD, anno Peregrinationis suæ LXXXI' (*'Here lies the shed outward garment of the flesh of the Venerable Handmaid of the Lord, Jane Lead, in the year of her pilgrimage, 81'*).[67]

Thereafter Lead's body, which she had compared to a 'heap of nasty rubbish', continued to decompose.[68] Or as Francis Lee put it in an elegiac letter of September 1704 to an unknown aristocrat (probably the widowed Baroness von Knyphausen); 'It having pleased the Infinite Good to call up his dear and faithful handmaid ... by loosing the bonds of her mortal flesh ... thereby delivering her from all the evils and calamities' endured during her 'long exile from the land of her eternal nativity'.[69]

Lead's spiritual form, however, reportedly had an afterlife, appearing in accounts of visions granted to several followers. The most vivid was that recounted by one Hannah, later identified as Johanna Halberts of Utrecht.[70] This woman had borrowed and read a book containing Lead's two earliest publications, *Heavenly Cloud* and *Revelation of Revelations*, though whether in German translation by Loth Fischer of Utrecht (with whose daughter Halberts was acquainted), or a Dutch version is unclear. Despite being warned that Lead's speculative writings were nothing but the dreams of an old English woman, Halberts was so awed by them that she wondered there was yet such a person living in the world. Eventually an inner voice told her she would see Lead. On 19 August 1704 according to the Julian calendar, Halberts disclosed to a certain woman that she had had a premonition of Lead's death. This had supposedly been revealed to her in a 'wonderful vision' during a dream on the night of 3–4 August, five days before Lead's demise:

> I beheld a Matron sitting, to my appearance very pious and modest of a grave deportment and civil look. She was pretty well in Age, not very tall ... but lusty and fatt. She was of a pale dead colour, and cloathed ... with a black vestment, like a Rain-Cloath from the Top of her Head to the Feet; the cloath being a vail of black silk, as if she was in mourning.[71]

To her great surprise underneath this garment Lead was entirely naked. Overcoming her abhorrence of indecency, Halberts timidly approached so as to observe what was upon Lead's heart. Casting her eyes on Lead's exposed breast she saw Christ crucified hanging on the cross, with the Blessed Virgin Mary on one side and Christ's disciple John on the other. On closer examination Halberts perceived blue swollen veins and that Jesus together with his two companions were alive, 'not painted or imprinted' upon Lead's bosom. Marvelling at this vision she folded her hands and lifted her heart up to God in worship. She then began to pray in earnest at which Lead opened her eyes and turned to speak— but remained silent.[72] Halberts's account of a flabby elderly woman of moderate stature accords with other descriptions of Lead except for the omission that she was then also blind. Moreover, during her terminal illness Lead had assured her followers that her agonies would not surpass Christ's suffering on the cross. Here, as Sarah Apetrei has suggested, in 'her final sublime indignity, the Passion was literally subsisting in Jane Lead's flesh'.[73]

Other visions followed. One to Francis Lee and his wife Barbary, in which Lead encouraged them to wait upon God patiently; one to Mrs Joanna Oxenbridge; and one to Richard Roach to whom, after 'a sudden lightning flash as it were of Divine Power', Lead appeared in spirit 'descending from ye Heavens'. In an early self-serving draft of his 'Account of the rise and progress of the Philadelphian Society' Roach claimed he had witnessed a 'small Globe beginning to descend from ye Highest Region' and that he heard the words 'the Still Eternity displays it Self' (the '*Still Eternity*' was envisaged by Lead as the beginning and highest of the eight worlds allotted to human souls). Thereupon the 'Holy Power and Sacred Union' opened Roach's understanding as the 'mantle of that great Saint' Lead fell upon him.[74]

These visions had a two-fold purpose. First, they sustained the devotion of believers by attesting to Lead's sanctity, comforting them with the knowledge that with the 'pangs of death' her 'astonishing' and prolonged suffering was finally at an end as her spirit transcended what she called her great burden: the 'old stitched' coat of her fleshy prison.[75] As a correspondent of Roach's consoled, she was 'a woman of ye cross, & acquainted with sorrows'. In other circumstances the 'loss of so great a person' might have been 'very considerable'. Yet Lead's demise, together with that of Anne Bathurst, another 'eminent pillar' of the Philadelphian Society, could presage the 'near approach of a wonderful resurrection'. Indeed, just as Isaac was not blessed by God until Abraham's death (Genesis 25:11), so the passing of the 'first generation' presented an opportunity for their successor to renew their millenarian mission with greater vigour and usher in an age of peace.[76] Second, Roach invoked Lead's authority as a prophetic figure highly favoured with the '*Virgin Wisdom* of God', as a notable example of the '*Female Embassy*' sent to prepare the way for the recovery of paradise on earth, to bolster his claims to leadership of the Philadelphians.[77]

* * *

What happens to a small religious group on the death of a central charismatic figure is a well-worn question. Disappointment as prophecies come to naught, falling away from the faith, leadership struggles, schism, new personalities and fresh predictions, promoting certain doctrines at the expense of others—including adapting and usually softening the original message to suit changed political and religious contexts, as well as rewriting the movement's history so as to give greater prominence to the triumphant second generation of leaders are all occurrences familiar to students of the subject. We see all this in the Philadelphians with the added peculiarity that so many of their guiding spiritual lights, so many readers and indeed authors of their texts, had been women. There would be a second incarnation, as the movement was reborn, reinvigorated by the arrival of the Camisards at London in 1706. As Lionel Laborie shows in this volume that too, however, would ultimately end with personality clashes, dissension, fragmentation, disappointment, ridicule and failure.

NOTES

1. Jane Lead, *A Message to the Philadelphian Society* (London: J[ohn] Bradford, 1696), pp. 3, 80, [87].
2. Lead, *Message*, pp. 7–14, 107.
3. M. Treadwell, 'London printers and printing houses in 1705', *Publishing History*, 7 (1980), pp. 15–16; Paula McDowell, 'Sowle, Tace (1666–1749)', *ODNB*.
4. Lead, *Message*, 'Advertisement'; Jane Lead, *The Tree of Faith* (London: J[ohn] Bradford, 1696), 'Advertisement'; Jane Lead, *A Fountain of Gardens* (London: J[ohn] Bradford, [1697]), 'Advertisement'; Francis Lee, *The State of the Philadelphian Society* (1697), p. 31.
5. Bodl., MS Rawlinson D 833, fol. 55r; Onesimus [*pseud.* = Richard Roach], 'Solomon's Porch: or the Beautiful Gate of Wisdom's Temple', in Lead, *Fountain of Gardens*, sig. *E2.
6. Bodl., MS Rawlinson D 833, fols. 55r–56r, 64r.
7. Richard Roach, *The Great Crisis* (London: N. Blandford, 1725), p. 99; Bodl., MS Rawlinson D 1262, p. 15, quoted in S. Apetrei, 'Mystical divinity in the manuscript writings of Jane Lead and Anne Bathurst' (this volume).
8. Jane Lead, *A Fountain of Gardens* (London: booksellers of London and Westminster, 1697), preface by 'Timotheus' [*pseud.* = Francis Lee].
9. Bodl., MS Rawlinson D 833, fols. 55r, 63r, 80v, 82r.
10. Anon. *Propositions Extracted From the Reasons for the Foundation and Promotion of a Philadelphian Society* (London: booksellers of London and Westminster, 1697), p. 10; [Francis Lee], *The State of the Philadelphian Society* (1697), pp. 3, 7; Bodl., MS Rawlinson D 833, fol. 6r.
11. [Lee], *State of Philadelphian Society*, p. 9.
12. Anon. *Propositions*, p. 9; LPL, MS 942 (130), *Reasons for the Foundation and Promotion of a Philadelphian Society* (1697), pp. 3–4; Bodl., MS Rawlinson D 833, fols. 57r, 63v.
13. LPL, MS 942 (130), p. 4; [Lee], *State of Philadelphian Society*, pp. 2, 6–7; Bodl., MS Rawlinson D 833, fol. 57v.

14. [Lee], *State of Philadelphian Society*, p. 7.
15. [Lee], *State of Philadelphian Society*, p. 2.
16. Anon. *Propositions*, pp. 7, 10–11; LPL, MS 942 (130), pp. 2, 3; [Lee], *State of Philadelphian Society*, p. 2; G & C, MS 725/752; Bodl., MS Rawlinson D 833, fol. 87r.
17. Bodl., MS Rawlinson D 833, fols. 54v, 63v–64v, 82r.
18. Bodl., MS Rawlinson D 833, fols. 23r, 82v.
19. *CSPD William III, 1697*, p. 54; Bodl. MS Rawlinson B 243, fols. 9–10; *CSPD William III, 1698*, p. 339; Bodl., MS Rawlinson D 832, fol. 4r; TNA: PRO, Prob 11/476 fol. 281v.
20. Bodl., MS Rawlinson D 833, fols. 27r–28v, 65r.
21. Bodl., MS Rawlinson D 833, fols. 65v, 82v, 86v.
22. [Lee], *State of Philadelphian Society*, p. 14.
23. Bodl., MS Rawlinson D 833, fols. 65v, 82v; Francis Lee (ed.), *Theosophical Transactions by the Philadelphian Society* (5 vols., 1697), vol. 5, p. 224.
24. *CSPD William & Mary, 1693*, pp. 119, 186.
25. Chetham's, 3.F.3.46 (a), endpaper.
26. Joseph Besse (ed.), *The Life and Posthumous Works of Richard Claridge* (3rd edn., London: Darton and Harvey, 1836), pp. 31–33.
27. Bodl., MS Rawlinson D 833, fols. 56v, 66r, 82v.
28. *CSPD 1672*, p. 273; Bodl., MS Rawlinson D 832 fols. 53r–v, 94r–95r.
29. Anon. *Propositions*, p. 11; Anon., *The Declaration of the Philadelphian Society of England, Easter-Day, 1699* (1699), p. 6; Bodl., MS Rawlinson D 833, fols. 56r–v, 65v–66r, 82v, 84r; Roach, *Great Crisis*, p. 99.
30. *CSPD 1682*, p. 609; Walter Wilson, *The History and Antiquities of the Dissenting Churches and meeting houses in London, Westminster and Southwark* (4 vols., 1808–14), vol. 2, pp. 557–58.
31. C. Garrett, 'Swedenborg and the Mystical Enlightenment in Late Eighteenth-Century England', *Journal of the History of Ideas*, 45 (1984), pp. 67–81.
32. Staatsbibliothek Preussischer Kulturbesitz Handschriftenabteilung (Berlin), Nachlaß A.H. Francke, Kapsel 30—England betreffend, fol. 673; Bodl., MS Rawlinson D 832, fol. 45r; G & C, MS 725/752; T. Dixon, 'Love and music in Augustan London; or, the "Enthusiasms" of Richard Roach', *Eighteenth Century Music*, 4:2 (2007), pp. 193–94.
33. Anthony Horneck, *Several Sermons upon the Fifth of St. Matthew* (2nd edn., 1726), vol. 1, pp. viii–x; W.R. Ward, 'Horneck, Anthony (1641–1697)', *ODNB*.
34. Nicholas Fontaine, *The history of the Old and New Testament* (1691), title-page; Berlin, Nachlaß A.H. Francke, Kapsel 30, fol. 300.
35. Warren Johnston, 'Beverley, Thomas (d. 1702)', *ODNB*; W. Johnston, 'Thomas Beverley and the "Late Great Revolution": English Apocalyptic Expectation in the Late Seventeenth Century', in Ariel Hessayon and

Nicholas Keene (eds.), *Scripture and Scholarship in Early Modern England* (Aldershot, 2006), pp. 158, 171–73; Warren Johnston, *Revelation Restored. The Apocalypse in later seventeenth-century England* (Woodbridge, 2011), pp. 193–94, 209, 215–18, 231–32.

36. Thomas Beverley, *An Exposition of the Divinely Prophetick Song of Songs* (1687), pp. 47–50; Thomas Beverley, *The Prophetical history of the Reformation* (1689), sig. a2^{v-2}, pp. 64–65, 72–73, 78.

37. Anon. *Propositions*, p. 11.

38. Richard Roach, *The Imperial Standard of Messiah Triumphant* (1727), p. xix.

39. Thune, *Behmenists*, p. 127.

40. Edward Waple, *The Book of the Revelation Paraphrased; with annotations on each chapter* (London, 1693), 'The Argument', pp. 54–55, 210, 236, 241–43.

41. LPL, MS 1048a, fol. 20; G & C, MS 725/752; Harry Bristow Wilson, *History of Merchant Taylors' School* (London, 1814), vol. 2, pp. 865–66.

42. TNA: PRO, Prob 11/527, fol. 239v.

43. Walton, *Notes*, pp. xxxii, 7, 329, 460, 491–92, 680–81, 684, 685; Charles Muses, *Illumination on Jacob Boehme: the work of Dionysius Andreas Freher* (New York, 1951), p. 15.

44. LPL, MS 1048a, fol. 147; FbG, Chart A 297, p. 12; Anon., *The Vindication and Justification of the Philadelphian Society* (London, printed for the Society, 1702), brs.; Thune, *Behmenists*, p. 134 n. 8.

45. Roach, *Great Crisis*, p. 99.

46. Walton, *Notes*, p. 203; John Pordage, *Göttliche und Wahre Metaphysica* (Frankfurt and Leipzig, 1715), pp. 596–97, 669–73; Thune, *Behmenists*, pp. 65–66.

47. LPL, MS 942 (130), pp. 2–3; Anon. *Propositions*, p. 10; [Lee], *State of Philadelphian Society*, pp. 1–2, 7, 9, 15.

48. Charles Leslie, *A reply to a book entitul'd, Anguis Flagellatus* (1702), 'Advertisement'; Anon., *Dissenters and schismaticks expos'd* (1715), pp. 94–95.

49. Maximilien Misson, *M. Misson's Memoirs and Observations in his Travels over England*, trans. John Ozell (1719), pp. 236–37.

50. John Cockburn, *Bourignianism detected* (1698), sig. A2v; John Cockburn, *A letter from John Cockburn* (1698), pp. 21–22.

51. Cornelius Nary, *A modest and true account of the chief points in controversie between Roman Catholics and the Protestants* (1696), p. 50; John Newte, *A Letter to a friend in the country* (1698), p. 36; Stephen Nye, *The grounds and occasions of the controversy concerning the unity of God* (1698), p. 52.

52. [Lee], *State of Philadelphian Society*, pp. 11, 30.

53. Lead, *Message*, pp. 8–9; Bodl., MS Rawlinson D 833, fols. 54v–55r, 59; Bodl., MS Rawlinson D 1152, fol. 30r.

54. [Lee], *State of Philadelphian Society*, pp. 15–19.
55. LPL, MS 1048a, fols. 94, 118, 121–22, 124–25, 140–41, 184, 189.
56. *Tatler*, no. 257 (30 November 1710; reprinted, London: Nichols & Son, 1806), pp. 484–85; cf. FbG, Chart A 306, pp. 232–33.
57. Bodl., MS Rawlinson D 832, fol. 53v.
58. LPL, MS 1048a, fols. 93–94, 95, 118–19, 120–21, 127, 146, 149, 158–62; S.J. Baumgarten, *Nachrichten von mertwürdigen Büchern* (Halle, 1756), p. 324; Berlin, Nachlaß A.H. Francke, Kapsel 30, fol. 567.
59. LPL, MS 1048a, fols. 146–49, 163; Baumgarten, *Nachrichten*, pp. 324–25; Staats- und Universitatsbibliothek (Hamburg), Supplex epistolica (4°) 17, fols. 9r, 28r, cited in Arlene Miller, 'Jacob Boehme: from Orthodoxy to Enlightenment', unpublished Stanford University Ph.D., 1971, p. 624.
60. *Theosophical Transactions*, vol. 1, pp. 46–52; LPL, MS 1048a, fols. 150–53; T. Wotschke, 'Der märkische Freundeskreis Friedrich Brecklings', *Jahrbuch für brandenburgische Kirchengeschichte*, 25 (1930), pp. 208–09 n. 131; cf. Thune, *Behmenists*, p. 128.
61. G & C, MS 725/752.
62. Bodl., MS Rawlinson D 832, fol. 21r; Bodl., MS Rawlinson D 833, fols. 6r–7v, 83r–v; LPL, MS 942 (141), fols. 1r–12v; Thune, *Behmenists*, pp. 87–89.
63. Bodl., MS Smith 48, fol. 349; *London Evening Post*, 432 (10 September 1730).
64. Bodl., MS Rawlinson D 833, fol. 56v; Anon., *The Protestation of the Philadelphian Society* (London, 1703?) [BL, MS Harleian 5946].
65. [Roach], 'Solomon's Porch', in Lead, *Fountain of Gardens*.
66. *An Elegy, Upon the Philadelphian Society* (London, 1703), brs. [BL, MS Harleian 5946].
67. [Francis Lee], *Der Seelig und aber Seeligen Jane Leade Letzere Lebens-Stunden*, ed. Johann Theodor von Tscheschen (Amsterdam: R. and G. Wetsteinen, 1705), pp. 40–41; Johann Wolfgang Jaeger, *Dissertatio historico-theologica, de Johannæ Leadæ Anglo-Britan. Vita* (Tübingen, 1712), pp. 28–29, 30–32; Thune, *Behmenists*, p. 135; Joanne Sperle, 'God's healing angel: A biography of Jane Ward Lead', unpublished Kent State University Ph.D., 1985, pp. 17–18, 41, 49.
68. Swedenborg Society (London), MS A/25, fol. 4v.
69. DWL, MS 186 (1), p. 15.
70. LPL, MS 1559, fol. 1r–v; Bodl., MS Rawlinson D 833, fol. 89r–v; Jaeger, *Dissertatio*, pp. 33–36.
71. Bodl., MS Rawlinson D 833, fol. 89r–v. Halberts dated her disclosure 30 August 1704 and her premonition 14–15 August 1704. She was using the Gregorian calendar, which was 11 days ahead of the Julian calendar (1704 was a leap year).
72. LPL, MS 1559, fol. 1r; Bodl., MS Rawlinson D 833, fol. 89r–v.

73. Sperle, 'God's healing angel', pp. 43–46; Sarah Apetrei, *Women, Feminism and Religion in Early Enlightenment England* (Cambridge, 2010), pp. 270–71.

74. Jaeger, *Dissertatio*, p. 31; DWL, MS 186 (1), pp. 24–26; Bodl., MS Rawlinson D 833, fols. 27r–v, 56v, 57r–v, 65r, 65v; Jane Lead, *The Wonders of God's Creation Manifested* (London: T. Sowle, [1695]), pp. 7, 39–40, 82–85; Sperle, 'God's healing angel', pp. 18, 221–22.

75. Swedenborg Society, MS A/25, fols. 4v–5r.

76. Bodl., MS Rawlinson D 832, fol. 33r.

77. Roach, *Great Crisis*, pp. 96–99.

CHAPTER 5

Jane Lead and the Tradition of Puritan Pastoral Theology

Amanda L. Capern

Saints should rejoice in nothing more, than to see a crucified Christ in one another.*

The historiography of puritanism has contained a puzzle for some time. While some historians would argue that it is not meaningful to speak of the existence of puritans (or their -ism) after, say, 1660, when the radical impetus of puritan revolution was supposedly brought to a halt, others would agree with John Spurr that there was an evolutionary but continuous tradition of radical Protestantism.[1] The continuity theory is one in which 'the hotter sort' of Protestants of the Elizabethan church did not disappear with the discontinuation of their name.[2] Instead, they were succeeded by a late seventeenth-century network of individuals and sects who were keen to preach pure doctrine in their efforts to return the Christian faith to its primitive form and to continue to perform their godliness in public.[3] In Spurr's analysis the 'good old cause' of the religious civil wars survived both the exportation from England of the Calvinist-Bezan Westminster Confession and the expulsion of godly ministers from the English church in 1662.[4] In this model, later English puritans—or, dissenters and after-dissenters from the Anglican Church—shared certain key beliefs and practices. It has been argued,

A.L. Capern (✉)
University of Hull, Hull, UK

© The Editor(s) (if applicable) and The Author(s) 2016
A. Hessayon (ed.), *Jane Lead and her Transnational Legacy*,
DOI 10.1057/978-1-137-39614-3_5

for example, that Protestant nonconformity had a distinct ecclesiology based on the doctrine of the invisible church and also that there was a continuity of evangelical identity expressed as spiritual witnessing and informal extemporaneous prayer practices.[5] There are key questions to ask, then, about what ideas gave shape to puritan theology over time. This chapter aims to throw light on the origins and afterlife of the ideas of Jane Lead and to demonstrate by this means that the puritan continuity thesis can be upheld and even extended not only chronologically but also geopolitically.

I

Jane Lead is remembered for three things. The first is that she was one of the main English exponents in print of Jacob Boehme (*c.* 1575–1624), the German mystic whose cosmological visions from 1600 led to the publication of several influential works, perhaps most notably *The Way to Christ* (1624).[6] The second is her association with another English Behmenist, John Pordage, whom she met in August 1673 or 1674 and whose household she subsequently joined.[7] The third is that she formed, with Anne Bathurst, Francis Lee and Richard Roach, the Philadelphian Society in 1697. The Society, which gained financial backing from Baron Knyphausen, set up a spiritual community in lodgings in Hoxton Square, though it also gathered in several other domestic and public spaces.[8] Lee and Roach believed equally with Lead and Bathurst in the effectual nature of feminine spiritual agency. Francis Lee, for example, argued that Christ had been born of woman to mediate between God and man after the ejection from paradise.[9] The feminised spirituality of the Philadelphians was not unique. In Germany Johanna Eleanora Petersen believed in the promises made by God to the daughters of Eve in Genesis 3:15 and used this to make the chiliastic argument that all things would be restored in the last days.[10] German Pietism promoted female agency in private Bible study meetings which were based in small domestic congregations to bring to life the Spenerian idea of 'little churches within the church'.[11] Jane Lead and the Philadelphians were, therefore, not just part of a longer English puritan tradition, they were also part of what Diarmaid MacCulloch has recently called the Protestant Reformation's 'spectrum of radicalisms' across Europe.[12]

The English radical Protestant (or puritan) tradition from which Lead emerged was essentially Calvinist and, like all puritans, she was intensely interested in personal salvation. During the 1640s her religious beliefs were shaped by hearing the sermons of Tobias Crisp, among others, and it can be argued that she was radicalised by the wider spiritual revolution, as well as by dissemination of Boehme's works by radical publishers and booksellers such as Giles Calvert.[13] Lead shared the context of religious debate and heightened spiritual expectation with male radical co-religionists in overlapping social networks, and sermon and prayer groups.[14] She also shared the context with a number of female prophets and visionaries, including Eleanor Davies whose prophetic career gained new currency in the wake of the collapse of the English church. There was also a transatlantic dimension, the support of New England religious exiles being reflected in the prayers of thanksgiving and fasting amongst those saints who returned to Old England to establish congregations in 'the New England way'.[15] Religious experimentalism undermined the formal authority of the visible church and sacralized informal and domestic space. Ariel Hessayon has uncovered the remarkably complex network that gathered around John Pordage and his Biblical Family between 1649 and 1650. This included the female prophet, Elizabeth Poole, as well as Abiezer Coppe, inspired author of *A Fiery Flying Roll*. Pordage styled himself as Abraham, the biblical patriarch; his wife, Mary, as Deborah, a mother of Israel. Lead inherited Pordage's Abrahamic vision of an inward household offering salvation to Israel and it can be argued that it was this inward-seeking communitarian and associative behaviour that linked all radical Protestant sects.[16] Even Eleanor Davies attracted to her estate a group of Diggers, including Gerrard Winstanley who, in 1650, came to hear her preach in a barn that she was the spiritual incarnation of the high priest Melchizedek.[17]

There was a problem inherent in Calvinism—predestination was inescapable. Alexandra Walsham has recently defined English puritanism as 'an affective, evangelical piety rooted in an experimental application of the Calvinist doctrine of predestination'.[18] Experimentalism, of course, engendered a continuous search for truth and authority. Some radical Protestants located both in the Holy Scriptures, while others wished to transcend what MacCulloch has called 'the noise of theological controversy' to wait patiently for the silent workings of the Holy Spirit.[19] Lead looked for inspiration and truth in the Holy Spirit, though one of the features of her pastoral theology as it developed was that she retained the intellectual remnants of Calvinist predestination alongside ideas acquired from Boehme and Pordage. Her first work—*The Heavenly Cloud*

Now Breaking—was published in 1681, a few months before Pordage's death and while she was facilitating publication of his *Theologia Mystica*. Pordage's pastoral impulse had actually been to abandon predestination altogether: 'Here is no *Election or Reprobation takes place amongst these Spirits, as being all of them the Sons of God's Eternal Love*'.[20] However, Lead retained more than echoes of the doctrine of reprobation in her first works. 'The spirit of Daniel came upon me', she said, before prophesying that Prince Michael would defeat the evil monarchy.[21] This was very similar to Eleanor Davies's use of Daniel 7 in *A Warning to the Dragon* of 1625, as well as some of Davies's 1640s works in which she equated Prince Michael not with Charles I but with James I, whose Calvinist credentials were rather more credible.[22] Davies's path to salvation lay along a linear chronology—'the beginning of the Creation to the building of the New Jerusalem, the second comming of Messiah, it shall be seaven Weekes or Seaven Moneths'—and she quantified exactly the number of those saved (144,000), implying a finite number also for the damned.[23] Lead, however, abandoned linear eschatological thinking in favour of a more spatial imagining of the last days. Of the reprobate she spoke much more obliquely in *The Heavenly Cloud* than Davies had ever done. Nevertheless the reprobate were there, hiding behind a pseudo-Pelagianism which manifested itself as the saved taking the 'Golden Stone'.[24] At the end of *The Heavenly Cloud* Lead admitted that there was a sealed number who were saved and in this way she offered assurance of the glory that awaited the elect if they followed 'the Love-harmony and Spirit of Faith'.[25] However, she did also say that God's 'Divine Ray' would pass over the reprobate and, indeed, it would 'glide away without making any impression'.[26]

Comparing Jane Lead with Eleanor Davies—the only woman prophet to write more works (if not words) than her—is enlightening. Together they exemplify the way in which shared Calvinist doctrinal roots could lead to seemingly different soteriological positions. Although much has been made of Lead's arrival at a doctrine of universal salvation, she sometimes buried the doctrine of election's logical partner—reprobation—in a language that lent only a visual imagery to God's judgement of the damned and she emphasised the operation of the Holy Spirit rather than lingering over Daniel 7. Davies's works, by contrast, always featured descriptions of the tortured fate of the damned and these were rooted in a legalistic Biblical exegesis. However, Davies was not averse to offering some hope (even to the reprobate) and her prophetic theology was actually intended to be pastoral. For example, Davies used the idea of Christ's descent into hell as a way of slipping in double covenant theology—a 'first Adam' to 'second Adam' translation of the law into God's promise through Christ's spilt blood. Covenant theology—very much around because of the Westminster Confession—offered, according to Davies in 1647, 'the mystery of the general redemption'.[27] Rather like Winstanley, who proposed 'a heterodox marriage of universal redemption with particular election', Davies spoke of a 'common Salvation', hidden in Christ's retention of the keys to the mystery of death and hell.[28] Lead's pastoral theology relied on a fine distinction being made between redemption through Christ and salvation through Christ in order to maintain a tenuous link with the doctrine of predestination. For example, Lead also utilized the concept of the power of the keys in *The Heavenly Cloud*: 'the Prince of the new and Everlasting Covenant' would guide believers 'through the passage-gate of Death'.[29] The First Adam/Second Adam escape clause, then, used by both Lead and Davies, was a way of ameliorating the full impact of double predestination for pastoral purposes and only matters of presentation—legalism *versus* visual symbolism—created an appearance of totally different theological formulation.

If Lead's theology drew, at least to some extent, on Calvinist covenant theology, where does this leave the appeal and influence of Boehme on her thought? Lead's version of radical Protestantism was arguably what Nabil Matar once defined as a 'doctrine of realised eschatology'.[30] Eschatological thinking of the exact (and exacting) kind promoted by Eleanor Davies and others was found wanting by some religious visionaries as a form of practical divinity. After all, millenarian thinking could sew its own seeds of doubt. When Davies's first prediction for the end of the temporal world came and went with the execution of William Laud in 1645, she needed to re-set the date to 1700. She was not the only one to do this—in 1711 Thomas Beverley's *The Grand Apocalyptic Question* made a case *post facto* for the currency of his prediction that the world would end in 1697.[31] By drawing on Boehme, Lead's pragmatic eschatology could take the form of an elaborate vision of Paradise, one that replaced the old chronologies with a more elastic and spatially (instead of temporally) imagined doctrine of salvation. Nigel Smith has argued that the richness and density of Boehme's visionary writing lent authenticity to his prophetic message and the same can be said of Lead's writing which appropriated his theology in pastorally strategic ways.[32] Lead could also divert attention away from reprobation by claiming to have personally seen and felt God's promise of the union of the invisible church with Christ. The early foundations of this paradisical theology can be seen in both of the works published during Lead's initial, short-lived, writing career between 1681 and 1683. For example, in *The Heavenly Cloud* Lead vested salvation in 'Christ's Ascension Ladder'. The ladder involved a two-way exchange that effectively removed the passivity inherent in the Calvinist doctrine of election: the elect ascended the ladder and the Holy Trinity descended to join in 'the celebration of the Marriage with the Lamb'.[33] God appeared as a 'Paradisical Body' to meet and greet, in an actual, tangible sense, 'those in whom I will be glorified ... in one Spiritual Body at one Table'.[34]

As all puritan theology was pastoral theology *per se*, this was rather more forgiving than some formulations, but the more evangelical end of the spectrum of radical Protestantism did struggle to provide Biblical precedents. According to Daniel Neal's *The History of the Puritans* (1738) a crucial Biblical prophet was John the Baptist because he could be used extensively to demonstrate the value of suffering in the service of God.[35] John's message gave assurance of election because reprobates were oblivious to God and the Spirit of truth. This left believers free to think they were of the elect because they *saw*, *heard* and *felt* (even *channelled*) the Holy Spirit. Lead retained the concept of the absoluteness of God's sovereignty (with all that implied), but she stressed, for example, God's mystery and his oneness with eternity. The promises of John ran like a thread through her works. *The Heavenly Cloud* led with John's message of resurrection of and in Christ, inviting believers to prepare for ascension to heaven. The work embodied sin in flesh, but carnality was then potentially erased by transformation into spiritual flesh and the mystical spiritual death fused the fate of the elect with that of Christ. The elect experienced 'a new Creation' and became 'the first springing Plants of this new Creation'.[36] Christ, himself, Lead claimed, had experienced 'a four-fold transmutation in his Heavenly humanity'.[37] The route to spiritual incarnation for humans consequently involved a four-step plan to regeneration, or a process of salvation that could be explained, rather than an arbitrary pre-ordained journey that ended—potentially at least—in eternal death. Paternal elders were central to this narrative. They came 'to full and perfect Age', implying that everyone could attain perfection as they emerged from their spiritual war and the 'Sealing Angels' arrived 'with Viols filled with the Love Oil of the Holy Ghost'.[38] Some of Lead's imagery was alchemical and linked to traditional and commonly held principles about the four humours and the transforming effects of distilled cures. In spiritual change effected through the body itself the mystical transformations of Christ's body at Holy Communion were invoked. Those saints who were already 'Ascended and Glorified' would descend for the saints to follow and 'th' Elected Seed shall all be then brought in, Christ then shall reign, and put an end to Sin'.[39] The mystical union was brought about by love, that expression of God's relationship with the elect. This vision, then, of the potential for universal salvation, strengthened by messages of God's love, co-existed with an older Calvinism.

In *The Heavenly Cloud* Lead claimed that there would be 'yet more wonder and hidden Things, that have been under a Seal' and that she would be able to reveal details of the 'last Age' guiding the way to 'consummation' of the mystical union.[40] It was the classic pastoral hook, or the promise of more to come, as the Spirit transported the elect on a journey of 'inward Spiritual Death, Resurrection, Ascension, and Glorification'.[41] The second work, when it came—*The Revelation of Revelations*—similarly buried old doctrine behind and within the imagery of new ideas, but it drew on Boehme also to develop a highly feminised language of salvation by introducing the 'Virgin Wisdom' as 'Sophia' for the first time, claiming that when the higher 'priestly order' arrived, 'as to outward Sex, there shall be no distinction'.[42] The imagined ecclesiology was the 'true Temple' or invisible church of believers.[43] The walls and liturgical contents of the invisible church were plain, even erased as a visible space, but the imaginative visual landscape of worship was cluttered. The 'Tabernacle Body' was familial and domestic, a place where believers would 'all come to be Kings in God's House, and of his own Family' awaiting Melchizedek and the Ark of the Covenant.[44] As will be seen, when Lead's thinking developed, the powerful feminine paradigm of maternity and birth (as an antidote to death) emerged to dominate in some of her writing and helped to gender and feminise the narrative of seventeenth-century puritan religious radicalism.

II

In 1694 Lead embarked upon her second writing career with *The Enochian Walks with God*. In *The Enochian* she called herself 'a Spiritual-Traveller Whose Face Towards Mount-Sion Above was Set'.[45] She told her readers that, like Enoch, they too could walk with God. The language of reaching out to the elect suffused all of her works in the 1690s and the approach was pastorally effective among her followers. She spoke of the 'Power of the Everlasting Gospel' and of her personal 'Gift' and 'heavenly

Power' to set 'the sure Foundation for both his [Christ's] present and future Appearance in the World'.[46] Her theology continued to combine Behmenist and Paracelsian ideas with covenant theology. For example, *The Tree of Faith* of 1696 (which had a title modelled on the third part of Boehme's *The Treatise of the Incarnation*) spoke of her vision of 'the Eagle-Bird' which nested to hatch a 'great Wonder' and included the concept of 'a pure bright attractive Eye' that would bring together those numbered to be in faith's tree.[47] Apart from the obvious association of the light with God's saving goodness, the idea of 'the wonder eye of eternity' was first expounded by Boehme in 1620 and had been repeated in Pordage's *Theologia Mystica*.[48] In another passage of *The Tree of Faith* she spoke of 'the high and approving Eye' and, later, in *The Ascent to the Mount of Vision*, in 1699, she again beckoned believers to 'turn thine Eye into that Central Light'.[49] The eye was everywhere, sometimes figured as 'the Light Orb' from which 'wonders' flowed.[50] In *A Fountain of Gardens*—her longest and most well-known work of 1696—she spoke of 'the Priestly and Prophetical Kingdom upon the Earth' which would help believers to 'draw in any Light'.[51] Lead appeared to include herself in this temporal priestly order: 'I saw in vision, a bright round Ball, pourtraid [portrayed] like a Man's Face, breaking through a Cloud, and immediately two Stars broke through after it, which were very bright and blazing'.[52]

Boehme's other central belief—in the Virgin Wisdom—made its way as well into all of Lead's texts of the 1690s. In *The Ascent to the Mount of Vision* and *The Signs of the Times*, which also came out in 1699, Lead enumerated and diarised millennial prophecies that were couched in a Behmenist *topos*. *Signs of the Times* was framed as a numerically ordered series of signs, sign XXVI being that 'the Tyde must turn, and the Satanical Powers and Kingdom must give way to the Virgin with her Male-Birth'.[53] The marriage and birth paradigm was proxy-human, sign XXVIII promising that 'Heaven-born Children' would escape the temporal world to be 'instructed in all the divine Arts in the Royal Court of God their Father, and the new Jerusalem their true Native Mother'.[54] Thus, Lead blurred the distinction between humanity and the son of God.[55] *The Ascent to the Mount of Vision* announced that 'the Woman Cloathed with the Sun' will 'travail … bringing forth the Man-Child' and God '[i]n swallowing up all into his Eternal Virgin-Womb … brings forth distinct Figures in the Image of his own Glory'.[56] The link between maternity and the doctrine of election runs through other texts. In *The Tree of Faith* the doctrine of election was re-cast and feminised as 'a new Birth-Nature' for 'all the Children of God by Faith in Christ Jesus, and so Born from the Virgin-Womb of the Jerusalem-Mother'.[57] This formulation allowed Luther's first pillar of salvation—faith—to peep through and hinted at the connection between maternity and salvation for all. *A Revelation of the Everlasting Gospel Message* of 1697 spoke similarly of 'the Eternal Womb' that gave birth to those possessing the image of God or 'Angelical Essence'.[58] *A Fountain of Gardens* turned textual formulations into visual ones by paraphrasing Revelation 12 and speaking of the woman bathed in light giving birth. In this way, Lead collapsed Biblical texts comfortably into Behmenist ideas expressing the notion of the Virgin Wisdom (Sophia) giving birth to the incarnate God in Christ.

Sylvia Bowerbank has argued that Lead's first entry into the 1690s world of print with *The Enochian* was 'pivotal ... because she went beyond what had been revealed by Boehme to declare the doctrine of apocatastasis, the universal restoration of all creation to its original harmony'.[59] However, if Lead shifted to a Creationist *topos* to escape the uncomfortable logic of double predestination, she also vested Christ's efficacy in his role as 'the second Adam'.[60] *A Revelation of the Everlasting Gospel Message* did speak of 'the eternal womb', but it also alluded to the need for God's power to counter 'the dark Abyss' and bring the saved from Lucifer into the light.[61] Thus, the fate of the damned continued to be referred to obliquely in her later works, just glimpsed occasionally through the opaque filters of her imaginative writing. For example, in *The Tree of Faith* she warned of a potential collective damnation at the day of judgement: 'O England, England, understand the Day of thy Visitation ... Take care, O England, lest this Star do from thee glide away'.[62] The metaphor she used to hide the doctrine of reprobation was the star over Bethlehem, which 'calleth the Ransomed Ones from all Nations, Languages and Tribes to come to the Brightness of its Rising', but 'Clouds of ignorant Suspicion' over 'the true Heir of the New Jerusalem Mother' could shut out the corrupt as the sand ran out of the 'Glass ... now turn'd up'.[63] The pastoral message lay in Lead's millennial visionary encouragement of unity. In *The Messenger of An Universal Peace* in 1698 she offered readers the city of Philadelphia and 'the Unity of Philadelphian Love'.[64] 'O England, England ... a wonderful Morning-Light is springing', she said, though it was conditional upon joining 'the New Philadelphian Temple'.[65]

It can be argued, then, that one of Lead's key strategies for pastoral success was to embed the idea of promise through an expanded and reimagined covenant theology. *A Revelation of the Gospel Message* took as its didactic texts Jeremiah 33:9 and Revelation 21:5 which, read together, offered considerable hope that God intended universal salvation. Although Jeremiah was often used as a text of doom about Jerusalem's ruination and the exile and judgement of the Jews, Lead chose its closing sections to proffer the message about God's New Covenant. Overturning the Adamic covenant, the new promise wrote the law into the hearts of Jews and gentiles alike and Lead added in parenthesis on the title page 'the whole Race of the Apostacy'.[66] Judgement was tempered by Revelation 21:5 because of the Biblical promise 'Behold I make All Things New'.[67] This hinted that exile and suffering would end and were not, in themselves, indicative of exclusion from the New Jerusalem. The central argument of *A Revelation of the Gospel Message* was that sin was not eternal, but removed for all through judgement from Christ's 'Mediatorial Throne'.[68] The *all*, however, was a rather elastic and equivocal concept.

Understanding Lead—as with other evangelical Protestants—is to understand that sin and its consequences were frighteningly ineluctable. The beauty of God's covenants was that they could temper the implications of his overwhelming power. Abraham's covenant with God was alluded to repeatedly in Lead's works. In *The Tree of Faith* she talked of 'the Branches of faith, growing up from the Root and stock of Abraham'.[69] Her tree of faith was genealogical, like the Jesse tree, 'from the very Day of our being born into it'.[70] Perhaps even more tellingly *The Tree of Faith* had appended to it *The Ark of Faith* and in this work she went beyond the usual Calvinist sliding scale of covenantal Old Testament doctrines of salvation—Adamic, Mosaic, Abrahamic—to the Noahic covenant in which God gave assurances, literally, to all human beings. Noah was, according to Lead, 'Heir of the Righteousness which is by Faith'.[71] Through Noah, the 'Stumbling block even to those who call themselves the Children of Abraham', was removed.[72] The Ark was built in the paradise of the Virgin Wisdom. In *Ascent to the Mount of Vision* she spoke of 'healing in the Elijah-Spirit, as a Type fore-runing [sic] Christ' and she also pushed this work beyond the covenants of work and grace.[73] She said the 'first Adam' was given 'Prerogative', but the second, or Christ, not only had vastly more power, he was not given it alone; instead it extended to all those who were 'incorporated into his Life and Nature'.[74] The concept of the Spirit was essential to this doctrine: the laws 'after the manner of the old Covenant, written in Tables of Stone [Mosaic]' came to an end with Christ 'and so is become a fiery *Law in the Spirit of Life* [my emphasis], engraven upon the Mind and the Heart; there Springing and Rising according to the pure dictate of the Holy Spirit'.[75]

One of the most arresting features of Lead's writing was her attempt to visualize—even to give a tangible visual form to—paradise and heaven, or those spaces where the elect would be brought to 'a full and perfect Redeemed State' and where 'Life doth lie'.[76] In *A Fountain of Gardens* she gave a daily account of what she had seen. On 16 February 1676 she was 'cast upon the Crystalline shore' and told to wait because she could not pass through 'his Borders and land peaceably' in her state of 'Mortal Sensitive Life' 'without commencing War'.[77] She was called by 'our New-Jerusalem Bride' and ordered to dwell 'by this pure Golden Shore' 'till Times-Number shall be fulfilled' while 'the Earthly angry Sea, which foameth from the deep sense of a Quagmire Center' crashed around in the 'Strife and Mutiny' that would be consumed by the 'Holy Fire's Breath'.[78] The whole spiritual journey could be seen by her readers and vicariously felt in this passage. Transformation involved the senses: 'This Sensation like the New Song, the New Name, and the White Stone, they only who do experiment ... are able to distinguish'.[79] Religion becomes an empirical science and change can be tasted and touched, in the way that a physician might scrutinize the body.[80] After all, according to one seventeenth-century tract on the senses 'a cleare sighted Soule' began with 'the *Sense of Sinne*' and could hear edification because of 'the Soule-ravishing hopes of eternity', smell 'the sweet perfume of an undefiled conscience' and taste 'the apprehension of Gods mercy ... by *tasting* how sweet hee [God] is'.[81]

The pastoral intent of Lead's message was one shared by all puritan ministers. They hoped to offer the saints the secrets they needed to imagine their journey to paradise. Such secrets were designed to offer the saints assurance that they were close to God and were not of the reprobate. Dissenters claimed a witnessing function which came from their apocalyptic vision of standing together as the elect in the last days. The Quaker women of London, for example, described themselves as '*faithful Witnesses* both to God and Man, in our own *Gift of Grace*, in which God hath and doth own us'.[82] The idea of suffering was vital to this message. All of an evangelical faith spoke and wrote as if they were outsiders and people separated from the reprobate, their very exclusion being a sign of an inward knowledge of God. Samuel Willard's *The Child's Portion* of 1683—an early Boston imprint that made its way quickly to London—claimed that 'the Children of God are so little regarded here in the

World ... because the World knows not who they are ... Their glory for the present is within; outwardly they look like other men, they eat, drink, labour, converse in earthly imployments, as others do; the communion which they have with God in all of these, is a secret thing'.[83] The secrets to salvation were the secrets withheld from the damned. Lead created a personalised dialogue of communion between the Saints above and the Saints below in which she spoke of the several gifts to the saints, such as the gift of revelation and the gift of vision. For Lead these were part of the inheritance from the 'Glorious Virgin' or 'She of whom the Lord Christ was born in Flesh'.[84] The key to Lead's ecclesiology, then, was an invisible church of believers, or saints, that could be made visible by selected prophets—such as herself.

One further feature of Lead's pastoral theology in the 1690s distinguished it from the panoply of late seventeenth-century puritan thought. This was the degree to which she imposed the feminine imaginary on the invisible church of the elect.[85] Lead borrowed her imagery from Boehme and Pordage, but edged even closer than either of them had done to vesting the potential for salvation in the feminine. Boehme had argued that the life of man, which 'existeth in the Mothers womb', was brought into 'one Spirit with God'.[86] Articulating a similar maternal message Pordage had said that 'Spirits' were fed and nourished by the 'Eternal Mother' whose 'powers are the very Blood, Life and Spirit of Love'.[87] In *The Enochian* Lead told her readers that the way to walk like Enoch was under the auspices of the 'Eternal Virgin ... our supernatural Mother' who was responsible for overcoming the lapsed state of Adam and Eve because the 'Virgin-Purity' of her womb 'brought forth, and made manifest in time, Angellical Births again for a new-created Host of spiritual born Creatures, begotten by the Holy Ghost'.[88] Thus Lead collapsed the second Adam into Marian imagery to offer a maternal creationist doctrine of salvation. Later, in *A Fountain of Gardens*, she used *Canticles*, or the Song of Songs, to conjure up how this spiritual conception might take place. The elect were 'Watered by the Rivers of Divine Pleasure', she said, in remarkably sexualised language.[89] For Lead, then, the secrets of the marriage bed, of the domestic and the maternal, endowed her pastoral theology with the power to turn her into a female spiritual leader and in her works we see the female body used as a palimpsest upon which God bestowed his love and offered salvation to the elect, if not really to all.

III

The context of the 1690s is important for explaining Lead's message and its potential appeal to beleaguered nonconformists suffering from persecution in Old England—what Ethan Shagan has characterised as 'the violence of moderation' after the Act of Toleration—and attempts by the Church of England to 'refashion puritan New England'.[90] Nonconformists of the 1690s suffered from a lack of unity and from their own mortality. After 1695 so many of the remaining ejected ministry of 1662 died that very few of them were left in 1700.[91] Lodowick Muggleton, the last survivor of the 'two last prophets and witnesses of the spirit', died in 1697 and was seen to the grave by a crowd of 248 people.[92] The idea of the old puritans came to inform Daniel Neal's *The History of the Puritans*. Gerontocracy meant that the nonconformist burying ground of Bunhill Fields began to fill and Lead, herself, was to be buried there in 1704. Neal was later to claim that the disparate dissenting groups did all consciously adopt a 'Covenant of Uniformity' and there was certainly an ecumenical drive in the Christian reformation societies that popped up in the 1690s.[93] Suffering, testimony and preparedness became central motifs in late seventeenth-century puritan writing. The Quakers, for example, reeling from imprisonments in the 1680s, began publishing notes from women's meetings to highlight suffering. Mary Foster's *A Living Testimony* of 1685 recorded the 'secret *Smitings* of that Spirit which seeks to *Divide* and lay *Waste* the *Heritage* of God'.[94] Appropriating the revelation to John to legitimise the voice and 'peace testimony' of elderly Quaker women, Foster claimed that their suffering stood against the '*vain Talkers*', the '*Mockers, Scoffers, Writers* and *Printers* against us' who denied that they stood in the truth and spirit of God as 'the spiritual Eye do see'.[95] The agency of puritan women had expanded and contracted contingently for at least a hundred years, really, from Ann Lok's translation of Calvin's sermons in the 1550s through to the Quakers when they organized around the moral agency of Margaret Fell in the 1650s. Male Quakers became genuine co-religionists with women and female agency in the movement waxed and waned according to circumstances.[96] For some puritan groups in the late seventeenth century the household became the key locus for evangelical identity, just as convents acted as political as well as domestic spaces for English Catholic women and their dispersed kin networks.[97] Growing out of late sixteenth-century godly household manuals, familial (including friendship network) puritan worship turned into 'a very particular form of religious sociability' involving book collection and communal reading practices.[98] Familial language in worship blurred the line between inward piety and outward membership of a spiritual household, providing identity to puritan groups as their members collaborated in evangelical worship. One Quaker woman told Charles II that she was 'Christ's Minister' and she warned him in 1660 that his reign would only prosper if he allowed her 'liberty for my own practice of my own Household Ordinances'.[99] The idea looked backwards to the legitimacy claims of sixteenth-century puritan prophesyings and forwards to eighteenth-century domestic sectarianism. Jane Lead's own anti-formalism was so highly developed that in *The Tree of Faith* she argued that 'Formal Worships set up by Man, and constituted by Rational Inventions, as a shadow must pass away'.[100]

Anti-formalist thinking meant that puritans in New England as well as Old England in the late seventeenth century sought to build a New Jerusalem that was not imagined as possessing denominational or national boundaries. Michael Winship has recently pointed out that the puritans in New England were not building 'a city on a hill' (Mount Sion) to remain separate. They did not expect to remain pure and in splendid isolation from the Old World.[101] The language of inclusivity was actually exclusive and the suffering that puritans experienced said more about their hopes than their pain. Lead exemplified this. In *A Living Funeral Testimony* she claimed that she knew and felt 'Internal Communication with the Spirit of Christ' and that it would end her suffering by elevating her spirit to a place—a 'mansion'—of perfection.[102] Cosmological imagery such as 'the Globe of Eternity' and God's 'all-seeing Eye' became ubiquitous themes as Lead reproduced her version of Boehme's flaming eye of God encapsulated within the *primum mobile* that contained angelical and other eternal spirits. The eye of God was perceived as watching the saints at war during the building of the New Jerusalem. Lead called for peace and unity in 'the latter days' of spiritual warfare.[103] The drive for unity on the radical fringes of Protestantism can also be seen in the transatlantic nature of the debate in print, for example about the threat of Antichrist during the Salem crisis of 1692 and 1693.[104] Graduates from Harvard released works in Boston and London simultaneously, Benjamin Harris selling them out of his London Coffee House.[105] It can be argued that the powerfully paradigmatic 'New England mind', as captured by Perry Miller, was partly predicated on this shared transatlantic eschatology.[106] Puritans both sides of the pond equated personal salvation with the fashioning of a godly community of the elect, wherever the elect happened to be.[107] The

Baxterian idea of the republic of godly Christians—'spiritual and eternal good is the chief part of the common good'—not only eroded the difference between the embodied external and internal self, it also eroded any sense of separation between groups of the godly, separated by continents and oceans, exilic and self-moderating in reality as well as in their minds.[108]

It can be argued also that the domesticated invisible church eroded the boundaries between the sexed body and the soul. Long before the Shakers unsexed their spirituality through celibacy, the Pordage 'Family' had denounced 'flesh and carnal relations'.[109] Enlighteningly, Lead's description of John Pordage's last days entirely erased the distinction between the temporal and the spiritual body. She said he 'put off only the weak and less honourable Bodie, and put on Immortalitie and Glorie'.[110] Puritan women and men watched each other for signs of transformation in life, but they watched each other even more closely at times of death when Christ seemed not just immanent, but reincarnated in the departing soul. Lead said of Pordage that his 'Soul's Hunger to taste of Death' emulated Christ's endurance in life and descent into hell before resurrection.[111] Puritan Christological death could have uniquely feminine bodily symptoms. John Batchiler recorded that as Susanna Perwich's torment intensified she suffered 'convulsive motions ... and risings of the mother' and these were witnessed as signs of her salvation by the other girls around her.[112] The soul was unsexed, but it was not ungendered. The barriers erected by the sort of rationality that hindered the soul and blocked the word and work of God could be thought to exist in men, but perhaps less so in women. According to Sarah Apetrei 'women were allied to Christ's intellect, which confounded the worldly wisdom so esteemed by rational men'.[113] Female physiology, which was imagined as spongy and porous, made women more emotional and volatile in bodily ways.[114] However, understandings of the gendered soul were not quite as binary as this might seem to suggest. Early-modern people believed the senses could be directed by reason and that knowledge—the key to closeness with God—was arrived at through passion. The faculty of reason was sensate according to Richard Braithwait, directing the soul to 'the best taste' which was 'to distaste sin'.[115] Apetrei suggests that it 'may be possible to regard this dialectic as part of a process which finally established the association between male qualities and rational thought'.[116] Certainly Roland Knox's seminal twentieth-century work on *Enthusiasm* argued that 'enthusiasts' collapsed grace into nature as they abandoned reason and waited for the oracular.[117] Knox tersely commented that 'the unfettered exercise of the prophetic ministry by the more devout sex [women] can threaten the ordinary decencies of ecclesiastical order'.[118] The loss of bodily control, the poetic ecstasy and rapture signalled an emotionalism that could *only* be associated with women in this later binary model. However, if irrationality was sometimes gendered feminine by early-modern people, equally it could become the key for *both* sexes as they unshackled the doctrine of election from its opposite and unlocked more fully the idea of the operation of the Holy Spirit. Phyllis Mack once pointed out that the concept of Christ's lactating nurture of the elect crept into male as well as female expressions of their relationship with God.[119] After all, the milk and blood of Christ were just different versions of the same fungible fluid concocted in the liver according to the early-modern humoral system. Rational dissent and rational piety of the emerging Enlightenment may have invoked everything from 'popular Kabbalism' to 'the hermetic symbol of the quest for eternal life'.[120] However, in some strands of puritan thought, reason itself was used to insist that the heightened senses were indicative of a state of grace. This led to an anti-rationalist and anti-Cartesian piety that was an intellectual hybridity, one that collapsed science and creationist understandings of nature and constructed religious appeal.[121]

Lead's theology urged transcendence of reason because this made possible the escape from temporal corruption. Her preaching—oral and textual—was designed to be read by believers and unbelievers alike as a performative and embodied escape from human reason.[122] Loss of control was a vital element of the performance of suffering in the manner of Christ. Lead revealed her 'secret Combates that have followed me hard, to shake my Faith'.[123] Like Jesus she was being tested in the wilderness. In one of her last works—*The Wars of David*—Lead told her readers that 'the whole Life of a Christian is a perpetual Warfare'.[124] During the 'warrings in the Soul' man was transported 'from a natural to a spiritual Estate, which at first is legal', though this was followed by the state of grace during which there is 'perpetual War' as the 'Children of Israel' (whom she called the 'Elect Seed') are brought out of bondage.[125] The bondage included human reason. Therefore, if Lead's was a form of rational dissent, it was predicated on her own claims to salvation through the manifestation of the exact opposite.

Puritan visionaries such as Lead experienced auditory and visual sensory overrides and, as William Lamont once pointed out about the Muggletonians, '[t]heir real world was in the mind'.[126] When Lead and other puritan prophets of the spiritual age picked up the Bible to speak with

God, he actually answered. Tanya Luhrmann has recently pointed out that rationality and irrationality are both part of ordinary lived human experience.[127] Oral performance of sensory override can be seen, for example, in the simply-expressed Quaker theology of walking in the light, which manifested itself at times as embodied gushes of verbal violence. Elizabeth Hooton explained it as the power of the Lord literally rising within her body.[128] Quakers quaked because they physically felt the release of their own sinfulness and this led to ecstasy. Later, in the eighteenth century, Ann Lee turned her body into a Cartesian *tabula rasa* that invited rejection of corporality in favour of transmogrification into spiritual flesh.[129] Lee burned with her feminised messianic conviction. She invited Shakers to shake because their oral outbursts of God's word could result in the release of speaking in tongues. The Shakers felt themselves bodily possessed by something elemental, which they often explained in terms used to describe nature, such as wind and fire. They described their collective spiritual ecstasy as becoming like clouds, in motion around one another as if 'agitated with a mighty wind'.[130] The trembling that preceded their eruption into singing and shouting, chanting, jumping about and pacing the boards with uncontrollably shaking limbs, marked a specific Scriptural rite of passage that expressed 'the indignation of God against all sin' moving on to 'joy at the near prospect of salvation'.[131] The narrative was scripturally based, but the feminised radicalism of their witnessing for God required that reason be disembodied, de-sexualised and speech-disrupted into a new public transcript.[132] One Shaker hymn linked this bodily freedom to the celibacy that 'Mother Jane' [Wardley] had encouraged in married couples: 'A few first receiv'd it, | And their lusts forsake; | And soon their inward power | Brought on a mighty shake'.[133] Members of the Cannon Street household congregation believed that their salvation lay as much in physical manifestation through absence as in wild physical motion. The absence was sex and the physical motion was dance: 'For dancing is a sweet employ, | It fills the soul with heavenly joy, | It makes our love and union flow, | As round, and round, and round we go'.[134] In the familial worship at home, the ecstatic joy felt by the Shakers at their perceived salvation embraced them like a tidal wave: 'At Manchester, in England, This blessed fire began, | And like a flame in stubble, | From house to house it ran'.[135]

The Shakers belonged to the same domestic and anti-rationalist puritan tradition as Jane Lead and the Philadelphians. Like Lead they emphasised John's prophetic message and their covenant beliefs were Noahic: 'When the old world of flesh and blood, | Was swept away by Noah's flood'.[136] Shaker hymns were also intensely feminine and maternal in their descriptions of spiritual warfare. One of their hymns—recorded later about this deeply secretive and by now American sect—invited singing about 'The Heavenly Bridegroom and Bride' and continued: 'Now Christ is revealed in the woman, | And makes her as pure as the light; | This sets the old serpent a foaming, | But let him come on to the fight'.[137] The Shakers looked to the prophesy of the two olive trees seen by Zechariah to ask 'Pray do they show us the fitness | Of male and the female in one?'[138] Shaker meetings of ecstatic singing and dancing were punctuated by strict and prosaic domestic routines. Privacy had little value in the Shaker world because it was the collective interiority rather than outward formal arrangements for worship that mattered in their quest to build a sinless utopia.[139] The Shakers simply ensured that men and women in supervisory roles sat in offices across the hall from one another, communicating the logistics of running sex-segregated dormitories—but not directly opposite, just in case they caught sight of one another's sexed bodies.[140] Perhaps the one thing that most demonstrates the importance of feminine spiritual leadership to these later puritans was their invention of the automated washing machine in the nineteenth century. After all, as far as the Shakers were concerned a washing machine left more time for God to work through the spiritual agency of women in domestic spaces.[141]

IV

Jane Lead was writing just as radical Protestantism found it necessary to invent the term theodicy to explain away human suffering under an omnipotent God.[142] *A Fountain of Gardens* was an extended, complex and reasoning exercise that attempted to release the elect from fear of damnation. This was what all puritans wanted from their pastoral theology. *A Fountain of Gardens* bent Calvinist doctrine and cemented it to a rhetorically anti-rationalist, ocular and sensate pathway to paradise.[143] Lead incorporated and extended Boehme's idea of the Virgin Wisdom and combined it with hermeticism and the alchemical, but she liberally and loosely applied covenant theology as well. Deploying covenant theology was a common tactic in puritan works because God's promises—especially to Noah—helped to obscure the full impact of double predestination. Puritan theology emphasised the transforming nature of the spirit as it worked through a much more ancient covenant of grace.[144] Assurance came in the form of the invisible church, or, in Lead's words, 'the living stones' of the Tabernacle.[145] The invisible church bound the elect, wherever they were, by erasing the material world at the same time as sacralising multiple (often domestic) places of worship where a sensate worship took place that defied all Cartesian logic.[146]

In her penultimate work—*A Living Funeral Testimony*—Lead offered assurance to 'the Beloved Philadelphian Society' that they were 'gather'd into one Unity of Spirit'.[147] Hers was a world in which the elect benefitted from 'peculiar Providences ... Whereupon chosen out I was, with some other Precious Stones' to win 'the Spiritual Warfare' thrust upon them by 'the Evil one'.[148] The Philadelphians were saints who surely could rejoice in recognizing Christ in one another. Sophia was there in Lead's message, but Christ remained central and, indeed, Lead was engaged in imagining Christ's arrival. This extraordinary event could happen just at home and involve a very ordinary-looking ladder. It is this domestic and feminised worship under charismatic female leadership that links Lead and the Philadelphians with later groups of the English Evangelical Revival and the American Second Great Awakening, especially the Shakers. The feminine content of the radical religious narrative lay in Lead's suggestion that the sensation she felt at her transforming knowledge of God was actually a song—a *new* song. Word was transformed into *bel canto* and the elect felt, saw, tasted and heard that their souls were sinless and that the sensate worship brought them to a full and embodied knowledge of the passion of Christ. What was significant was not Christ's humanity, but that some of them—the saints—might be merged corporally with Christ. The invisible church stretched across time and place and there were only a few short steps between the ideas of Lead—with her breath-taking imagined paradise—and those of the Shakers as they sang and quaked and danced in whirling circles and revelled in the glory of glossolalia.

NOTES

* Jane Lead, *The Heavenly Cloud Now Breaking* (1681), p. 17. My thanks go to J. Colin Davis and Ariel Hessayon for insightful reading of this chapter and very useful suggestions.

1. John Spurr, 'From Puritanism to Dissent, 1660–1700' in (eds.) Christopher Durston and Jacqueline Eales, *The Culture of English Puritanism 1560–1700* (Basingstoke: Macmillan, 1996), chapters 6–8. For the idea of 'continuity of Puritanism' until 1642 see Jacqueline Eales, 'A Road to Revolution: The Continuity of Puritanism' and for the adjectival concepts of 'puritan

revolution', 'puritan rule' and 'radical Puritanism' through to 1660, see John Morrill, 'The Puritan Revolution' and David R. Como, 'Radical Puritanism, *c.* 1558–1660', in John Coffey and Paul C. H. Lim (eds.), *The Cambridge Companion to Puritanism* (Cambridge: Cambridge University Press, 2008), chapters 4, 14 and Christopher Durston, 'Puritan Rule and the Failure of Cultural Revolution, 1645–1660', in Durston and Eales (eds.), *The Culture of English Puritanism*, chapter 7.

2. For the origins of Puritanism in a 'hotter sort' of Protestant see Patrick Collinson, *The Elizabethan Puritan Movement* (Oxford: Clarendon Press, 1967), *English Puritanism* (London: The Historical Association, 1983) and *Godly People: Essays on English Protestantism and Puritanism* (London: The Hambledon Press, 1983).

3. See Ariel Hessayon and David Finnegan (eds.), *Varieties of Seventeenth- and Early Eighteenth-Century Radicalism in Context* (Farnham: Ashgate, 2011); Alexandra Walsham, 'The godly and popular culture', in Coffey and Lim (eds.), *The Cambridge Companion to Puritanism*, pp. 277, 286; F. Bremer and E. Rydell, 'Performance Art? Puritans in the Pulpit', *History Today*, 45:9 (1995), pp. 50–54.

4. John Spurr, 'Later Stuart Puritanism', in Coffey and Lim (eds.), *The Cambridge Companion to Puritanism*, chapter 5. For the puritan godly content of civil war politics, see also, John Morrill, 'The Religious Context of the English Civil War', *Transactions of the Royal Historical Society*, 5th Series, 34 (1984), pp. 155–78.

5. See Martin Sutherland, *Peace, Toleration and Decay: The Ecclesiology of Later Stuart Dissent* (Waynesboro, Georgia: Paternoster Press, 2003); Andrew Cambers and Michelle Wolfe, 'Reading, Family Religion and Evangelical Identity in Late Stuart England', *Historical Journal*, 47:4 (2004), pp. 875, 882.

6. Ariel Hessayon and Sarah Apetrei (eds.), *An Introduction to Jacob Boehme: Four Centuries of Thought and Reception* (Abingdon, Oxon. & New York: Routledge, 2014).

7. See Ariel Hessayon, 'Pordage, John (*bap.* 1607, *d.* 1681)' and 'Pordage, Mary (*d.* 1668)', *ODNB* and Sarah Apetrei, *Women, Feminism and Religion in Early Enlightenment England* (Cambridge: Cambridge University Press, 2010), pp. 191–96.

8. Sylvia Bowerbank, 'Lead [née Ward], Jane (1624–1704)' and 'Bathurst, Ann (b. *c.* 1638-d. in or before 1704)', *ODNB*; B. J. Gibbons, 'Roach, Richard (1662–1730)', *ODNB*, and 'Lee, Francis (1661–1719)', *ODNB*; Apetrei, *Women, Feminism and Religion*, p. 196.

9. Francis Lee, *The Labouring Persons Remembrancer: Or, a Practical Discourse of the Labour of the Body* (1690), pp. 7, 14–15.

10. See Johanna Eleonora Petersen, *The Life of Lady Johanna Eleonora Petersen, Written by Herself*, ed. Barbara Becker-Cantarino (Chicago: University of Chicago Press, 2005).
11. Pietist meeting structure followed Philipp Spener's model of the *collegia pietatis* recommended in *Pia Desideria* (1675).
12. Diarmaid MacCulloch, *Silence: A Christian History* (New York: Penguin, 2013), p. 144.
13. For example, *The Way to Christ* was printed in English in London in 1647, 1654 and 1656. Although John Pordage is regarded as the main follower and conduit of Boehme's works from the 1650s, there were others such as Durant Hotham and Charles Hotham. See Richard L. Greaves, 'Hotham, Charles (1615–1672)', *ODNB*, and Gordon Goodwin Gibbons, 'Hotham, Durant (1616/17-1691)', *ODNB*. See also Ariel Hessayon, 'Jacob Boehme's Writings during the English Revolution and Afterwards: Their Publication, Dissemination, and Influence', in Hessayon and Apetrei (eds.), *An Introduction to Jacob Boehme*, chapter 5 and Roger Pooley, 'Crisp, Tobias (1600–1643)', *ODNB*.
14. See Ariel Hessayon, 'Winstanley and Baptist Thought', *Prose Studies*, 36:1 (2014), p. 22.
15. Francis J. Bremer, 'The Puritan Experiment in New England, 1630–1660', in Coffey and Lim (eds.), *Cambridge Companion to Puritanism*, p. 138.
16. Hessayon, 'Pordage, John', *ODNB*, and 'Pordage, Mary', *ODNB*.
17. *The Complete Works of Gerrard Winstanley*, eds. Thomas N. Corns, Ann Hughes and David Lowenstein (Oxford: Oxford University Press, 2009), 'Letter to Lady Eleanor Douglas', 4 December 1650, vol. ii, pp. 422–29.
18. Alexandra Walsham, 'The godly and popular culture', in Coffey and Lim (eds.), *Cambridge Companion to Puritanism*, p. 277.
19. MacCulloch, *Silence*, pp. 140–150 quoting from p. 139.
20. John Pordage, *Theologia Mystica, or the Mystic Divinitie of the Eternal Invisibles* (1683), p. 89.
21. Jane Lead, *The Heavenly Cloud Now Breaking* (1681), pp. 7–8.
22. Amanda L. Capern, 'Eleanor Davies and the New Jerusalem', in Julie A. Chappell and Kaley S. Kramer (eds.), *Women during the English Reformations: Renegotiating Gender and Religious Identity* (Basingstoke: Palgrave, 2014). Eleanor Davies's *A Warning to the Dragon* (1625) was an exegetical paraphrasing of Daniel 7.
23. Eleanor Davies, *A Warning to the Dragon* (1625), pp. 38, 42.
24. Jane Lead, *The Heavenly Cloud Now Breaking* (1681), p. 8.
25. Lead, *Heavenly Cloud*, p. 36.
26. Lead, *Heavenly Cloud*, sigs. A²-A³.
27. Eleanor Davies, *The Mystery of the General Redemption* (1647).

28. Hessayon, 'Winstanley and Baptist Thought', p. 21; Davies, *The Mystery of the General Redemption*, pp. 4–5, 15.
29. Lead, *Heavenly Cloud*, p. 8.
30. Nabil Matar, 'Sterry, Peter (1613–1672)', *ODNB*.
31. William Lamont, 'The Muggletonians 1652–1979: A "Vertical" Approach', *Past and Present*, 99 (1983), p. 29.
32. Hessayon and Apetrei (eds.), *An Introduction to Jacob Boehme*, p. 7 and Nigel Smith, 'Did Anyone Understand Boehme?', chapter 5.
33. Lead, *Heavenly Cloud*, sig. A².
34. Lead, *Heavenly Cloud*, sigs. A²-A³.
35. Daniel Neal, *The History of the Puritans, or, Protestant Nonconformists, From the Death of King Charles I to the Act of Toleration by King William and Queen Mary, in the Year 1689* (London: Printed for Richard Hett, 1738), vol. iv, frontispiece. See also John 15:26 and 16:1–5.
36. Lead, *Heavenly Cloud*, pp. 34, 37.
37. Lead, *Heavenly Cloud*, sigs. A2-A3.
38. Lead, *Heavenly Cloud*, sig. A3.
39. Lead, *Heavenly Cloud*, pp. 36, 40.
40. Lead, *Heavenly Cloud*, sig.A3ᵛ, p. 7.
41. Lead, *Heavenly Cloud*, p. 8.
42. Jane Lead, *The Revelation of Revelations* (1683), pp. 49, 105–7.
43. Lead, *Revelation of Revelations*, pp. 104, 114.
44. Lead, *Revelation of Revelations*, pp. 67–68.
45. Jane Lead, *The Enochian Walks with God* (1694), title-page and Introduction.
46. Lead, *Enochian Walks with God*, Introduction [pp. 2–3].
47. Lead, *The Tree of Faith: or, the Tree of Life, Springing up in the Paradise of God* (1696), pp. 14–16.
48. See, for example, the idea of 'God's Mystery' in Jacob Boehme, *The Tree of Christian Faith* (London: 1654) and the idea of 'the Eternal Nature' and 'Spirit of Eternity himself' in John Pordage, *Theologia Mystica* (1683).
49. Lead, *Tree of Faith*, p. 6; [Jane Lead], *The Ascent to the Mount of Vision* (1699), sig. B.
50. Jane Lead, *A Revelation of the Everlasting Gospel Message* (1697), p. 28.
51. Jane Lead, *A Fountain of Gardens* (1696), p. 16.
52. Lead, *Fountain of Gardens*, p. 384.
53. Jane Lead, *The Signs of the Times* (1699), p. 16. The construction here was very like the anonymous *A Short Survey of the Kingdom of Christ* (1699), p. 47.
54. Lead, *Signs of the Times*, p. 17.
55. Cf. F. L. Cross and E. A. Livingstone (eds.), *The Oxford Dictionary of the Christian Church* (Oxford: Oxford University Press, rev. ed. 1990), pp. 1445, 1492.
56. [Lead], *Ascent to Mount of Vision*, pp. 28, 35.

57. Lead, *Tree of Faith*, pp. 64–66, quotation from p. 66.
58. Lead, *Revelation of Everlasting Gospel Message*, pp. 28–9.
59. Bowerbank, 'Lead [*née* Ward], Jane', *ODNB*.
60. Lead, *Enochian Walks with God*, title page, Introduction [p. 3].
61. Lead, *Revelation of Everlasting Gospel Message*, p. 29.
62. Lead, *Tree of Faith*, p. 221 [121].
63. Lead, *Tree of Faith*, p. 221 [121].
64. Jane Lead, *The Messenger of An Universal Peace* (1698), p. 30.
65. Lead, *Messenger of An Universal Peace*, pp. 30–31, 34 and *Signs of the Times*, sig. A2.
66. Lead, *Revelation of Everlasting Gospel Message*, sig. A^1. See Cross and Livingstone (eds.), *Oxford Dictionary of Christian Church*, pp. 730–31.
67. Lead, *Revelation of Everlasting Gospel Message*, sig. A^1. See Alister E. McGrath, *Christianity: An Introduction* (Malden, Massachusetts: Blackwell, 2nd ed. 2006), pp. 98–9.
68. Lead, *Revelation of Everlasting Gospel Message*, sigs. A^1-A^{2}v.
69. Lead, *Tree of Faith*, p. 68 and 'To the Reader', sig. A3^v.
70. Lead, *Tree of Faith*, p. 66. This passage benefitted from an interesting discussion with my colleague David Crouch.
71. Jane Lead, *The Ark of Faith Or a Supplement to the Tree of Faith* (1696), title page.
72. Lead, *Ark of Faith*, sig. 2^v, p. 8.
73. Lead, *Ascent to Mount of Vision*, p. 25.
74. Lead, *Ascent to Mount of Vision*, p. 32.
75. Lead, *Ascent to Mount of Vision*, p. 20.
76. Lead, *Tree of Faith*, pp. 13, 4–5, 19–26.
77. Lead, *Fountain of Gardens*, vol. I, pp. 126–7.
78. Lead, *Fountain of Gardens*, vol. I, pp. 128–9.
79. Lead, *Fountain of Gardens*, vol. I, p. 503.
80. *Cf.* Mark S. R. Jenner, 'Tasting Lichfield, Touching China: Sir John Floyer's Senses', *Historical Journal*, 53:3 (2010), pp. 647–70 and Jonathan Reinarz, 'Learning to Use their Senses: Visitors to Voluntary Hospitals in Eighteenth-Century England', *Journal for Eighteenth Century Studies*, 35:4 (2012), pp. 505–20.
81. Ric[hard] Brathwayt [Brathwaite], *Essaies upon the Five Senses* (2nd ed., 1635), 'A Table of Contents', n.p.
82. Mary Foster *et al.*, *A Living Testimony From the Power and Spirit of our Lord Jesus Christ in our Faithful Womens Meeting and Christian Socity* [sic] (London: s. n., 1685), p. 6.
83. Samuel Willard, *The Child's Portion* (1683), pp. 66–7 in *The Puritans: A Sourcebook of their Writings*, 2 vols., eds. Perry Miller & Thomas H. Johnson (New York: Harper Torchbooks, 1965), vol. I, p. 369.
84. Lead, *Enochian Walks with God*, pp. 26–9.

85. *Cf.* Joan Wallach Scott *The Fantasy of Feminist History* (Durham and London: Duke University Press, 2011). Scott argues that at the intersection of gender and the symbolic structures of society there lies an historical subjective identity which has no fixed location but depends instead on the imaginary, labile and created self.
86. Jacob Boehme, *The Tree of Christian Faith* (London: 1654), pp. 6–7.
87. Pordage, *Theologia Mystica*, pp. 88–92.
88. Lead, *Enochian Walks with God*, p. 29.
89. Lead, *Fountain of Gardens*, vol. I, frontispiece.
90. Ethan Shagan, 'Beyond Good and Evil: Thinking with Moderates in Early Modern England', *Journal of British Studies*, 49:3 (2010), pp. 488–513 and *The Rule of Moderation: Violence, Religion and the Politics of Restraint in Early Modern England* (Cambridge: Cambridge University Press, 2011); Jeremy Gregory, 'Refashioning Puritan New England: The Church of England in British North America, *c.* 1680 – *c.* 1770', *Transactions of the Royal Historical Society*, sixth series, 20 (2010), pp. 85–112.
91. Spurr, 'Later Stuart Puritanism', in Coffey and Lim (eds.), *Cambridge Companion to Puritanism*, p. 89.
92. Lodowick Muggleton, *The Acts of the Witnesses of the Spirit: in Five Parts* (1699), title page, p. 9; Lamont, 'The Muggletonians 1652–1979', p. 29 and 'Muggleton, Lodowicke (1609–1698)', *ODNB*.
93. Neal, *History of the Puritans*, vols. iv, vii-viii and *The History of New England containing an Impartial Account of the Civil and Ecclesiastical Affairs of the Country to the Year of our Lord, 1700*, 2 vols. (London: Printed for J. Clare, 1720), vol. I, iii-iv.
94. Foster *et al.*, *A Living Testimony*, pp. 1–4.
95. Foster *et al.*, *Living Testimony*, pp. 3–7. See also Erin Bell's analysis of Quaker strategies for cohesion in 'The Early Quakers, the Peace Testimony and Masculinity in England, 1660–1720', *Gender and History*, 23:2 (2011), pp. 283–300.
96. See Patrick Collinson, *The Elizabethan Puritan Movement* (London: Jonathan Cape, 1967), p. 71 and Kate Peters, *Print Culture and the Early Quakers* (Cambridge: Cambridge University Press, 2005), p. 141.
97. Claire Walker, *Gender and Politics in Early Modern Europe: English Convents in France and the Low Countries* (Basingstoke: Palgrave, 2003).
98. Andrew Cambers and Michelle Wolfe, 'Reading, Family Religion and Evangelical Identity in Late Stuart England', *Historical Journal*, 47:4 (2004), pp. 875–76.
99. *A Strange Prophecie Presented to the Kings most Excellent Majesty, by A Woman-Quaker (all in white) called Ahivah* (London: 1660), pp. 1–3.
100. Jane Lead, *Tree of Faith*, sig. A³.

101. Michael Winship, *Godly Republicanism: Puritans, Pilgrims, and a City on a Hill* (Cambridge, Massachusetts & London, England: Harvard University Press, 2012), p. 233.

102. *Cf.* Julie Hirst, *Jane Leade: Biography of a Seventeenth-Century Mystic* (Aldershot, Hampshire & Burlington, Vermont: Ashgate, 2005), pp. 32–40. See also Nigel Smith, 'Jacob Boehme and the Sects', *Perfection Proclaimed: Language and Literature in English Radical Religions 1640–1660* (Oxford: Clarendon Press, 1989), chapter 5.

103. Jane Lead, *A Living Funeral Testimony* (1702), pp. 27–8.

104. See, for example, Cotton Mather, *The Wonders of the Invisible World being an Account of the Tryals of Several Witches lately executed in New-England* (1693) and Increase Mather, *Cases of Conscience concerning Evil Spirits Impersonating Men* (1693). The debate had parallels with that generated a hundred years earlier by Reginald Scot's *The Discoverie of Witchcraft* of 1584.

105. Samuel Willard (1640–1707), for example, published multiple works in Boston in the 1680s and 1690s, such as *The Child's Portion* (1684) and *The Doctrine of the Covenant of Redemption* (1693) which were printed and distributed in the London Coffee House. See Mark Knights, 'Benjamin Harris (*c.* 1647–1720)', *ODNB*.

106. Jeffrey K. Jue, 'Puritan Millenialism in Old and New England', in Coffey and Lim (eds.), *Cambridge Companion to Puritanism*, p. 271; Perry Miller, *The New England Mind: The Seventeenth Century* (Cambridge, Massachusetts & London, England: The Belknap Press, 1939, rep. 1982); Bremer, 'Puritan Experiment in New England', in Coffey and Lim (eds.), *Cambridge Companion to Puritanism*, p. 131.

107. *Cf.* Coffey and Lim, 'Introduction', in idem *Cambridge Companion to Puritanism*, p. 3.

108. Richard Schlatter, *Richard Baxter and Puritan Politics* (New Brunswick, New Jersey: Rutgers University Press, 1957), pp. 21, 62, 76; Shagan, *The Rule of Moderation*, p. 151.

109. Hessayon, 'Pordage, John'.

110. Jane Lead, 'To the impartial and well-disposed Reader' in *Theologia Mystica*, p. 2.

111. Lead, 'To the Reader' in *Theologia Mystica*, p. 3.

112. John Batchiler, *The Virgins Pattern* (London: 1661), p. 35.

113. Apetrei, *Women, Feminism and Religion*, pp. 247–55 quoting from p. 255.

114. Phyllis Mack, *Visionary Women: Ecstatic Prophecy in Seventeenth-Century England* (Berkeley: University of California Press, 1992), pp. 23, 27. See also Thomas Laqueur, *Making Sex: Body and Gender from the Greeks to Freud* (Cambridge, Massachusetts, 1990); Anthony Fletcher, *Gender, Sex*

and Subordination in England, 1500–1800 (New Haven & London: Yale University Press, 1995); Laura Gowing, *Common Bodies: Women, Touch and Power in Seventeenth-Century England* (London: Yale University Press, 2003).
115. [Rich[ard] Brathwayt [Brathwaite], *Essaies upon the Five Senses* (1st ed., 1620), pp. 48–9.
116. Apetrei, *Women, Feminism and Religion*, p. 255.
117. Roland Knox, *Enthusiasm: a Chapter in the History of Religion* (Oxford: Clarendon Press, 1950), p. 3.
118. Knox, *Enthusiasm*, p. 20.
119. Mack, *Visionary Women*, passim but especially chapters 1, 9.
120. Knud Haakonssen (ed.), *Enlightenment and Religion: Rational Dissent in Eighteenth-Century Britain* (Cambridge: Cambridge University Press, 1996), passim and quoting Iain McCalman, 'New Jerusalems: Prophecy, Dissent and Radical Culture', in idem, p. 318; *Cf.* Apetrei, *Women, Feminism and Religion*, p. 194.
121. By contrast see Brad Gregory, *The Unintended Reformation: How a Religious Revolution Secularized Society* (Cambridge, Mass.: Harvard University Press, 2012).
122. *Cf.* Alexandra Walsham, 'The godly and popular culture', in Coffey and Lim (eds.), *Cambridge Companion to Puritanism*, pp. 277, 286.
123. Lead, *Tree of Faith*, p. 3.
124. Jane Lead, *The Wars of David and the Peaceable Reign of Solomon* (1700), p. 63.
125. Lead, *Wars of David*, p. 64.
126. Lamont, 'The Muggletonians', p. 35.
127. T. M. Luhrmann, *When God Talks Back: Understanding the American Evangelical Relationship with God* (New York: Vintage Books, 2012), p. 236. My thanks to Phyllis Mack for a great discussion around this one enjoyable afternoon.
128. Mack, *Visionary Women*, pp. 128–9 citing Emily Manners, *Elizabeth Hooton: First Quaker Woman Preacher (1600–1672)* (London: Headley Brothers, 1914), pp. 36–7, 49.
129. Julie A. Chappell, *Perilous Passages: the Book of Margery Kempe, 1534–1934* (New York: Palgrave Macmillan, 2013), pp. xx-xxxvi; Knox, *Enthusiasm*, pp. 558–9. Ann Lee was illiterate: Carla Gerona, 'Lee, Ann (1736–1784)', *ODNB*.
130. [Calvin Green and Seth Young Wells], *A Summary View of the Millennial Church, or United Society of Believers (Commonly Called Shakers)* (Albany: Packard & Van Benthuysen, 1823), p. 5.
131. [Green and Wells], *Summary View of the Millennial Church*, p. 5.
132. See the 'public transcript/hidden transcript' paradigm of James C. Scott, *Weapons of the Weak: Everyday Forms of Peasant Resistance* (New Haven:

Yale University Press, 1985) and John Walter, *Crowds and Popular Politics in Early Modern England* (Manchester: Manchester University Press, 2006).

133. Terrie Dopp Aamodt, 'Wardley, Jane (*fl.* 1747–1770)', *ODNB*; Seth Young Wells, *Millenniul Praises: containing a collection of gospel hymns, in four parts; adapted to the day of Christ's second appearing* (Hancock: Josiah Tallcott Junior, 1813), p. 79.

134. Wells, *Millennial Praises*, p. 69.

135. Wells, *Millennial Praises*, p. 79.

136. Wells, *Millennial Praises*, p. 3.

137. Wells, *Millennial Praises*, p. 19.

138. Wells, *Millennial Praises*, pp. 18–19.

139. *Cf.* Lena Cowen Orlin, *Locating Privacy in Tudor London* (Oxford: Oxford University Press, 2007), pp. 1, 193, chapter 8 especially pp. 324–6 and referring to Alan Sinfield, *Faultlines: Cultural Materialism and the Politics of Dissident Reading* (Berkeley: University of California Press, 1992), pp. 152–80; Retha Warnicke, 'Private and Public: The Boundaries of Women's Lives in Early Stuart England' in Jean R. Brink (ed.), *Privileging Gender in Early Modern England*, vol. xxiii, Sixteenth Century Essays and Studies (Ann Arbor, Michigan: Edwards Brothers, 1993), pp. 138–9.

140. From personal observation and information from the docent at the Canterbury Shaker Village in New Hampshire, 4 September 2012.

141. Information about the washing machine from the docent at the Canterbury Shaker Village, 4 September 2012.

142. Luhrmann, *When God Talks Back*, p. 267. The term was coined in 1710 by Gottfried Leibniz (1646–1716), rationalist mathematician and philosopher.

143. *Cf.* Christopher Haigh, *English Reformations: Religion, Politics, and Society under the Tudors* (Oxford: Clarendon Press, 1993).

144. *Cf.* Miller, *New England Mind*, pp. 92–3, 360–2; *The Works of Anne Bradstreet*, ed. Jeannine Hensley (Cambridge, Massachusetts & London, England: The Belknap Press, 1967, rep. 2005), pp. xxix, xxxiii, xxxvii.

145. Lead, *Fountain of Gardens*, vol. I, p. 399.

146. *Cf.* Nicky Hallett, *The Senses in Religious Communities, 1600–1800* (Farnham, Surrey and Burlington, VT: Ashgate, 2013); Matthew Milner, *The Senses and the English Reformation* (Farnham, Surrey and Burlington, VT: Ashgate, 2011).

147. Lead, *Living Funeral Testimony*, preface, sig. A².

148. Lead, *A Living Funeral Testimony*, pp. 1–2.

CHAPTER 6

Jane Lead and English Apocalyptic Thought in the Late Seventeenth Century

Warren Johnston

There can be no doubt that the transformation and restitution of the world in accomplishment of divine revelation was the central theme in Jane Lead's thought and convictions. This is apparent simply in Lead's self-identification as a prophet. Lead, however, also combined those recent and original revelations with the more familiar scriptural imagery and prophetic representations of future events found in the Book of Revelation. Her prophesying is permeated with references to the 'New Jerusalem State', Christ's coming kingdom on earth, and the promise of a 'New Paradisical World'. Lead confirms the advent of the 'Marvellous Reign of Christ in his Saints' in both the 'ancient prophecy' of Revelation and in 'these latter prophecies' she was bringing forth.[1] Even the name chosen for themselves by Lead and her followers, the Philadelphian Society, was a reference to Revelation 3 and the church that epitomized the patient and faithful followers of Christ among whom the New Jerusalem would be fulfilled.

Lead's prophetic writings have received much attention from modern scholars. Of particular interest have been her application of the ideas of

W. Johnston (✉)
Department of History and Philosophy, Algoma University,
Sault Ste. Marie, ON, Canada

© The Editor(s) (if applicable) and The Author(s) 2016
A. Hessayon (ed.), *Jane Lead and her Transnational Legacy*,
DOI 10.1057/978-1-137-39614-3_6

119

the German mystic Jacob Boehme, the importance of the female figure of Wisdom in guiding spiritual enlightenment, as well as the importance of gendered and androgynous portrayals of the prophetic figures represented in her prophesying.[2] Included among such analyses have also been references to Lead's place in seventeenth-century English apocalyptic thought. Her writings are described as containing 'powerful subversive "visions" characteristic of millenarian writings', part of a 'repressed' radical millenarian tradition after the Restoration and of the inclination to internalize mystical experience, disengaging it 'from overt political culture'.[3] Lead herself has even been described as 'one of the last public millenarians from a gentry family'.[4] However, it is crucial to note that the perceived decline of apocalyptic beliefs after 1660, along with their supposed connection solely to the failed radicalism of the Civil War and Interregnum period, has been greatly overstated by many historians. Thus, it is not the departure from radical millenarian beliefs that is unique about Lead's thought, but instead her divergence from the predominant norms of late seventeenth-century English apocalyptic interpretation. Though some authors have examined Lead's apocalyptic ideas more closely,[5] they have failed to note the continued existence of contemporary hermeneutical convictions, as well as neglecting to examine her ideas in contrast to those traditions. What has remained elusive, then, is a thorough explanation of Lead's apocalyptic thought in the context of such exegetical conventions: this chapter will begin to fill that gap.

I

In order to present Jane Lead's ideas in the context of a broader tradition of later seventeenth-century apocalyptic thought, it is first necessary to provide a brief overview of contemporary interpretive traditions. By the end of the seventeenth century, a historicist understanding of the Book of Revelation, as well as other supporting apocalyptic scripture, was predominant. The success of this exegetical method, which saw the prophecies of Revelation as representing a series of events and figures stretching from the time of the apostles to the fulfillment of the Millennium in the impending future, was largely founded in England upon the work of the Cambridge scholar Joseph Mede. Though he died in 1638, Mede's *Clavis apocalyptica* (1632) was translated into English by order of parliament in 1642 (as *Key of the Revelation*) and his ideas influenced English apocalyptic interpreters into the eighteenth century.[6]

English historicist interpretation saw the seven seals (Revelation 6:1–17 and 8:1) and the seven trumpets (8:2–9:21, and 11:15–19) as the overarching chronological prophecies of Revelation. These joined together, with each of them marking significant episodes in the history of Christianity. The seals and the trumpets began at the founding of the Church, continued through the Roman persecutions, the conversion of the Empire, its subsequent fall to Germanic tribes, the corruptions of the medieval period, and, finally, to the Reformation and the return to purified forms. In addition to these major prophecies, other significant prophetic imagery included: numerous references to the beast and Babylon, representing worldly and sinful institutions; the seven vials (16:1–21), whose pouring would result in the destruction of the beast; the whore of Babylon (17:1–18) representing worldly degeneracy; and the New Jerusalem, which embodied the perfected millennial church and state that would rule over Christ's thousand-year kingdom on earth. The prophecy of the woman in the wilderness pursued by the dragon (Chap. 12) coincided with the exclusion and persecution of proper Christian forms of worship during the degeneration of the medieval church, as did the two witnesses (Chap. 11). The anchoring of these prophecies to specific historical events was aided by references to various time periods of 1,260 days, three and a half days, a 'time, times, and half a time', and 42 months—all of which were most often viewed as signifying the same period of 1,260 years.[7]

Apocalyptic interpreters did vary in the precise specifics of their application of these prophecies to particular historical circumstances. For example, while Anglican exegetes might see the fulfillment of millennial ecclesiastical and temporal government in the episcopal church and the English monarchy, nonconformist authors might view the persecution of the two witnesses and the woman in the wilderness as ongoing and awaiting further church reform before these prophecies would conclude. And, of course, dissenters might disagree among themselves on which particular forms best suited the coming perfection of the millennial church and the government that would support it. However, despite such differences, a vast majority could agree on the basic Protestant historicist presumptions that the beast and Babylon were embodied in the papacy and Roman Church, that the Reformation (in whatever form) marked a significant circumstance in the accomplishment of apocalyptic prophecy, and that the millennium signified a future, glorious state of the Christian church on earth.

It is apparent in Jane Lead's writings that she was aware of the continuing interest in apocalyptic ideas during her time, as well as the particulars of the historicist interpretive framework. In 1683 she noted 'much controversie' over the prophecy and timing of the Millennium, stating that 'many have Calculated, and puzled their Spirits about it in vain'.[8] A decade later she mentioned a 'little Tract lately manifested in what way and manner we may expect the Lord Jesus his Appearance about which so many prophecies and sounds in this present Age have gone forth'.[9] Her later works continued to acknowledge such apocalyptic views. In her spiritual diary, Lead remarked on different opinions concerning Christ's personal appearance and kingdom on earth, and in her final publication, *A Living Funeral Testimony*, she criticized the expectations of 'any overturning of the Worldly Kingdoms, for Reformation' as an idea 'from the vile Conversation that now so Universal is, by which the greater part of the Inhabitants lie buried in the Love of earthly Things'.[10] This statement not only recognized the state of contemporary apocalyptic thought but also demonstrated her conviction about the limited material impact of prophetic realization.

There is also evidence of knowledge of specific expositors in Lead's works. A letter discussing the legitimacy of ongoing revelation, likely by one of her close followers, is included in one of Lead's writings. This epistle cites Joseph Mede's position on that topic, adding that 'All of the World who have but look'd into him, or even heard of his Name, must needs know what was his Sentiment as to the Glorious Reign of Christ'.[11] Connections have also been made between Lead and Thomas Beverley, the most prolific apocalyptic author of the 1680s and 1690s. The constitutions of the Philadelphian Society were completed on 23 August 1697, the day that Beverley dated for the destruction of the beast and the advent of the Millennium. Moreover, in 1698 Lead observed that 'the Spirit of Prophecy has in some declared that from the Year 1697. to 1700. a good Progress will be made' towards the beginning of the thousand-year reign, a position that was reiterated repeatedly in Beverley's writings.[12] Yet even with recognition of these exegetical traditions, Lead's apocalyptic ideas would diverge greatly from their path.

II

In the preface to a 1695 work, Lead's editor succinctly stated the place of her thought in its late seventeenth-century context: 'What is contained in this Treatise ... will appear more than ordinarily Strange, to the greatest part of those who shall look upon it'.[13] The 'strangeness' of Lead's ideas originated from the particular and peculiar perspective from which she made and accounted for her apocalyptic beliefs. In her first publication, she referred to herself as a 'Heavenly Spy' who had been privileged with access to 'substantial high, and worthy precious things', and whose responsibility it was to record and present these to the world.[14] In short, she was not simply an interpreter of scriptural and apocalyptic meaning, but, instead, a prophet in her own right. Lead described the qualities of her mystical encounters in powerful terms:

> the Spirit of Truth and Revelation openeth himself in the fiery Essence of the Soul, in a sweet silent stillness, where out all thoughts are excluded; then doth the light Ray of the Deity rise, and overshadow and fill the Temple of the Mind with light and glory, then will the soul sink away deeper & deeper into the abyss being, where the greatest of Wisdom's secrets are to be known.[15]

These visitations provided her access to important, new divine information that was on par with scripture itself. The Old Testament was 'appropriated to the Ministration of the Father, the new [Testament] to the Son', and Lead now was part of the ministration of the Holy Ghost, who would 'Unseal and Reveal what yet never was known or understood'.[16] She was moved by 'the same Spirit that did Heretofore inspire the Holy Men of God' and her prophesying was 'Now in this last Day more abundantly shed forth to multiply the Volumes of Scripture: For whatsoever is purely dictated by the Holy Ghost, may be called by that Name'.[17] Lead's delivery of such revelations was used as evidence that apocalyptic accomplishment would soon be achieved in the impending establishment of Christ's reign on earth.[18]

The prestige of her prophesies, with their neo-scriptural status, was also demonstrated in their origins. The purveyors of information in the many visitations that Lead received were often the Holy Spirit, Christ, or the embodiment of divine knowledge, whom Lead designated as 'Wisdom'.[19] However, she also encountered other personages that gave some sense of the importance and purpose of her prophecies and message. These included John the Divine, to whom the Book of Revelation's prophecies were delivered, and the archangel Michael, whose apocalyptic roles included delivering God's people and battling the dragon (Daniel 12:1 and Revelation 12:7).[20] She also compared her prophetic insight to that of John himself. Lead claimed that her prophecies came from the 'sort

of Vision the Beloved John was in', and she recounted the experience of
a 'Light Orb [that] opened and all overspread me … so that it brought
to my remembrance the Lord's Day, which John saw, and had all his
Revelations in'.[21] Indeed, Lead's role went beyond that of John himself,
as she was given knowledge of mysteries that he had not been made privy
to or that he had been told to keep hidden. Introducing her explanation
of the seven seals, she pronounced Revelation's treatment of them as 'very
obscure', asserting that 'there is no fathoming of it to the utmost' until
Christ comes to provide an explanation. Yet she continued by remarking
that some 'have been favoured with this light of Revelation' and that the
meaning of the seals was given to her 'according as how it was acted …
in a particular experience of my own in the divine Mystery'.[22] She also
expounded on the meanings of the seven thunders, about which John had
been told to 'write them not' (Revelation 10:3–4), as well as professing
special knowledge of the prophecy of the 'Thousand Years Reign' which is
only briefly mentioned in Revelation 20:2–3.[23]

Lead's divinely inspired aptitudes were not limited to new insights
upon existing scriptural prophecies but also extended to being given new
revelations. In a visitation on 19 May 1677 she was shown a 'Glassy Book',
which she was told 'would put an end to all other Books: it was beyond
all literal Ministration' and comprised 'all Wisdom, Knowledge, and Sight
of Eternal things'.[24] Thus Lead claimed here a privileged and prestigious
access to divine knowledge that she presented to the world in the form of
new and ongoing revelation; one, moreover, that could supersede existing
scriptural prophecy. While 'the old Prophecies' had their place, it did not
'put a stop to, and restraint upon the further Manifestation, and Revelation
of what is to be brought forth in this latter day … [when] knowledge of
the Divine Mysteries must have its unvailing; which are too deep to be
fathomed by the meerly litteral Wise Ones'.[25] The means to attain the
New Jerusalem, a theme that is ubiquitous in Lead's writings and central
to her ministry, was presented to her 'not by Vision only as in past times …
but now the Spirit hath moved itself in another degree … into an Essential
Fruition' that would reward those who adhered to her guidance.[26] She
answered her critics by maintaining that the possibility of new revelations
had not ended after the age of the apostles and with the completion of the
biblical canon.[27] She warned 'Let none therefore presume to set bounds
to the Wisdom and Power of the Immense Being, to shut him up to this
or that Measure or Degree, Age or Time, who always moveth in Eternal
Liberty', and she held up her own experiences as proof 'that Revelation

hath no cessation, but that it is daily Renewed in Vessels, or Instruments, rightly qualified to receive it'.[28] These new prophecies and revelations would educate those on the path to the New Jerusalem, 'so none may be frustrated of what they expect in a Future State'.[29] Fulfillment of prophecy would extend to 'both what hath been in past Ages given, and hath been of late so plentifully Renewed' by Lead herself.[30] This demonstrated her own principal and essential role in impending apocalyptic accomplishment.

Despite the emphasis placed on the importance of her new revelations, Lead's prophesying also made reference to existing scriptural imagery. Familiar apocalyptic motifs were conspicuous in her writings but their meanings were largely abstract, adapted to suit her primary prophetic message. This usage provided no historical reference points or applications in the way that most other late seventeenth-century English apocalyptic interpretations did. Prominent among the imagery that Lead used were the New Jerusalem, the beast and the dragon, Babylon, and the woman in the wilderness, along with less frequent references to the seals, thunders, and vials.

In her *Revelation of Revelations* (1683) Lead undertook an explanation of her vision of the New Jerusalem. She recounted how her spirit had been 'oft taken up to see the wonderful Plat-form of the New Jerusalem'. Her concern was to discover the meaning of this prophecy for her time, and these spiritual visits allowed her to see it 'descend and cover the whole Earth', with 'multitudes' fleeing from it but another 'Numerous Company gathered to it from all Quarters ... the first-born of this Mother-City'.[31] Noting that there had been many attempts to present and configure the New Jerusalem in the past but 'the Heavenly Thing it self hath not been brought forth, as now [i]t will be, because the set time approacheth', she later described the gates of the city as a series of ordeals and characteristics of the spirit to test those who desired entry there.[32] Passage through the seventh and last gate would see pilgrims transformed into a pure, spiritual, 'Cœlestial Body' that would shed 'whatsoever doth stick in the Curse ... together with the Body of fallen Man' and prevent Satan and his agents from being 'able to overthrow the Lord's personal reign in his Saints'.[33] Throughout her writings Lead referred again and again to the New Jerusalem, elaborating and giving further detail about the city and those who would come to inhabit it. As the preceding description suggests, citizenship of the city required a spiritual transformation guided, as Lead had been, by the figure of Wisdom.[34] Connecting the New Jerusalem to Christ's millennial kingdom, Lead cited Revelation 20:4, the souls who would reign at that time must be 'beheaded', 'an inward and spiritual Martyrdom ... who have their Head Life, where Rational Understanding is seated ... cut off'. This would see people abandon worldly reasoning in favor of spiritual knowledge, preparing them for this New Jerusalem state.[35] In the first pages of her first published work, Lead promised her readers that 'great things are prepared [for them] in the New Jerusalem, there to have Communion in one Spiritual Body at one Table, each according to their measure and degree' of spiritual advancement.[36] The progress of the saints towards this enlightened state would allow the New Jerusalem to 'begin to descend and spread' throughout the world.[37]

The spiritual purity of the New Jerusalem was contrasted in the attributes of worldly wisdom, embodied in the figures of the beast, the dragon and Babylon. All 'Evil, Earthly, Carnal sensual Thoughts, and Cogitations do proceed from the Center of this Earthly Principle, and from the Nature and Spirit of this great World in us, called the Beast in the Revelations', which had 'many Generations' to impose his 'strange Laws, and Injunctions ... Witchcrafts, and Deceits'.[38] Lead deemed human 'Reason' the beast's 'Fore-Head mark' and 'mighty Sword and Spear', 'suitable for the Degenerated Estate to guide and govern the Outward Terrestrial Man'. Reason acted as a hindrance to spiritual edification, 'a Wall of Defence ... maintaining its Soveraignty without Check or Controll, so long as the Beasts Reign is to endure'.[39] Similarly, Babylon represented a 'Confusion' of worldly forms, 'all Formal worships set up by Man, and constituted by Rational Inventions ... [that] must pass away'.[40] The battle against these influences occurred internally, within the mind of each individual. Lead told her readers 'how thy Michael **in thee** will Fight against the Dragon' (Revelation 12:7–8), describing 'a head-Power great and mighty in the Soul-Region, to repel and keep down, what the Dragon and Beast would do to make Mutiny and Riot'.[41] The fulfillment of the destruction of Babylon (Revelation 14:8; 18:2) was an individual accomplishment, 'that in thy self thou maist first behold its Fall'.[42] Just as participation in the Babylonish kingdom had required the mark of the beast, citizenship in the New Jerusalem would require 'the Seal of the Father, Son, and Holy Ghost upon their Forehead, to signify that they are ordained free denizons here'.[43] The pervasiveness of worldly interests and pleasures were 'a Sign of the near Approach of the Overthrowing of the Kingdom of this Antichristian Beast', as was the arrogance of the dragon and its opposition to the spiritual efforts of the saints.[44]

Another prophecy that appears a number of times in Lead's work is the account of the woman clothed with the sun. Revelation 12 describes this figure in the throes of childbirth, fleeing into the wilderness and pursued by the dragon. As with her explication of other prophecies, this meaning is focused on the achievement of spiritual refinement and the approach of Christ's kingdom on earth. The woman's 'coming forth out of the Wilderness, will signify this great day of Dominion and Power over the Earth'.[45] More than simply a symbolic representation of the Church, the woman is Virgin Wisdom herself, the source of all spiritual enlightenment and Lead's guide in many of her visions.[46] Wisdom 'is given Command and Power ... within the Celestial Region' and Wisdom's child will 'all opposing Nations crush, and bring under'.[47] After ascending to heaven, that 'man child' will return to save the 'Remnant of the Virgin-Seed, against whom the Dragon still makes War'; these people will then be entrusted with rulership over Christ's kingdom.[48] Although believing that this prophecy was yet to be fulfilled, Lead insisted that it would soon be accomplished, with its last 'Half Time' about to expire.[49]

Other imagery from Revelation also found meaning within Lead's explanations. Her account of the opening of each of the seven seals contains specific characteristics associated with each and described in relation to personal and scriptural reference points, but without historical allusions.[50] However, despite this lack of chronological anchoring, Lead does assert that the prophecy of the seven seals and the seven thunders were already being fulfilled within certain individuals.[51] The opening of the seventh seal would initiate the sounding of the seven thunders, and together marked the establishment and populating of the New Jerusalem kingdom on earth.[52] Lead also referred to the seven vials in a fairly standard exegetical way, as the means that would destroy the beast, the dragon, and Babylon—though again she did not situate these prophetic events historically or chronologically.[53] It is noteworthy, however, that other imagery which featured frequently in typical late seventeenth-century English apocalyptic interpretations—notably the two witnesses and the whore—were rarely mentioned by Lead.[54]

III

The preceding section described significant imagery from the Book of Revelation that featured prominently in Jane Lead's prophesying and her explanations of prophetic fulfillment. Most of this application of apocalyptic prophecy is presented as depicting aspects of individual and personal spiritual accomplishment. There is little or no specific indication of its placement within the unfolding of history in past, present, or future events. Lead did, however, imply that the world would be transformed by prophetic accomplishment. Exactly how she interpreted the realization of these prophecies within historical time now needs to be considered.

The idea of apocalyptic prophecy being fulfilled within the souls of individual believers, and at different times in different people, was a unique perspective in the context of late seventeenth-century English apocalyptic thought. Lead stressed the need to separate the spiritual from the temporal spheres. She assured her readers that it should 'not seem grievous, to rend and divide from what is of this evil world', even describing the body as 'but an outside covering, as the Badgers Skin was a covering upon the Tabernacle Glory' (Exodus 26:14; 36:19).[55] Lead regarded interaction with the world through the senses as 'the great and only impediment to all of Divine Vision, Prophecy, and Revelation'.[56] The material world was that place 'where the Dragon and the Beast … exercise their Soveraignty', and the saints could not allow 'temporal or secular Matters to interfere' with the business of 'Heavenly Affairs'.[57] Lead also noted that few individuals would be given the ability to first fully access the spiritual realm. Only 'some who are alive in this present Generation' would be granted admittance to Christ's 'secret Counsel', those who 'had finished their inward Transformation, to the utmost Perfection'.[58] Indeed, she proclaimed that Christ's reign had already begun 'in some personalities … now with Christ on the Throne, and doth absolutely rule … even to the utmost parts of the Souls inward Earth'.[59] These worthy souls would form a new 'Disciplehood' and Christ would 'walk again upon an invisible Earth, where none but the Spiritual Man can understand my Speech, or see my transformed Shape'.[60] Though this limited number of initial inhabitants of the New Jerusalem would eventually expand to be 'Numberless', it would be only the 'Glorified' saints 'whom he hath by his Spirit, quickned' to whom Christ would first appear.[61]

These exposures to spiritual illumination and to the guidance of Christ himself would occur within those chosen individuals. The 'Kingly Soul' would rule 'invisibly over all its inward Motions and Properties, as over Peoples, Nations and Languages'.[62] Not only would the true believer 'become a Christ, (or an Anointed) from this Deified Root opening within their own Soul', but also their bodies would change into one that would 'be able to pass into the invisible Orb where the King of Glory dwells'.[63]

In effect, Revelation's prophecies played out within each person, 'in the Souls inward Essence, from whence the Serpent and Beast are cast out'.[64] As noted above, though Christ's reign and the New Jerusalem would ultimately come to cover the whole earth and all people, they would initially visit only 'some', a limited and varied fulfillment to a few 'in your own Heavens and Earth' (Revelation 21:1).[65] Similarly, the opening of the seventh seal, the sounding of the seventh trumpet, the keeping of the inward court (11:1–2), and the final battle with Satan all had been, and would continue to be, accomplished separately and at different times for each person.[66] Yet even with this emphasis on internal prophetic fulfillment, Lead hinted at external results in the world. She noted that, just as the seven vials will be poured 'inward[ly]', there are also 'outward Vials to be poured forth on the World', though she stopped short of expounding upon them, claiming 'that is not my Commission'.[67]

Despite her determination not to discuss the effects of prophecy on the 'outward' earth, Lead's writings make it clear that the world must be altered by their accomplishment. She told her readers 'now the antient Prophesies of a new State of things are to be fulfilled'.[68] Though again referring to 'a signal Change we in ourselves shall find', this new state would also effect a change beyond each individual, with God forever maintaining 'his Superiority and Kingly Power over all Principalities of the Worldly Region; putting all things under, which hath exalted themselves above him.' Lead concluded by asserting 'This is that great and mighty over-turn, which we are looking and hastning for'.[69] Such an expectation, suggesting a fundamental and sweeping alteration of the worldly order, is a familiar theme in later seventeenth-century apocalyptic writings. Similarly, Lead pointed to the importance of the Millennium as the instigation for this change. Her millenarian expectations included the reappearance of the church fathers and the prophets, along with those who have been spiritually transformed 'to do Worthy Exploits ... for the state of the Prophesies relating to Christ's thousand Years Reign ... will overspread the Earth with the Kingly, Prophetical, and Priestly Train'.[70] Despite such statements, however, Lead was vague about what aspects of the material world would be transformed. Elsewhere she indicated only its implications on individuals. She affirmed that the Millennium would not be universal, that only 'some' would be 'sprinkled' in each nation to demonstrate that this reign had begun, and that its 'great Renovation, and Change' would only occur 'Gradually' throughout the length of the thousand years.[71]

Whatever the external impact of the Millennium on the world, it is clear that Lead believed this period would see Christ's effective reign on earth. She stated that Christ must reign 'personally' over the earth, as he did in heaven, though again she added the qualification that he would set up his reign 'Spiritually'.[72] Yet, once more, Lead suggested that Christ's reign would not be limited just to its impact on individual believers. She declared that the unrighteous 'will in no wise enter into Christ's Kingdom ... which shall rule over them. For this Kingdom shall not only be inward, in the Properties of the Soul, but shall also exercise its dominion over this visible Principle.'[73] Furthermore, she asserted that the saints would 'come to bear the sovereignty and dominion' not only 'in the microcosm within them' but also 'in the great world without them', and 'in this day it shall be said, Christ lives and walks upon the Earth in and among his selected Number, upon whose Shoulders the Government of his Kingdom is to rest'.[74] This not only suggests an active presence of Christ, but also Lead's confirmation of the millennial rule of the saints. She called for God to make the saints 'Kings to Reign over ... the Earthly Life' and 'to let them know their Thrones are set, ... their Conquering–Crowns ... are fitted, and that all Power and Judgment is given to them'.[75] Those who had undergone their spiritual transformation would be entrusted with the responsibility of governing Christ's kingdom, with access to his personal presence and his power.[76] Again, the indication that this new government would result in a change for the world was hinted at but never fully described. Lead alluded to putting 'this lower World into a new Model of Government ... all Powerful ... upon Earth',[77] a proposition with obvious implications for existing rulers and states throughout the world. Indeed, the saints would be given the ability to perform miracles, as well as 'Superiority over all the outward Constellations, and changeable motions of the Planets; all Sublunary things being put under their Feet'.[78] Such miraculous and physical powers would certainly have a noticeable impact on the material world but the effects of this are not explained. Still, Lead's expression of the idea of Christ reigning over the earth with and through the saints during the Millennium demonstrated her sharing another common aspect of English apocalyptic thought, though without a clear indication of its historical implications.

Lead left no doubt that Christ's actual return to the earth would not occur until after the Millennium. Though the saints would rule with his power, and with the benefit of his spiritual presence, Christ's actual physical presence on earth again would have to wait until the millennial transformation of the world made it fit for his spiritual form. Lead elaborated on these distinctions in an explanation of the 'threefold coming of Christ, besides his first coming in the Flesh'. She asserted that Christ's second coming had been a spiritual one to all of his followers that had been occurring since his departure from the earth; 'his second, or it may be called his third coming' was to the saints in order to transform their bodies into their celestial form so that they could rule with and for him in the New Jerusalem. Christ's final (fourth) coming would take place after the entire world had been transformed. This would see the consumption of the material world and the formation of a new heaven and a new earth that would precede the Last Judgment.[79] The New Jerusalem would see 'a New and Heavenly Generation' created that would 'multiply itself over the Face of the whole Earth' and 'make the old hereby to vanish and sink away'; until that was achieved, Christ 'cannot come down in his Visible and Personal Glory'.[80] In this view, the Millennium would be a transitional period to prepare the earth for Christ's physical return, further affirming the idea that the world would see substantial change during the thousand-year reign of Christ and the saints.

Lead's pronouncements concerning the millennial kingdom also demonstrated her belief that Christ's reign on earth was imminent, as many of her contemporaries likewise believed. At times this recognition was couched in more general terms. She warned the faithful to be prepared and stated that the time for the establishment of Christ's kingdom was not far off.[81] At other times, her statements are more explicit: 'The great Day of Christ's Appearance in the World draweth near', and 'the Line of Time is now far spent, and the Scenes of turbulent Commotions will have their pass away'.[82] In addition to the accomplishment of scriptural prophecies, Lead also interpreted her own prophesying as 'Confirmation ... that doth assure us, that this Day is very nigh', seemingly confirmed by a visitation on 1 June 1676 in which a voice advised her 'The End of all Things is at hand'.[83] Finally, she went so far as to indicate a much more precise dating of the beginning of Christ's reign in the year 1700 by declaring:

> One full Circle of a thousand Years is already run out, and when the full point of the seventh Hundred Year shall be superadded to it, then the Thrones and Dominions here below shall begin to bow and stoop to that Reign and Kingdom, which shall (by the Spirit in meek and Holy Souls) be set afoot.[84]

Yet again, however, even in this work published one year before that significant date, there is still no exact description of the political impact of

Christ's millennial kingdom, nor how it would affect the material world around it.

As has been noted several times, Lead's prophetic assertions and explanations have limited reference to tangible historical events or meanings. As the preceding quotation demonstrates, in the very same breath she could declare that the kings and kingdoms of the world would begin to bow down to Christ, and that it would happen through 'the Spirit in meek ... Souls'. How this profound change would come about, and what it would look like, was not revealed. The ambiguous state of worldly affairs during the Millennium is repeated throughout Lead's writings. She asserted that while Christ's 'Kingdom is not come ... in Power and Soveraignty, so as to Rule and Reign *openly* over all Principalities, and Earthly Powers; it will be the Royal Prerogative of the Saints ... wherein expected may be nothing less than Turmoils, and Perplexities of Nations, and Tribulations throughout the whole Universe'.[85] Elsewhere she predicted 'very near approaching ... a terrible Blow and Stroke upon the Nations of Earth will suddenly come', a 'great Increase, and Mighty Power that will turn the World upside down', and that 'the Saints shall bear Rule, as Kings, Priests, and Prophets ... Then shall all the Kingdoms of the Earth submit, and bow to the New Laws of his Kingdom.'[86] Though the saints are to be made kings, priests, and prophets, it is not evident what the nature of the saints' authority will be, whom they will rule over, and to whom they will minister and prophesy. In another rather nebulous statement, it is noted that God will not allow rulers of the world to continue to reign 'but by degrees, and in his own determinate time, chase them out, and bind them up, and triumph over them in the sight of all men', concluding that this will end 'the time allotted to the Beast, the Dragon and Antichrist'.[87]

Lead implied political alterations for the governments existing during Christ's reign. Christ's kingdom would be 'quite different ... than what was allowed to be' and he would 'come to make a total alteration, and throw out all Forms and Constitutions'.[88] The citizens of the New Jerusalem would receive 'Laws, Institutions, and Ordinances, that relate to this new Modell'd World and Kingdom',[89] implying a legal and political system during the Millennium that was distinct from existing worldly forms. This suggestion is borne out in the claim that 'a new Model shall be brought in ... Setting up a Monarchical Soveraignty that shall Rule over Nations, by a Rod of Power in the hand of such as shall be found in the Spirit of Moses and Elias, David and Daniel' and this 'may cause a great turn, and overturn, in the Kingdoms of this World' that are under the power of the beast and the dragon.[90] Rulers would throw their crowns at Christ's feet, his saints would 'overturn and bear down all Earthly Powers', 'rule and subdue all Nations under them', and 'make the Kingdoms of this World submit themselves, and bow down'.[91] Though Lead's editor warned not to 'lay too great a stress upon ... the Rise or Fall of any Earthly Monarch, Potentate, or State' as a sign of the Millennium,[92] the language in her writings left readers to conclude that drastic change would occur within and against the governments of the world during Christ's millennial reign on earth.

Existing churches were also forewarned of impending change. Referring to the fifth commandment (honor thy father and thy mother), Lead identified 'the Idolatrous Party who ... refuse to submit to the Reign of Jesus ... [at] his Second Appearance'.[93] With reference to the church of Laodicea in Revelation 3, the sounding of the trumpets was to awaken 'Luke-warm degenerate, and Formal Christendom', and the false prophet is identified in rational 'fine spun ... Idolatry, even among the Reformed Party'.[94] In a more comprehensive comment on ecclesiological preparations for Christ's reign, she instructed the 'Ecclesiastical Order, and all other Pastors and Teachers under what Denomination soever ... to consider to what your Ministry tends to, which is no more to be according to a dead draught of literal Knowledge'.[95] In *A Message to the Philadelphian Society* (1696) Lead enumerated a vision of seven English Protestant denominations in an allusion to Revelation 2–3. Included were the Anglican, Presbyterian, Congregational, Baptist, and Fifth Monarchy churches, as well as an enigmatic reference, likely to the Quakers,[96] a 'Body greater then any of these, come up with great Boldness ... and so visibly distinguishing themselves from all the rest'—all six of these would be 'shut-out', 'excluded', or 'dismissed' from the heavenly New Jerusalem. The seventh and true church was represented in the prophetic figure of the woman in the wilderness, and would be the 'Real Mount Sion Church, made up of Philadelphian Spirits' who had come out from the other ecclesiastical forms.[97] The saints were 'Wisdom's Royal offspring to whom the name of the Philadelphian Church doth of right belong'.[98] Here again Lead placed herself and her sect paramount in this ecclesiastical order and, indeed, at the forefront of apocalyptic fulfillment.

This critique on church forms also demonstrated some willingness to remark upon specific circumstances in England in relation to apocalyptic accomplishment. At times Lead's writing takes on the tone of a jeremiad. 'O England, England, understand the Day of thy Visitation, for this is the Acceptable Year ... Take care, O England ... let not the Clouds of ignorant Suspicion ... concerning the true Heir of the New Jerusalem Mother ... hinder thee.'[99] 'Over thee O City of London! a Mighty Angel doth fly, with this Thundering Cry, saying, Do not despise Prophesy ... the Spirit ... must renew Paradise upon the Earth'.[100] These warnings were even addressed to William III, 'him who sits at the Helm of Government in this nation', asking him to consider the significance of the revolutionary events that brought him to the throne ten years earlier, 'by what a wonderful Hand you have been brought in, and planted here ...for what End the Key of the Government in these Nations has been intrusted into Your Hands.'[101] Lead's spiritual diary noted a vision delivered to her two decades prior to this, on 9 October 1678:

> relating to the outwards State of the Political Body, in this Nation, that was designed to be set in a Flame, Which Flame was in part ... to be extinguished: that both the Justice and Mercy of the supream Majesty might the better appear ... to see what God is now doing ... in the Kingdoms of the Earth (and in this England especially) for the advancement of the Righteous, and Peaceable Kingdom of his Son.[102]

Whether perfect visionary hindsight or true prophetical inspiration, this clearly refers to the situation surrounding the Popish Plot and Exclusion Crisis. However, Lead did not elaborate, either in 1678 or 1700, on the exact details of divine intervention in English affairs during that period.[103] Another comment, this time from 1681, makes vague mention of 'Strife, Wars, and great Divisions that are this day enkindled among the Sion-Professors',[104] again hinting at the political disturbances of the early 1680s and again not providing additional detail as to how prophecy was being accomplished in these specific events. Though introductory verse by 'Onesimus' (the spiritual name given to Richard Roach, a Church of England minister and one of Lead's principal supporters) provides the poetic assurance that 'Again shall British Piety Aspire. / As it sunk Low; so shall it now Rise Higher. / His First-born, God in Thee again shall Own / ... / And England's Monarch High shall wear the Nations Crown',[105] the only basis that Lead indicated for this special status of England and London was that she and her followers were 'hid in thee', a 'mighty Star that in thy Bethlehem City is born'.[106]

In contrast to this absence of comment, it is evident that, even among Lead's acolytes, there was the recognition of a need to anchor apocalyptic fulfillment to contemporary events. Richard Roach, identified above as 'Onesimus', was instrumental in the founding of the Philadelphian Society and has been described as singularly important in articulating Lead's visions as an expression of feminist theology.[107] Roach's 1727 work *The Imperial Standard of the Messiah Triumphant* was very much akin to Lead's spiritual expressions of prophetic meaning and, indeed, included extracts from Lead's writings. However, two years earlier he had published *The Great Crisis: or, the Mystery of the Times and Seasons Unfolded* in which he had clearly connected the accomplishment of apocalyptic prophecies to unusual natural occurrences, as well as recent political affairs such as the Revolution of 1688–89 and the rise of Toryism and Jacobitism in Queen Anne's later reign.[108] Roach even equated the Philadelphian Society with the two witnesses of Revelation 11, proving a chronological correspondence between the founding of the group and that prophecy.[109] Roach's concern in linking worldly circumstances of the recent past and present had much more in common with the predominant interpretive frameworks of the apocalyptic authors of his time than did Lead's apocalyptic utterances.

*   *   *

This chapter has considered Jane Lead's usage of apocalyptic prophecies, and her interpretation of their meaning and fulfillment. It demonstrates Lead's focus on her special prophetic inspiration and the primary function of scriptural revelation in confirming that vision. Though there is not room to undertake a detailed elaboration of prevailing later seventeenth-century English apocalyptic exegesis, it can be stated for certain that Lead's great emphasis on the spiritual fulfillment of prophecy and her lack of explication of the impact of that accomplishment on existing material conditions and institutions make her ideas unique. It is for their idiosyncrasies, then, that Lead's apocalyptic ideas have gained attention. And it is their disconnection with a continuing tradition of apocalyptic thought that are their claim to fame.

Lead's ideas leave many questions unanswered. While, of course, any understanding of the enigmatic imagery and messages of the Book of Revelation was not an exact science, most early modern exegetes attempted to find historical, political, social, and ecclesiastical correlation—in the past, present, and even the future—for their interpretations. But, other than enigmatic and abstruse references, Lead did no such thing. Instead, her explanations show a highly individualized and internalized application of major prophetic events. Lead's exegesis had meaning largely within her own prophesying and unique understanding of scripture. It is uncertain whether only she herself would experience these prophetic fulfillments or if prophecy was fulfilled repeatedly as each believer was enlightened. It is also unclear how Christ's millennial reign would affect the world that would be subject to that reign, or how the suggestions of worldly transformation would be carried out. Even if Lead and her followers did understand her millenarian ideas fully and clearly, such an appreciation remained inaccessible to a majority of Christian believers.

It was not unusual for any group or person to feel that they were singularly identified in scriptural messages in general and in apocalyptic accomplishment in particular. Of course orthodox apocalyptic interpretations privileged certain people or denominations above others: persecuted dissenting groups, for example. However, such explanations included apparent and transparent apocalyptic fulfillment that would be available for all to see as it played out in political events and religious activities. The achievement of apocalyptic prophecy for Lead, however, was exclusive and unavailable for scrutiny to a majority of the world. Within her explanation, the internal, spiritual accomplishment of prophetic meaning was restricted to only the very few initiates to the New Jerusalem and Christ's second coming in their souls. While Lead's Millennium would eventually spread throughout the world, apocalyptic understanding and accomplishment would come, first and foremost, privately to a very limited group of her immediate followers, as well as those who read and believed her writings. It was not represented in historical terms or through means that were accessible to the rest of Christianity. Though interesting in themselves, Jane Lead's unique apocalyptic beliefs should not be viewed as an example simply because of their presence in her thought. Instead, historians should see her ideas as an anomaly, a departure from the prevailing apocalyptic views that were still plentiful in England in the later seventeenth century. It was Lead's claims to a prophetic voice equal, or even superior, to biblical prophecy that colored and motivated the ambiguity and opaqueness of apocalyptic meaning in her writings. She was, like John in the Book of Revelation, a purveyor of mystical and mysterious visions, not the interpreter of them.

NOTES

This chapter has greatly benefitted from Ariel Hessayon's careful editing and reading. I would also like to thank Marisha Caswell, Kelly DeLuca, and Bruce Douville for their comments and suggestions on a previous draft.

  1. Jane Lead, *The Glory of Sharon in the Renovation of Nature, Introducing the Blessed Kingdom of Christ in the Sealed Number of the First Fruits* (first

published in1700), in *The Wars of David, and the Peaceable Reign of Solomon; Symbolizing the Times of Warfare and Refreshment of the Saints of the Most High God* (London: Thomas Wood, 1816), p. 102.

2. See for example: Thune, *Behmenists*, pp. 72–75, 174–75 and *passim*; S. Bowerbank, 'God as Androgyne: Jane Lead's Rewriting of the Destiny of Nature', *Quidditas* 24 (2003), pp. 5–23; J. Hirst, 'Dreaming of a New Jerusalem: Jane Lead's Visions of Wisdom', *Feminist Theology* 14:3 (2006), pp. 349–65; J. Hirst, '"Mother of Love": Spiritual Maternity in the Works of Jane Lead (1624–1704)', in S. Brown (ed.), *Women, Gender and Radical Religion in Early Modern Europe* (Leiden: Brill, 2007), pp. 161–87; T.D. Kemp, '"Here must a beheading go before": The Antirational Androgynist Theosophy of Jane Lead's *Revelation of Revelations*', *CLIO* 34:3 (2005), pp. 251–75; C.F. Smith, 'Jane Lead's Wisdom: Women and Prophecy in Seventeenth-Century England', in J. Wojcik and R.-J. Frontain (eds.), *Poetic Prophecy in Western Literature* (Cranbury, New Jersey: Associated University Presses, 1984), pp. 55–63; Sarah Apetrei, *Women, Feminism and Religion in Early Enlightenment England* (Cambridge: Cambridge University Press, 2010), pp. 192–95.

3. Paula McDowell, *The Women of Grub Street: Press, Politics, and Gender in the Marketplace 1678-1730* (Oxford: Clarendon Press, 1998), pp. 164, 177–78; Bowerbank, 'God as Androgyne', pp. 5, 7; Paul Salzman, *Reading Early Modern Women's Writing* (Oxford: Oxford University Press, 2006), p. 131.

4. Hirst, 'Dreaming of a New Jerusalem', pp. 350–51.

5. J. Hirst, 'The Divine Ark: Jane Lead's Vision of the Second Noah's Ark', *Esoterica* 6 (2004), pp. 21–22; Bowerbank, 'God as Androgyne', pp. 11–12, 21; Kemp, '"Here must a beheading go before"', pp. 253–54, 259; Hirst, 'Dreaming of a New Jerusalem', pp. 349–51. Though Julie Hirst acknowledges the survival and moderation of apocalyptic ideas after 1660, she suggests that this is a product of the defeat of radicalism rather than part of a longstanding moderate interpretive tradition. In turn, Theresa Kemp recognizes the need to consider Lead's writings, including her millenarian thought, within the context of English nonconformist thought. This more thorough examination remains to be done.

6. For a thorough examination of Mede's thought and its influence, see Jeffrey Jue, *Heaven Upon Earth: Joseph Mede (1586–1638) and the Legacy of Millenarianism* (Dordrecht, 2006); Warren Johnston, *Revelation Restored: The Apocalypse in Later Seventeenth-Century England* (Woodbridge: Boydell, 2011), pp. 11–13, 23–27.

7. For a fuller summary of later seventeenth-century historicist opinion concerning Revelation's prophecies and imagery, see Johnston, *Revelation Restored*, pp. 27–37.

8. Jane Lead, *The Revelation of Revelations Particularly as an Essay Towards the Unsealing, Opening and Discovering the Seven Seals, the Seven Thunders, and the New Jerusalem State* (London, 1683), pp. 24–25, 28.

9. Jane Lead, *The Enochian Walks with God, Found Out by a Spiritual-Traveller* (London, 1694), 'Introduction and Apology', no pagination.

10. Jane Lead, *A Fountain of Gardens*, volume III, part I (1700), p. 40; Jane Lead, *A Living Funeral Testimony* (London, 1702), p. 24. See also Jane Lead, *The Signs of the Times: Forerunning the Kingdom of Christ, and Evidencing When It Is Come* (London, 1699), p. 8.

11. Jane Lead, *A Fountain of Gardens* (London, 1696), vol. I, p. 500.

12. Jane Lead, *The Messenger of an Universal Peace: or a Third Message to the Philadelphian Society* (London, 1698), p. 8. I thank Ariel Hessayon for this reference to the exact dating of the finalization of the Philadelphian Society's Constitutions: *Propositions Extracted From the Reasons for the Foundation and Promotion of a Philadelphian Society* (London, 1697), p. 11. For Thomas Beverley's dating of the advent of the Millennium, see W. Johnston, 'Thomas Beverley and the "late Great Revolution": English Apocalyptic Expectation in the Late Seventeenth Century', in Ariel Hessayon and Nicholas Keene (eds.), *Scripture and Scholarship in Early Modern England* (Aldershot: Ashgate, 2006), p. 158 and *passim*. For the correspondence between Beverley's dating and the foundation of the Philadelphian Society, see Hillel Schwartz, *The French Prophets: The History of a Millenarian Group in Eighteenth-Century England* (Berkeley: University of California Press, 1980), pp. 45–50. For Beverley's commentary on the apocalyptic significance of the events of the period from 1697 to 1700, see Johnston, 'Thomas Beverley,' pp. 173–74.

13. Jane Lead, *The Wonders of God's Creation Manifested* (London, 1695), sig. A2r; see also Jane Lead, *A Fountain of Gardens* (London, 1697), vol. II, sig. A6r. These editorial comments can be attributed to Francis Lee, Lead's amanuensis, son-in-law, and overseer of her works through publication from 1695 onwards: McDowell, *Women of Grub Street*, p. 171; Thune, *Behmenists*, p. 85; Hirst, 'Dreaming of a New Jerusalem', p. 353; Hirst, '"Mother of Love"', p. 164; Kemp, '"Here must a beheading go before"', p. 268.

14. Jane Lead, *The Heavenly Cloud Now Breaking* (London, 1681 edition), p. 39.

15. Lead, *Revelation of Revelations*, p. 126.

16. Lead, *Wonders*, p. 8.

17. Lead, *Wonders*, pp. 52–53.

18. Lead, *Fountain*, vol. III, part 1, sig. A2r; Lead, *Fountain*, vol. I, sig. A3r-v.

19. Encounters with Wisdom pervade Lead's writings. See for example: Jane Lead, *A Message to the Philadelphian Society* (London, 1696), pp. 82–83, 92–[94]; Jane Lead, *The Tree of Faith* (London, 1696), p. 80; Lead, *Fountain*, vol. II, p. 163. In some of Lead's treatises, the pagination is in error. Corrected page numbers will be shown within square brackets—[ ].

20. See for example: Lead, *Fountain*, vol. I, pp. 58–60, 62–63; Lead, *Heavenly Cloud* (1681 edn.), pp. 8, 9.
21. Lead, *Fountain*, vol. I, pp. 12, 86, cf. p. 239. See also Lead, *Fountain*, vol. II, pp. 316–17, 374.
22. Lead, *Revelation of Revelations*, p. 12.
23. Lead, *Fountain*, vol. II, p. 249; Lead, *Revelation of Revelations*, pp. 20–22, 24.
24. Lead, *Fountain*, vol. II, pp. 248, 249.
25. Jane Lead, *The Heavenly Cloud Now Breaking* (London, 1701 edition), pp. 61–62.
26. Lead, *Enochian*, p. 7.
27. Lead, *Revelation of Revelations*, pp. 123–24.
28. Lead, *Wonders*, p. 51. See also Lead, *Fountain*, vol. I, p. 7.
29. Lead, *The Ascent to the Mount of Vision* (London, 1699), sig. A2r.
30. Lead, *Tree of Faith*, pp. 31–[32].
31. Lead, *Revelation of Revelations*, pp. 6–7.
32. Lead, *Revelation of Revelations*, pp. 10–11, 46–53.
33. Lead, *Revelation of Revelations*, pp. 53, 33.
34. See for example: Lead, *Fountain*, vol. II, p. 117; Lead, *Wonders*, p. 32.
35. Lead, *Revelation of Revelations*, pp. 25, 67; Jane Lead, *The Laws of Paradise Given Forth by Wisdom to a Spirit* (London, 1695), p. 16. See also Lead, *Heavenly Cloud* (1681 edn.), p. 11; Lead, *Fountain*, vol. III, part 1, pp. 40, 41; Lead, *Revelation of Revelations*, pp. 27, 58.
36. Lead, *Heavenly Cloud* (1681 edn.), sig. A3r.
37. Lead, *Living Funeral Testimony*, p. 23.
38. Lead, *Fountain*, vol. III, part 1, pp. 85–86; Lead, *Fountain*, vol. I, pp. 369–70.
39. Lead, *Revelation of Revelations*, p. 25; Lead, *Laws of Paradise*, p. 56; Lead, *Fountain*, vol. I, pp. 256–57.
40. Lead, *Tree of Faith*, sig. A3r.
41. Lead, *Laws of Paradise*, p. 45 [emphasis added]; Lead, *Fountain*, vol. III, part 1, p. 119. See also Lead, *Revelation of Revelations*, pp. 13, 17; Lead, *Heavenly Cloud* (1681 edn.), p. 10.
42. Lead, *Laws of Paradise*, pp. 17–18.
43. Lead, *Glory of Sharon*, p. 94.
44. Lead, *Signs*, pp. 6, 7.
45. Lead, *Ascent*, p. 28.
46. Lead, *Revelation of Revelations*, p. 38.
47. Lead, *Fountain*, vol. I, p. 470; Lead, *Signs*, p. 16.
48. Lead, *Fountain*, vol. II, pp. 128–29. See also Lead, *Ascent*, pp. 28–29.
49. Lead, *Fountain*, vol. I, p. 468; Lead, *Fountain*, vol. II, p. 126; Lead, *Message*, p. 14.
50. Lead, *Revelation of Revelations*, pp. 12–16.

51. Lead, *Ascent*, p. 14; Lead, *Tree of Faith*, pp. 119–20.

52. Lead, *Revelation of Revelations*, sig. B1r, pp. 9, 11, 19–22.

53. Lead, *Fountain*, vol. II, p. 188; Lead, *Revelation of Revelations*, pp. 14, 18; Lead, *Heavenly Cloud* (1681 edn.), sig. A3r; Lead, *Message*, pp. 14–15; Lead, *Messenger*, p. 10.

54. Reference to the two witnesses can be found at Lead, *Signs*, pp. 3–4; Lead, *Fountain*, vol. I, p. 456; Jane Lead, *A Fountain of Gardens* (1701), volume III, part II, entry dated 19 August 1681. One reference to the whore can be found at Lead, *Fountain*, vol. I, p. 373.

55. Lead, *Fountain*, vol. II, p. 51; Lead, *Wonders*, p. 36.

56. Lead, *Heavenly Cloud* (1681 edn.), p. 14.

57. Lead, *Laws of Paradise*, p. 61; Lead, *Heavenly Cloud* (1701 edn.), p. 60.

58. Lead, *Ascent*, p. 13; Lead, *Revelation of Revelations*, p. 7. See also Lead, *Wonders*, pp. 75–76; Lead, *Revelation of Revelations*, p. 63.

59. Lead, *Revelation of Revelations*, p. 75.

60. Lead, *Fountain*, vol. II, pp. 100–01.

61. Lead, *Ascent*, p. 13; Lead, *Wonders*, p. 26; Lead, *Enochian*, p. 15.

62. Lead, *Revelation of Revelations*, p. 26.

63. Lead, *Enochian*, p. 33; Lead, *Revelation of Revelations*, pp. 37–38. See also Lead, *Tree of Faith*, p. 91.

64. Lead, *Revelation of Revelations*, p. 26.

65. Lead, *Tree of Faith*, p. 27; Lead, *Revelation of Revelations*, p. 28. See also Lead, *Revelation of Revelations*, p. 17.

66. Lead, *Revelation of Revelations*, pp. 16, 19; Lead, *Message*, p. 5; Lead, *Fountain*, vol. II, p. 516; Lead, *Laws of Paradise*, p. 45.

67. Lead, *Revelation of Revelations*, p. 16.

68. Lead, *Fountain*, vol. III, part 1, p. 9.

69. Lead, *Heavenly Cloud* (1681 edn.), pp. 32–33.

70. Lead, *Tree of Faith*, sigs. A3v-A4r.

71. Lead, *Revelation of Revelations*, p. 27; Lead, *Wonders*, p. 56; Lead, *Signs*, p. 14; Lead, *Living Funeral Testimony*, p. 25.

72. Lead, *Ascent*, p. 24.

73. Lead, *Revelation of Revelations*, p. 27.

74. Lead, *Glory of Sharon*, p. 104; Lead, *Ascent*, p. 23.

75. Lead, *Enochian*, p. 35; Lead, *Revelation of Revelations*, p. 25.

76. References to the government of Christ's kingdom by the saints are found throughout Lead's works. See for example Lead, *Fountain*, vol. III, part 1, p. 41; Lead, *Heavenly Cloud* (1701 edn.), pp. 37, 62; Lead, *Revelation of Revelations*, p. 34; Lead, *Wonders*, p. 24; Lead, *Living Funeral Testimony*, p. 25; Lead, *Enochian*, p. 31; Lead, *Tree of Faith*, pp. 117–18; Lead, *Signs*, pp. 9, 15; Lead, *Glory of Sharon*, pp. 89, 101, 104.

77. Lead, *Ascent*, p. 13.

78. Lead, *Ascent*, pp. 23, 29. See also Lead, *Enochian*, p. 15; Lead, *Revelation of Revelations*, p. 35.
79. Lead, *Fountain*, vol. III, part 1, pp. 42–45. See also: Jane Lead, *A Revelation of the Everlasting Gospel-Message* (London, 1697), p. 17; Lead, *Revelation of Revelations*, p. 25.
80. Lead, *Message*, p. 77. See also Lead, *Glory of Sharon*, p. 101.
81. See for example Lead, *Laws of Paradise*, pp. 26–27; Lead, *Fountain*, vol. I, p. 4; Lead, *Tree of Faith*, pp. 94–95; Lead, *Ascent*, p. 30; Lead, *Signs*, p. 6; Lead, *Glory of Sharon*, p. 106.
82. Lead, *Enochian*, p. 15; Lead, *Signs*, p. 4. Use of the expression 'the Line of Time' in the context of apocalyptic fulfillment has resonance with the writings and idioms of Thomas Beverley during this same period. See for example Thomas Beverley, *The First Part of the Scripture Line of Time ... From the First to the Last Sabbatism* (1687); Thomas Beverley, *A Scripture-Line of Time, Drawn in Brief From the Lapsed Creation, to the Restitution of All Things* ([1687]); Thomas Beverley, *The Scripture-Line of Time: From the First Sabbath, to the Great Sabbatism of the Kingdom of Christ* (London, 1692).
83. Lead, *Wonders*, p. 24; Lead, *Fountain*, vol. I, p. 251.
84. Lead, *Ascent*, p. 13.
85. Lead, *Living Funeral Testimony*, p. 26.
86. Lead, *Wonders*, p. 3; Lead, *Enochian*, p. 32; Lead, *Living Funeral Testimony*, p. 25.
87. Lead, *Messenger*, sig. A3r-v.
88. Lead, *Revelation of Revelations*, p. 72.
89. Lead, *Heavenly Cloud* (1701 edn.), pp. 60–61.
90. Lead, *Signs*, p. 5; Lead, *Heavenly Cloud* (1701 edn.), p. 62.
91. Lead, *Ascent*, pp. 13–14; Lead, *Wonders*, pp. 56, 25; Lead, *Message*, pp. 78, 102.
92. Lead, *Fountain*, vol. I, sig. A8v.
93. Lead, *Laws of Paradise*, p. 15.
94. Lead, *Messenger*, sig. A6r; Lead, *Fountain*, vol. I, p. 103.
95. Lead, *Fountain*, vol. III, part 1, sig. A3r.
96. Sarah Apetrei also suggests this sixth church is the Quakers, see Apetrei, *Women, Feminism and Religion*, p. 197.
97. Lead, *Message*, pp. 6–14. Elsewhere, Lead included other, non-English denominations, including the Jews [sic], Catholics, 'Greek' [Orthodox], Ethiopian, Lutheran, Calvinist, and Waldensians, among the 'disperst' churches of the world, see Lead, *Messenger*, pp. 2–3, 31–46.
98. Lead, *Glory of Sharon*, p. 106.
99. Lead, *Tree of Faith*, p. [121].
100. Lead, *Wonders*, p. 55.

101. Lead, *Messenger*, p. 48.
102. Lead, *Fountain*, vol. III, part 1, p. 273.
103. Paula MacDowell provides an interesting analysis of some references to the execution of Charles I and 'the aggressive language of Whig parliamentarians' in Lead's publications from the early 1680s, see P. McDowell, 'Enlightenment Enthusiasms and the Spectacular Failure of the Philadelphian Society', *Eighteenth-Century Studies* 35:4 (2002), pp. 521–22. While compelling, this still only identifies a brief, veiled, and fragmentary commentary on prominent contemporary events—especially in comparison to other apocalyptic writers of the period.
104. Lead, *Heavenly Cloud* (1681 edn.), p. 7.
105. Lead, *Fountain*, vol. I, sig. H1r-v; B.J. Gibbons, 'Roach, Richard (1662–1730)', *ODNB*.
106. Lead, *Wonders*, p. 54; Lead, *Tree of Faith*, p. [121].
107. Apetrei, *Women, Feminism and Religion*, pp. 195–96, 207.
108. Richard Roach, *The Great Crisis* (London, 1725), pp. 5–8, 10, 26, 32.
109. Roach, *Great Crisis*, pp. 36–38.

CHAPTER 7

The Restitution of 'Adam's Angelical and Paradisiacal Body': Jane Lead's Metaphor of Rebirth and Mystical Marriage

Stefania Salvadori

From the end of the seventeenth to the beginning of the eighteenth century heated debate concerning the connection between mystical and human marriage broke out among Pietists,[1] especially among more radical authors.[2] As recent literature has clearly demonstrated, this debate was rooted in a broader discussion about the regeneration process, specifically postlapsarian nature and the restoration of the image of God in humankind.[3]

Pietism usually interpreted rebirth (Wiedergerburt) as a spiritual process, through which God permeated human beings with a new nature. Believers' souls were so connected with God, that they were not only forgiven of their sins, but restored to the lost *imago Dei*. According to Philipp Jacob Spener, the father of churchly Pietism, this inner process involved putting off the old nature and putting on the new one, so as to complement rebirth by renewal (Erneuereung) and live a godly life with the support of the Holy Spirit.[4] Although Spener had stressed that believers needed to become a new creation in Christ and incited them to grow

S. Salvadori (✉)
Herzog August Bibliothek, Wolfenbüttel, German

© The Editor(s) (if applicable) and The Author(s) 2016   143
A. Hessayon (ed.), *Jane Lead and her Transnational Legacy*,
DOI 10.1057/978-1-137-39614-3_7

in holiness, he distinguished sharply the inner process of rebirth and its consequence in the practice of the Christian life from any physical transformation of the believers in new creatures, which could eventually occur in an undefined eschatological future. During their life on earth, reborn Christians could and should live within society acting as a spiritual elite within the Church so as to promote the community's renewal.[5]

Radical Pietism departed from Spener's teaching, reinterpreting it in an original way. If, according to Spener, Christians who experienced an inner revival had to promote a reforming impulse within the Lutheran Church, radical Pietism placed the true spiritual community outside and often in opposition to all human churches, considering their claim to reform empty words, dramatically refuted in practice. The true 'Christian Church' gathered only the reborn believers, whose outward behavior was as pure as their inward faith since their souls were married with the Savior's and enjoyed therefore a substantial union with him. This spiritualistic understanding of the connection between God and the believer was connected with chiliastic expectations, which became the focal point of the theology and piety of many pietistic groups and thinkers, acting as an accelerating factor to their radicalization.[6] Radical Pietists could not content themselves merely with representing a spiritual elite inside the churchly—i.e., sinful—community, and by trying to promote a future—yet historically undetermined— purification of it; they strove rather to immediately form the first group of the chiliastic true Church which had to be established before setting up Christ's millennial kingdom on earth. The more imminent the supposed apocalyptic end became, the more compelling the need to define forms and content of the true elect community.

To depict the essential connection between Christ and the spiritual Church, radical Pietists did not hesitate to recall traditional bridal mysticism: the rebirth and the outbreak of the chiliastic era were depicted as the final union between the bride—respectively interpreted as the single soul and the whole community of true believers—and the Holy bridegroom.[7] Within this context the concept of rebirth (Wiedergeburt) underwent a radicalization and was usually interpreted as a consequence of divine direct and personal revelations, which acted free of and beyond all human definitions and radically transformed human beings. But how was this transformation to be accomplished? Were reborn believers restored to the lost *imago Dei* only inwardly, or was their outward appearance adapted to Adam's prelapsarian perfection? Indeed, in some radical pietistic groups the central theological problem became whether or not the private renewal of individual believers could imply physical transmutation, since the human body was considered to be ruled by weakness and postlapsarian sins and, therefore, unsuitable to enter the millennial kingdom. Consequently, many authors questioned whether rebirth (i.e., a personal inward communion with God) could coexist with the human marital state (a sign of the postlapsarian world), prompting true believers to 'ascetical' attitudes so as to prepare not only their spiritual but also their physical transmutation.

Jacob Boehme's theosophy played a central role within the different traditions that collectively constituted radical Pietism.[8] During the late seventeenth century, however, his continental reception was often indirect, mediated by the so-called 'English Behmenists' and in particular, Jane Lead.[9] Recent studies have pointed out how Lead freed the teaching of the 'first German philosopher' from many of its intricate cosmo-ontological implications. Moreover, focusing on Boehme's interpretation of Adam's creation and fall, as well as on the mediating role of the 'heavenly Sophia' in the restitution of the original divine likeness of humankind, Lead closely related the eschatological expectations of Christ's second coming with the doctrine of the mystical regeneration of human souls. Hence she provided an essential starting point for radical pietistic discussion.[10]

The idea of the renewal of humankind into the birth of a 'new Adam' deserves particular attention,[11] since the opposition of a restored righteous nature, on the one hand, and the sinful essence of the 'old Adam', on the other, is not restricted in Lead's thinking to symbolic meaning, nor reduced to a simple spiritual purification of the believer. Rather, it suggests the beginning of a concrete 'transfiguration of the body', which enables true Christians to enter an essential connection with God. The metaphor of the heavenly marriage between the regenerated soul and the Bridegroom Christ expresses, in Lead's works, the final goal of a process of *unio mystica* interpreted as a slow—yet progressive—renovation of the earthly body into a spiritual one.

This chapter discusses these aspects of Lead's thinking underpinning her description of the regeneration process of the believer. Following a brief overview of Lead's anthropological premises and her interpretation of Boehme's work, this chapter then analyzes the four stages of the 'mystical path', through which believers enter the perfect union with the celestial Bridegroom and receive the total restitution of the paradisiacal perfect body. After the dissolution of the corrupted nature in the mystical death, reborn Christians enter a dual state: while still living in their carnal body, they receive a new spiritual body, made of heavenly substance. The heavenly

Wisdom's maternal role is radicalized in order to depict the generation of the new creatures in believers' souls and prepare the final restitution of the paradisiacal body, which is completed by Christ, the heavenly Bridegroom. And even if the complete—both physical and spiritual—transfiguration takes place only at the end of time, it can however be experienced prior to that by the 'elected folk', i.e., the reborn Christian. This chapter also provides a new insight into Lead's teaching of twofold corporality, showing how she tried to combine spiritual regeneration and gradual refinement of the new spiritual magical body with the corporal earthly life.

JACOB BOEHME'S ANTHROPOLOGY

Before examining Lead's works some context is necessary. Teaching distinguishing spiritual from material corporality has a long history, going back to Neoplatonic philosophy, patristic debates and Kabbalistic tradition. Such teaching, however, cannot always be reduced to mere opposition and mutual exclusion. On the contrary, it entails several attempts to connect spiritual and corporal dimensions by a *tertium quid*: the halfway reality of the 'subtle' or 'spiritual body'.[12] This concept was used by Paul in 1 Corinthians 15:44 to indicate the resurrected body prepared for eternity and inherited in the resurrection in order to replace the pre-death physical body, which is a mark of the postlapsarian nature and destined to perish. The new 'subtle body' is on the contrary imperishable, glorious and powerful (1 Corinthians 15:42–43) and in orthodox theology was closely connected with Christ's body and blood in the Eucharist and with the mystical body of the Church. However, the idea of a 'subtle body' often became controversial, indicating both Adam's nature before the fall and an invisible, spiritual body subsisting beside the natural body before the resurrection.[13]

Jacob Boehme (*c.* 1575–1624) was a clear reference point in the early modern 'spiritual body' debate. The life and writings of this German shoemaker are well known and have been closely examined. Many of the influences on his thought (particularly Christian Kabbalah,[14] as well as the teachings of Paracelsus, Caspar Schwenckfeld and Valentin Weigel) have been explored, so that his theosophical system now appears as a kind of reassembled compendium of different mystical and esoteric traditions. Ranging from alchemical ideas to Neoplatonic thought, from mysticism to the Hermetic tradition, Boehme's theosophy had an enormous impact during the early modern period among readers from a variety of cultural milieus. In the eyes of contemporaries and subsequently of his English and German followers, he represented a kind of prophet, disclosing the deepest secrets of divine and natural principles. It was, however, his cosmological and anthropological teachings, both resting on an indissoluble connection of material and spiritual worlds, that drew most attention.

Boehme's theosophy is extremely complicated and cannot be summarised without oversimplification. But it is nonetheless useful here to highlight at least its central features, particularly with regard to its 'soteriological narrative'. Briefly, the creation represents a continuing process of divine self-expression which transcends the inner-trinitarian life. God's revelation outside himself is his expression in an extra-divine existence, up to his externalization in nature. The first step of this process is the revelation of himself in the 'virgin Sophia', as divine Wisdom. The latter is a first hypostasis which enables God's self-contemplation outside the trinity and assures at the same time the original connection between divine and human, spiritual and material natures.[15] Virgin Wisdom comprises all divine essences, 'models' and archetypes and enables therefore not only God's self-contemplation but also the second step of the process, namely God's self-expression in the creation.[16]

Sophia, moreover, represents the perfect connection between God and the first man, Adam, who replaced the fallen Lucifer in Eden and restored a new harmony after the implosion of the 'angelic kingdoms' into chaos (Genesis 1:2). In Boehme's view, Adam is created fully in God's image and enjoys perfection of vision and knowledge as a consequence of his participation in heavenly Wisdom. This essential connection with Sophia is primarily the expression in the first man of the teleological direction of the creation, according to which all desires have to be set 'into the light', into God's glory. Adam's soul is consequently connected to God's will.[17] Even his body partakes of the paradisiacal substantiality of the divine, since it is made not of earthly materials, but of celestial *Quinta Essentia*.[18] Adam therefore embodies the archetype of the human being and represents the microcosm in which God's manifestation is originally reflected in the creation. This is not in opposition to the spiritual essences, but rather an expression and externalization of them. Adam's spiritual, 'crystalline', heavenly corporality or *Kraftleib*, to use Boehme's term,[19] can be compared to angelic corporality,[20] and is, therefore, incorruptible. It suffers no hunger, tiredness or sleepiness.[21] Above all, it is characterized by androgyny and the ability to procreate magically through the power of imagination.[22]

Yet this 'subtle body' is dramatically lost as soon as Adam desires to follow his own will rather than God's.[23] According to Boehme, the images of Adam falling asleep in Eden and of God taking a rib and forming Eve already represent the departure of the virgin Sophia, the split of androgyny and the fulfillment of the first fall.[24] The loss of original perfection worsened with the second fall: by eating the fruit of the forbidden tree Adam and Eve undergo a spiritual and a physical degradation. The 'crystalline' body of the first man becomes mortal and bestial, filled with sinful desires and exposed to weakness, hunger and death.[25] It is here that postlapsarian human history begins. God is unwilling to let his perfect image in human beings fall into definitive alienation and to interrupt his continuing process of self-manifestation. Therefore, he opens his work of redemption by 'putting on' human nature and dying on the cross, to cover his wrath with his love. In Boehme's soteriological narrative Christ is the 'second Adam' who restores the divine image in souls, leading fallen nature back to its previous, perfect essence, restoring the intimate communion between human and divine will, but also overcoming the corruptibility of flesh and sexual differentiation.[26] This work of the conversion and transformation of human nature represents a central part of the cosmic restitution of the whole of the creation, which Christ fulfills together with the virgin Sophia. And it steadily draws believers into a salvific relationship with the Lord.

To conclude, Boehme's salvation narrative stretches from the creation to the apocalypse and includes perdition and the subsequent return to the paradisiacal state. Christ is the link between the restoration of original perfection and its eschatological fulfillment in human beings. His redeeming work cannot be reduced, however, to the doctrine of imputative justice. As in the process of alchemical transmutation, he reveals through his passion, death and resurrection, the way to self-purification and of renovation that true believers must freely imitate.[27] By embracing the example of Christ's crucifixion and shaping their lives according to the sacred events of the Lord's earthly drama, human beings can experience the inward rebirth until the final restoration of the image of God in their souls is completed following the general resurrection after death. However, Boehme's teaching introduced a critical problem: does the soul's regeneration imply a progressive recovery of the paradisiacal body during life on earth?

THE ANDROGYNOUS ADAM AND THE HEAVENLY SOPHIA IN JANE LEAD'S THOUGHT

The idea of a perfect, androgynous, prehistoric man; his original connection with the heavenly Sophia; Adam's double fall; and spiritual rebirth as a restored connection between the human soul and divinity provided a widely shared soteriological framework in the early modern period. Although Boehme postulated the restoration of a 'subtle body' for reborn souls not before the (still undetermined) eschatological end, the doctrine of corporal transmutation became increasingly important among his readers. When chiliastic expectations were the focal point of their theology, many groups and thinkers also radicalized the doctrine of physical transmutation, arguing that the transformation of their natural bodies could accelerate— or confirm the imminence of—Christ's second coming.[28] This is evident in the case of radical Pietist Heinrich Horch (1652–1729).[29] While imprisoned in Marburg Castle from November 1699 to July 1700 because of his chiliastic views, the former theology professor pulled out his hair and removed his teeth (both signs of the transience of mortal bodies according to Boehme) to anticipate—or accelerate—his physical transmutation into a new heavenly body, and in so doing confirming his inward rebirth.[30]

In identifying the conceptual frame of such radical attempts to make the physical transmutation an essential consequence of spiritual purification, it should be emphasized that the pietistic reception of Boehme's teaching was deeply conditioned by a transcultural process. Most German readers— including Horch—did not engage with the writings of the German philosopher directly. Rather, they re-discovered them through works by English Behmenists.[31]

Literature on the subject has highlighted how Boehme's works quickly spread in England, starting with their translation between 1644 and 1662 by John Sparrow and John Ellistone. They sparked great interest among many radical groups and thinkers, with each giving a personal interpretation and shape to Boehme's doctrine, mainly by combining elements with other traditions.[32] The most famous English Behmenist was John Pordage (1607–1681),[33] under whose tutelage Jane Lead (1624–1704) came into contact with the works of the German philosopher.

Lead's mystical career together with her leadership of the Philadelphian Society is well known and discussed earlier in this volume.[34] Considering herself an instrument of God, she quickly assumed the role of spiritual guide for the followers gathered around her, preaching the conversion and experience of inward union with Christ. Her writings—especially the reports on her mystical visions—were translated into German from the mid-1690s and found an enormous resonance on the continent.[35]

Recent studies have noted the central features of Lead's thinking.[36] Indeed, it is now clear that there were both significant similarities as well

as differences between Lead and Boehme.[37] Lead, for example, shared
Boehme's anthropological premises. She describes the first man in Eden
as the 'virgin Adam' who had in himself a feminine essence as long as he
lived in perfect connection with holy Wisdom. The first man, however,
lost his androgynous perfection as soon as he 'looked outward, as if he
were not sufficient of himself to increase and multiply for the replenishing
of Paradise, God having created him Male and Female in himself.'[38]
Subsequently, Lead assumes that Adam's first fall overturned God's perfect
design, causing the spiritual and physical degradation of the human being
and, as the spiritual body was replaced by the material and 'animal' one, it
marked the beginning of the 'fleshly generation' of human beings.[39]

Similarly, Boehme and Lead state that human history is defined by the
loss of God's image as a consequence of the first man's adultery with the
heavenly Sophia and subsequent disobedience by eating forbidden fruit. To
escape the consequences of the double fall of the first human pair, which
determines the sinful earthly life, Lead encourages true believers to strive for
the reunion with Sophia and for the spiritual marriage with Christ, to restore
the *imago Dei* in the human soul.[40] Yet behind this common soteriological
framework, Lead develops her own doctrine, putting at the core of her
messages some ideas that remained peripheral in Boehme's thinking.

Additionally, millenarian stirrings, particularly in the 1690s, made Christ's
salvific work imperative: he was expected to shortly restore the whole
creation.[41] According to Lead, to prepare for their Savior's return and to enter
his kingdom, Christians have to experience their regeneration both spiritually
and physically, since the sinful soul and the material body cannot take part
in the 'nuptial feast' and enjoy their reunion with Christ. For this purpose,
true believers have to be born into a new life, killing the old Adam. Unlike
Boehme, Lead describes Sophia neither in terms of ontological speculation
on the nature of God, nor as a spiritual medium, in which the divinity reveals
itself. Rather, she characterizes divine Wisdom as a mother in whose womb
rebirth takes place and who introduces regenerated souls to union with the
heavenly bridegroom. Mystical marriage, however, is the ultimate goal of a
process of self-denial and transmutation. So it is to this I now turn.

The Beginning of the Mystical Process
and the Nothingness of the Soul

Among Lead's earliest published works, the 40-page tract titled, *The
Heavenly Cloud Now Breaking* supplies a concise, yet clear introduction

to her teaching, describing the mystic ladder with which to ascend into heaven and take part in the 'wedding banquet'.[42] The work is addressed to all those who are ready to divest themselves of their essence of 'sin, curse, bondage and sorrow'.[43] No soul can in fact attain real freedom and peace if plunged into the 'dying Pool' of the world, far away from Christ, the healer of all spiritual maladies. True believers are, therefore, invited to eat at the 'Supper of God'.[44]

Presenting herself as a friend and servant of heavenly Wisdom, Lead develops the image of the 'godly supper', avoiding any discussion on the sacraments, instead applying it to the different stages of the mystical path of regeneration. According to Wisdom's order, Lead discloses the way to enter into the 'nuptial feast' with Christ and, for this reason, introduces in the preface a preliminary distinction: there are four groups of souls, each of them is invited to taste a specific course according to its different degree of 'spiritual refinement'. The simplest food is prepared for those who still have to die from their sins and consists of the 'broken and crucified body of the Lord'. Souls that are raised from 'mystical death' can then enjoy the second course, that is to say, Christ's paradisiacal body and its powerful nature. Once any sinful mark has been removed and a pure spiritual body has been obtained, the regenerated souls are finally carried away into the New Jerusalem and are fed Christ's glorified body, which represents the third and fourth courses of the Lord's banquet. Believers are filled with all the 'fullness of God' and introduced to the nuptial day, when the holy Trinity descends to celebrate the marriage with the Lamb.[45] Regenerated Christians become part of the glorified person of Christ and are gifted with the 'generating Power of the Holy Ghost to go forth for the replenishing of the New Heavens and Earth'.[46]

In Lead's thinking, this image of a four-course Supper corresponds to both a four-stage process of spiritual growth, and to four different steps on Jacob's ladder (Genesis 28). This ladder enables souls to ascend gradually, according to their stage of maturity. Its initial step consists of 'Mystical Death', which dissolves the threefold captivity that characterizes postlapsarian human nature.[47] Satan not only introduced the 'original venom of sin' by corrupting Adam and Eve in Eden, but he still tempts believers and prevents their regeneration by oppressing their souls and harming their outward bodies with sickness, sorrow and death.[48] The restitution of the relapsed creation, therefore, requires the complete dissolution of corrupted nature. Citing Romans 6–7, Lead invites readers to enter the 'passage gate of Death', to let Christ direct the 'Sacrificing Knife' upon the 'viperous Body of the Sin', in order to destroy it and restore instead 'that pure Angelical Image, in which the most Holy One took such delight to see his own Similitude in'.[49]

In *The Heavenly Cloud* the restoration of the *imago Dei* in the human soul requires the imitation of Christ's death, which is intended as a 'living Type and example [...] to follow', not as a mere imputative sacrifice. It, therefore, implies personal engagement, as well as 'conformity and fellowship with him in his Death' in order to kill postlapsarian sinful nature.[50] Christ offered his 'personal Body' to his Father and suffered the sacrifice. True believers must 'intervert' their life into Christ, offering it as a voluntary sacrifice and enduring the 'dying Agonies' with the Spirit's support.[51] In this way, believers will be able to cut off 'every Member in the Body of Sin'. At the same time, this passage into total death requires God's intervention, since humans cannot overcome all weakness and temptation. Regarding this, Lead stresses how the Savior slowly introduces souls into this distressing process, showing them the necessity of the crucifixion on the one hand, and revealing the final goal, that is to say, the restoration of original glory, on the other.

Behind this first mystical process of self-denial, Lead offers a more detailed description of 'inward Death' and distinguishes three domains for its application. Apart from animal life—the 'more gross and right-down earthly Life, consisting of a beastly Nature'[52]—the rational part of the human being also deserves to be crucified. Although reason is usually regarded as a wise controlling force upon the wild movements of the soul, it is not completely free from sin. Only those who are properly 'enlightened and well-instructed' by God can easily recognize this truth.

Lead introduces three arguments to support her thesis. First, she takes into account daily experience: human reason is so closely connected to earthly interests that, despite its godly appearance, if forced to choose between material and spiritual advantage, humans opt for the former. Turning to Scripture, reason is then clearly a feature of postlapsarian nature. In Lead's interpretation of Genesis, Adam had no rationality before his fall, since in his perfection 'he had no occasion to use subtilty or craft, all things were provided to his hand. So now in the way of our return to the more transcendent Liberty and Glory, for which the Holy Ghost, operating in the power of Faith to perfect, will admit to have nothing contributed from the Rational Spirit.'[53] Moreover—and this is the third argument—human reason is incompatible with the 'Spirit of Faith': it constantly raises questions and doubts concerning God's promises and his revelations and consequently prevents the resurrection of souls, which have, on the contrary, put themselves completely into God's hands.[54] In conclusion, even if Lead acknowledges the positive role of human reason in governing and tempering the impulses of fallen animal life, intellective faculties come from 'the womb of fallen time' and are, therefore, not only worthless, but also dangerous for the souls that try to ascend the spiritual ladder.[55]

The middle position of reason is also reproduced in sensual life, which is divided in three 'branches': exterior, bodily and interior senses. The first two have to be killed without hesitation because exterior senses (above all human will) are corrupted by a depraved sensual desire that pursues its own delight and satisfaction rather than God's teaching, and natural senses reflect the essence of the mortal body and its corruption and represent therefore the greatest impediment to any experience.[56] But the interior senses also imply a hard spiritual struggle. They are, in fact, strictly connected to reason and the postlapsarian condition. Even if they can be in part renewed and enlightened (enabling the comprehension of immortal and divine things), they are constantly confronted with the human sinful essence, so that they always try in vain to escape mortal nature and fly up to heaven, causing the interior struggle of which many saints gave testimony.[57] It is at the climax of this interior struggle and mystical self-denial that true believers finally reach the 'cessation from senses' and the 'eternal Nothingness',[58] which opens the door to a clearer knowledge of God and to a new paradisiacal state.[59]

THE RESURRECTION OF (THE NEW) ADAM

The metaphor of mystical death and of the nothingness of souls illustrates the killing of the old Adam in analogy with Christ's Passion. According to Lead, souls that have accomplished this process of self-denial are finally reunited with Christ's dead body. They are buried with the Lord. However, this means that the following step is that of the Resurrection, since there can be no doubt that 'the same Spirit which raised him [Christ], must and will raise up such as are dead in him'.[60]

It is in this connection that Lead introduces the problem of the physical transmutation of believers. Even if the perfect restitution of original—both spiritual and physical—perfection cannot be completely attained before the end of the world, the risen soul is already dressed with 'the fine Robe of the Resurrection' during earthly life.[61] Lead argues that according to the godly mysteries, a 'new Adam' comes to life as soon as one takes the 'Resurrection-step'. Reborn believers live from that moment on in a dual state: the godly seeds grow up inwardly, even if they are still fastened to their carnal body, which now represents only an impediment to the regenerated souls. This dual state corresponds to a dual substance or corporeal reality.

The birth of the new spiritual man is a pivotal theme in Lead's teaching. In the beginning, the new Adam is hidden, growing up inwardly, so slowly that sometimes the soul itself cannot discern him.[62] He can be compared to the restored *imago Dei* as a principle of divine animation, yet is not an abstract reality, since in accordance with Boehme's teaching no spirit can subsist without a body.[63] To explain this mystery, Lead uses a metaphor: as a child in a natural womb lies passive and contributes nothing to its own life, so the new Adam receives his new substance from his creator by a superior and incorruptible action. This continues until a 'new body' is fashioned in human souls as in the 'gross bodily Figure', but of a different consistency, the new creature being 'airy, thin, and of a transparent purity'.[64] The difference between body and soul is progressively dissolved into the new Adam, whose substance is compared to the angelic essence, consisting of 'one pure Element, which can swallow up the visible gross substance of Flesh.'[65]

Christians are now fed with the second course of the nuptial banquet, namely Christ's resurrected body, which means that the new creature, which arose in the regenerated soul, participates in Christ's flesh and mutates according to the different realities that Christ assumed from his crucifixion to his glorification. The old Adam was killed and laid in the grave during the process of mystical death, so Jesus was crucified and buried; the new Adam is now risen, so Christ is resurrected and appears again to his disciples.[66] However, the simile between Christ's and the new creature's resurrected body is not symbolic. Rather it implies a bodily transmutation: the new Adam is the real *Christus in nos*, the effective and concrete presence of the Lord in human beings. This new spiritual body in believers' souls is part of Christ's universal body, sharing the same heavenly substance.

Here, Lead's teaching shows signs of the doctrine of the celestial flesh, which Boehme also inherited from the Radical Reformation and in particular from Caspar Schwenckfeld.[67] The idea that human physical bodies could be transformed into heavenly substance was widespread in England among Platonist and Behmenist groups that interpreted the concept of the *unio mystica* as a cosmic principle. In their opinion, the whole of creation runs to the re-establishment of prehistoric harmony, and its universal restoration requires the complete assimilation and transfiguration of all creatures into God, therefore assuring an ontological continuum between them.[68] Lead shares this doctrine and interprets the process of purification and regeneration of the soul as a gradual incorporation of the believers in the divine life and substance.

This process is, at the beginning, still incomplete. The 'spiritual body of the resurrection' cannot immediately subjugate the 'visible and vile' mortal body, but it subsists, relying on Christ's promise to turn it into its paradisiacal essence again.[69] Even if the 'frail mortal Body of Flesh' still remains as the Kingdom of 'the Beast and Dragon', the new spiritual 'Magical body' is not inactive.[70] On the contrary, even before the full and total resurrection and transfiguration into the glorious body of the glorified Christ, the new spiritual 'Magical body' represents an 'advance [...] beyond the Life of Faith' since it is the 'medium' through which true believers have visions and representations of heavenly realities.[71] The spiritual body of the resurrection 'sees in the Light of God's Eye, as being translated into that principle, where one perpetual everlasting Day doth shine, where it doth behold greatness, goodness, and purity, as being entered into the same.'[72] The spiritual body of the new Adam, although only inward, therefore enables reborn Christians to participate in the eternal Worlds, in the divine essence. At the same time, the spiritual body discloses their dramatic situation, exacerbating both their suffering for beings still imprisoned in the postlapsarian state and their longing for the final transfiguration.

Before the definitive and everlasting 'correspondency with God, and Christ, and all the Heavenly Family' could be attained,[73] an inward struggle characterizes those regenerated Christians who have taken the Resurrection step, but have still not reached the following one, namely Ascension. Lead describes it as a 'Probation-Time', in which the risen soul should be 'very cautious, to keep up to the Celestial Region, improving all those sublime Faculties' of the new Adam.[74] They should become unconcerned with all worldly affairs, with all sinful desires and relationships, with all bodily necessities and live as a stranger among mortals. 'Their Home is properly with the Lord', and they can visit it, since they 'can with their invisible Spirit and Body, pass through divers unknown Spheres, some times more immediate with the Deity; and other times with the Orders of glorified Angels, and Saints of high Degree, [...] and then again return to be seen and known of such as are in this lower Orb'.[75]

To conclude, according to Lead, regenerated Christians live a twofold corporality similar to Christ who appeared with a mortal body after his Resurrection and before his Ascension. They keep their material body, struggling to avoid all its postlapsarian impulses and to reduce it to a shell from which they will escape as soon as they are completely transfigured into paradisiacal perfection. Despite all mortal and terrestrial appearances, they are already able to move in and out, to ascend and descend the heavenly ladder, not only to fulfil their transmutation, but also to act as Christ's delegates and messengers, to witness that the Lord is raised in them and to carry out 'God's great wonders upon the visible Stage of this World'.[76]

As long as the 'Resurrection-Flock' lives in the mortal body, it is exposed to risks, temptations and attacks from evil spirits, as Lead shows through reports of her personal experiences.[77] Yet only this refinement process ascertains the 'Resurrection-Mark' while living in the earthly body, by being welcomed into the paradisiacal Region even if one departs mortal life without having completely put on Christ (Galatians 3:27). However, a further step on the heavenly ladder can be taken on entering the 'Gate for Ascension'.

Ascension and Glorification in the Marriage Feast

Lead also extends the birth and generation metaphor to divine Wisdom, which represents an eschatological mediator of salvation on earth, preceding and preparing the final union with the Lord. Scholars have highlighted this point, showing how the figure of Sophia in Lead's writings contributed to the gender definition and deeply influenced the self-representation of many female mystical writers.[78] It is known that Lead's Sophiology is highly indebted to Boehme, yet some studies have also pointed out its originality, referring above all to a tendency to 'individualize and anthropomorphize the Sophia concept',[79] transforming God's Wisdom from a cosmic-ontological principle to a personified interlocutor in Lead's visions and mystical experiences. This shift in interpreting the role of Wisdom also influenced the doctrine of the spiritual body, connecting the birth of the 'new Adam' in human souls with Sophia's maternal role.

Lead's writings suggest that Wisdom was originally God's eternal essence, hidden in the Father, and was produced, *alias* manifested, during the time of the creation.[80] Like Boehme, Lead also argues that this 'heavenly Virgin' allowed Adam's magical reproduction before his fall, assuring him of the 'Generation force' by imagination. Yet according to Lead,

Sophia keeps her maternal role even today. After Adam's fall and the loss of original perfection, she still makes believers' souls 'fruitful', introducing all Christians to the mystical purification process which represents the only way to be born into new life and to enter into the nuptial feast with Christ.[81]

Defining Sophia as the 'perpetual virgin', the 'Jerusalem-Bride' or 'the virgin mother', Lead highlights again and again the generative force of the heavenly Wisdoms, in whose womb the rebirth of human souls takes place.[82] Behind this metaphor of maternity-rebirth, the association between divine Wisdom and the Virgin Mary in opposition to Eve becomes explicit. If the latter gave birth to postlapsarian creatures, Mary and Sophia—the new Eves—are the mothers of the 'elected flock'. Like Mary, who was a 'Figure of the Eternal Virgin', Christ is born in the Flesh, so the souls are now generated anew by divine Wisdom.[83] According to Lead, it is for this reason that Sophia deserves the title of 'natural Mother' of a new heavenly progeny, whose spiritual body fully corresponds to Christ's (the archetype of the 'new Adam').[84]

The maternal role of Sophia also plays a central role in *The Heavenly Cloud Now Breaking*. Lead maintains here that divine Wisdom can fulfill her generative task because she is in marriage union with God's omnipotence, so that if God's omnipotence is the 'only productive force and ground' the Wisdom is his acting force in the world.[85] Sophia creates all things anew, she lays her 'Platform in order to the restoring that Virgin Nature, and Godlike Simplicity, that have been deflowered through the subtilty of Reason'.[86] This prehistoric perfection will be fully accorded to regenerated souls who have held out against the 'Probation hour' and who then enter the 'Gate of Ascension' towards final spiritual and physical glorification.

The restoration of God's eternal and pure nature in the regenerate souls now has to be completed for the mystical wedding with the heavenly Bridegroom. While divine Wisdom is the 'mother' of the new creature in the believers' souls, Christ himself refines the restitution of spiritual and physical paradisiacal perfection. Using nuptial imagery Lead often describes her personal union with the 'Eternal spiritual Husband' in her diary as a restoration of the 'lost Virginity' and the incarnation of Christ's virginal body within her.[87] A 'full and perfect Change into [...] a spiritual Corporiety, in which the offence of Sin might altogether cease' is in fact essential because 'the Lamb, the Bridegroom can take no other into the Marriage-Bond of inflamed Love with him, but an immaculate Bride, all

Fair and Serene'.[88] That is why reborn souls have to put Christ's Mystical Body on and depart—at least mystically and spiritually—from earth.

The complete transfiguration will take place only at the end of time. Yet, although still living in the mortal body, the new spiritual creature can start its ascent into heaven. Or better still, only the spiritual body generated in the Resurrection-step can move and soar to the highest heavenly regions, where it will be rewarded with the promised transfiguration by means of Christ's intervention. These last steps of the mystical ladder—the Ascension and the Glorification—cannot be perceived by mortal senses, nor understood by rational knowledge, but only experienced by the 'Elect Flock'.[89] The twofold state of reborn believers is therefore radicalised: their 'visible Figure may be seen by Mortals, while their inward transformed Spirit, Soul and Body are translated out sight, and are taken into the Heavens.'[90]

Focusing on the transmutation which occurs at this stage, Lead argues that regenerated human beings are readmitted into the heavenly regions, from where they had been banished after Adam's fall. If Adam corrupted humankind by eating the fruit of the forbidden tree, now true Christians can be confirmed in eternal life by eating from the Tree of Life.[91] Thanks to the Bridegroom's priestly mediation, 'as Adam's Angelical and Paradisiacal Body was changed into that which was mortal and vile; so by virtue of feeding upon this Tree of Life, we shall again reassume a pure and unfadable Body, far more transparent that he had in that first Creation-state'.[92]

The transfigured body of regenerated souls therefore appears not only like the prehistoric body –androgynous and made of divine essence—but the finest. Lead lists in the conclusion of her tract its 12 main properties. The new spiritual body is, first of all, immortal and has both a 'christaline sight' to contemplate without any *medium* all celestial glories, and a 'supernatural hearing' to understand the 'Heavenly Language' of the creation. Third, God's Wisdom is fully restored in its essence, so that all earthly understanding and knowledge are replaced.[93] Moreover, the new spiritual creature enjoys all heavenly rewards, immunities and gifts: a perfect and everlasting righteousness, a delightful pleasure and joy, a 'flowing torrent of Love' towards all divine essences and creatures, a free will in perfect accordance with God's, the 'Balsam Tincture' of godly mercifulness and the 'sweet-scented Odours and Perfumes' of the Tree of Life as an 'Antidote against all Putrefaction of Sin'; and finally, all heavenly 'Riches and Honour' in opposition to such earthly ones.[94]

Lead's doctrine reinterprets Boehme's 'soteriological narrative' and particularly highlights the mystical process of human regeneration. Above all Lead faces the thorny problem of the physical transmutation of reborn believers. First, she maintains that the postlaparian nature is incompatible with the regenerated souls. Old Adam and new Adam are antipodes; therefore, rebirth necessarily implies the dissolution of both the animal senses as the rational part of the human beings. Lead regards the nothingness of the creatural state as a precondition to the gradual incorporation of the souls in the divine substance and states that regenerated believers must become part of Christ's body. Focusing on the essence of the new Adam and assuming that no spiritual reality can subsist without a 'body', Lead maintains that the new spiritual creature within reborn souls has a heavenly essence. The more the 'new Adam' grows in souls, the more its 'spiritual body' gains substance in the perfect union with God. Thus Lead describes the 'new creature' as a part of Christ's glorified body, with whom it is united in mystical marriage. In truth, this does not imply a complete and instantaneous transmutation of physical corporeality. Paradisiacal perfection of the reborn will be refined gradually and completed only with Christ's second coming, when the new 'magical body' will completely 'swallow up' the mortal one. In the meantime, the final resolution of the conflict between these two natures can be foretasted only by the elect in their mystical visions.[95]

This gives new insights into Lead's idea of corporality. Especially concerning the coexistence of the spiritual and material body, as well as Sophia's maternal role. Elected Christians are forced to live in a twofold state: they still endure postlapsarian corporeality—although they have reduced it to a mere 'figure'—while they inwardly experience the paradisiacal life of their new angelical nature. They can finally recognize each other on account of their spiritual senses, remaining concealed to all mortal sight and rational understanding. This coexistence of a physical and spiritual body in reborn Christians represents a temporary situation, whose resolution is not clearly fixed, but is only described as 'forthcoming' in Lead's works. Yet, with chiliastic expectation mounting, Lead's ideal of the restitution of 'Adam's Angelical and Paradisiacal Body' became a reference point for many, especially radical Pietists, who attempted to put Lead's mystical process into effect by urging real physical transmutation. Indeed, her doctrine of twofold corporality may have contributed to similar debates in radical pietism, offering new arguments to individual thinkers and groups who tried to explain the soteriological process as a physical restitution of the original paradisiacal perfection.

NOTES

1. The standard reference work on German Pietism remains the four-volume handbook M. Brecht et al. (eds.), *Geschichte des Pietismus* (Volume I: *Der Pietismus von siebzehnten bis zum frühen achtzehnten Jahrhundert*, Göttingen 1993; Volume II: *Der Pietismus im achtzehnten Jahrhundert*, Göttingen 1995; Volume III: *Der Pietismus im neunzehnten und zwanzigsten Jahrhundert*, Göttingen 2000; Volume IV: *Glaubenswelt und Lebenswelt*, Göttingen 2004). A recent excellent survey in English is D.H. Shantz, *An Introduction to German Pietism. Protestant Renewal at the Dawn of Modern Europe* (Baltimore, 2013).

2. H. Schneider, *German radical Pietism* (Lanham, 2007); W. Breul et al. (eds.), *Der radikale Pietismus. Perspektiven der Forschung* (Göttingen, 2010).

3. Bridal mysticism and the marriage metaphor played a central role in theological discussions within radical Pietism. Literature on the topic is extensive. See, W. Breul and C. Soboth (eds.), *Liebe, Sexualität und Ehe im Pietismus* (Wiesbaden, 2011). For a collection of pietistic sources and a historical introduction on the topic see also the text edition W. Breul and S. Salvadori (eds.), *Geschlechtlichkeit und Ehe im Pietismus* (Leipzig, 2014).

4. Beside the classical introduction to Spener's life and work of Martin Brecht, *Philipp Jakob Spener, sein Programm und dessen Auswirkungen*, in *Geschichte des Pietismus*, volume I, 281–389, see also Johannes Wallmann, *Philipp Jakob Spener und die Anfänge des Pietismus* (Tübingen, 1986).

5. For an overview on Spener's eschatological thinking from the 1670s see H. Krauter-Dierolf, *Die Eschatologie Philipp Jakob Speners* (Tübingen, 2005), pp. 29–53, 267–79.

6. H. Schneider, *Der radikale Pietismus im 17. Jahrhundert*, in *Geschichte des Pietismus*, vol. I, 391–437. New research perspectives and recent literature on the meaning and importance of eschatological expectation in Pietism can be found in W. Breul and J. Carsten Schnurr (eds.), *Geschichtsbewusstsein und Zukunftserwartun in Pietismus und Erweckungsbewegung* (Halle, 2013).

7. See for example Burkhard Dohm, *Poetische Alchimie. Öffnung zur Sinnlichkeit in der Hohelied- und Bibeldichtung von der protestantischen Barockmystik bis zum Pietismus* (Tübingen, 2000).

8. For the reception of Boehme's teaching in Pietism, see L. Martin, 'Jacob Boehme and the anthropology of German pietism', in Ariel Hessayon and Sarah Apetrei (eds.), *An introduction to Jacob Boehme: four centuries of thought and reception* (New York, 2013), pp. 120–41; B. Dohm, *Poetische Alchimie. Öffnung zur Sinnlichkeit in der Hohelied- und Bibeldichtung von der protestantischen Barockmystik bis zum Pietismus* (Tübingen, 2000).

9. B. Dohm, 'Böhme-Rezeption in England und deren Rückwirkung auf den frühen deutschen Pietismus: Jane Lead und das Ehepaar Petersen', in W. Kühlmann and F. Vollhardt (eds.), *Offenbarung und Episteme: zur*

europäischen Wirkung Jakob Böhmes im 17. und 18. Jahrhundert (Berlin, 2012), pp. 219–39.

10. For an introduction to the Pietistic anthropology and the teaching of the 'inner rebirth' in connection with the opposition between old Adam and the 'new man', see E. Benz, *Adam. Der Mythus vom Urmenschen* (Munich, 1955) and U. Sträter (ed.), *Alter Adam und Neue Kreatur. Pietismus und Anthropologie. Beiträge zum II. Internationales Kongress für Pietismusforschung 2005* (Halle, 2009).

11. M. Meier, 'Der "neue Mensch" nach Jane Lead: Anthropologie zwischen Böhme und Frühaufklärung', in U. Sträter (ed.), *Alter Adam und Neue Kreatur. Pietismus und Anthropologie. Beiträge zum II. Internationales Kongress für Pietismusforschung 2005* (Halle, 2009), vol. 1, pp. 138–49.

12. On the spiritual body and celestial flesh in the late antiquity, see H. Hunt, *Clothed in the body: asceticism, the body, and the spiritual in the late antique era* (Farnham, 2012). For a general history consult T. Griffero, *Il corpo spirituale. Ontologie "sottili" da Paolo di Tarso a Friedrich Christoph Oetinger* (Milan, 2006).

13. For an overview of the early modern debate on the 'spiritual body' see Brian Gibbons, *Gender in Mystical and Occult Thought. Behemenism and its Development in England* (Cambridge, 1996). On the doctrine of the 'celestial flesh' during the Reformation see J. D. Rempel, 'Anabaptist Theologies of the Eucharist', in L. Palmer Wandel (ed.), *A companion to the Eucharist in the Reformation* (Leiden, 2013), pp. 115–38.

14. W. Schmidt-Biggemann, 'Jakob Böhme und die Kabbala', in W. Schmidt-Biggemann (ed.), *Christliche Kabbala* (Ostfildern, 2003), pp. 157–81.

15. For the concept of Sophia in Boehme's work see U. Fuchs, 'Sophia—das Gesicht der Weisheit. Matrix und Signatur des Weiblichen bei Jakob Böhme (1575–1624)', in E. Gössmann (ed.), *Weisheit. Eine schöne Rose auf dem Dornenstrauche* (Munich, 2004), pp. 70–122; F. van Ingen, 'Die Jungfrau Sophia und die Jungfrau Maria bei Jakob Böhme', in J. Garewicz and A. M. Haass (eds.), *Gott, Natur und Mensch in der Sicht Jacob Böhmes und seiner Rezeption* (Wiesbaden, 1994), pp. 145–63.

16. P. Deghaye, 'Die Natur als Leib Gottes in Jacob Böhmes Theosophie', in Garewicz and Haass (eds.), *Gott, Natur und Mensch in der Sicht Jacob Böhmes und seiner Rezeption*, pp. 71–112.

17. Jacob Boehme, *Mysterium Magnum*, 15.5, in *Sämtliche Schriften. Faksimile-Neudruck der Ausgabe von 1730 in elf Bände*, ed. W.E. Peuckert (Stuttgart, 1955–56), vol.7, p. 94.

18. Boehme, *Mysterium Magnum*, 17.17, ibid., vol.7, pp. 110–11; Jacob Boehme, *Beschreibung der Drey Principien Göttliches Wesens*, 12.26, ibid., vol. 2, p. 136.

19. Jacob Boehme, *Aurora oder Morgenröte im Aufgang*, 17.18, ibid., vol. 1, p. 242.

20. Boehme, *Mysterium Magnum*, 18.7, ibid., vol.7, p. 118.

21. Boehme, *Mysterium Magnum*, 18,12-13, ibid., vol.7, p. 120.
22. Boehme, *Mysterium Magnum*, 18.2-6, ibid., vol.7, pp. 117–18.
23. Boehme, *Mysterium Magnum*, 17.39, ibid., vol.7, p. 115.
24. Boehme, *Mysterium Magnum*, 19, ibid., vol.7, pp. 124–32; see also Jacob Boehme, *De tribus pirncipiis, oder Beschreibung der Drey Principien Göttliches Wesens*, 12.45, ibid., vol. 2, p. 141.
25. Boehme, *Mysterium Magnum*, 19.22-25, 20.30-37, ibid., vol.7, pp. 130–31, 139–41.
26. Jacob Boehme, *Mysterium Magnum*, 19.7, ibid., vol.7, p. 126. See also C. Bendrath, *Leibhaftigkeit: Jakob Böhmes Inkarnationsmorphologie* (Berlin/New York, 1999).
27. Jacob Boehme, *De signatura rerum*, 11.1-10, in *Sämtliche Schriften*, vol. 6, pp. 138–43.
28. W. Temme, *Krise der Leiblichkeit. Die Sozietät der Mutter Eva (Buttlarsche Rotte) und der radikale Pietismus um 1700* (Göttingen, 1998).
29. M. Meier, 'Horch und Petersen. Die Hintergrunde des Streits um die Apokatastasis im radikalen Pietismus', in *Pietismus und Neuzeit* 32 (2006), pp. 157–74.
30. Jacob Boehme, *Aurora oder Morgenröte im Aufgang*, 6.17-18, in *Sämtliche Schriften*, vol. 1, p. 70; Temme, *Krise der Leiblichkeit*, p. 99.
31. Thune, *Behmenists*, pp. 68–151; P. McDowell, 'Enlightenment Enthusiasms and the Spectacular Failure of the Philadelphian Society', *Eighteenth-Century Studies* 35 (2002), pp. 128–46. For the German reception of the Philadelphian Society, see C.W.H. Hochhuth, *Geschichte und Entwicklung der philadelphischen Gemeinden*, in *Zeitschrift für die historische Theologie* 35 (1865), pp. 171–90.
32. Nigel Smith, *Perfection proclaimed: language and literature in English radical religion* (Oxford, 1989), pp. 185–225; A. Hessayon, 'Jacob Boehme's writings during the English Revolution and afterwards: their publication, dissemination and influence', in Hessayon and Apetrei (eds.), *Introduction to Boehme*, pp. 77–97.
33. Besides the literature on the English Behmenists, for further information on John Pordage and his contribution to the reception of Boehme's thinking, see C.G. Manusow, 'Jacob Böhme and Britain', in J. Garewicz (ed.), *Gott, Natur, Mensch in der Sicht Jacob Böhmes und seiner Rezeption* (Wiesbaden, 1995), pp. 197–208; Arthur Versluis, *Wisdom's Children. A Christian Esoteric Tradition* (Albany, NY, 1999), pp. 39–56, 172–80.
34. See also Julie Hirst, *Jane Leade. Biography of a Seventeenth-Century Mystic* (Aldershot, 2005).
35. Burkhard Dohm, 'Böhme-Rezeption in England und deren Rückwirkung auf den frühen deutschen Pietismus. Jane Lead und das Ehepaar Petersen', in W. Kühlmann and F. Vollhardt (eds.), *Offenbarung und Episteme. Zur*

europäischen Wirkung Jakob Böhmes im 17. und 18. Jahrhundert (Berlin-Boston, 2012), pp. 219–39.

36. B. Becker-Cantarino, 'Das Neue Jerusalem. Jane Leade, die Philadelphian Society und ihre Visionen von religiöser Erneuerung in den 1690er Jahren', in Sträter (ed.), *Alter Adam und Neue Kreatur*, vol. 1, pp. 151–64; M. Meier, 'Der "neue Mensch" nach Jane Lead'; W. Temme, 'From Jakob Böhme via Jane Lead to Eva von Buttler—Transmigrations and Transformations of Religious Ideas', in J. Strom (ed.), *Pietism in Germany and North America 1680-1820* (Farnham, 2009), pp. 101–06; Sarah Apetrei, *Women, feminism and religion in Early Enlightenment England* (Cambridge, 2010), pp. 187–98.

37. Temme, *Krise der Leiblichkeit*, pp. 318–20, 343–49.

38. Jane Lead, *The Revelation of Revelations* (London, 1683), p. 38; see also Jane Lead, *A Fountain of Gardens* (London, 1696), vol. 1, pp. 253–55, 311–14.

39. Lead, *Revelation of Revelations*, pp. 38–39; see also Jane Lead, *A Revelation of the everlasting Gospel* (London, 1697), pp. 26–28.

40. Jane Lead, *The laws of paradise* (London, 1695), pp. 21–27.

41. See Warren Johnston's chapter in this volume.

42. Jane Lead, *The heavenly cloud now breaking* (London, 1681).

43. Ibid., *Epistle*, p. 3.

44. Ibid., *Epistle*, p. 6.

45. Ibid., *Epistle*, p. 5.

46. Ibid.

47. Ibid., pp. 7–20.

48. Ibid., pp. 7–8.

49. Ibid., p. 9. See also Lead, *Revelation of Revelations*, pp. 14–18.

50. Lead, *Heavenly cloud*, p. 9.

51. Ibid., p. 10.

52. Ibid.

53. Ibid., p. 12.

54. Ibid., pp. 11–13; See also Lead, *Revelation of Revelations*, pp. 15–16.

55. Ibid., p. 12; see also Jane Lead, *The tree of faith* (London, 1696), pp. 67–69.

56. Lead, *Heavenly cloud now breaking*, pp. 13–14.

57. Ibid., pp. 16–18.

58. Ibid., p. 14. It is interesting to note here the similarity with Jeanne Marie Guyon's doctrine of 'morte mystique' in connection with the metaphor of the heavenly marriage with Christ, especially in J.M. Guyon, *Le Cantique des Cantiques de Salomon, interpreté selon le sens mistique et la vrai representation des Etats interieurs* (Lyon, 1688). See N. Carol James, *The Conflict Over the Heresy of 'Pure Love' in Seventeenth-Century France. The Tumult over the Mysticism of Madame Guyon* (Lewiston/NY, 2008).

59. Lead, *Revelation of Revelations*, pp. 35–36.
60. Lead, *Heavenly cloud now breaking*, p. 18.
61. Ibid., pp. 20–21. See also Lead, *The tree of faith*, pp. 63–66.
62. Lead, *Heavenly cloud now breaking*, p. 21.
63. Boehme, *Aurora oder Morgenröte im Aufgang*, 26.50, in *Sämtliche Schriften*, Vol. 1, p. 392.
64. Lead, *Heavenly cloud now breaking*, p. 21.
65. For the 'Magical Body, such as the Lord Christ had after his Resurrection', see Lead, *Revelation of Revelations*, p. 32.
66. Lead, *Heavenly cloud now breaking*, pp. 22–25.
67. For Schwenckfeld's doctrine of 'celestial flesh' see A. Sciegienny, *Homme charnel, homme spirituel: étude sur la christologie de Caspar Schwenckfeld (1489–1561)* (Wiesbaden, 1975). See also S.H. Webb, *Jesus Christ, eternal God. Heavenly flesh and the metaphysics of matter* (Oxford, 2012).
68. Apetrei, *Women, feminism and religion*, pp. 243–55.
69. Lead, *Heavenly cloud now breaking*, pp. 23–24
70. Lead, *Revelation of Revelations*, pp. 32–33.
71. Lead, *Heavenly cloud now breaking*, p. 23.
72. Ibid.
73. Jane Lead, *The Enochian walks with God* (London, 1694), p. 1.
74. Lead, *Heavenly cloud now breaking*, p. 26.
75. Ibid.
76. Ibid.
77. Ibid., pp. 26–27.
78. J. Hirst, ' "Mother of love": spiritual maternity in the works of Jane Lead (1620–1704)', in Sylvia Brown (ed.), *Women, Gender and Radical Religion in Early Modern Europe* (Leiden, 2007), pp. 161–87. See also Gibbons, *Gender in Mystical and Occult Thought*, pp. 145–50.
79. Temme, *From Jakob Böhme via Jane Lead to Eva von Buttler*, p. 103.
80. Jane Lead, *The wonders of God's creation manifested, in the variety of eight worlds* (London, 1695), pp. 31–32.
81. Lead, *Revelation of Revelations*, pp. 48–52.
82. Lead, *Fountain of Gardens*, Vol. 1, pp. 18–19.
83. Lead, *Enochian walks with God*, p. 26.
84. Jane Lead, *The Glory of Sharon, in the renovation of nature, introducing the kingdom of Christ in his sealed virgins, redeemed from the earth*, in *The wars of David* (London, 1700).
85. Lead, *Heavenly cloud now breaking*, p. 22.
86. Ibid.
87. Lead, *A Fountain of Gardens*, vol. 1, pp. 124–26.
88. Lead, *Fountain of Gardens*, vol. 2, p. 464.
89. Lead, *Heavenly cloud now breaking*, pp. 28–30.

90. Ibid., p. 37.
91. Ibid., p. 30; see also Lead, *Tree of faith*, pp. 24–25.
92. Lead, *Heavenly cloud now breaking*, p. 30.
93. Ibid., p. 31. This property—the tenth in Lead's list—can be interpreted in opposition to human reason as postlapsarian faculty.
94. Ibid., pp. 30–32.
95. Lead, *Revelation of Revelations*, pp. 29–31.

CHAPTER 8

Mystical Divinity in the Manuscript Writings of Jane Lead and Anne Bathurst

Sarah Apetrei

Mystics throughout the ages, not least in the early modern period, have somehow managed to find an awful lot to say, and indeed write, about the ineffable. But the process of translating spiritual experience and mystical knowledge into text has always, naturally enough, been a problematic one, testing the boundaries between metaphor and reality. Spiritual writers after Pseudo-Dionysius wrestled self-consciously and often creatively with the challenge of *apophasis*, or unsaying; preferring to allude to divine presence or divine personality by analogy, or indeed by negation, rather than by positive assertions using known categories.[1] The problem is heightened when mystical knowledge is regarded not universally as incommunicable, but as inaccessible except to a practised elite. Jane Lead and her circle wrote in a prophetic idiom, but also a mystical one, combining paradoxically the visionary boldness of seventeenth-century millenarianism, claiming special revelation on the public stage, with the secrecy of esoteric and alchemical discourses, and with Dionysian apophatic theology. As a result of this paradox, what literary critics call the 'topos of ineffability' fostered vividly imaginative writing among the Behmenists and Philadelphians, and a curious ambivalence about producing text and making it public.

It might be argued that the epistemological and linguistic challenges of writing ineffable experience were diminished in the case of female

S. Apetrei (✉)
University of Oxford, Oxford, UK

© The Editor(s) (if applicable) and The Author(s) 2016
A. Hessayon (ed.), *Jane Lead and her Transnational Legacy*,
DOI 10.1057/978-1-137-39614-3_8

visionaries. Women embodied the 'unknowing', the absence of intellectual illusions and interfering images that was so highly prized in mystical theology, and that encouraged in theory if not in practice the veneration of fools, madmen and virgins.[2] They might, as vessels of revelation highly idealized and even fetishized in their purity (as the elderly Jane Lead undoubtedly was), act as the virginal, chastening 'Other' of worldly masculine wisdom. In a period famous for the more public appearance of female authorship in England, the most prominent voices were visionary ones, and the most powerful defences of women's writing were made by the male mentors or associates of these mystics. One such advocate was the Welsh Benedictine Augustine Baker (1575–1641), who collected the works of Gertrude More (1606–1633), a nun of Cambrai, later published with the subtitle 'the sainctly ideots devotion'. Her devotions were conceived by and properly set forth for 'ideots', wrote Baker:

> because they are for such as feruently and simply with all their affections, desire to *aspire* after *God* in the *Cloud of faith and feelings of Loue* without troubleinge themselues with busye and impertinent operations of the vnderstandinge, commonly called Meditations or discourses of the vnderstandinge, to move & excite the will, which in the case of these deuine & Seraphicke Ideots, are superfluous, they beinge alreadye sufficiently, yea aboundantly excited and bent to loue *God*, and practise vertue, through their *light of Faith, which* telleth and assureth them, that all is vanitye of Vanities, *but. Only to Loue and serue God*[.][3]

The 'ideot', who 'to others seemes ignorant, and foolish; to you is knowingly ignorant, and wisely vnlearned', with 'more … satisfactorie knowledge then all the subtile Scholasticks, and suttle politicks put together could haue done'.[4] Baker had observed that 'in these latter times God hath as freely (and perhaps more commonly) communicated the Divine Lights and Graces proper to a Contemplative life to simple women, endued with lesser & more contemptible Gifts of Judgment, but yet enriched with stronger Wills and more fervent Affections unto him, then the ablest men'.[5] Along similar lines, the Scottish Jacobite mystic George Garden (1649–1733) wrote an extensive *Apology* for the 'innocent virgin' Antoinette Bourignon (1616–1680), whose ingenuous writings confronted a fruitless and 'speculative Knowledge of Divine Things', humiliating mere 'Humane Wisdom', which, 'is directly opposite to the Wisdom of the Holy Spirit which descends only into humble Souls'.[6] Bourignon herself is said to have observed that 'Men are now less dispos'd to receive his Divine Light than Women, since their Hearts are blown up with Pride'.[7]

The Philadelphians were, of course, followers and interpreters of Jacob Boehme (1575–1624), the inspired cobbler of Görlitz, whose own writings were notoriously abstruse but, for those who believed in his inspiration, unmistakeably stamped with the divine imprimatur precisely because of his 'illiterate' and untrained persona.[8] His writings provided the seventeenth-century template for the visionary expression of the ignorant sage. They were designed to be obstructive and exclusive, to foster an experimental rather than an abstractive reading. His English translators in the 1640s and 1650s insisted that Boehme's texts were precisely not to be approached as normal theological texts, by the light of Reason, for Boehme had 'not received his Knowledge from men, or from the imperfect fallible Principles of the Schools, but from the true Fountain of Wisdom and Knowledg'.

Nor did he write, as most do, by transcription out of other men's Books; nor were his Dictates neither, the Products of his own Fancy, but by Divine influence; and (as is his own expression) out of his *Three-leav'd Book*, which the Hand of God had opened in him: wherein he found the Knowledge, not only of all that *Moses*, the Prophets, Christ and the Apostles taught in Sacred Scripture, but of all Mysteries also in Heaven and Earth, as he himself affirms in his *Epistles*, and many other of his writings.[9]

As another translator put it, 'Herein lieth that simple child-like way to the Highest Wisdome, which no sharp Reason, or worldly learning can reach unto; nay it is foolishness unto Reason, ... the wiselings of this world, have alwaies trampled it under foot with scorn and contempt, and have called it Enthusiasm, madness, melancholy, &c'.[10]

Arguments for the special disposition of women and fools to receive spiritual impressions were not new of course, but the conventional distinction between proud Reason and holy humility took on a freshly oppositional character in the polemics of anti-popery and Counter-Reformation, and in the post-revolutionary outpouring of anti-enthusiasm and its own counterpart, radical spiritualism. Such oppositions can be found developed in Catholic defences of medieval and Counter-Reformation female mystics after the Restoration, and in Quaker justifications of women's speaking. However, its more powerful expression is to be found in the censorious writings of the anti-enthusiasts, for whom 'simple women' were rather more likely to be 'led captive' (1 Timothy 3.6) by their own delusions and melancholy than to be anointed with extraordinary revelations. In a hostile environment for mystical religion—hostile not least because of the association with female prophets and preachers—women's visionary writing confronted dominant discourses. Female leadership and social and political disorder were closely linked, a consequence of the civil wars which cast a long shadow, and shaped responses to women's visionary activity for generations. In a letter dated 1702, Anthony Ashley-Cooper (1671–1713), the third Earl of Shaftesbury, described his encounter with an 'Angelick Sect', presided over by 'adept ladys' and one female visionary in particular, dressed like a Quaker. The resemblance to the Philadelphian Society (apart from the distinctive costume) is striking. The members of the sect boasted of 'the Wonders and Miracles which God had wrought in, and by Her [the female prophet]; such as were of greater Certainty than either of the old or New Testament'. The 'Grand Sybill, and Soverain Instructess' then herself held forth, in 'Empiricall Astrologicall Bombastick Strains' and began to recall 'the Manner of her first Salutation by the Angell of God', speaking of the angel 'allways as a *She-one*; using the Terms *she*, and *Her*: which … was to shew us the Authority of her Sex in heaven'. Shaftesbury concluded his letter with a diatribe on:

> the burning Fury and Rage, the Dreadfull Ravage and Destruction of that greatest Incendiary of the Earth ENTHOUSIASME; which is not only able (as we see) to destroy private Persons and whole Familyes; but which getting head, and rising at first from Small Beginnings, has so far reduc'd even to Ashes and Desart the most flourishing Cityes and Countryes, 'orethrown establish'd Churches, violated the most lawfull Rites, revers'd all that is sacred, prophan'd Religion with Blood and Crueltyes, and in a word, confounded all things Divine and Human.[11]

There could be no more powerful inducement to quietism among female visionaries.

Much attention has been paid among literary scholars in past decades to manuscript writings by early modern women, a reaction against the exclusive focus on female authors who chose to publish in print.[12] Manuscript culture has come to the foreground in the scholarly field devoted to English women's writing, as it has become increasingly clear that scribal publication was an alternative mode of distribution and the most common means of disseminating women's writing. Harold Love's observation that 'the stigma of print bore particularly hard on women writers, as they themselves pointed out' remains influential.[13] Elaine Hobby has estimated that among the *printed* works by English women between 1649 and 1688, more than half were in fact prophecies.[14] Prophetic words were naturally the most 'sayable' for women in the public sphere, for obvious reasons: they were ventriloquized divinity, authenticated by the very weakness of the vessel. An interesting counterpoint to this trend is the case of Grace Cary, a prophetic petitioner whose (apparently genuine) resistance to print publication has been investigated by Margaret Ezell.[15] Cary's dramatic experiences of 1639, which included a disturbingly prescient vision of Charles I's disembodied head, led her to seek an audience at court. Nonetheless, she felt that it was 'very unfit, that such diuine & miraculous truth should be made common in these times wherin so manie falasies and false printed papers are set fourth'; it would 'eclipse the truth' of her visions by exposing them to vulgar interpreters.[16] Despite her political message and the undoubted circulation of her visions in manuscript prior to their eventual publication in 1646, Cary was possibly prudent to exercise restraint in a febrile environment in which other female prophets were vilified, but there is perhaps also some substance to her fear that 'divine and miraculous' experiences might fall into the wrong hands in the burgeoning print culture of the 1640s, with its vulnerability to profane appropriations and hostile, gendered readings.[17] As Ezell writes, for Cary, 'print seems to be the province of man-made, artificial intelligence, false stories made up by men for their own dangerous purposes, or perhaps the formulaic language of religion she had abandoned with her first ecstatic experience'.[18]

Cary's grounds for hesitation were intensified for female visionaries writing in the exhausted wake of the revolutionary period, with all the dangers of raising their heads amid the sharp, satirical daggers hurled by Restoration polemicists. Female visionaries and the masculine public sphere stood implacably opposed. Jane Lead and Anne Bathurst, from the 1670s part of the close circle of mystics and prophets which had its origins in the household of the Interregnum heresiarch John Pordage, chose initially at least to keep a private record of their experiences, journals of visions or meditations quite different in tone and purpose from the printed jeremiad. For them, writing was a spiritual exercise first of all, and the texts that were produced in the course of this ascent were understood to be problematic and subjective. This could not be like ordinary, scholastic theological writing, an effortful process burdened with erudition and linguistic precision; there must be something prophetic and instrumental in the act itself. It was reported that Antoinette Bourignon wrote fluently and without errors, like a secretary taking dictation: 'when she put Pen to Paper she wrote as fast as her Hand could gide the Pen, and what was once written, was written without blotting out or Change … She needed not, it seems, the Buckets of Study and Meditation, wherewith to draw out of the broken Cisterns of others; but she had within her a Fountain of living Water, still springing up to everlasting Life'.[19] Jane Lead's own *Fountain of Gardens* flowed forth spontaneously and, like Bourignon, she seems at first to have considered her visionary activity to be chiefly private, without thought of publication. In the first printed edition of her diary (1697), she claimed that she had recorded her privileged insights into 'the Deep Things of GOD: Which are only Knowable to that Holy Spirit', over 30 years:

> keeping a Private Recollection to her self, as they did from Time to Time open, and come down as a Burning Shower; not knowing whether they should have been made Publick in her Age, but thinking rather they might be kept as a Garden Enclosed, and as a Fountain Sealed.[20]

This is a reference to Song of Songs 4.12 (KJV): 'A garden inclosed is my sister, my spouse; a spring shut up, a fountain sealed'. It also evokes the tradition of the Virgin Mary as the *hortus conclusus*, and makes the statement that Lead's writing was itself essentially *virginal* and innocent, too chaste to be prematurely exposed to public view, and a maidenly contrast to the promiscuous print culture of her age.[21] However, the time for public consummation/consumption had come; Lead rejoiced that God had finally 'put into the Hands of a Good-willer to these Divine Mysteries' (possibly her Prussian patron, Baron Dodo von Knyphausen, but more probably her son-in-law, Francis Lee), 'to bring forth into the Publick, what might otherwise have been left in Oblivion and Secresie'.[22]

This might very well be thought to be disingenuous, but for other evidence presented for the first time here which suggests that Lead was not only secretive in her habits, but also seems to have recorded and kept her visions haphazardly, without an eye to wider circulation and preservation for posterity. In letters to Richard Roach, she was certainly remarkably guarded about the activities of the Philadelphians even after they had 'gone public'. Roach was under pressure from the ecclesiastical authorities in August 1697, not least because of the dominance of Lead and other women in their meetings, and he was warned by Lee that 'The Spies are many, and of serious kinds'. Roach was even cautioned against revealing too much to von Knyphausen, although he had shown himself to be 'of a very good disposition', adding that he was 'a stranger to all our affairs'.[23] Lee, who assembled and edited her writings, supported the account Lead gave of her private diary-keeping, recalling her writing habits in his correspondence with the scholar and high churchman Henry Dodwell, who had expressed doubts that a woman could have composed anything so complicated that consisted 'of many Latin terms, of terms of art, of the old Platonic mystical divinity, of all the modern enthusiasts, of JACOB BEHME, of the judicial astrologers, of the magic oracles, of the alchymists'.[24] John Pordage, he thought, must be the true author of her visions. Lee answered that 'it was the constant course of my mother to write down with her own hand day by day, all her own experiences and discoveries, with several memorandums also relating to her external as well as internal life'. There were many works left unpublished, he claimed, which she had 'described in secrecy with her own pen'.[25] He confirmed that it was Pordage who collected her diary, written on 'loose slips of paper, like the Sibilline leaves', transcribing them 'for his own private use, without any thoughts of their publication: whence in haste he frequently copied the very grammatical errors, and false orthography, leaving void spaces for the words he could not read'.[26]

The impression Lee gives of an unsystematic approach to visionary writing is confirmed by the discovery of two manuscript fragments which I suggest can be attributed to Lead. The first is a small sample of those 'sibilline leaves', a series of seven journal entries from November 1676, the second year after Lead's installation at the household of John Pordage. These can be found bound together with other loose notes and short mystical reflections in a volume among the British Library Sloane manuscripts, MS 2569. This intriguing little volume includes legal papers belonging to Thomas Lamb, the General Baptist and cloth merchant, a man who renounced his Independency after the Restoration and nearly converted to Catholicism; a Life of St Mary of Egypt, which depicts precisely the sort of encounter between a learned priest and a simple holy woman which might vindicate female prophecy; a vision of the Pietist prophet Hans Engelbrecht; and some curious 'Private Ejaculations', with a treatise dated June 1697 'Concerning Man's Eternall-Forme And what it is Like' which concludes that men and women would be reunited with their true marriage partners in heaven, regardless of whether or not they were united in life. The manuscript journal entries contained in the book were not published in *A Fountain of Gardens*, but comparison with nearly-dated entries clearly indicate that they are by the same author. Their absence from the printed text suggests not so much censorship (there is nothing particularly contentious or remarkable about them), but rather either ignorance of their existence or selective omission by the editors; the entries in *Fountain of Gardens* are the edited highlights, as it were. The two passages reproduced in Appendix A at the end of the chapter show in bold the resemblances in content and language between an entry from the printed first volume of *A Fountain of Gardens*, dated 9th November 1676, and one from Sloane MS 2569, dated 10th November 1676. Even without the corroborating journal entry from *Fountain of Gardens*, dated the very day before the manuscript fragment, the Behmenist and astrological content of the passage is so characteristic of Lead that it would be perfectly reasonable to attribute it to her on that basis. If further proof were needed, there is a reference in another vision dated 19 November 1676 to a dream in which 'Dr John' was driving 'a coach travelling very swiftly' across a flood, to arrive at the shores of a land where all were 'the Virgin Spouses of the Lamb'.[27]

The content of these entries is perhaps not as illuminating as the very fact of their existence, which is indicative of Lead's undisciplined, or at least unself-conscious, habits of writing and collection. The preservation of her work, she apparently did leave to Pordage and perhaps even other associates; the survival of these random and unpublished pages, one of which is merely a fragment in which text is broken off mid-sentence, may point to the involvement of another collector of her writings altogether. Another new source of Philadelphian writing is a volume containing 'Visions' in several hands in the Rawlinson manuscript collections (Bodleian, MS Rawlinson C. 266). The revelations include, once again, a 'A short account of ye wonderfull life and visions of Hans Engelbrecht, taken out of a large Treatise writ by himselfe in ye German tongue' (this is not the translation published as *The German Lazarus* in 1707), which tells the story of a madman or depressive, his near-death experience and miraculous recovery.[28] There are also two diary entries which I think may be attributed to Lead, dated December 3rd 1678 and November 12th 1679, though it is more difficult in this case to rule out other members of the circle, Anne Bathurst for instance, as possible authors. Their themes and ecstatic style are strongly evocative of Lead, especially when juxtaposed to a series of diary entries in a different hand and clearly not by the same author also bound in the volume (dating between 1681 and 1682), which contain relatively unsophisticated apocalyptic prophecies amounting to little more than crude paraphrases of the book of Revelation.[29] Their scruffiness also suggests that they may in fact be autograph. The second of the two diary entries is reproduced in full as Appendix B at the end of this chapter.

One cannot be quite as confident about the attribution as one can in identifying the fragments in BL Sloane MS 2569, but some additional clues suggest that the entry for November 1679 may have been recorded around the time that Lead began to write her *Revelation of Revelations*, published finally in 1683. The third volume of her *Fountain of Gardens* contains a very brief entry for that month, merely mentioning a vision in which 'the *New Jerusalem* City descended out of the Heavens, and the manner of its future Manifestation upon the Earth was Marvelously exhibited', with references to the published version. In the manuscript diary entry, it is envisioned that Christ 'is coming through clouds now to Apear to his People and to marry them to himself, in the most intemate Joyes of the New Jerusalem' (fol. 12v). There is also a clear account of the 'Express Efects of this vitall tranceport and over shadowing visitation of the Lord Jesus' (fol. 13r). Jane Lead frequently, though of course not uniquely, used the terms 'transport' and 'visitation' for her visions. The effects include 'the renewall of the heavenly Body my spirrituall senses were allso renewed, & partickularly my inward hearing seeing and feeling' (fol. 14r). In *Revelation of Revelations*, she describes the opening of all of her spiritual 'faculties': seeing, hearing, smelling, tasting and feeling.[30] This is not definitive evidence, but all these small coincidences chime with the general redolence of the diary entry to anyone familiar with Lead's writings; the reference to communion with other saints, to a divine penetration of the spirit, to universal charity and resignation as the fruits of contemplation.

The theme in this short manuscript vision which is of most relevance to the present discussion is that of the vexed interplay between writing and experience. Jane Lead (we shall assume it is she) concludes:

Thus have I Briefly described and set down the heads of what som others would Dilate into many sheets and of which I mite write a volume but if I should, I could not express, but in a meer shadye Representation what I then most intimately distinctly and feelingly enjoyed which Like the white stone and new name, can be known to none but those that have it but for it Blessed be the Great name of the Lord for ever, and for that ineffable Love and Eternall sweetness I felt transfused into my hart by the holy spirrit whilst I wrote this, and at this Instant whilst I think of it for which thrice Blessed Be the Liveing God in Trinity forevermore. (fol. 15r–v)

Writing here is described as its own reward, and as in a circular fashion reproducing the experience: a sweetness is supernaturally transfused into the heart through its narration. But it is also a process fraught with difficulty, so that Lead is economical in her language, reluctant to elaborate a 'meer shady Representation' of the feeling. It is telling that elsewhere in the published journal, Lead reports that she has periods in which she comes to 'a stop as to the Writing', especially when she lacks 'Privacy and Suitableness', and that she is instructed by God to write for the most part 'upon a private Account, for my own *Memorandums*, and not to Divulge it, but to the Believing Seekers and Waiters, who in unity of Love and Life do with me walk, and feel some Savour of Life from my other Writings, which sent out for Publick Benefit are to be'.[31]

Why, then, did Lead choose to publish? In *Revelation of Revelations*, she admits the same reclusive impulse: 'IT was in my purpose to have suspended, as yet, any further manifestation of the Revelation that still followed me, and would have hid the golden Talent ... but *Christ*, the bright Banner of Glory stood before me, and said, *Keep in Record the Journal of the now raised Life ... go on, and forbear not writing; for it shall be as the unclouding of the present dark Day*'.[32] She sends forth her revelation into print with the prayer: 'though in the form of a dead Letter, yet O God, as the Auther hereof, did in the writing meet with a mighty flow of the anointing Presence; so let the same out-flowing Spring accompany such whom thou hast ordained to be taken into this holy Priestly Order'.[33] The manuscript fragment might just give us a new insight into that flow of inspiration. Lead believed that her writing heralded an age of the Spirit, a 'mystical dispensation', in which inspired speech would be the only intelligible text. She wrote in her preface to *A Fountain of Gardens*:

> I think my self obliged to Publish for these Ends, what can be recovered of the Process and Diary of my Life, since I have been under these Love-Visitations from the Spirit of my Lord. ... For it is the Morning-Watch and Day-break of the Spirit, that is to spread forth its Light and Glory, whereby is to be enlightned the Dark Ignorant State of the World, who have sat in the Region of Traditional and Literal Knowledge, according to the Rational Wisdom of Man, which through the Innundation of the Spirit must all be drowned[.][34]

This is printed text that actively aims to subvert—to 'drown'—the culture in which it intervenes, encouraging readers to turn away from the 'dead Letter', the 'visible teachings of men', and apply themselves instead to God's inward teachings, the 'Book written within thee' by eternal Wisdom.[35]

The visions and meditations of Anne Bathurst, by contrast, only ever circulated in manuscript. A number of extracts from and copies of her ecstatic diary are known to be extant, several of which have been discovered in the past decade: fair copies and fragments in the Rawlinson collections in the Bodleian; extracts among the Deskford papers in the National Archives of Scotland; a volume in Chetham's Library, Manchester; and two volumes in the Library of the Russian Academy of Sciences in St Petersburg, originally obtained by Baron Metternich, an aristocratic German mystic connected to Scottish Jacobite visionaries and the French Quietists.[36] Of these, the Chetham's manuscript appears to be the earliest (possibly autograph) and contains the most interesting material, some of which was censored by Bathurst's copyists, such as references to her suicidal thoughts, and to the visitations of her own private angel. In a retrospective account of the Philadelphian Society, Richard Roach mentioned the leading role of 'Mrs Anne Bathurst; who has also left her Works in Manuscript', commenting that these works were 'too highly tinctur'd in the Seraphick Love for this Rougher Age to bear': they are 'Reserv'd ... for their time'.[37] The judgement that they were texts too sensitive for a wide contemporary audience was born out by the response of her readers. One of the recipients of the Petersburg fair copy, a Moravian, professed that he could not understand the style; and a note made by the nineteenth-century Bishop of Moray on one of her manuscripts indicates the limits of its appeal: 'All gross, raving Enthusiasm', he wrote. 'Who can read it through?'[38]

Like Lead's, Anne Bathurst's diary attests to an ambivalence about recording her ecstasies by means of the written word, though as Julie Hirst has argued she 'clearly made the connection between the act of writing and divine inspiration'.[39] She can express her experience only under considerable pressure, and it is a form of expression that is at odds with worldly communication. Like Lead, her writing is deeply self-referential, interpreting itself continually. Bathurst describes writing as the outcome of the mystical process of self-annihilation, and a kind of intoxication which, in her words:

at last constraines me to write that which I long time doe but first mutter to myself, saying; How can I write? I am Goded with God! Has he inrobed himself in me? And am I any other then he? Feel I myself all him? What then must I write? And how shall I utter, seeing I am not to be silent, but express. O my friends! I ascribe not this to myself, as if I were better, and had merited this state, O no! But only to express a little what God is in his Saints. and what I write is but to declare to you that such Honour have all the Saints.[40]

In the height of ecstasy, 'Eternity opens', and her inhibitions about writing cease: her spirit is 'out of time … & dips its pen in Eternity … & here I am without limits to write large folios of Eternity'.[41] Elsewhere, she describes how 'when the excess or extasie of the Revelation is over, for sometime after, it may be dayes, nay weeks before I can read what I have writ, for the great spirit of Love-wine and Heavenly tincture is annext to it'. After the intensity has subsided, she reports, 'Then I can chew the Cudd, and see & behold with a remained strength: For He or Shee that so serves at the Altar, lives on the Altar' (an interesting comment, which resonates with the potent eucharistic imagery in her evocation of divine presence).[42] Experimentation with form characterizes Bathurst's regime of mystical writing. Like some female visionaries of the revolutionary period, she sang her experiences as well as writing them, and the 'extempore hymns by Madam Bathurst' from her journal were collected in 1713 by a Scottish Episcopalian reader.[43] This is not sophisticated poetry: a typical verse couples 'This Love sets all my Heart on fire' with 'I'm almost ready to expire'.[44] The formlessness of the verse has an authentically spontaneous feel; not only are the rhymes obvious or strained, there is no effort to avoid repetition or to produce verse with a consistent rhythm. Sometimes the songs are as brief as three lines: 'Tis his Loving Heart/ Is placed within my breast/ And like a dove hath made its nest'.[45] This artless singing is a more immediate, sensual expression of the incommunicable rapture, but it does also ultimately produce a text, a sacramental sign of the heavenly 'written word / Which in our hearts we still may find'.[46]

The self-consciously artless and possessed quality of the visions of Jane Lead and Anne Bathurst links them to the mystical discourse of medieval women, which opposed corrupted, worldly Reason with Virgin Wisdom, divinely apprehended. However, as representatives of this sacred innocence they were faced with the fresh difficulty of participating in the public sphere: could the printed prophetic word, exposed to the world, be truly chaste? Lead and Bathurst, under the more or less controlling guidance of their male mentors, adopted different attitudes to publication, while sharing a vocation as spiritual writers. As a result, Bathurst, who felt compelled to 'attend to my Inward Teachings, and not to Look out after National Concerns, or the publick affairs of the world', has been more or less obscure until rediscovered in the twentieth century, while Lead has exercised a modest, intermittent influence on Pietism and charismatic Protestant sects until the twentieth-century pentecostal movement.[47] What made the difference between them? In part, of course, there is a difference in the content and style of their visions. Lead's are opaquely allegorical and often narrative; Bathurst's are ejaculations so passionately affective that they embarrass the contemporary reader, and the reception by a polite eighteenth-century audience is easy to imagine. Lead's inspiration is in a sense intellectual, the opening of the imagination, her spiritual sense of sight: Bathurst's is sensible, an opening of the bowels. Perhaps their writing embodies something of the tension between prophecy and mysticism. Nonetheless, in their writing both sought not only to express but also to generate (for themselves and others) spiritual experience. These were in a sense apologetic texts, demonstrating the reality of God in three dimensions in a sceptical age: not through reasoned argument, the discredited masculine way, but by mystery speaking to mystery.

APPENDIX A: DIARY ENTRIES FROM NOVEMBER 1676

Printed Version: Jane Lead, *A Fountain of Gardens* (London, 1696), pp. 433–34 November the 9th. 1676

Then was shewed me an Engraving like a Seal, with the Emblem of an Olive-Tree with three branches, and it was said to me, When ye are Sealed with this living Print, you then shall know a fixed Life. These Winds can no more hurt, if once they may but stop, till ye are feelingly impressed with this Olive-Tree. This is another manner of Life, then what is subject unto Mutability. For what is greater then for the Life of the Holy Trinity, to be appropriated penetratingly by way of Sealing? Now for this great preparation thereto, is required the **one pure unleavened Lump,** all passive without Life, to receive the Impression. Which accordingly was performed, by the overshadowing of the Dove, that gave the living Witness of being Baptized into the Name of the Father, Son, and Holy Ghost. By which the Contrary Winds were restrained, that they could not blow up the dark Mists and Fogs any more. So from hence feeling in me a pure Serene Calmness, the Powers of the Eternal World did let fall sweet pleasant Dews, from which the Fruitful *Sharon* did spring, to entertain the Trinity, within the circumference of this holy Ground, which is now so strongly enclosed, and fortified, that nothing common or unclean can pass hereunto: for **the pure Winds from the Heavenly Element gave forth a new fresh Air, all**

clear and bright; so that in the Light thereof, liberty was given for Holy Walks, as in a Supercelestial Region, there to take up the Souls true Central Rest. Even so sweet Jesus, never let me venture out, lest **those perilous Winds** should me overtake; to unfix me out of the even Temperature, wherein all stability will the Mind most safely and securely Fix.

Manuscript Version [Unpublished]: British Library, Sloane MS 2569, fols. 87r–87v November 10th, 1676

The **Cry of the seale** was still in my eares, the voice saying where and upon whom shall this be fastened, but upon **the new Lumpe, that hath beene kept from the old Leaven**. Behold, and so a new mould is prepared for the Spirits formation in you. Turn yor eye in, and you may se the holy matter, that is sifted frm that wch is mortal and evill. This being preserved from **all those hurtfull winds,** that would blow up such heavy mountaine sands upon it Let it but have its allowed time, for every high ingredient so comingle proportionably, acceeding to the measure of every part, through an unknowne conveying center. Wch addeth and contributeth hereunto, according as the evill Spirit entring into that abysicall deepe, from whence this pure thing doth spring wch is the foundation matter, for the Life Seale to worke upon. Oh thou eternall Spirit of might, who is not yet come to fathom thy are not being as **a restored lumpe, made up of that leaven Composition**, of **wch is the Invisible Element**. Wch also must be sustained, through all its growing degrees, that so being come up unto the Number of three times seaven as the full age of him, whoe here by may give prooffe, he ever lives to raise his body againe, wch is the new created similitude of ye exalted Jesus. These sayings being somewhat obstruse [*sic*] that I could not well sound the matter of the new mould, I earnestly sought a more cleare making of it out, so as I might comprehend it, wch through grace I obtained. Ffirst seing as sometimes before, a sparkleing light, suddainely rose as an auray, and againe passe away, with this word, following saying, there is no end of Revelation, because it proceedes from that infinite, generating being, that still casteth up new treasury out of the unknowne Magia from whence this holy Lumpe doe proceede, and will be fed and nourished by a source, as its deepe from beneath, in conjunction with the celestiall Planetts, ruling from that one element. Ffrom whence the life quickning riseth as an **Eternal breath of pure ayre, wch is altogeather free from mingling with any of those grosse and polluted Elements.** This pure Lumpe must be secure in a pure Virgin wombe, wr unto I have elected mine eye, that if possibly such an other unmixed wonderfull birth may be brought forth, as was visibly, but hereunto high chastity, with great humility is required. ffor on this wise the mould is all of holy matter, as well for to be as that Lumpe into wch it is cast for sublime fashioning. Ffor after this manner ye Lord Jesus conception and birth were, deriving his life Spirit from that ever and unchangeable pure Spirit, that constituted him into that unparalelled composition of spirit, in order to all the sealing power of ye holy ghost, wch was effected accordingly, in the most naturall flowing out of all actings powers from this magick birth roote, wch was in him.

APPENDIX B: DIARY ENTRY OF NOVEMBER 1697

(Bodleian MS Rawlinson C. 266, fols. 10v–15v)

Being in serious contemplation of the spirituall world, I enjoyed Great communion with the spirit of one of the saints, and felt a divine penetration of Life, vertue and power with a Mutuall reciprocation of most vivid substantiall holy influence, being a short preludium, of that communion of saints which is in heaven and will Last forever nothing of this world is Like unto it, this being far more Excellent, makeing me feel the Power of that Petition that they all may be one as thou Father art in me and I in thee that they also may be one in us.

But through this I ascended into a deep perseption and communion with the spirit and person of Christ from whom had such an over shadowing and penitration of Life and Love that neither words nor Imaginations could reach it, it was really part of the supper of the Lamb and of the eternall marriage: for it was an ineffable enjoyment in my whole inward man into which the very outward seemed for a while absent also, I felt the highest sweetness Goodness Life, Love drawing out all my faculties and Imploying them upon this Blessed object the sonne of God, whom I felt diffuseing his Life quite through mee: with the Idea of his Glorifyed Person being fixed in my mind I felt such Inexpressable Love, to his sacred majesty, and such a neer and Close fruition of his Essentiall profound Goodness and sweetness that it seemd heaven its selfe and that nothing could bee Beeyond it, for in it I had a vitall perseption of the Eternall Deity penitrating, Imbibing, and comprehending my inward man, with the most sacred Joyes of Eternall Love, soe that my whole man could desire nothing more: for he brought me into his banqueting hous and his Banner over me was Love which with other scriptures (representing the signall Love of Christ) to the Church, I then felt reallised and witnessed by a powerfull and vital sensation and they rose in me with still Ideas of a divine sound penitrateing my spirit with an harmonious sweetness far transcending all the efects of vocall or Instrumentall musick soe that in a divine harmonious power such scripture Ideas emerged, in my mind his name is Like ointment powered forth therfore doe the vergins Love him, Let him kisse me with the kisses of his mouth for his Love is better then wine.

In the opening of which Idea I felt ineffable sweetness even a deep central enjoyment inexpressable beyound the ammors of this world or any thing Immaginable in it, after that of John was sounded in me, I am the way the Truth and the Life, that soe it was Like those that sing silently coming with a most still musicall aire that Life divine power and breathing were in spoken and transfused into my whole inward man, then that of the Romans rose from amongst internall words and Images to be spirit and life, yee are become dead to the Law by the body of Christ, that ye may be Married to another, even to him who is raised from the dead whom I signally felt to be a quickening spirrit and that in that Attrebute he is coming through clouds now to Apear to his People and to marry them to himself, in the most intemate Joyes of the New Jerusalem, more over a midst these things I had a dear and deep perception of that most transcendent Love Jesus hath and Ever had to his Church, where he followed and came down after them into flesh for the Chilldren being made pertakers of flesh and blood he himself took part with them and this from the most intimate dear Love and conjugall afection whence he came down to seeke his Lost sheep or spouse which Love he Longs to Exhibitt and over shadow us with, as Josephs bowels Earned to make himself known to his Brethren but our unfittness generally Impeads the fruition of this most Meet supersensuall bliss with which the hart of Christ is full and which we shall all feed of as we are purified for it and tis to fitt us for this that he soe mercyfully dispenseth such various chastisements that being Lost, he may find us, being sick he may heale us, being falne he may cement us, being emtied of all the Irregular Images of the Cretures, he may fill us with himself and with the indearing Loves of his fathers bosome where from all Eternitie he hath dwelt and whence he proceeded to deliver us and make us pertakers of his own never failling Joyes.

And now I shall briefly write the Express Efects of this vitall tranceport and over shadowing visitation of the Lord Jesus.

1. Then I found new degrees of Love Excited to the mediatour, with a strong perception of his most profound Love and afection to all his people

2. New degrees of divine Charity or Brotherly Love to all the saints ye of universall Charity and mercy to all men

3. A great meekness, or meet sweetness opening in my soule, with a strong sence of our Great Exemplar Christ as the meek Lamb of God.

4. An humble prostrateing my selfe before the throne of Grace with a renewed oblation of my whole man Body and soule and spirit to the Lord.

5. A wonderful still silent fram of spirit Attended with humillity introvertion and deep resignation.

6. Out of which arose an universall vigor throughout my whole Inward man, by which and some other certain indications, I felt and clearly perceived that I then put on the Divine body in some new degrees, by which my very outward became more lively and was freed from an illness which three Dayes had hung upon me.

7. Out of the renewall of the heavenly Body my spirrituall senses were allso renewed, & partickularly my inward hearing seeing and feeling but I shall instance only in the first, though I could in all, as to my hearing then I perceved most unutrable still harmonious sounds, as though my whole head were turned into harmony by the Living touches of the Eternall Logos, or word of God.

8. The Power of Prophesy was vigorously Renewed in me, and I felt a mighty Power Impelling me to Pray and utter The Glorious Truths of the Everlasting Gospel, so that at that season I wanted Auditors and opportunity to ease my soule of its most weighty yet sweet burthen of Evangellicall prophecies.

9. My faith was much strengthened in the Lord Jesus by reflecting of his Amazeing Goodness and condesention which afforded me Great Boldness and more fixed Reliance upon his future Asistances.

10. I found Great Courage in me to suffer for our Deare Emanuell and to press through all difficulties to be neerer and with him, whose inefable Love I found and perceved soe redy to Receive us, and to conclude I found soe Great a sweetness and still Resignedness in my whole man that my Joy was unutterable Manifestly perceaveing the whole Image of God Renewed in me with a perticular tenderness towards my Greatest Enimies for whom I most hartyly Prayed that the paine I felt mite open in them soe then we should be one.

Thus have I Briefly described and set down the heads of what som others would Dilate into many sheets and of which I mite write a volume

but if I should, I could not express, but in a meer shadye Representation what I then most intimately distinctly and feelingly enjoyed which Like the white stone and new name, can be known to none but those that have it but for it Blessed be the Great name of the Lord for ever, and for that ineffable Love and Eternall sweetness I felt transfused into my hart by the holy spirrit whilst I wrote this, and at this Instant whilst I think of it for which thrice Blessed Be the Liveing God in Trinity forevermore.
Amen

NOTES

1. On the tensions in mystical discourse see, for instance, Michael A. Sells, *Mystical Languages of Unsaying* (Chicago: University of Chicago Press, 1994).
2. Nicholas of Cusa, *Idiota*; Tauler and the beggar. See Michel de Certeau, *The Mystic Fable: The Sixteenth and Seventeenth Centuries*, trans. Michael B. Smith (Chicago: Chicago University Press, 1992), pp. 31–48.
3. Augustine Baker, 'Directions' in Gertrude More, *The holy practises of a devine lover, or, The sainctly Ideots Deuotions* (London, 1657), pp. 24–25.
4. Ibid., p. 168.
5. Augustine Baker, *Sancta Sophia* (London, 1657), p. 156.
6. George Garden, *An Apology for Antoinette Bourignon* (London, 1699), pp. 26, 28–29, 34. Garden's *Life* of Bourignon and translations of her works by Garden in manuscript also survive. See 'The Life of Mrs Antoniet Bourignon', in National Archives of Scotland, MS CH 12/20/14; and *Antichrist Discover'd*, Aberdeen University Library MS 512.
7. Ibid., p. 165.
8. On the falsity of this persona, see Andrew Weeks, *Boehme: An Intellectual Biography of the Seventeenth-Century Philosopher and Mystic* (New York: SUNY, 1991), and Ariel Hessayon, 'Boehme's Life and Times', in Ariel Hessayon and Sarah Apetrei eds., *An Introduction to Jacob Boehme: Four Centuries of Thought and Reception* (Abingdon and New York: Routledge, 2014), pp. 13–37.
9. Humphrey Blunden, 'To the Reader' in Jacob Boehme, *Four Tables of Divine Revelation*, trans. Humphrey Blunden (London, 1654), pp. 2–3.
10. John Ellistone, 'Preface' in Jacob Boehme, *Signatura Rerum, or, The Signature of All Things*, trans. John Ellistone (London, 1651), sig. A2ᵛ.
11. Anthony Ashley Cooper, Earl of Shaftesbury, 'The Adept Ladys, or the Angelick Sect', in *Complete Works, Selected Letters and Posthumous Writings*, eds. G. Hemmerich and W. Benda (Stuttgart: Fromman-Holzboog, 1981), vol. 1, part 1, pp. 384, 396, 404–6, 416.

12. See, for instance, George L. Justice and Nathan Tinker eds., *Women's Writing and the Circulation of Ideas: Manuscript Publication in England, 1550–1800* (Cambridge: Cambridge University Press, 2002); Victoria Burke and Jonathan Gibson eds., *Early Modern Women's Manuscript Writing* (Aldershot: Ashgate, 2004); Jill Seal Millman and Gillian Wright eds., *Early Modern Women's Manuscript Poetry* (Manchester: Manchester University Press, 2005).

13. Harold Love, *Scribal Publication in Seventeenth-Century England* (Oxford: Clarendon Press, 1993), p. 54.

14. Elaine Hobby, *Virtue of Necessity: English Women's Writing 1649–1688* (London: Virago Press, 1988), p. 26.

15. Margaret Ezell, 'Performance Texts: Arise Evans, Grace Carrie, and the Interplay of Oral and Handwritten Traditions during the Print Revolution', in *English Literary History*, 76:1 (2009), pp. 49–73. On the alterations to Carrie's text for publication, see also Rory Tanner, '"She Mente Well, and Was a Good Woman": The Vision and Revision of Grace Cary', in *ANQ: A Quarterly Journal of Short Articles, Notes and Reviews*, 24:1–2 (2011), pp. 81–88.

16. Quoted in Ezell, 'Performance Texts', p. 56.

17. Cary's prophecies were published, with extensive revisions, as *Vox Coeli: To England, or England's fore-warning from Heaven. Being a Relation of true, strange, and wonderfull Visions, and Propheticall Revelations* (London, 1646).

18. Ezell, 'Performance Texts', p. 57.

19. Garden, *Apology*, p. 41.

20. Jane Lead, *A Fountain of Gardens Watered by the Rivers of Divine Pleasure* (London, 1697), p. 3.

21. I am grateful to Mark Philpott for pointing out the Marian allusion to the *hortus conclusus*.

22. *Fountain of Gardens*, p. 16.

23. J.L to Richard Roach (31 August 1697), in Bodl., MS Rawlinson D 832, fol. 53.

24. Walton, *Notes*, p. 192.

25. Ibid., pp. 202–03.

26. Ibid., p. 203.

27. BL, MS Sloane 2569, fol. 90^r.

28. Bodl., MS Rawlinson C. 266, fols. 1^r-9^r.

29. Ibid.

30. Jane Lead, *Revelation of Revelations* (London, 1683), pp. 43–45.

31. 9 November 1680, in *Fountain of Gardens*, vol. III.

32. *Revelation of Revelations*, p. 1.

33. Ibid., p. 130.

34. *Fountain of Gardens*, pp. 4–5.
35. Ibid., pp. 6, 46.
36. Bodl., MS Rawlinson D. 1262, D. 1263, D. 1338, Q. e. 28; National Archives of Scotland, Edinburgh, MS CH 12/20/9, CH 12/20/11; Chetham's, Mun. A.7.64; Library of the Russian Academy of Sciences, St Petersburg, MS Q. 472, Q. 538. On the St Petersburg manuscripts, see Leena Kahlas-Tarkka and Matti Kilpiö, ' "O Thou Sea of Love": Oxford and St Petersburg manuscripts of Ann Bathurst's religious visions', in *VARIENG: Research Unit for the Study of Variation, Contacts and Change in English e-series*, 9 (2012), http://www.helsinki.fi/varieng/series/volumes/09/kahlas-tarkka_kilpio/. I am grateful to Ariel Hessayon for alerting me to the existence of the Chetham's version.
37. Richard Roach, *The Great Crisis* (London, 1727), p. 99.
38. National Archives of Scotland, MS CH 12/20/11, n.p.
39. See Julie Hirst, ' "If my pen's liquor is to be from Eternity, it cannot be written dry": Anne Bathurst, a Seventeenth-Century Visionary', in Katherine Quinsey ed., *Under the Veil: Feminism and Spirituality in Post-Reformation England and Europe* (Newcastle: Cambridge Scholars Publishing, 2012), p. 15.
40. Bodl., MS Rawlinson D. 1263, fol. 525v.
41. Ibid., fol. 27r.
42. Ibid., fol. 527r.
43. National Archives of Scotland, MS CH 12/20/9, pp. 1–25.
44. Ibid., p. 23.
45. Ibid., p. 16.
46. Ibid., p. 12.
47. Bodl., MS Rawlinson D. 1262, p. 15.

CHAPTER 9

'God's Strange Providence': Jane Lead in the Correspondence of Johann Georg Gichtel

Lucinda Martin

> How else did unholy Pietism arise in our churches, except through the testimonies, raptures, and enthusiasm of the little women [...]? How else has it made its progress, except through the enthusiastic maidens [...]? And how else is it still now being discussed, but precisely through all sorts of suspicious books by women [...]?*

This is the question posed by the German historian Johann Feustking in his 1704 book, *History and Description of false Prophets, Quakeresses, Fanatics and other sectarian and enthusiastic Women*. Writing against the tradition of early modern catalogues of learned women, Feustking compiled a kind of anti-catalogue, based on the premise that women were responsible for the heterodoxy of the day. He listed over 175 'seductive and suspicious women', among them Jane Lead and a number of German women who became associated with her. Feustking saw Lead as an adherent of the Quietism of the Spanish mystic Miguel de Molinos

L. Martin (✉)
Gotha Research Centre, University of Erfurt, Erfurt, Germany

© The Editor(s) (if applicable) and The Author(s) 2016
A. Hessayon (ed.), *Jane Lead and her Transnational Legacy*,
DOI 10.1057/978-1-137-39614-3_9

(1628–1697) and of the 'cobbler-theology' of Jacob Boehme. Feustking cited contemporary religious literature arguing both for and against Lead to prove that the Englishwoman was attempting to 'introduce a devilish theology' into Germany.[1]

It was not only critics of Pietism who commented on Lead's influence in Germany. In the mid-1690s, Lead became a lightning rod figure among religious dissidents on the continent. Some, such as the Pietist historian Gottfried Arnold, believed that she and other women prophets were fulfilling Biblical passages about the 'last days', while other Pietists saw her as a fraud, or even an instrument of the devil.[2] Depending on their viewpoint, authors of polemical texts either lauded or condemned Lead, taking stands both on her specific teachings and on her status as a female prophet. The literary debate about Lead helps explain why, as late as the mid-eighteenth century, a German lexicon of learned women still remembered her as an 'English Quakeress', who had made herself famous through her 'writings filled with fanatical, chiliastic, Quietist and Behmenist enthusiasm'.[3]

Despite Lead's acknowledged influence in Germany as a religious writer, much remains unknown about the spread and import of her thought. How were her texts published in German translation? Who distributed them? Which tenets were appealing or controversial for contemporaries? How were her writings interpreted and transformed by German readers? In this chapter I hope to partially answer some of these questions by analysing the discussion of Lead in the correspondence of a key player in continental nonconformist circles—Johann Georg Gichtel.[4] As the 'self-appointed Grail Keeper of Boehme's legacy',[5] Gichtel saw it as his duty to judge other interpreters of Boehme and to promote or denounce them within the dissenting religious community.

'PHILADELPHIA' IN GERMANY

Near the end of the seventeenth century, Lead was at the centre of a group based in London known as the Philadelphian Society. The circle took much of their inspiration from English translations of the writings of the German theosophist Jacob Boehme. For a time, Boehme's writings were available more readily to English readers than to Germans. British nonconformists such as the group surrounding Lead thus debated Boehme's ideas and incorporated aspects of his thought into their own theologies.

Yet Boehme's writings were censored and often difficult to obtain in his German homeland. Although some of his works had been published from the 1630s in Amsterdam, these editions were scarce, so that continental devotees of the 'Teutonicus philosophus' relied mainly on hand-written copies of his texts that they exchanged underground. That situation began to change when Johann Georg Gichtel edited and published Boehme's complete theosophical writings in a 15-volume edition at Amsterdam in 1682–83.[6]

Through Gichtel's edition, Boehme's writings soon reached more people than had previously been possible, spurring debate in German Pietist circles and beyond. Yet it was English Behmenists and their German allies who brought many of Boehme's ideas to a broader German-speaking public. Indeed, the Philadelphians were much more influential in German territories than in the British Isles.[7] Philadelphian-inspired works by Gottfried Arnold, the Petersens and others were among the best-sellers of their day and went into multiple editions.[8] To be sure, these writers interpreted and transformed Boehme's thought, so that it was often something quite different from what Boehme had himself intended.

As Warren Johnston discusses in Chap. 6, the circle around Lead combined Boehme's thought with their own chiliastic expectations to conceive of 'Philadelphia' as a union of true believers in all confessions that would come together before the Final Judgement (Revelation 2 and 3:7–13). Boehme had not written explicitly of 'Philadelphia', but already in the first generation after his death, some of his German followers had associated the idea with Boehme.[9] Although the concept had long circulated among German-speaking dissenters, the translated writings of Lead and her co-religionist John Pordage (1607–1681) inspired German Pietists to try out new forms of community in an effort to enact 'Philadelphia'.

Most of Lead's texts were published in German translation between 1694 and 1705. They made an immediate impact, but Pietists understood and implemented them in a variety of ways. Soon, the 'radical' wing of Pietism was saturated with Philadelphian ideas[10]: the notion of a supra-confessional Philadelphian community; a chiliastic understanding of history according to the Book of Revelation; the doctrine of universal salvation (*apokatastasis*); a Melchizedek order of 'chosen' priests; the belief in a female element in the godhead (Sophia); and the idea that God—and thus humanity in its original form—is androgynous. Debates about these tenets led to many of the alliances and divisions in the Pietist movement.

These ideas reached German speakers above all through the writings of the prominent Pietist couple Johann Wilhelm Petersen and Johanna Eleonora Merlau Petersen.[11] Histories of the influence of Jane Lead and the Philadelphians in Germany thus centre on the Petersens.[12] Through their prolific publishing, the couple popularized Philadelphian thought and through their extensive correspondence and travels, they built up a network of like-minded cohorts.

In her autobiography, Merlau Petersen described how in 1695 'a distinguished gentleman' gave her and her husband a manuscript copy of Jane Lead's tract *Eight Worlds* asking them to comment on it.[13] The work unleashed an intense experience in Merlau Petersen, who thereafter became convinced of the doctrine of universal salvation, called in German 'the Return of all Things' or 'the Return of all Creatures'.[14]

In his autobiography, Johann Wilhelm Petersen revealed that it was Baron Dodo von Knyphausen, a patron of religious nonconformists, who gave the couple the text.[15] The Petersens initially worried that Lead relied too much on her own visions without having biblical citations to back them up. However, they soon became convinced that the work was of great value and needed only to be adjusted on a few minor points. Searching the scriptures, they were able to find precedent for Lead's ideas and even to correct certain 'errors'.[16] Merlau Petersen initiated a correspondence with Lead and in the following years the Petersens would write dozens of tracts on Philadelphian themes, without however associating themselves formally with the English movement.

Although the account beginning with the Petersens' receiving *Eight Worlds* in 1695 is the starting point for most histories of the Philadelphians on the continent, there is evidence of even earlier Pietist engagement with her texts. Indeed, the preface to *Eight Worlds*, penned by Francis Lee, remarks on the great success of Lead's previous works in the Netherlands.[17]

MERLAU'S DUTCH CONNECTION

In the late seventeenth century, Amsterdam became a refuge for sectarians and religious free thinkers, many of them exiles from German territories. Like their brethren back home, nonconformist Germans living in the Netherlands discussed Jane Lead and took a range of positions on her writings. For example, the Boehme enthusiast Friedrich Breckling rejected her as a charlatan (he did not believe that women should speak out on religion), even as Quirinus Kuhlmann and others saw Lead and other women prophets as harbingers of the 'New Jerusalem'.[18]

Yet Lead's texts met with most interest in the circles surrounding Johann Georg Gichtel. A German exile living at Amsterdam, Gichtel led a celibate household of 'Angelic Brethren', so called because they strove to achieve the purity of angels (Matthew 22:30). In 1682–83 Gichtel published his monumental edition of the theosophical writings of Jacob Boehme, and through a vast correspondence, he spread his interpretations of Boehme to a web of 'Friends in Christ' dispersed throughout much of Europe.

In 1700 Gichtel began publishing selected letters from his correspondence. These eventually culminated in the massive seven-volume *Theosophia Practica*, but gaps make clear that the collection is far from comprehensive.[19] In their letters, Gichtel and his correspondents debated religious issues, exchanged news on other radicals and sent one another texts, money and gifts.

More than 40 letters from Gichtel to Merlau Petersen (her letters have been lost) survive in Gichtel's published correspondence.[20] The first letters are from the years 1677–79, before Merlau married, while a second phase in the correspondence begins in 1691 after a break of more than 10 years. During the first phase (1677–79), Merlau lived in Frankfurt, the centre of early Pietism in Germany. She was good friends with the Pietist leader Philipp Jacob Spener, but because Spener did not allow women to speak in his churchly conventicle, Merlau began to host an alternate meeting where women and those of all social ranks could speak and interpret the Bible.[21]

It is unclear how Merlau first made contact with Gichtel, but they associated with many of the same people. Merlau was well integrated into international nonconformist networks. She corresponded with Anna Maria van Schurman, Antoinette Bourignon and William Penn—the latter visited her conventicle in Frankfurt. Merlau's spiritual advisor, the Frankfurt attorney Johann Jakob Schütz, knew several members of Gichtel's circle. Furthermore, Johann Wilhelm Überfeld, one of Gichtel's closest followers and his successor in leading the Angelic Brethren after Gichtel's death, participated in William Penn's so-called 'Frankfurt Company' of investors in Pennsylvania, as did Merlau.[22]

As Ruth Albrecht has previously studied the Merlau–Gichtel correspondence more broadly, I focus here primarily on aspects relevant to Lead.[23] Four letters from Gichtel to Merlau are preserved for the years 1677–79.[24] In these early letters, Merlau and Gichtel discuss a range of religious topics—practical matters, such as how to live as Christians in the world, and the ideas of other reformers. From Gichtel's responses, it is clear that Merlau wrote of humility and the mystical experience, while Gichtel was most interested in the workings of the devil and the individual's struggle to defeat Satan in silent, inner prayer.

In the letters Gichtel presents himself as a role model and advisor to Merlau, but the two had different conceptions about how to live as Christians. Merlau participated in and even hosted conventicles. She thought that the 'born again' should reach out and teach others whenever possible, while Gichtel makes clear that the only correct way to live as a Christian is in 'sacrifice', isolating oneself from others as much as possible and living in continuous prayer.[25]

In 1680 Merlau and her new husband, Johann Wilhelm Petersen, travelled to Amsterdam. Since Merlau corresponded with Gichtel between 1677 and 1679, it would have been customary for the couple to pay Gichtel a visit. Yet in their autobiographies the Petersens do not list Gichtel as one of the people they met. However, in a letter from 1693, Gichtel recalls them visiting him in Amsterdam and finding him ill.[26] There are no surviving letters between the two from the years 1680–90. Did something happen during the Petersens' visit in Amsterdam that led to the 10-year gap in their correspondence? Or was Gichtel's claim that he had to 'live like the dead' for his spiritual struggle the real reason?[27]

It may be that their different understandings of the correct Christian lifestyle were simply too great to bridge. When Merlau decided to marry Johann Wilhelm Petersen, she reversed her earlier decision to remain celibate and devote herself to a 'career in Christ'. Gichtel broke with Gottfried Arnold and others over the marriage issue, advocating celibate 'spiritual' marriage between friends, rather than a marriage of 'flesh'. Furthermore, in 1680 the Petersens still saw a role for the institutional church, which Gichtel dismissed as 'Babylon'. Yet the gap in the letters may not be the result of a disagreement but could simply be due to one of Gichtel's many periods of withdrawal to live in 'stillness'.

At any rate, Gichtel apologized for the hiatus when he renewed the correspondence in January of 1691, attributing it to his need 'to be silent, to suffer and to place myself in God's will'. In the meantime, the Petersens had moved to the forefront of Pietist debates, especially in the discussion about the possibility of post-Biblical prophecy, and Gichtel writes to them wanting to know more about events in Germany.

In these later letters—now often addressed to both husband and wife— Gichtel discusses themes such as the priesthood of believers, but mostly he is concerned with how contemporary apocalyptic visions fit into biblical prophecies. In contrast to the earlier letters, Gichtel now discusses the role of the divine Sophia and he cites Boehme often.[28] Evidently, he trusts the Petersens enough to raise controversial subjects. He thus warns Merlau

Petersen to take care his letters do not fall into the wrong hands.[29] He affirms that he and the Petersens are pursuing the same goals and offers them moral support for the persecution they are suffering.[30]

While there are only four letters from 1692, the correspondence increases in 1693, with 16 letters to Merlau Petersen alone or to both Petersens.[31] In January 1693, Gichtel and Merlau Petersen began discussing a theme that would have far-reaching consequences, not just for their friendship but for the Pietist movement more generally— namely, the problem of how a loving God could punish sinners with eternal damnation.[32]

Merlau Petersen apparently believed that she had found concrete answers to the problem in certain scriptural passages. Gichtel encouraged her investigation, but remained ambivalent about any conclusions, warning her not to look for references to specific persons and dates, since the Scriptures can be interpreted spiritually. Whenever there is doubt about dense passages, he recommends reading Boehme.[33] Yet Gichtel did believe in the possibility of 'renewal' for those who die unconverted if the 'born again' pray for them enough.[34] In his biography, Gichtel even claimed that he was able through prayer to free a man from hell who had committed suicide.[35]

In 1694 Gichtel and Merlau Petersen often exchanged news about those active in the dissenting religious community, especially their fraternal visits and confrontations with authorities.[36] The two continued to discuss signs of the coming apocalypse and issues related to universal salvation. Gichtel believed that all humans, including Jews and heathens would be saved, but tied this to the effectiveness of the priesthood of believers. For Gichtel, however, the priesthood consisted in selected 'chosen' priests who have access to secret knowledge, while Merlau Petersen believed that all Christians are called to minister to one another.[37] Gichtel made clear that 'the saints will judge the godless and rule over the devil, death and hell, and [they will] have the power to lessen or increase pain, to accept grace or [let them] stay in the purifying fire longer'.[38] Merlau Petersen would come to believe that God's unlimited love had to result in universal salvation, but for Gichtel it was certain elite 'saints' or 'angels' like himself who had the power to control the conditions and length of damnation.

In September 1694, that is, immediately upon its printing, Gichtel sent the Petersens a copy of Jane Lead's *Himmlische Wolcke* (the translation of *Heavenly Cloud*). In his study of the Philadelphians, Nils Thune noted that Jane Lead was mentioned in Gichtel's letters in 1695, but based on Gichtel's published correspondence this must be antedated to at least 1694.[39] It is true that Gichtel did not yet name Lead, but it is clear who was being discussed when he sent the Petersens a new tract by a female author. At this point, Gichtel had nothing but praise for Lead. He saw her as a fellow disciple of Boehme and was anxious to help spread her texts. Addressing J.W. Petersen, Gichtel wrote:

> Your honor [Petersen] should already have been provided a copy, more from this already-mentioned author should follow soon, the content will not be unpleasant ... it gives good instruction ... especially in those other tracts that are underway: She alone describes the path exactly and witnesses powerfully that none can enter Christ's kingdom who has not struggled here with Christ and become like his image ... and has not experienced the purification of the soul.[40]

In their later autobiographies, the Petersens underscore that Baron Knyphausen gave them a Lead manuscript in 1695, but Gichtel's letter from September 1694 reveals that they were already familiar with her writings. Furthermore, in the context of relating how Knyphausen had asked them to comment on the Lead manuscript, J.W. Petersen referred to Lead in his autobiography as a 'dear friend'.[41] This indicates that the Petersens and Lead must have been in contact when they received the manuscript from Knyphausen in 1695.

Gichtel's letters also raise a question about the origins and development of the doctrine of universal salvation in these circles. In 1694 neither Gichtel nor Merlau Petersen seems to have found Lead's position remarkable. The letters further show that Merlau Petersen was concerned with the concept of universal salvation as early as 1693, since she and Gichtel discussed the subject on several occasions. It is thus not clear who first initiated discussion on this subject—Merlau Petersen, Gichtel, Lead, or others.

In May 1695 Gichtel sent the Petersens three more Lead tracts (again without specifically mentioning her name), and he and Merlau Petersen discussed them in their correspondence.[42] In a letter dated 21 June 1695, Gichtel referred to a discussion with J.W. Petersen about Lead's *Offenbahrung der Offenbahrungen*, this time mentioning both author and text by name.[43] Gichtel approved of Lead's 'discreet' way of interpreting Scripture, that is, metaphorically instead of literally.[44] He discussed the content at length, revealing more about his role in the production of these texts: 'The Englishwoman Lead has written about this, our and all true disciples' faith struggle and process, which has moved us to translate it into our mother-tongue [...] yes, even our opponents here, who consider us to be vagrants and gossipers have cried out and have changed their minds [...], because they now see that our teachings and our efforts are justified'.[45]

In August 1695, Gichtel wrote a long letter regarding Lead. Pleased that Merlau Petersen enjoyed a Lead book, Gichtel related details of Lead's biography, from her birth in a 'noble house' to her conversion experience in 1665, to the theological ideas in her writings. Gichtel stressed the difference between the superficial 'letter' and the deeper 'magical' sense of scripture that can be apprehended only through 'inner spiritual eyes'. He ended the letter by declaring, 'It is God's strange providence that Lead's writings have come to light in our language'. Gichtel feared however that some would follow her writings at first, but when they saw that light and darkness cannot mix, they would begin to despise her.[46]

GICHTEL'S TURN AWAY FROM LEAD: THE FISCHER LETTERS

Yet other letters preserved in Gichtel's correspondence help explain how Gichtel and Lead—two of Boehme's most influential interpreters—came to part ways. Some of Gichtel's most revealing missives concerning Lead were written to Loth Fischer, a German radical from Nuremburg who had been in the Netherlands since the 1680s. At first, Fischer frequented Gichtel's circle, but he eventually broke with Gichtel to devote himself to the English Philadelphians. It was Fischer who translated Lead's texts into German.

Only five letters to Fischer appear in Gichtel's published correspondence. In the earliest two letters from 1683, Gichtel does not name Lead, but he does resentfully mention that the German radical Quirinus Kuhlmann has been incommunicado in London for some time.[47] Gichtel complains that if he had wanted to build up a new 'sect' in Germany, he could easily have done so. This is an early indication of the jealousy that would develop between Gichtel and other radicals, especially those who saw themselves as spiritual descendants of Boehme.[48]

After the letters from 1683, the next letter from Gichtel to Fischer is from 1695. Although the *Theosophia practica* presents a 12-year gap in the correspondence, it is clear that the two were in close contact during this period. Gichtel and his associates chose to include those letters that they deemed most valuable for their readers in distinguishing Gichtel's thought from that of other religious thinkers. Thus, the Gichtel–Fischer correspondence picks up again right after the publication of Lead's texts in Germany and deals intensively with conflicts between her thought and Gichtel's.

In a letter to Fischer from 1695, Gichtel cited Lead to back up his own views on the 'inner and outer mirror' and the 'virginal birth' in the first human being.[49] As in his letters to Merlau Petersen, Gichtel saw Lead as a kindred spirit. Yet, in the very next letter to Fischer, Gichtel began to criticize Lead for her conception of the devil and the role of evil in God's universal plan. In this long, detailed letter dated 3 October 1696, Gichtel explained how Lead's version of events would contradict the divine principles underlying the cosmos as described by Boehme.[50]

Between 1695 and 1696 Lead's views had evidently gained traction in Pietist circles, because Gichtel complained that he had heard Fischer's objections from others. Gichtel saw Lead's writings as a sign of God's revelation, but believed that she was still at an early stage of development. Yet he lamented that some would set her writings up as infallible commandments to be followed blindly. Gichtel found this demand unjust, since he was 'set ablaze' by God and had passed through 'fiery trials' long before he or Fischer had heard of Lead. Gichtel argued that God had sent the heavenly Sophia to Lead, so that his disciples could see with their own eyes and not be 'blown about by the winds of doctrine' (Ephesians 4:14). Yet many had sent Gichtel letters asking him to justify Boehme's writings with 'this new doctrine'.[51]

Gichtel recounted how these requests prompted him to pray, seeking answers, so that he would not be brought to a 'foreign opinion' and would not 'push Christ and his believers from the throne and place the devil on it'. According to Gichtel, Lead correctly saw that God forgiving the devil would not undo Lucifer's fall, any more than it would undo Adam's, and therefore she presupposed the creation of the devil. But Gichtel maintained that God did not create the devil; rather, it was Lucifer who chose evil over good.

For Gichtel, there was also an anthropological component to this debate. He claimed that the angelic Lucifer took on a serpent body; when he chose evil. Jesus had to take on a human body in order to atone for human sin, but if God had *intended* for Lucifer to be evil, then Jesus (and his believers) would have to take on a monstrous 'serpent body' like

Lucifer in order to atone the world's sin. Gichtel saw this as an abomination and an impossibility that would contradict both physical laws ('the light of nature') and the divine revelation that Gichtel himself had received through his long spiritual battle.[52] Gichtel concluded that he did not want to argue further with Fischer, since the most important issue, that of the inner spiritual struggle, must be 'learned from another book', because 'Lead does not mention these things'.[53]

Critical of Fischer, Gichtel argued that the heavenly Sophia does not trust someone who has not learned to recognize the 'ground' in himself. Gichtel grumbled that he had suffered a great deal because he could not get along with those who constantly change their alliances.[54] He wished that Fischer could borrow his eyes, so that he could see Gichtel 'in all three principles'. Then he would see, perceive and know that Gichtel cannot favour any 'despicable spirit that raises itself above other talents'—a clear reference to Lead.

Gichtel compared the behaviour of Fischer and others who follow 'sects' to the movements of heavenly bodies, drawn to one another by invisible forces. Just as gravity can pull a planet into a new orbit, so too can people follow erroneous doctrines if they do not make an effort to turn away quickly: 'the soul tosses about in the body like the outer planets in the heavens and takes no note of the divisive effects of the third principle, combining first with this one, then with that one and in the end stays true to none'.[55]

According to Gichtel, Fischer could not see his own fault because he was 'in opposition' to Gichtel and his followers; Fischer was in a 'new conjunction' with Lead, and carried her in love 'because of the opposition of your astral bodies and their reflective light'.[56] Gichtel cautioned that everything must be taken into the 'centrum' and tested against God's will, so that one does not fly away with every new 'astrum'; even a 'good-meaning astral body' can divert a seeker from his goals. For Gichtel, all the contemporary religious divisions were caused by this and only serve the devil. Gichtel thus begged Fischer not to interpret his brotherly love in anger. He then reiterated in great detail his theological arguments against Lead's understanding of the devil and universal salvation.[57]

Gichtel's next letter to Fischer, from June 1697, repeats some of these arguments but also brings new ones to bear.[58] Gichtel was worried about a particular 'K' who wanted to be part of Gichtel's community but could not let go of the 'dark kingdom of fantasy'. Gichtel remarked sarcastically that he himself is no prophet, yet he can already see that K will end up joining those in London so that he can live according to 'imagination and reason', as opposed to the spiritual work of the inner battle. K will 'reach his own self-set goals, but not those of God'.[59]

Gichtel commented that since Lead's diary has been published, new problems in her writings had come to light.[60] He remarked that only another 'female mind' (*weiblicher Geist*) who was following the same path could possibly profit from her text: 'no spirit can take root in us that is not free of the feminine matrix and that has its imagination purely in Sophia'. He added that the 'feminine tincture' is volatile; it can ignite the masculine tincture quickly and easily, but is weak and quickly extinguished. K needed to learn through spiritual struggle how dangerous it was to keep company with women who 'hunger after the male limbo'.[61]

Gichtel's biography—volume seven of the *Theosophia practica*—repeats this theme in less astrological terms: men can easily be led astray by women and should avoid them whenever possible. Gichtel thus emphasized to Fischer that God wants his disciples to live from 'heavenly bread', shunning women and rejecting the desires of the physical body, including not just sexuality, but also the desire for sleep and social companionship. Gichtel stressed solitary prayer and vigilant suffering as the true path to God. Strangely, he cited Lead in this context—despite her 'feminine matrix'—to support his argument: 'As Lead also explains in detail in her tract on the *Revelations*, which, next to the *Clouds* is still the best tract that aims for our goal and to shore up our transformation'.[62]

At the end of this last letter to Fischer, Gichtel added a note claiming that he wrote but did not send the letter, believing that it might have pushed K into joining a sect. Yet another postscript adds that K died 'in dark melancholy in London soon thereafter'. K supposedly stopped praying, gave up the spiritual battle and began to have visions.

Gichtel consistently differentiated between visions and his own 'inward seeing' as the result of inner spiritual struggle. In his letters, Gichtel describes the vivid images that he saw 'inwardly'—perhaps hallucinations induced by fasting and sleep deprivation—but then contrasts these with uncertain 'appearances from without'.[63] He warns against reliance on 'outer visions' such as Lead's, which can deceive.

He thus maintained that Lead wrote of the inner struggle but had not fought it herself.[64] Gichtel blamed Lead for K's turn away from silent prayer to 'visions' and thus made her culpable for the man's death.[65] In a letter to yet another correspondent about this same K, Gichtel wrote that K was put under a spell by a woman with whom he prayed alone, and that he had complained greatly of having to fight the struggles of 'Venus' to resist the woman's charms.[66]

GICHTEL'S VERSION OF EVENTS

Between 1695 and 1696, Lead's views spread, both through her own writings and through those of the Petersens, Gottfried Arnold and others who adopted and transformed aspects of her thought. Loth Fischer may have been the first to challenge Gichtel about discrepancies between Lead's writings and Gichtel's own interpretations of Boehme, but Gichtel was soon inundated with inquiries from his correspondents. Gichtel repeated the explanations that he had given Fischer, but over time refined and added new elements to them.

In 1697 one of Gichtel's closest allies, an 'Angel Brother' named Johann Gottfried Pronner, wrote to Gichtel asking how Lead's writings on the devil could be reconciled with Boehme's.[67] Gichtel replied that Boehme addressed the issue in his last theosophical question and that Lead's explanation diverged. Gichtel claimed that he posed a series of questions through Loth Fischer, prompting Lead to write her *Everlasting Gospel* to address his concerns.[68] Gichtel was, however, dissatisfied with Lead's answers to his queries. Indeed, both his correspondence and biography contend not only that Lead wrote her *Everlasting Gospel* in answer to his concerns, but that she changed her earlier stance to incorporate his insights.[69] Gichtel declared that it was this sudden change that made him mistrust her visions and realize that they were mere opinions and not anything divine. Gichtel claimed that he was worried about the devil's eternal damnation long before Lead, but that after much seeking he understood that the problem was not that God will not forgive the devil, but that the devil does not want to change.

A number of correspondents wrote to Gichtel asking his advice on Lead and on other leading figures in nonconformist circles. Gichtel remarked that he knew little of Pordage and that Lead was 'weak'. He found contemporary books generally unsatisfactory and could only recommend Boehme. He underscored that Lead's writings relied on her visions and that visions can deceive, especially where egoism played a role. He professed that Boehme had already refuted Origen's opinion about the devil's conversion, but that Lead was 'warming it up' again.[70]

On the other hand, Gichtel complained that J.W. Petersen and Gottfried Arnold—the most respected theologians on the 'radical' wing of Pietism—relied too much on reason and scholarship.[71] In his earlier correspondence, Gichtel had happily agreed with Lead, the Petersens and Arnold on a variety of points and had used their writings to back up his own arguments. But over time he came to see the 'inner struggle' as something different from both Lead's visions and the Petersens' and Arnold's biblical interpretation.

In a letter from 1706, Gichtel gave his own version of the history of his acquaintanceship with Lead. He declared that her writings were a trap laid by the devil for the Angelic Brethren. He recalled that it all began when two of Lead's 'little books' fell into the hands of the impressionable Loth Fischer.[72] 'Now, since I didn't understand any English, he talked up the English woman. How such a weak tool is walking our manly path. If these texts would go public, how our secret faith path would become more known. Under this pretense, they got printed'.[73] In his biography, Gichtel supplied further details, claiming that when he first presented the books to the Angelic Brethren, Fischer pretended Jane Lead was a man. Each day Fischer translated some passages out of Lead's *Revelations* into German for the brothers, who were enthusiastic about the writings, since they seemed to confirm the faith path of the Angelic Brethren. Only Brother Überfeld was suspicious that something might be amiss.[74] Yet Gichtel thought that they should wait until the texts appeared in German before making a final judgement.

Gichtel made clear that Loth Fischer had 'sown Lead's writings in Germany', but admitted that he was at first deceived because Lead wrote of divine revelation. According to Gichtel, it was only after her texts were published that Fischer's true goal was revealed: 'he sought a following and money'.[75] Gichtel related that Fischer wrote to him, promising that if his group would support Lead, then Baron von K. [Knyphausen] would give them money, just as he had given money to *Herrn P.* [J.W. Petersen]. Indeed, after he was dismissed from his post as a Lutheran pastor, Petersen and his wife lived from the charity of sympathetic supporters, including Knyphausen.[76] As Gichtel tells it, he and his followers refused to accept 'that woman' (*diese Braut*), so Brother Überfeld replied to Fischer that they did not 'follow Christ for money'. Fischer then became their 'worst opponent and persecutor'. Dr Petersen then composed a theological defence of Lead's ideas on the devil, 'and proved his opinion, but not the truth'.[77]

Believing that God would provide for his disciples, Gichtel opposed paid work. He and the Angelic Brethren thus lived from the support of patrons. Yet Gichtel was highly critical of Lead for soliciting donations, because she was not using them to live in silent prayer, but to publish her texts.[78] He asserted that any illuminated reader who read Lead's diaries would see that her ideas were not deep and had no power. Furthermore, Germany did not need these writings and had much nobler texts of its own—notably those of Boehme. Gichtel was vexed that others were angry with him because he disagreed with Lead, although he believed anyone could see that she had shifted her opinion in response to his criticisms.[79] Gichtel complained bitterly that, 'if B.K. [Baron Knyphausen] had not contributed so generously and given L.F. [Loth Fischer] 400 *Reichstaler* yearly, then L.F. would have gotten stuck with his translation'. Gichtel consoled himself in the knowledge that 'God will topple Babylon'.[80]

In yet another letter, Gichtel claimed that he even helped to correct Lead's German texts. He only became wary when he learned that she was planning on using contributions not for her livelihood, since she had enough to live on, but for publishing costs instead. Gichtel asked Fischer about it and the two got into an argument. In the end, Fischer himself paid the costs to get the 'tracts with the diaries, etc.' printed in Utrecht and broke off communication with the Angelic Brethren.[81] According to Gichtel, Fischer edited Lead's writings and became her disciple, not because he wanted to grow in love but rather because he wanted to 'help build the tower of Babylon'. He accused the Philadelphians of condemning to hell those who did not accept Lead's visions.[82]

Gichtel's 1722 biography is softer in its judgement of Lead, but all the more devastating in its portrayal of Fischer. It depicts Lead as an unknowing and simple woman who was manipulated by Fischer: 'L.F. is about to find out what it means to play with spirits; since he made himself into a devil and poisoned the Lead woman and made her an accomplice, though she was actually innocent, and knew nothing of the affair. Thus her lamp was extinguished ... Her society in England has since been scattered'.[83] Gichtel presents Lead as well-meaning but harmless, while Fischer, who betrayed his loyalty, is nothing short of evil.

Gichtel's collected correspondence ends with an additional appendix of letters written by Gichtel and two 'true servants'. Significantly, these final letters address Lead and her influence. Gichtel and his 'servants' claim that her writings were suspect to them from the beginning, even before they were public. They 'taste sweet, but give no sustenance'.[84]

Furthermore, there is even an appendix discussing Lead attached to Gichtel's biography—in essence the final word of the seven-volume collection: 'We thank God in Jesus Christ that our oracle is not born of Lead, but rather of our inward man. This is more certain for us than all the visions of Lead, which will not be able to protect dear L.F. in the fire ... I really wish him the true living power of faith in his heart. How would this good woman have known that there is a Gichtel in the world if she had not been informed so by L.F.?'[85]

THE DISSOLUTION OF PHILADELPHIA

Between 1695 and 1699 Gichtel began to criticize but not break from Lead. After 1701, however, he broke completely and publicly with both the Petersens and Lead. Since the published correspondence between Gichtel and the Petersens ends abruptly in the mid-1690s, it is likely that it actually continued for some time, and that a later decision was made not to print these letters.[86] If so, we can assume that they would have been discussing—and arguing over—Lead's writings, just as Gichtel did with Fischer. At any rate, a subsequent desire to distance themselves from one another led both the Petersens and Gichtel to obscure their earlier friendship.

In later years, the Petersens and Gichtel became openly hostile to one another. In his *Theosophia Practica*, Gichtel had essentially accused the Petersens of selling out when they accepted Baron Knyphausen's financial assistance. The Petersens defended themselves aggressively against these charges. In his autobiography, J.W. Petersen openly questioned whether Loth Fischer would have offered Gichtel a bribe from Knyphausen to follow Lead, thus implying that Gichtel lied about the affair. Petersen argued that it was rather Gichtel and his Angelic Brethren who dealt fraudulently with funds.[87]

In this context, Petersen portrayed Gichtel as a hypocrite for accusing others of building sects. He pointed out that Gichtel and his Angelic Brethren had sought followers far and wide, despite their criticism of the Philadelphians for doing the same. As far as sect-like qualities go, Petersen accused the group of giving Boehme the same authority as the Bible.

Petersen also tried to set the record straight on the issue of universal salvation—ostensibly the reason for Gichtel's rejection of Lead and the Petersens. To prove that Gichtel had originally believed in the 'Return of all Things', Petersen published a letter from Gichtel to another correspondent in which Gichtel discussed biblical passages that might pertain to universal salvation. The same letter is printed in Gichtel's published correspondence and demonstrates that Gichtel found scriptural support for the doctrine. Nonetheless, Gichtel left the matter open, concluding, 'As far as the punishment of the fallen angels goes, a new, future time or century will make [this question] clearer to us'.[88]

In his account, Petersen ventures that Gichtel retreated from his earlier position because he had exaggerated the tenet. Petersen cited yet another letter in which Gichtel allegedly went so far as to 'call the devil his brother during prayer'.[89] No such letter is printed in Gichtel's *Theosophia Practica*, although it is easy to see why he would have chosen not to print it—if indeed it ever existed.

In fact, Gichtel's own published correspondence makes his objections about universal salvation seem like an afterthought, since he did not initially object. It may well be that Gichtel only became aware of a potential conflict between Lead's thought and that of Boehme when others wrote to him, pointing out discrepancies and asking him to take a stand. As in many other cases, Lead and the Philadelphians went beyond Boehme with the doctrine of universal salvation. When in doubt, Gichtel always took Boehme as his authority.

Although J.W. Petersen was a renowned theologian, it was his wife, J.E. Merlau Petersen, who took the lead in developing and publicizing the couple's views on the controversial doctrine of universal salvation. Their first publication on the subject was Merlau Petersen's *Ewiges Evangelium* of 1698, a tract inspired by Lead's similarly-titled work that was being attacked by Gichtel and others.[90] Although published anonymously, contemporaries knew that one or both Petersens were responsible for the text.[91] Merlau Petersen's *Evangelium* drew enormous attention, not only from Pietists, who took a variety of positions, but also from outraged Lutheran orthodoxy, and from territorial rulers who censored the work.[92] The tract went into three editions, provoking dozens of other tracts supporting or opposing it.[93]

These debates go beyond the bounds of this chapter, but the Petersens' goals are relevant: as with Lead's *Eight Worlds*, the Petersens found theological argumentation to back up Lead's revelations and to refute her opponents' objections. Despite their conviction that Lead relied too much on her visions, they did not deny their authenticity, but rather sought to verify them. And although they never officially joined Lead's Philadelphian Society, the couple considered themselves to be members of 'Philadelphia'. The title page of Merlau Petersen's *Evangelium* thus includes a cryptogram, giving the author as a 'member of the Philadelphian congregation'.[94] Unlike Gichtel, the Petersens were able to tolerate disagreement about the exact form 'Philadelphia' should take. They were thus able to correspond with Lead as late as 1703, the year before her death.[95]

While Lead claimed divine inspiration and the Petersens pointed to biblical authority, Gichtel fought the literary battle through his correspondence. Because of Gichtel's break with Lead and the Petersens, there are substantial differences between the 1710 and 1722 editions of Gichtel's published letters. In the 1710 edition Gichtel praised Lead and distributed her texts within his network. In the later 1722 edition, the many positive references to Lead in Gichtel's letters to Merlau disappear.[96] Instead there is sharp criticism of Lead, especially in the letters to Loth Fischer that had not appeared in the earlier edition.

Despite an obvious attempt to distance Gichtel from Lead, the later edition provides far more details about Gichtel's role in the translation and publishing of Lead's texts. Apparently the relationship between Gichtel, Lead and the Petersens was such a matter of public speculation that Gichtel and his followers felt compelled to tell their version of the story by printing the letters to Fischer. The Fischer letters are crucial because they reveal how, after being an early promoter of Lead, Gichtel became disenchanted with her.

Gichtel believed that the spiritual struggle was an individual one and he was even against conventicles.[97] While the Petersens and Lead believed in publicizing their insights, Gichtel wanted to keep divine mysteries secret.[98] Although he advised an extensive network of correspondents, Gichtel did not see the Angelic Brethren as a 'sect', and indeed it was only under the leadership of his successor, Johann Wilhelm Überfeld, that the Angelic Brethren developed into something more cohesive than a loose association.

Beyond these concerns, Gichtel may have simply felt threatened by Lead. He was incensed that Lead's writings were receiving more attention than those of the great Jacob Boehme. One reason for their different reception among German speakers was surely social rank: critics referred to Boehme derisively as a 'cobbler-theologian', and Gichtel was seen as a strange ne'er-do-well, while Lead was known for stemming from a 'noble house' (as was Merlau).[99]

Gichtel's letters to Fischer also reveal that Gichtel was disturbed at Lead's ability to garner patronage. He even accused the Petersens of prostituting themselves for her cause when they accepted Baron Knyphausen's financial assistance. However, the Baron aided nonconformists with a wide range of views and there is no evidence that he ever demanded adherence to particular doctrines. It is more likely that Gichtel was jealous of this support. Far from the ideal of a Philadelphian brotherhood of Christians from different backgrounds, Gichtel and others competed for funding and followers from the same limited pool of people interested in nonconformist religion. In other letters that he chose not to reprint in his published correspondence, but that remain preserved in archives, Gichtel urged potential patrons not to fund Quakers and others who, according to Gichtel, were well-meaning but wrong-headed.[100]

It was thus not only a 'devilish theology', but also psychological and practical factors at the root of Gichtel's break with Lead and the Petersens—jealousy over who would be Boehme's rightful 'heir', friction over religious forms, and competition for patronage.

CONCLUSION

When the 1710 edition of Gichtel's letters was published, the Lutheran periodical, *Unschuldige Nachrichten* ('Innocent Messages') reacted with glee that Lead, Gichtel and the Petersens were all fighting among themselves rather than living in 'Philadelphia'.[101] The mouthpiece of the Lutheran state church had long treated the three as part of the same camp, and indeed, Gichtel's letters reveal that for a time, they had all worked together toward a common cause. In its review, the journal wrote of Gichtel, 'He did indeed translate Lead's writings, but afterward they left a bad taste in his mouth'.[102]

It was, of course, not Gichtel himself, but a member of his community, Loth Fischer, who translated the texts, apparently with Gichtel's approval and under his guidance. Gichtel's support for the project was enthusiastic and multifaceted, from reading correction to distributing the texts within his network, and—if Gichtel is to be believed—even to stimulating Lead to produce a new text. It appears that Gichtel's probing questions contributed to Lead's controversial *Everlasting Gospel (Ewiges Evangelium)* and that this work in turn fed into Merlau Petersen's influential *Ewiges Evangelium*. Both works created shock waves in Pietist circles.

Beyond Gichtel's role in the publishing and distribution of Lead's texts, his correspondence suggests that Gichtel may have influenced Lead as much as Lead influenced him. Gichtel, Merlau and Lead were exchanging views on the divine Sophia, universal salvation and other tenets.[103] Thus, it may be more accurate to speak of a multi-party conversation than a dialogue. Furthermore, Gichtel's lack of fluency in English and Lead's lack of fluency in German made both of them reliant on Loth Fischer and others to translate and defend their ideas, adding yet another layer to these discussions.

The published correspondence of Johann Georg Gichtel reveals that Jane Lead's history on the continent began earlier and is more complex than is usually reflected in accounts that reduce her influence largely to one manuscript that fell into the Petersens' hands in 1695. The notion of a one-way transfer of ideas from Lead to the Petersens is also overly simplistic. Historians have long taken eighteenth-century spin control for fact. The Petersens' and Gichtel's own attempts to distance themselves from one another in the public eye have obscured Gichtel's role as a medium, transformer—and stimulant—of the thought of Jane Lead.

NOTES

* J.H. Feustking, *Gynaeceum Haeretico Fanaticum* (Frankfurt and Leipzig: Gottfried Zimmermann, 1704; reprinted, ed. E. Gössmann, Munich: iudicium verlag, 1998), p. 117.
1. Feustking, *Gynaeceum*, pp. 412–17.
2. G. Arnold, *Unparteyische Kirchen- und Ketzer-Historie* (2 vols., Frankfurt a.M.: Fritsch, 1699–1700).
3. P.P. Finauer, *Allgemeines Historisches Verzeichniß gelehrter Frauenzimmer* (Munich: Mayr, 1761), vol. 1, pp. 132–33. In seventeenth- and eighteenth-century German, the word 'Quäker' stood for fanaticism in general.
4. On Gichtel, see the following which include further sources: L. Martin, 'Jacob Boehme and the Anthropology of German Pietism', in Ariel Hessayon and Sarah Apetrei (eds.), *An Introduction to Jacob Boehme. Four Centuries of Thought and Reception* (New York: Routledge, 2014), pp. 120–41 (at 123–25); J.J. Seidel, 'Gichtelianer' in *Enyzklopädie der Neuzeit* (Stuttgart: Metzler, 2006), vol. 4, pp. 894–96; G. Zaepernick, 'Johann Georg Gichtels und seiner Nachfolger Briefwechsel mit den hallischen Pietisten, besonders mit A.M. Francke', *Pietismus und Neuzeit*, 8 (1982), pp. 74–118.
5. H. Schneider, 'Der radikale Pietismus im 17. Jahrhundert', in Martin Brecht et al. (eds.), *Geschichte des Pietismus* (4 vols., Göttingen: Vandenhoeck & Ruprecht, 1993), vol. 1, pp. 391–437 (at 415).
6. Gichtel, J.G. (ed.), *Des Gottseeligen Hoch-Erleuchteten Jacob Boehmens Teutonici Philosophi Alle Theosophische Wercke* (15 vols., Amsterdam: [n. pub.], 1682–83). Gichtel's followers put out subsequent expanded editions: Johann Otto Glüsing (ed.), *Theosophia Revelata* ([Hamburg]: [Holle], 1715); Johann Wilhelm Überfeld (ed.), *Theosophia Revelata* ([n. pub.], 1730).

7. Donald F. Durnbaugh, 'Jane Ward Lead (1624–1704) and the Philadelphians', in Carter Lindberg (ed.), *The Pietist Theologians* (Malden, MA: Blackwell Publishing, 2005), pp. 128–47, esp. 139–40.

8. In his study of the radical Pietist book market, Schrader shows that Philadelphian books were some of the most popular of the era. H.-J. Schrader, *Literaturproduktion und Büchermarkt des radikalen Pietismus: Johann Henrich Reitz', Historie der Wiedergebohrnen' und ihr geschichtlicher Kontext* (Göttingen: Vandenhoeck & Ruprecht, 1989).

9. Boehme's friend and biographer, Abraham von Franckenberg (1593–1652), included the ideal of 'Philadelphia' in his own writings. Paul Felgenhauer (1593-c.1677) also tried to gather a Philadelphian community near Bremen. Cf. H.-J. Schrader, *Literaturproduktion.*, pp. 375–76.

10. Schneider, 'Der radikale Pietismus im 17. Jahrhundert'; Schneider, 'Der radikale Pietismus im 18. Jahrhundert', in Brecht, vol. 2, pp. 107–97 (at 112–15).

11. Merlau was a well-known activist before her marriage and afterwards continued using her noble maiden name in her publications. This has led some researchers to call her 'Merlau', and others 'Petersen'. Here I refer to her as 'Merlau' before her marriage and 'Merlau Petersen' after she married.

12. See the articles by Schneider, cited above, and Thune, *Behmenists,* pp. 113–14; D.F. Durnbaugh, 'Jane Ward Lead'; D.F. Durnbaugh, 'Philadelphia-Bewegung', in Erwin Fahlbusch (ed.), *Evangelisches Kirchenlexikon* (3rd edn., Göttingen: Vandenhoeck & Ruprecht, 1992), vol. 3.

13. Jane Lead, *The Wonders of God's Creation Manifested, In the Variety of EIGHT WORLDS* (London: Sowle, 1695).

14. J.E. Petersen, *Leben Fr. Joh. Eleonora Petersen, [...] Von Ihr selbst mit eigener Hand aufgesetzet* (n.p.: n. pub., 1718), pp. 56ff.

15. J.W. Petersen, *Das Leben Jo. WILHELMI PETERSEN* (Halle: Renger, 1717), p. 297. Petersen writes, '[...] Lord Knyphausen sent us something from Mrs. Jane Leade in England that was still in hand-written form, which dealt with the Return of all Creatures [...]'. On Knyphausen's involvement, see Durnbaugh, 'Philadelphia-Bewegung'. The Petersens were also connected to Lead through other channels, although they do not reveal this in their autobiographies. In 1695 Francis Lee penned a preface for the English translation of J.W. Petersen's *Send-Schreiben an einige Theologos [...]* (n. pl.: n. pub, 1691): J[ohann] W[ilhelm] P[etersen], *A Letter to some Divines [...].* London: John Whitlock, 1695. These connections are explored by Ariel Hessayon earlier in this volume.

16. J.E. Petersen, *Leben,* pp. 41–42.

17. Lead, *EIGHT WORLDS,* unpaginated preface; cf. Thune, *Behmenists,* pp. 113–14. English Behmenist thought however was present before

Lead, for example through Thomas Bromley's *Der Weg zum Sabbath der Ruhe* (Amsterdam, 1685).

18. H.-G. Kemper, *Deutsche Lyrik der frühen Neuzeit* (Tübingen: Niemeyer, 1988), vol. 3, pp. 279–311 (at 282–87).

19. I cite primarily from the 1722 edition, which contains the most letters (883): J.G. Gichtel, *Theosophia practica Halten und Kämpfen* (7 vols., [Leiden]: [n. pub.], 1722). The letters are not chronological and it is unclear what principle underlies the ordering. Volume VII is a biography of Gichtel penned by one of his followers. The biography quotes from additional letters and also includes an appendix of letters from Gichtel to Johann Wilhelm Überfeld ('Zugabe zum Lebens=Lauf', 367–468). I also cite the 1710 edition, which includes some information deleted in later editions: Gichtel, *Erbauliche Theosophische Send-Schreiben* (Bethulia [invented]: n.pub., 1710). In citing Gichtel's works, I abbreviate the *Theosophische Send-Schreiben* of 1710 as 'TS' and the *Theosophia Practica* of 1722 as 'TP', along with the volume number. Editions of the correspondence were published in 1700, 1701, 1708, and 1710, as well as an edition with no date; some editions carried the title *Erbauliche Theosophia practica*.

20. Some original letters from Gichtel survive in archives and are cited where relevant.

21. Merlau lodged with Maria Juliana Baur von Eyseneck. Merlau and Eyseneck hosted the meetings in the latter's home. R. Albrecht, *Johanna Eleonora Petersen: Theologische Schriftstellerin des frühen Pietismus* (Göttingen: Vandenhoeck & Ruprecht, 2005), pp. 65–78; A. Deppermann, *Johann Jakob Schütz und die Anfänge des Pietismus* (Tübingen: Mohr Siebeck, 2002), pp. 81–125.

22. Deppermann, *Schütz*, pp. 78–79, 243, 139, 313, 330. In most documents the investment company is called the 'Pennsylvania Company', but since Francis Daniel Pastorius, who managed the enterprise, referred to it as the 'Frankfurt Company', researchers have adopted this usage. Gichtel himself rejected the plan to go to Pennsylvania, writing, 'I fear that Babylon is there where I am' (in a 1709 letter to Überfeld, TP VII: 454).

23. R. Albrecht, 'Zum Briefwechsel Johann Georg Gichtels mit Johanna Eleonora Petersen', in W. Breul, M. Meier, L. Vogel (eds), *Der radikale Pietismus: Perspektiven der Forschung* (Göttingen: Vandenhoeck & Ruprecht, 2010), pp. 327–60.

24. TS II: 184–86; TS III: 32–35; TS III: 35–36; TP I: 87–94; TP II: 1310–11.

25. TP I: 92–94; TP III: 1950–51. L. Martin, 'Female Reformers as the Gate Keepers of Pietism: The Example of Johanna Eleonora Merlau and

William Penn', *Monatshefte* 95:1 (2003), pp. 33–58; Albrecht, 'Briefwechsel', pp. 335–36.

26. TS III, 54–65, at 64 (dated 17 January 1693); Albrecht, 'Briefwechsel', p. 338.

27. TP III, 1899–1902; TS III, 37–40 (addressed to both Petersens, 11 January 1691). There are indications, discussed below, that the correspondence may have continued beyond 1680.

28. TS IV: 586–94; TS III: 66–67; 82–86.

29. TS III: 65.

30. TP III, 1901–02; TP III, to J.E. Merlau Petersen, 27 January 1693: 1917–29, esp. 1918–19.

31. TS III: 54–109; TP III: 1917–29.

32. 27 January 1693: TP III: 1917–29, esp. 1924; TS III: 54–65, esp. 61.

33. To both Petersens, 19 February 1693: TP III: 1931–38, at 1934; TS III: 67–74, at 70. On Boehme: TS III: 76–78; 88.

34. TP III: 1917–29, at 1924 (27 January 1693).

35. TP VII: 109–12.

36. On these friends, see for example, TS III: 126–28; TP III, 1991–93. There were nine letters to Merlau Petersen and one to her husband in 1694: TS III: 109–33; TP III: 1974–98.

37. TS III: 100–01, 129; TP III: 1993–97, at 1994–95.

38. TS III: 128–32, esp. 130.

39. Thune was aware of some of Gichtel's comments about Lead in his letters, but did not know to whom they were addressed, since most of the recipients' names are encoded; see Thune, *Behmenists*, pp. 111–12.

40. TS III: 132–33 (24 September 1694); TP III: 1997–98.

41. J.W. Petersen. *Leben*, p. 299.

42. TS II: 111–20.

43. Jane Lead, *Offenbahrung der Offenbahrungen* (Amsterdam: Wettstein, 1695), a translation of Jane Lead, *The Revelation of Revelations* (London: Sowle, 1683).

44. TS II: 126–33, esp. 132–33. Compare Albrecht, 'Briefwechsel', pp. 352–53.

45. TS II: 126–33, at 132–33.

46. TS II: 136–43, at 142.

47. TP I: 121–28; 213–34.

48. TP I: 124–28 at 125–26 (20 September 1683).

49. TP I: 213–21, at 217 (dated simply 1695).

50. TP I: 221–30 (3 October 1696).

51. TP I: 221–30 (3 October 1696); cf. TP VII: 328.

52. He later repeats and refines these arguments, for example, in a letter from 1697: TP V: 3131.

53. TP I: 224–25.
54. Throughout the letters, Gichtel complains in particular about Alhart de Raedt, who helped to edit Boehme's writings but then fell out with Gichtel.
55. TP I: 225.
56. TP I: 226.
57. TP I: 227–30.
58. TP I: 230–31.
59. TP I: 231. Without further evidence it is impossible to identify 'K.' conclusively. The different editors of Gichtel's correspondence masked people's identities in different ways. Some used initials, while others simply used 'N.' for all, so that the letters have to be carefully studied and cross-referenced for identification.
60. Jane Lead, *EIN GARTEN-BRUNN [...] oder Ein rechtes DIARIUM* (Amsterdam: n. pub., 1697).
61. TP I: 231–32. Gichtel's evident fear and loathing of women have led some researchers to conjecture that he may have been homosexual. Martin, 'Anthropology', 124–25. On his attitudes toward sexuality, cf. Aira Võsa, 'Johann Georg Gichtels Verhältnis zum anderen Geschlecht in Leben und Lehre', in Breul et al. (eds), *Der radikale Pietismus*, pp. 361–68.
62. TP I: 233; Lead, *Offenbahrung der Offenbahrungen;* Jane Lead, *Die nun brechende und sich zertheilende himmlische Wolcke* (Amsterdam: H. Wetstein, 1694); a translation of Jane Lead, *Heavenly Cloud Now Breaking* (London: n. pub., 1681).
63. See for example a letter to J.E. Merlau Petersen, dated 27 January 1693 (TP III: 1917–29).
64. TP V: 3719–25 (3 August 1706).
65. TP V: 3687–99, at 3693 (Gichtel to Johann Friederich Schultz, 10 October 1705).
66. TP III: 2000 (Gichtel to Theodor Schermer, May 1699).
67. TP I: 325 (11 September 1697).
68. Jane Lead, *Eine Offenbarung der Bottschafft des EWIGEN EVANGELII* (Amsterdam: n. pub., 1697); a translation of Jane Lead, *A Revelation of the Everlasting Gospel Message* (London: n. pub., 1697). Gichtel repeated this assertion often: TP V: 3699–3712 (29 December 1705); TP V: 3731–34 (4 February 1707); TP V: 3784–92, esp. 3787–88 (6 January 1708).
69. TP VI: 1463 (Gichtel to George Vechtmann, 25 February 1702); TP VI: 1667 (25 February 1707); TP III: 2444–48 (Gichtel to Friedrich Andreae, 3 January 1708); TP VII: 328; TP V: 3739–42 at 3741 (1 April 1707); TP V: 3644–53, esp. 3650 (17 July 1708).

70. TP III: 2430 (Gichtel to Friedrich Andreae, 3 November 1705); TP III: 2437 (Gichtel to Friedrich Andreae, 8 February 1707); compare also: TP V: 3835–38, at 3836 (14 May 1709).
71. For example: TP V: 3792–3800 (31 January 1708).
72. The books were *Heavenly Cloud* and *The Revelation of Revelations*. TP V: 3540–41 (24 December 1706).
73. TP V: 3536–44, at 3541 (24 December 1706).
74. Lead, *The Revelation of Revelations*. This account according to Gichtel's biography (TP VII: 326–27).
75. TP VII: 328.
76. J.W. Petersen, *Leben*, pp. 219; 235–36.
77. TP V: 3536–44, at 3541 (24 December 1706); TP V: 3650 (17 July 1708); TP VIII: 329.
78. TP V: 3699–3712 (29 December 1705).
79. TP V, 3699–3712, at 3706–07 (29 December 1705).
80. TP V: 3739–42, at 3741–2 (1 April 1707). Elsewhere Gichtel refers to 400 guilders (*Gulden*): TP VII: 328.
81. TP V: 3784–92, esp. 3787 (6 January 1708). As the imprint is Amsterdam, the connection to Utrecht is unclear.
82. TP I: 412ff (6 December 1701).
83. TP VII: 329.
84. TP V: 3853–55.
85. TP VII, 'Zugabe zum Lebenslauf', 465–66.
86. There are hints of unpublished letters. Gichtel's biography refers to interactions not mentioned in the published letters. For instance, Gichtel mentions that Merlau wrote a letter of recommendation for his former housekeeper to get a position in Frankfurt (TP VIII: 134). Cf: Albrecht, 'Briefwechsel', pp. 336–37.
87. J.W. Petersen, *Leben*, p. 338.
88. TP III, 1897–98 (Gichtel to Christoph Krausemarck, 8 February 1696); J.W. Petersen, *Leben*, pp. 336–37.
89. J.W. Petersen, *Leben*, pp. 336–37.
90. [J.E. Merlau Petersen], *Das Ewige Evangelium der Allgemeinen Wiederbringung* (n.pl.: n.pub., 1698); Lead, *Bottschafft des EWIGEN EVANGELII* (translation of *Everlasting Gospel*).
91. Historians over the years variously attributed it to one or the other of the Petersens, but Ruth Albrecht has proven conclusively that Merlau Petersen was the author; see, Albrecht, *Petersen*, pp. 274–95 (esp. 279–80).
92. Albrecht, *Petersen*, pp. 293–94.
93. In 1701 Merlau Petersen wrote yet another anonymous text defending the first one: [J.E. Merlau Petersen], *Bewährung des Ewigen Evangelii* (n.

pl.: n. pub., 1701). The Petersens would expand on the concept in numerous other tracts.

94. That is, a 'Mit-Gliede D.Ph.G.' The defence text of 1701, *Bewährung des Ewigen Evangelii*, includes a similar cryptogram ('E.M.G.D.P.G.' = ein Mitglied der Philadelphischen Gemeinde).
95. FbG, Chart A 297, p. 86f.
96. See esp. TP III, 1997–98.
97. TP V: 3224–38, at 3233–34 (likely to Andreas Morell, dated anno 1697).
98. See for example: TP VII: 148.
99. Merlau's family entered the lower aristocracy when an ancestor was knighted, while Lead belonged to the gentry. The German word 'adlig' refers both to the gentry and the aristocracy, which may explain why Germans, including Gichtel, seem to have had an inflated understanding of Lead's social rank.
100. Archive of the Franckesche Stiftungen in Halle: D 60, 101ff., esp. 107r-08v. Martin, 'Anthropology', p. 124.
101. *Unschuldige Nachrichten von Alten und Neuen Theologischen Sachen* (Leipzig, 1710), pp. 569–74, 641–50.
102. *Unschuldige Nachrichten*, p. 574.
103. For example, see TP III, 1912–17.

CHAPTER 10

Philadelphia Resurrected: Celebrating the Union Act (1707) from Irenic to Scatological Eschatology*

Lionel Laborie

INTRODUCTION

The Philadelphian Society is often assumed to have collapsed at the death of their matriarchal leader Jane Lead in 1704.[1] The loss of a charismatic leader typically entails that of a clear spiritual guidance and consequently opens room for internal rivalries and divisions. Many of Lead's most prominent followers actually outlived her by an entire generation and remained spiritually active both within and outside the remains of the Philadelphian Society, a period that has received little attention thus far. This chapter, therefore, aims to shed some light upon this comparatively lesser known period through close examination of the Philadelphians' involvement with the millenarian movement of the notorious French Prophets. It picks up from the end of Ariel Hessayon's Chap. 4 to explore their union with the Prophets at Baldwin's Gardens in 1707 and then traces that relationship after their separation until Richard Roach's death in 1730. Based on new archival and prosopographical research, it seeks to give a better sense of

L. Laborie (✉)
Goldsmiths, University of London, London, UK

© The Editor(s) (if applicable) and The Author(s) 2016
A. Hessayon (ed.), *Jane Lead and her Transnational Legacy*,
DOI 10.1057/978-1-137-39614-3_10

213

who the Philadelphians actually were. Overall, this chapter argues that the Philadelphians joined the Camisards as part of their celebrations of the Union Act and that the two societies mutually influenced one another in preparation for Christ's Second Coming.

PHILADELPHIA IN RUINS

The Philadelphian Society for the Advancement of Divine Philosophy, named after the sixth church of Revelation 3:7–13, was founded as a private religious society and subsequently became a public movement. Yet by 1703, one year before Lead's death, the Society was already dormant, having failed to fulfil its original promises. Ever since its inception, the Society had aimed to reconcile English Protestant denominations into a Universal Church ahead of Christ's Second Coming, which Thomas Beverley had predicted would begin in 1697.[2] As they opened to the public that year, the Philadelphians proclaimed their irenic mission to the wider world: 'This Spirit is Catholick: and thence the Church must also be Catholick [...] The Design of our Assembling is not to Divide, but to Unite; Not to set up for a New Religion, or Church, but to keep warm the Spirit of Love towards those of all Religions and Churches; [...] Catholick Love and Apostolical Faith, are the two Grand Pillars of our Society'.[3] Although using 'catholic' in its etymological sense of 'universal' here, the untimeliness of such terminology within years of the Glorious Revolution could not but spark immediate hostility. Not only was William III at war against France and the fear of a universal monarchy, but the Philadelphians had strong continental support. Some key members like Francis Lee were even nonjurors.[4] The Society's public assemblies, its *Theosophical Transactions*, the works by Lead and others, clearly failed to debunk accusations of separatism. Consequently the Philadelphians were largely dismissed as antinomian Sweet Singers of Israel, Familists or radical Quakers and sectarians.[5]

Despite six years of prolific public activity, the Philadelphians never formed a cohesive movement, their Society being plagued by internal tensions from the beginning. Lead herself was no stranger to these tensions. A prominent matriarchal figure for some, Lead proved more controversial for others. Indeed, most Philadelphians refused to support Lead's public testimony in 1697.[6] According to Richard Roach, one of the few with Lee who followed her to Hoxton, the Society subsequently divided between four millenarian ethe or 'talents': those focusing on love and charity ahead of the Second Coming were based at Baldwin's Gardens in the parish of St Andrew's, Holborn. A second, more dispersed group celebrated the passive power of the Gospel and worked on reviving primitive Christianity through the gift of inspiration. Some of these held public meetings in Hungerford Market, but closed after six months due to popular protests and violence. The Bow Lane group proved more radical, in the etymological sense of the term, that is they 'stemmed from a harsher root'—i.e., Quakers— but their ardour had been moderated and improved by their exposure to the other three talents. The fourth and last group had followed Lead to Westmoreland House, Twisters Alley, Loriners' Hall and finally Hoxton. They were more contemplative and concentrated on the advent of the Virgin Sophia, God's bride and the mother of all, who would usher in the restitution of all things. Thus, the Philadelphian Society already faced severe divisions as soon as it opened itself to the public in 1697. The failure of their irenic experiment was rapidly mocked in the press.[7]

If Hoxton was the mother group and public face of the Society, the houses of Anne Bathurst and Joanna Oxenbridge in Baldwin's Gardens remained the most dynamic, albeit private, nodes.[8] Philadelphians assembled separately thereafter, but continued to communicate. Efforts were repeatedly made on both sides to reconcile the Society into united assemblies, especially after the death of Dr Murray, which was perceived as 'a Lamb of sacrifice for ye Division & Contentions of those among whom he stood in a peaceful reconciling Spirit'.[9] Roach seemed particularly concerned about unity and reconciliation, and portrayed himself as the middle man between the remaining Philadelphian branches. He offered with Lee's support to leave aside contentious issues to concentrate instead on the fraternal beliefs and values shared by all.[10] His efforts, however, did not pay off.

On 9 June 1703, as they entered their seventh year of public existence, Lead announced to her disciples that the time had come to withdraw from public engagement to celebrate their Sabbath.[11] The Hoxton group ceased their activities three days later. The following year, in June 1704, Caleb Gilman, Mr Pitkin and Mr Forester invited Roach to return to Baldwin's Gardens but the latter refused because their outreach excluded the remaining Hoxton brethren.[12] The Philadelphians had lost prominent irenic figures such as Dr Murray, Dr Gilman and Anne Bathurst in the preceding months. Lead's death in August 1704 effectively left Philadelphia in ruins. Roach was ordered by the Spirit to pursue her mission, at which point he left Hoxton and moved to Joanna Oxenbridge's in Baldwin's Gardens.

If Lead's death sealed the Philadelphians' first and chaotic ministry, the Society nevertheless expected its glorious revival in 1707. The period of silence or 'mystical death' ordered by Lead in June 1703 was to last three and a half years and therefore placed considerable hopes for the beginning of 1707. Lead's prediction was based on the resurrection of the two witnesses (Revelation 11:3) and their ascension to Heaven. It proclaimed an age of peace and unity to be brought forward by a resurrected Philadelphian Society. Yet the Philadelphians' mystical resurrection also depended upon favourable conjunctures. Central to these was the political context in England and more generally the balance of power in Europe. In the early 1700s, virtually the whole of Europe was engaged in the War of the Spanish Succession (1701–14). The Allies, led by a Protestant, Anglo-Dutch coalition, were united against Louis XIV's expansionist policy and his support of a Jacobite restoration in England. Attempts for a deeper political integration between England and Scotland became a priority under Queen Anne. Negotiations officially began in 1705 and resulted in the Union Act of 1707, which gave birth to Great Britain and was to prove fundamental to the rapprochement between the Philadelphians and the Camisards.[13]

The Camisards in London

Meanwhile, three prophets had arrived in London from southern France in the summer of 1706, just as the Philadelphians in Baldwin's Gardens prepared for their mystical resurrection. Durand Fage (fl. 1681–1717), Jean Cavalier (fl. 1686–1740) and Elie Marion (1678–1713) were refugees from the Camisard rebellion (1702–1710) in Languedoc, which broke out at the beginning of the War of the Spanish Succession (1701–1714). The Camisards were radical Calvinist peasants fighting for the restoration of the Edict of Nantes and freedom of worship after decades of state persecution. Trapped in the Cévennes mountains and reluctant to flee their homeland, the Camisards had embraced the belief in martyrdom and taken up arms to fight the final battle against Rome, the 'Whore of Babylon'. They claimed to be directly inspired by the Holy Ghost and insisted on that basis that their leaders were also their most charismatic prophets.[14] The three refugees may have been second-rank Camisard prophets, but they nevertheless gave birth to a small religious circle in England, prophesying the end of the temporal world in violent agitations just months before the Philadelphian rebirth.

Two parallel millenarian movements, one English, one French, were thus about to emerge at the beginning of 1707. The Camisards had been causing great controversy within the London Huguenot community in the preceding months.[15] They were more active and public in their approach and probably also perceived as more threatening to the social order. They first came to the attention of the Philadelphians on 17 January 1707, and were discussed at greater length in Baldwin's Gardens 10 days later.[16] Although there is no evidence that the Philadelphians attended the Camisards' assemblies before the spring, earlier contacts seem very likely. How the two movements came into contact is unclear, but several hypotheses can nevertheless be formulated.

Nicolas Fatio de Duillier (1664–1753), one of the Camisards' earliest and most prominent supporters, almost certainly played a pivotal role in this transnational millenarian encounter. As a Swiss national and a Fellow of the Royal Society, Fatio had navigated between Huguenot and English circles since his arrival in England in 1687 and also maintained numerous contacts with the continent. He corresponded on religious matters with his relatives the Hubers, a Swiss Pietist family based in Lyon who had hosted the Camisard Durand Fage on his way to London, and he tutored among the Huguenot neighbourhood of Spitalfields.[17] Fatio also knew Sir Richard Bulkeley (1660–1710), the first anglophone follower of the Camisards, from the Royal Society and he stayed at Dr James Keith's on Red Lion Square in Holborn in June 1706, only a short walk to Baldwin's Gardens.[18]

Keith (d. 1726) became a member of the Royal College of Physicians three months later and, as a Scottish Quietist, may likewise have introduced the Camisards to the Philadelphians. Indeed, Keith had maintained religious ties with the continent, corresponding with Mme Guyon and acting as Pierre Poiret's main contact for the distribution of the works of the Flemish mystic Antoinette Bourignon (1616–1680) in England.[19] He visited Roach in January 1707 and his medical colleagues James Craven and Daniel Critchlow were prominent figures within the Philadelphian Society. Moreover, Keith had been John Lacy's family physician since 1705, shortly before the latter became the most notorious member of the French Prophets.[20] Lacy himself had joined the Camisards towards the end of 1706. It was consequently no coincidence if, along with Lacy and Bulkeley, Keith was among the first British targets of the Huguenot rioters protesting against the French Prophets on 25 April 1707.[21]

François-Maximilien Misson (c.1650–1722), the travel writer of international fame for his *Nouveau voyage d'Italie* (1691), may have been the third connection between the Camisards and the Philadelphians. He shared with Roach a common friendship with the German Pietist minister Heinrich Wilhelm Ludolf (1655–1712), court chaplain in London since 1705, who incidentally had provided the first known foreign account of pneumatic inspirations in the Cévennes before the outbreak of the rebellion.[22] Misson started collecting the testimonies of refugees from Languedoc and Dauphiné in September 1706 in order to accredit the existence of supernatural manifestations during the Camisards' rebellion. He compiled these testimonies throughout the winter of 1706–07 and had them simultaneously translated into English by Lacy. Their collaboration appeared in April as *Le Théâtre sacré des Cévennes* and *A Cry from the Desart*, which sparked the public outcry against those who became known as 'French Prophets'.[23]

All of these figures were acquainted by 1706 prior to the Camisards' arrival in London, whose private assemblies seemed to prefigure the Philadelphians' resurrection. Although Roach himself did not meet the prophet Elie Marion until 7 March 1707, the Camisards were already attracting attention among Philadelphians before that date.[24] Their emergence in England three and a half years or so after the suspension of the Philadelphians' public ministry in Hoxton and the concurrence of favourable astrological and political conjunctures only seemed to reinforce the Philadelphians in their imminent mystical resurrection. On 21 January 1707, Roach witnessed Scottish MPs coming to pass the Union Act; he noted the presence of several Jews on that occasion and discussed the Camisard Prophets with Charles Bridges in favourable terms over dinner that evening.[25]

MYSTICAL UNION

The Union Act came into effect on 1 May 1707 and was celebrated by the Philadelphians as a temporal sanction of their mystical resurrection. After a first testimony in 'Saccloth & Ashes, in Suffering & Contempt', the time for love and reconciliation had now arrived.[26] Their first meeting was held in Roach's chamber in James Jackson's house in Baldwin's Gardens on 6 April 1707 in the presence of James Craven, Jackson, William Clere (or Clare), Sarah Wiltshire and Roach's niece Mary Laughton. The venue itself reflected this ecumenical outreach: Roach, Anglican minister and self-proclaimed mediator between the four Philadelphian 'talents' described above, hosted the meeting with his Quaker landlord Jackson. With the collapse of the Hoxton meetings and Francis Lee's subsequent disengagement from the group, Baldwin's Gardens became the heart of the new Philadelphian assemblies.[27] Participants fasted, shared their dreams and visions, and above all sang hymns; they also discussed the Camisards' ministry and freshly published writings.[28]

A few weeks later, on 28 May, the widow Rebecca Critchlow opened her house, also in Baldwin's Gardens, where many Philadelphians attended on that occasion.[29] More Quakers—possibly of the Bow Lane group—joined the meetings over the following days, but it was not until 3 June that the resurrected Philadelphians—Richard Roach, his mother and his cousin, Mrs Cook and her two daughters, Mrs Ashley, William King, Mrs Wells and Mr Kemp—and the Camisards held their foundational assembly. The choice of Whit Sunday for the opening of their joint ministry was in itself highly symbolical: it nourished hopes that their union would become even greater than Britain's. As a sign of fraternal love, the French Prophet Jean Allut was ordered by the Holy Spirit to embrace his Philadelphian brethren one by one.[30] For a year or so, Camisards and Philadelphians celebrated their union, which they understood as preliminary to the Second Coming. Further assemblies were held in Hoxton, probably at Roach's mother's, Anne, with whom the Camisards seemed keen to engage, but the houses of Abraham Whitrow, Thomas Dutton, Peter Cuff and Francis Moult in Hatton Garden became prime locations for their meetings.[31] Situated a stone's throw from Baldwin's Gardens, these assemblies provided the Camisards with a steady influx of British mystics who soon represented the majority of their followers; their binational, ecumenical movement became known as the 'French Prophets' in reference to their origins rather than composition.

The rise and energy of the French Prophets was perceived as a powerful new force in Baldwin's Gardens, especially as the former engaged in miraculous cures from the summer 1707. The practice of healing proved equally important to both societies, albeit for different reasons. The former emphasised miraculous cures as evidence of the Spirit's presence among them and a sign of the imminent Second Coming. The latter, on the other hand, valued healings for its compassionate, apokatastic nature insofar as it restored the body to its original state of creation. Wonders were, therefore, expected from both sides. The Philadelphian Mrs Wells declared she had been cured upon leaving the foundational meeting with the Camisards on Whit Sunday; John Lacy allegedly removed a tumour from the throat of the young Philadelphian Prophetess Elizabeth Gray in

August; James Jackson recovered from his blindness in November and Mr Spong was likewise healed in December.[32] Several Philadelphians—Mary Laughton, Mrs Kemp, Elizabeth Blandford's eldest granddaughter and Mr Bondelin (or Bondeling)—all became inspired by the Spirit in the summer 1707.[33] Laughton and Peter Cuff even experienced the notorious agitations of the Camisards, much to the admiration of the Philadelphians, who saw in these ecstatic trances a natural expression of joy instilled by God.[34] The two religious societies continued to celebrate their union in music and harmony in a typically Philadelphian fashion, henceforth singing in both French and English for the opening of Sophia's gates.[35]

If the Camisards' arrival proved timely and promising at first sight for the Philadelphians' second testimony, the two societies nonetheless diverged in their millenarian aspirations. The former were refugees from the last French war of religion; they had taken up arms against Catholic oppression and had seen thousands of their brethren suffer martyrdom to defend their faith. They understood their persecution as a divine trial in the latter days, hence their strong emphasis on repentance ahead of God's Judgement. Their original intent when reaching England had been to raise an army of Huguenot refugees to resume the war in the Cévennes. The Philadelphians, by contrast, united Oxford-educated men with female mystics and showed little interest in the temporal world. They reached out to other denominations to promote a spirit of brotherly love, peace and charity across Christendom. Despite their diverging aspirations, these two millenarian world views were by no means mutually exclusive, but instead complementary.[36] Although they may not have realised it at first, the Camisards proved indispensable to the fulfilment of the Philadelphians' resurrection. Roach and his brethren of Baldwin's Gardens originally anticipated the return of the prophet Elias as a prerequisite for Christ's Second Coming. Elias—Elijah in Hebrew—was the harbinger of the Messiah (Malachi 4:5); he warned against the severity of the Lord's judgement, but also promised his forgiveness and miracles, and symbolised for this reason the transition from the Camisards' punitive warnings to the Philadelphians' merciful outreach. Just as he had preceded the physical Christ through the ministry of John the Baptist, Elias was expected to return before the Parousia.[37] John Mason and Thomas Moor both proclaimed themselves to embody this second Elias in 1694 and 1697, when the Philadelphian Society opened to the public.[38] Yet it was not till 1707 that the Philadelphians of Baldwin's Gardens found in the Camisard Elie Marion the true Elias blowing the seventh trumpet of God's wrath, based on his first name and in accordance with Lead's prediction. Marion himself made no such claim, even though he exhorted his audience to repent and reached out to Jews and heathens to convert them to Christianity ahead of the Parousia. Both societies fulfilled, in Roach's view, a complementary ministry, with the Camisards brandishing the threat of Christ's imminent, punitive Judgement and the Philadelphians emphasising his eternal mercifulness. By their own admission, they saw in the Camisards an outward medium for the expression of their inward inspirations. Yet it was also clear to Roach that their ministry was meant to disappear in order to give way to the advent of the Philadelphian reign.[39]

Beyond the immediate union of two societies of complementary ministries, it was the ultimate apokatastic promise that the Philadelphians were aspiring to. For the fulfilment of Christ's Second Coming required the conversion of the Jews and the reconciliation of Christian denominations into a universal Church. If Marion brandished the threat of a punitive God to coerce Jews and infidels into Christianity as the new Elias, the Philadelphians' irenic message offered a merciful counterpart to the French Prophets' ecumenical outreach. This extended first and foremost to the Quakers, as well as to Presbyterians and even the disciples of John Mason, among whom Roach recognised some presence of the Spirit.[40] Under the Philadelphians' influence, the Camisards began to attract a wider, heterogeneous audience. On 2 January 1709, the French Prophets gathered 200 people from seven denominations in Jackson's house in Baldwin's Gardens, possibly in commemoration of the seven Churches of Revelation.[41]

Such was the Philadelphians' dedication to the Camisards that Roach attempted to defend Elie Marion and his two scribes—Nicolas Fatio and Jean Daudé—before the Queen's Bench when they were charged with blasphemy and seditious libel following the publication of Marion's *Prophetical Warnings* in April 1707.[42] From the very beginning of their transnational union, Camisards and Philadelphians faced temporal obstacles to their mystical ambitions. For if the two societies embraced a different millenarian ethos, it made no doubt to Roach that the Camisards represented the first step toward the resurrection of the Philadelphian society as a whole and ultimately for the advent of the Virgin Sophia. They provided in other words the cement needed to rebuild upon the ruins of Philadelphia. Roach's remaining Hoxton coreligionists—Lee, Mr Knight and Mr Woodruff—warned him on the contrary that the judgement would soon fall upon the Philadelphians if they did not pray.[43] But

Roach wrote to Lord chief justice John Holt on 24 May 1707 and met with Marion the same evening. He considered defending him and his two scribes in court, but instead gave his instructions to Sergeant John Hooke (1655–1712) and attended the verdict on 4 July. Marion blessed him a few weeks later but, despite Roach's efforts, the three men were found guilty and were exposed on the scaffold on 1 and 2 December 1707.[44]

Roach saw in the Camisards' ordeal a sacrifice that further substantiated the Philadelphians' anticipation of the new Elias at the time the temporal opposition to the French Prophets reached its climax. Undeterred by what they had accepted as a divine trial, the Prophets entered a new phase by the beginning of 1708 under the impetus of their English members. The Socinian-turned-French Prophet and physician Dr Thomas Emes had died on 22 December 1707, and was buried on Christmas Day; soon afterwards his brethren had announced through the mouth of John Potter that he would rise from the dead five months later, on 25 May 1708. That Marion, Fage, Daudé and Fatio stayed away from such predictions already prefigured the growing national divide between the Camisards and their English followers. Only the latter (i.e., Lacy, Potter, Gray, King, Whitrow) engaged without restraint in promoting the miracle, with Lacy at the forefront healing the sick and poor in the meantime. Still, the Spirit speaking through Whitrow designated the old French Philadelphian Mary Sterrell to 'accompany the Body of my servant Emes who now sleepeth, even to his own Door'.[45] For Roach, the beginning of 1708 therefore marked the foundation of the universal church; Philadelphians, Camisards and some Quakers celebrated their union in a spirit of love, reconciliation and harmony ahead of Christ's imminent Second Coming.[46]

The Philadelphians' commitment in favour of the Camisards also reflected the shifting political situation in Europe. Beside the recent union between England and Scotland and that of the two East India Companies the following year, Philadelphians had their eyes turned towards France like the rest of their fellow countrymen.[47] Roach in particular celebrated the recent victories of the Duke of Marlborough—Blenheim (1704), Ramillies (1706)—and Heinsius's progress against France in his diary.[48] Yet his proximity to the Camisards also raised Francis Lee's suspicions that the Prophets might be disguised Papists, even though Roach insisted that their messianism had nothing to do with Louis XIV's universal monarchy.[49] On the contrary, as an avid reader of Jacob Boehme's theosophy, Roach saw in the heraldic symbolism of the lily a sign that France was the chosen country for the restoration of all things, which Marion had accordingly been designated to initiate as the new Elias. France represented in his view 'ye Kindom of ye Lily. Female. Effeminate. Talkative. Free in Love [...] therefore France [...] opens ye present Disp[ensation]'.[50] In Behmenist terms, the lily was a symbol of revival and wholesomeness; it also featured as the saviour against the Holy Roman Empire in the visions of Mikuláš Drabik (1588–1671) during the Thirty Years War, which Roach also believed would soon be fulfilled.[51]

Another sign of the restorative nature of the French Prophets' movement can be found in the gender balance between the followers. If their leading figures hitherto mentioned were all male, some of their most charismatic members were indeed women. With the exception of Jeanne Cavalier (née Verduron), Henriette Allut and Jeanne Raoux (who had found refuge in England before the rebellion in the Cévennes), the majority of these charismatic prophetesses were actually English and close to Baldwin's Gardens. Central to Boehme's doctrine of the apokatastasis was the rehabilitation of the female condition before the restitution of all things to their prelapsarian state. Signs of female redemption were read by some in England's recent political history: the Glorious Revolution had not only replaced the Catholic king with a Protestant one, but had also introduced the dual reign of William and Mary. Moreover, England's political union with Scotland meant Britain was now governed by a female monarch, Queen Anne.[52] In addition to praising France as an effeminate nation due to restore the female condition through Elias, Roach believed the 'Mystery of ye Lily' once announced by Lead herself prefigured 'the Day of ye Mother' before 'the Second Birth of Christ'. He traced the rise of a female embassy in the Philadelphians' genealogy right from the beginning with the widow Mary Freeman, whom John Pordage had married for her exceptional spiritual gifts. After her death Pordage had opened his house to Jane Lead, who embodied the Philadelphian matriarch 30 years later. Other prominent women emerged in their movement around that time, such as Anne Bathurst, Joanna Oxenbridge and Rebecca Critchlow.[53] Unlike Lead, who depended upon the financial support of Pordage and Baron Dodo von Knyphausen, they provided material structure and stability to their community by hosting assemblies in their houses in Baldwin's Gardens. They acted in this respect like the 'mothers in Israel' among Quakers; that is a well-established matriarchal figure nurturing the community.[54] Whatever their role, all these women were or became widows relatively early after joining the Philadelphians and embodied to some extent the female emancipation from male authority.

A similar pattern of charismatic female ministry can be observed among the French Prophets from the summer 1707, when the Camisards merged with the Baldwin's Gardens Philadelphians and some Quakers. Five of these prophetesses even claimed to be the woman clothed with the sun from Revelation 12:1.[55] Teenage girls and young women such as Elizabeth Gray, Ann Topham, Mary Turner and Mary Keimer were known to vocalise the Holy Spirit and enact Biblical allegories. Gray, for example, performed the fall of the whore of Babylon by exposing her naked body on the altar of the Catholic chapel of Duke Street in November 1707, while Keimer trod on a woman's body to crush the wicked as part of the same performance.[56] Both were promised a glorious future among the Prophets: Gray later had children with Lacy anticipating to give birth to the second messiah; Keimer was designated to deliver a warning to Louis XIV in Versailles and later led a prophetic mission to Pennsylvania.[57] If Keimer's association with the Philadelphians remains unclear, Gray's was established by 1702 while others' leave little doubt. Sarah Wiltshire, possibly a widow, became a charismatic figure among the French Prophets, while Dinah Stoddart, another widow, proclaimed herself the 'Saviour of Womankind'.[58] More controversial was Rebecca Cuff, wife of the Baldwin's Gardens prophet Peter Cuff, who was notorious for roaring warnings and kissing men under inspiration during public assemblies.[59] But by far the most outward manifestation of female authority lay in the case of Dorothy Harling—yet another widow—who presented herself as the 'Permanent Spring'. Her notorious performances effectively conflated the punitive and the restorative into an explicit position of sadistic and scatological domination: 'Permanent Spring' demanded public confessions from her brethren, whereupon she allegedly flogged them 'with a Whip knotted, with sharp Needles or Pins fastned thereto', then lifted her skirt screaming 'Come in Christ, come in,—Come in Christ, come in' before urinating on their wounds to purify them. An early candidate for such punishment was the Philadelphian William Spong, who suffered Harling's domination after confessing his adultery. Similarly, Mary Sterrell, an old French widow, former Quaker and early Philadelphian figure, 'was so unmercifully whipp'd, that she could not sit for a long Time after'. Such displays of licentious or deviant behaviour may stem from what Roach presented as the third, radical Philadelphian talent in Bow Lane and was not unlike those of Mother Eva von Buttlar's community in Germany.[60] The Sweet Singers of Israel, whom Sarah Apetrei was able to trace in London until 1707, had a similar scandalous reputation and likely contributed to such controversial rituals because of their proximity with the Philadelphians, who remained publicly regarded as Familists in 1710.[61] Still, the French Prophets allowed no room for Philadelphian claims to female emancipation. Harling was excluded on 27 July 1709, but nevertheless continued her rituals of female domination with her own followers. In fact, she may have been the Mrs Harling who visited Richard Roach in 1722.[62] Sterrell, Wiltshire and Stoddart were likewise excluded from the Prophets around the same time. As John Lacy once put it: 'Womens Preaching as ordinary Ministers is one thing, and God speaking in his own name through their Organs is another.'[63]

The intense, albeit ephemeral, union of the Camisards with Baldwin's Gardens raises the question of the numbers of active Philadelphians in the post-Lead era. Paula McDowell claimed the Philadelphian Society counted around 100 followers in London.[64] While this number seems plausible, it remains unsubstantiated. Indeed, the lack of biographical and prosopographical information complicates matters. The list presented in the appendix, based on Roach's papers, the French Prophets' records and contemporary accounts, suggests that some 70 Philadelphians joined or at least interacted with the Prophets during their second testimony prophesied by Lead. Of these more than a third were women, including many widows. Several prominent Philadelphian families like the Cravens, Critchlows, Cuffs, Gilmans, Maddoxes, Spongs and Whitrows also joined the French Prophets early in summer 1707.[65] These Philadelphians were often blessed by the French Prophets during their joint assemblies in 1707 and 1708 as a sign of their election.

The number and frequency of public blessings was proportional to the status, rank and wealth of the participants. Unsurprisingly, blessings tended to fall upon men and were often delivered by women, though not systematically. Two in particular deserve our attention: Francis Moult (d.1733) and Hall Reason. The former was a wealthy chemist in Hatton Garden who had built his fortune by extracting the Epsom salts; he was one of the French Prophets' most generous supporters and received their public blessing on 15 occasions between January 1708 and June 1709. Although his relationship with his Philadelphian neighbours in Baldwin's Gardens remains unclear, Moult was a reader of Jacob Boehme and maintained contact with Richard Roach until the latter's death in 1730.[66] Reason remains a more enigmatic figure. Yet his enduring proximity with Roach's entourage, the fact that he was publicly blessed a record of 23 times by the French Prophets—mostly in the first half of 1708 at the peak of their ecumenical symbiosis—and that the Spirit promised to make him 'a Pillar in my Jerusalem' suggests that he may have been an architect of the rapprochement between the two societies.[67]

The participation of such powerful figures came at a turning point in the French Prophets' history. The group as a whole had been publicly discredited by the spectacular failure of Thomas Emes's resurrection in front 20,000 people on 25 May 1708. The Prophets designated 160 followers to join their 12 missionary tribes due to disperse across Europe to announce the millennium. Although the tribes were conjointly named by Elie Marion and Jeanne Raoux based on Revelation 7:4–8 and 21:12, they may in fact have been inspired by the Philadelphians. Indeed Roach and Mr Hammond were discussing Emes's resurrection alongside missionary activities on 14 March and interpreted the Philadelphian Society as the tribe of Joseph. Roach may not have influenced Marion on the formation of their international millenarian network, but it worth noting that at least 19 Philadelphians featured in the Prophets' list of tribes in 1709.[68]

Mystical Divorce

By 1708, the Prophets had entered a new phase in the history of their movement. After their union with the Baldwin's Gardens Philadelphians and a series of alleged miraculous healings, the spectacular failure of Emes's resurrection forced the community to purge a number of followers who were henceforth accused of being animated by their personal ambition rather than the Holy Spirit. Scepticism had indeed grown among the Prophets—including Roach—in the months preceding the miracles, on which Lacy blamed the failure of the prediction.[69] The purge reasserted to a large extent the punitive tone of the Camisards, who may have felt manipulated by the Philadelphians as a springboard for their resurrection. It may not be a coincidence if the expellees—over 30 in total between 1708 and 1715—were almost without exception English. Aside from the overly charismatic prophetesses mentioned above, the Philadelphian Abraham Whitrow was also excluded in the summer of 1708; the Prophets declared his 'Doctrine of Levelling' to be inspired by the Antichrist as he began promoting the redistribution of wealth in favour of the most necessitous members. His departure caused the first schism within the group.[70]

It is precisely on the eve of this purge, when the group awaited Emes's imminent resurrection that on 1 April 1708 Roach began encrypting his diary in shorthand. The manuscript alternates in form from this point onwards, indicating the author's desire for secrecy rather than stenographic efficiency or speed. Roach's diary was almost entirely encrypted from early June until 1716 and contains significant chronological gaps in between.[71] A look at the Camisards' records can fortunately shed some light upon this obscure period that effectively marked a growing separation between the two societies. Around the same time, both Camisards and Philadelphians received simultaneous inspirations from the Spirit ordering them to keep their distance. French and English Prophets now held separate assemblies, but continued to meet on a regular basis, albeit in a more confrontational manner. If they remained theologically complimentary to the Philadelphians, the Camisards continued to reassert the primacy of God's judgement over his mercy. Warnings against Philadelphian teachings were first voiced as a result in this period, starting with the Swiss Philadelphian Mr Bondelin in March 1708.[72] This growing confrontation may have been partly fuelled by the visit of Abraham Mazel in London. The charismatic and first Camisard leader had been staying with Marion since February 1708 and delivered apocalyptic warnings and divine orders to the group. He sought to revive the insurrection in the Cévennes and Vivarais with the help of Huguenot soldiers; he departed for the South of France in August and was killed two years later.[73]

The Prophets' publication of warnings increased in this period and even key Philadelphian figures like Peter Cuff and Caleb Gilman embraced their menacing millenarian style.[74] Yet the persistence of the Prophets' punitive ministry and calls for repentance despite the failure of the apocalyptic predictions became increasingly resented by some Philadelphians as an obstacle to the advent of their third dispensation. Roach had on several occasions interrupted the French Prophets assemblies to preach against the primacy of judgement and emphasise instead the triumph of love and mercy to the audience. Eventually the tensions climaxed in a pneumatic confrontation during the public assembly on 1 June 1710. Roach and Mary Keimer, both under divine inspiration, argued:

M. K.—Who sent thee?
R. R.—The God of Love.
K.—By what dost Thou know?
R.—By the Witness of his Spirit with Me, in his Love.
K.—Take Thou Care, lest a False Peace have possess'd thy Soul, & Thou Goest on Believing Thou art sent from God, when Thou art not sent from Him.
R.—'Tis more than a Peace in ye Soul; 'tis a Testimony.

K.—Take heed: God is ye same. He manifests not himself in many things, nay in very many which thou blindly believest he does. For, He can in no wise, not in Any case Contradict Himself. Has He not Already declar'd, that this is not His Word? How darest thou then resume in this Manner to Appear declaring that it is the Voice of God when it is not?

R.—How knowest thou that this is not ye Voice of God? Or by what Spirit speakest Thou? Speakest Thou by ye Eternal Love, or speakest Thou in part from ye Eternal Justice?

K.—Consider Thou O Man! I will confound Thee [...] Who art Thou O Man that exaltest thyself? [...] I can this Moment, strike Thee Dead. What are Thou? I can with ye Breath of my nostrils blow thee into Dust. [...] For Quickly & Judgements shal be usher'd in. Then wilt Thou know Who has spoken & who Now does Speak. 'Tis the GOD of LOVE [...] Therefore, be Patient, be vigilant. [...] Acknowledge thy Fault, & Thou shal find yt I am a GOD of LOVE; [...] I am not that God as Thou tak'st me to be, in this Appearance: No! For, I do in each Dispensation manifest myself; yes in ye dispensations of LOVE & Mercy, and in ye Dispensing of my Judgements.[75]

Despite his continuous efforts to reconcile the Camisards with the Philadelphians of Baldwin's Gardens, the French Prophets never accepted Roach as one of theirs. Worse even, after blessing him several times for his support during their trial, they declared him to be possessed by the same evil spirit as Abraham Whitrow.[76] Sarah Wiltshire, a close disciple of Roach, endeavoured to bridge the widening gap between the two societies, but her irenic efforts only infuriated the Prophets, who multiplied warnings against the imminent fall of Babylon and the Antichrist.[77] John Glover warned Roach for taking Wiltshire's defence in July:

I will that thou, Roch, desist from vindicateing this Spirit; For, if thou stil goest on to vindicate that whish I have condemn'd, Thou shalt feel the weight of my Hand: whish, I have said, shal be imploy'd in punishing. [...] And Thou, Wiltshire, forbear thy Claim: For, Thou shalt know, to thy utter Confusion, that I have not sent Thee.[78]

It was not long before Glover's warning was literally put to practice. At an assembly held on 24 September 1710, where Lacy prophesied 'threatning Judgements particularly to ye City London speedily, for Disregarding ye Voice of ye L[or]d sent'em', Wiltshire announced under inspiration the failure of such predictions and called instead for a better balance between the spirit of Judgment and that of Love—for which she was violently beaten up by the prophet Louis Joineau.[79] Further warnings were subsequently issued against Wiltshire and Roach, with Henrietta Irwin calling for a separation of the wheat from the chaff in an assembly at Francis Moult's in June 1712. The location and host of this gathering may not have been coincidental, for Moult had by then been appointed 'ruler in Israel' as the Prophets' network expanded across Europe in 1713.[80] It was again in Moult's house in Hatton Garden that Roach was publicly condemned by John Lacy as a blasphemer in November of the same year for promoting the 'Universal Salvation of wicked men & Devils also: (according to Origen's Doctrine.)' in his preface to Jeremiah White's *The Restoration of All Things* (1712). While Universalists themselves, the French Prophets considered that Roach—and indirectly Lead herself—had crossed a red soteriological line in defending God's boundless mercy towards mankind over the constant need for repentance. Universal and unconditional salvation remained highly contentious among the Philadelphians and there is good reason to think that most of the Baldwin's Gardens brethren in fact rejected it.[81]

Most of these events are either encrypted or missing altogether from Roach's diary. Other sources nevertheless suggest the resurrected Philadelphian Society remained deeply scarred by its brief union with the French Prophets, with Roach and Wiltshire continuously mediating between both sides, as well as between the four Philadelphian branches. One divisive issue among the group remained the practice and authenticity of miraculous cures. Since January 1711, the case of the young Mary Heath, daughter of the Philadelphian Rev. Heath the rector of Bathwick, had crystallized the gaping theological divergences among the Society. Heath had been suffering from a lame leg and from melancholy, and had even been confined for some time in Bedlam. Sarah Wilshire had predicted her miraculous recovery on 18 October 1710 and her case had in the meantime been submitted to the Philadelphians' friends at the University of Halle, where a new spirit was rising. Mary Laughton begged her uncle Richard Roach to pray for her niece, who was instantly cured from her mental illness upon his visit. A month later, Sarah Wiltshire joined Roach and Laughton in songs and prayers and touched Heath's leg; Heath recovered from her lameness and was able to walk again two days later.[82] The miraculous nature of Heath's double recovery under the dual action of a male and female ministry was much debated among the Philadelphians. If the main protagonists all testified in its favour, others proved far more sceptical. Roach, Wiltshire and Laughton requested the medical expertise of their Philadelphian brethren John Coughen, Francis Lee and James

Keith, three members of the Royal College of Physicians, in an attempt
to preserve the remains of Philadelphia. The three physicians did not
question the sincerity of their Baldwin's Gardens brethren, but they
denied the miracle conjointly on 10 December 1713 after concluding to
a lack of tangible evidence.[83] Roach, Wiltshire and Laughton thus failed
to convince their Hoxton co-religionists of the miracle and remained
somewhat isolated within the Philadelphian Society thereafter.

Around the same time it was noted that the Camisards were also
silenced.[84] This may have had to do with Marion's death in Livorno in
November 1713, towards the end of a two-year mission that took the
Prophets to Stockholm, Halle, Constantinople and finally Rome.[85] Gaps
and encryptions in Roach's diary cast some shadow over the state and
activities of the Philadelphian Society beyond that date. He maintained
regular contact with some of his brethren—John Coughen, James
Keith, Francis Lee, the Cravens and the Critchlows—but also developed
other relationships between 1716 and 1726. Among these should be
mentioned the Anglican theologian and mathematician William Whiston;
the Origenist writer William Freke, who had proclaimed himself the new
Elias in 1709; Anne Walthoe, whose quasi-anagram—Anne Wealth—
was celebrated as a sign of fortune; and the mysterious Hall Reason.
Their meetings still involved singing hymns and playing the organ, but
also drawing and breathing experiments such as puffing.[86] No contact
was maintained, however, with the Bow Lane society, which imploded
between 1712 and 1715 as a result of theological tensions between Mr
Pitkin and Dionysius Andreas Freher (1649–1728).[87] Despite Roach's
irenic efforts to put differences aside, the last Philadelphians remained
largely divided and had lost key members—Caleb Gilman, John Giles—to
the French Prophets. Their harmonious assemblies were often plagued
by their internal disagreements and sometimes ended in physical fights.[88]

Despite years of destructive divergences, during which he had publicly
mocked Lacy and many followers, Roach never really turned his back on
the French Prophets and his Philadelphian brethren who stayed among
them.[89] In fact, he kept an eye on their activities thanks to an *entente cordiale*
with some of their members. He noted for example that the Prophets
were still prevailing and engaged in a mission to Lyon in 1717. He also
received the Prophet Guy Nutt to discuss their activities in May 1721;
wrote that Cuff prophesied seven years of famine; admired Hall Reason's
£30 donation to charity; and had a friendly meeting with Fatio and Moult
in September 1722.[90] It was with the latter that Roach appears to have

maintained the most contact, whether by correspondence, personal encounter or exchange of books. Looking back at the Prophets, Roach showed no sign of anger or resentment towards them some 20 years later. Instead, he located their dispensation within the Reformation alongside John Wycliffe, Jan Hus and Jerome of Prague or Luther, as well as the Philadelphians, Quakers, Presbyterians, Ranters and Fifth-Monarchists, 'each bearing still a testimony & some neglected Truth of Ch[ristianity]'. All of them played a role in the restoration of the True Church and formed, in Roach's Behmenist view, the 'All G[od] v[s] p[ar]t G[od] (as Teutonic)'.[91] Significantly, Roach finally conceded in a letter to Francis Moult in October 1728 that the Lord was 'Judge as well as Bridegroom', after his addressee had helped his neighbour Mrs Freeman, whose house had burnt down. Based on this late revelation, Roach planned to visit Moult a few days later and formulated once again hopes of reconciling the Philadelphians and French Prophets' ministries into a new, powerful and united society.[92]

CONCLUSION

All in all, the Philadelphians' encounter with the Camisards proved more than incidental and should not be underestimated for that reason. Not only does this episode reveal the state of the Philadelphian Society in the aftermath of Lead's death, but it also sheds a different light on her place and legacy within their movement. Our perception of Lead as a prominent matriarchal figure is largely shaped by Roach's papers and his contribution to the Society's publications with Francis Lee. Yet this should not occlude the fact that most Philadelphians refused to take part in the Hoxton meetings and thus submit to her authority. A re-examination of Roach's papers and diary suggests that Lead had left behind a chaotic community quartered between four societies and that the Philadelphians no longer constituted a cohesive movement. If Hoxton had been the Society's public face, Baldwin's Gardens remained its beating heart beyond 1704. It should come as no surprise, in this context, that despite the participation of many Philadelphians in their millenarian assemblies and a majority of English followers, neither Lead nor her works were ever mentioned at any point in the French Prophets' records and publications.

Still, the Camisards' arrival in England appealed to the remaining Philadelphians because it seemed to corroborate Lead's prediction of their long-awaited second testimony. As the Union Act came into effect, the public emergence of the French Prophets marked the union of two opposite, yet complementary millenarian ethe. The Camisards and Philadelphians respectively embodied judgement and mercy, outward and inner religious experience, war and peace; a union between two otherwise enemy nations encouraged by favourable political conjunctures. This symbiotic union only lasted a few years, but a degree of spiritual cross-fertilisation nonetheless survived from their ecumenical enterprise. Born in the purest Calvinist tradition, Marion eventually addressed the restitution of all things and the Camisards became increasingly recognised as Behmenist Prophets by 1711.[93] Conversely, they imposed the fear of judgement among some Philadelphians and eventually upon Richard Roach himself. Although both societies still existed in 1730 it was then too late for their reunion into a Universal Church.

List of Philadelphians and Associates Known to Have Joined or Interacted with the French Prophets in England[94]

'Unconfirmed Philadelphian, but close to them
†Appears in the French Prophets' list of tribes[95]
*Apostasy

1. ARCHDALE, Mr (fl. 1707)
2. BASIN/BAZIN, John (fl. 1707)
3. BLANDFORD, Elizabeth (fl. 1707)†
4. BODIN, Mrs (fl. 1707–1717)'
5. BONDELIN, Mr (fl. 1707–1708)
6. BRIDGES, Charles (1670–1747), Educator
7. BULL, Richard? (fl. 1708–1721)'
8. CALVERLEY, Mary (1631–1714), Lady, Widow'
9. CASE, Mary? (fl. 1708–1711)'
10. CLERE/CLARE, William (fl. 1707–1709), Minister†
11. COCK, John (fl. 1708–1716), Clockmaker'†
12. COUGHEN, John (fl. 1708–1713), Physician
13. CRAVEN, Elizabeth (fl. 1638–1713)
14. CRAVEN, James (fl. 1707–1722), Chemist
15. CRITCHLOW, Daniel (fl. 1707–1724), Chemist, surgeon†
16. CRITCHLOW, Mary (fl. 1708–1709)†

17. CRITCHLOW, Rebecca (fl. 1707–1710), Widow
18. CRITCHLOW, Sarah (fl. 1707–1712)
19. CUFF, Peter (fl. 1676–1722), Watchmaker†
20. CUFF, Rebecca (fl. 1675–1722)?
21. DOWNING, Mr (1676–1734)?
22. DUTTON, Thomas (fl. 1679–1741), Lawyer¦
23. EASTMAN, Susannah (fl. 1707–1712)?†
24. EYRES, Daniel (fl. 1707)
25. FORESTER, Mr (fl. 1707–1712)
26. GILES, John (fl. 1707–1721), Merchant?†
27. GILMAN, Caleb (fl. 1670–1722)
28. GILMAN, Mrs (fl. 1708–1712)
29. GRAY, Elizabeth aka 'Betty' (fl. 1692–1729), Candle-snuffer in a playhouse
30. HAMMOND, Mr/Dr (fl. 1707–1722)?
31. HAMMOND, Mrs (fl. 1708)?
32. HARRYS/HARRIS, Timothy† (fl. 1708)
33. HARTLAND, John (fl. 1707–1712)†*
34. HOFFMAN, Francis (fl. 1707–1712), engraver
35. HOLLIS, Isaac (1699–1774), Gentleman
36. HUMPHREYS, William (fl. 1708–1709)?†
37. INGLIS, James (fl. 1710), Minister
38. JACKSON, Benjamin (fl. 1707–1722), Inventor?†
39. JOHNSON, Elizabeth (fl. 1708–1712)?
40. JOHNSON, George (fl. 1708)?
41. KEITH, James (fl. 1684–1726), Physician
42. KEMP, John (1665–1717), Antiquarian
43. KEMP, M. (fl. 1707)?
44. KING, William (fl. 1707–1709), Tallow chandler†
45. KNIGHT, Mr (fl. 1707)
46. LAUGHTON, Mary (fl. 1707–1729), Richard Roach's niece
47. LESTER, Mrs (fl. 1707)?
48. MADDOX, Mrs (fl. 1708–1712)?
49. MANWAYRING, Mrs (fl. 1712–1721), Housekeeper?
50. OXENBRIDGE, Joanna (fl. 1687–1708), Widow
51. PENNY, Mrs (fl. 1707)
52. PITKIN, Mr (fl. 1704–1708)
53. REASON, Hall (fl. 1683–1728)?†
54. RICHARDSON, Robert (fl. 1707–1732)†

55. ROACH, Anne (fl. 1662–1708)²
56. ROACH, Richard (1662–1730), Minister†*
57. SPONG, Rebecca (fl. 1708)²
58. SPONG, William (fl. 1707–1725)†
59. STEELE, Benjamin (fl. 1680–1744), Watchmaker
60. STERRELL, Mary (fl. 1693–1712), Widow†*
61. STEVENSON, Mr (fl. 1708)²
62. STEVENSON, Mrs (fl. 1708)²
63. STODDART, Dinah (fl. 1707–1708)²*
64. TAYLOR, Mr (fl. 1707)²
65. WARD, Catherine (fl. 1707–1722)
66. WELLS, Mrs (fl. 1707)
67. WHITROW, Abraham (fl. 1689–1714), Woolcomber*
68. WHITROW, Deborah (fl. 1707)²*
69. WIDOWS, Anthony (fl. 1706–1707)²
70. WILTSHIRE, Sarah (fl. 1707–1710), Widow?*

NOTES

* This chapter was made possible by a Fellowship of the International Consortium for Research in the Humanities 'Fate, Freedom and Prognostication. Strategies of Coping with the Future in East Asia and Europe' (supported by the Federal Ministry of Education and Research) at the University of Erlangen-Nuremberg, Germany.
1. Thune, *Behmenists*, pp. 136–37; Paula McDowell, 'Enlightenment Enthusiasms and the Spectacular Failure of the Philadelphian Society', *Eighteenth-Century Studies*, 35:4 (2002), pp. 515–33.
2. Bodl., MS Rawlinson D 833, fol. 83r.
3. *Propositions Extracted From the Reasons for the Foundation and Promotion of a Philadelphian Society* (London, 1697), pp. 4, 8.
4. Brian Gibbons, *Gender in Mystical and Occult Thought: Behmenism and Its Development in England* (Cambridge, 2003), p. 10.
5. *The State of the Philadelphian Society* (London, 1697), p. 1; Daniel Lafite, *The Principles of a People Stiling Themselves Philadelphians* (London, 1697), pp. 1–3.
6. Gibbons, *Gender*, p. 144.
7. Bodl., MS Rawlinson D 833, fols. 58r-62v; *London Post with Intelligence Foreign and Domestick*, no. 54 (6 October, 1699), p. 2.
8. Bodl., MS Rawlinson D 833, fols. 84r-85r.

9. Bodl., MS Rawlinson D 833, fols. 59r, 70v. Possibly related to Sir Patrick Murray of Auchtertyre, 2nd Baronet (d. 1735), Scottish Quietist close to James Keith (see below). G.D. Henderson (ed.), *Mystics of the North-east, Including I, Letters of James Keith, M.D., and Others to Lord Deskford: II, Correspondence Between Dr. George Garden and James Cunningham* (Aberdeen, 1934), p. 20.

10. Bodl., MS Rawlinson D 832, fols. 94–95; Bodl., MS Rawlinson D 833, fols. 50–51.

11. Bodl., MS Rawlinson D 833, fol. 57v.

12. Bodl., MS Rawlinson D 833, fols. 69r-v.

13. William Gibson, 'Dissenters, anglicans and elections after the toleration act, 1689–1710', in Robert Cornwall and William Gibson (eds), *Religion, Politics and Dissent, 1660–1832. Essays in Honour of James E. Bradley* (Farnham: Ashgate, 2010), pp. 129–46.

14. Lionel Laborie, 'Who Were the Camisards?', *French Studies Bulletin*, 32:120 (2011), pp. 54–57; W. Gregory Monahan, *Let God Arise. The War and Rebellion of the Camisards* (Oxford, 2014), pp. 39, 52–56. See also Hillel Schwartz, *The French Prophets: The History of a Millenarian Group in Eighteenth-Century England* (Berkeley, 1980).

15. Lionel Laborie, 'The Huguenot Offensive Against the Camisards Prophets in the English Refuge', in Jane McKee and Randolph Vigne (eds), *The Huguenots: France, Exile & Diaspora* (Brighton, 2013), pp. 125–33.

16. Bodl., MS Rawlinson D 1152, fols. 15v, 20r.

17. Scott Mandelbrote, 'Fatio, Nicolas, of Duillier (1664–1753)', *ODNB*; Charles Andrew Domson, 'Nicolas Fatio de Duillier and the Prophets of London: An Essay in the Historical Interaction of Natural Philosophy and Millennial Belief in the Age of Newton' (PhD thesis, 1972). Fatio's niece, Marie Huber (1695–1753), became a prominent female Pietist theologian in the eighteenth century.

18. Eric G. Forbes, Lesley Murdin and Frances Willmoth (eds), *The Correspondence of John Flamsteed, the First Astronomer Royal* (Bristol, 2002), vol. 3, pp. 334–36.

19. Henderson, *Mystics of the North-East*, pp. 56–61; G.D. Henderson, *Chevalier Ramsay* (Nelson, 1952), p. 19; Mirjam de Baar, 'Conflicting Discourses on Female Dissent in the Early Modern Period: The Case of Antoinette Bourignon (1616–1680)', *L'Atelier du Centre de recherches historiques* (04/2009), http://acrh.revues.org/1399. Lead also corresponded with Poiret c.1700–1703, see Bibliothèque Cantonale et Universitaire de Lausanne (BCU), TS 1029, no. 1; FbG, Chart A 297, fols. 89–91.

20. Bodl., MS Rawlinson, D 1152, fol. 11v; Cheshire Archives and Local Studies, EDC 5/1720/2, fol. 1.

21. Bibliothèque de Genève (hereafter BGE), Ms fr. 605/7a, fol. 1v.

22. Archiv der Franckeschen Stiftungen (hereafter AFSt), StaB/Nachlaß Francke 30/4:1, fols. 681–84; AFSt, H D71, fols. 109–110; Daniel Brunner, *Halle Pietists in England: Anthony William Boehm and the Society for Promoting Christian Knowledge* (Göttingen, 1993), pp. 42–44; Richard Gawthrop, *Pietism and the Making of Eighteenth-century Prussia* (Cambridge, 1993), pp. 184–85.
23. Craig Spence, 'Misson, Francis Maximilian', *ODNB*.
24. Bodl., MS Rawlinson D 1152, fol. 32r.
25. Bodl., MS Rawlinson D 833, fol. 32; Bodl., MS Rawlinson D 1152, fols. 17v-18r, 20r-21r, 23r.
26. Bodl., MS Rawlinson D 833, fol. 85r.
27. Bodl., MS Rawlinson D 1152, fol. 39v.
28. Tom Dixon, 'Love and Music in Augustan London; Or, the "Enthusiasms" of Richard Roach', *Eighteenth-Century Music*, 4:2 (2007), pp. 191–209.
29. Chetham's, Mun.A.6.14/1, index V, fol. AA; Stack private collection, 1j, fol. 30; Bodl., MS Rawlinson D 1152, fol. 57r-v. Critchlow's house was not officially registered for dissenting meetings until 1 August, 1707, see; LMA, MJ/SP/1707/07/074.
30. Bodl., MS Rawlinson D 833, fol. 31.
31. Chetham's, Mun.A.6.14/1, index V, fols. AA-FF; Bodl., MS Rawlinson D 1152, fol. 58v; Bodl., MS Rawlinson D 1154, fols. 404v-05r.
32. Bodl., MS Rawlinson D 1152, fols. 57r, 69r, 92r, 95v.
33. Bodl., MS Rawlinson D 1152, fols. 59v, 62v, 71r, 83v.
34. Bodl., MS Rawlinson D 1152, fols. 55r, 82r, 84v, 105r.
35. Bodl., MS Rawlinson D 1152, fols. 61v-62r, 64r.
36. Hillel Schwartz, 'Millenarianism', *Encyclopedia of Religion*, vol. 9, p. 6029; Bodl., MS Rawlinson D 833, fols. 54–66.
37. *Elias, or the Trumpet Sounding to Judgment, From the Mount of God* (London, 1704); Markus Öhler, 'The Expectation of Elijah and the Presence of the Kingdom of God', *Journal of Biblical Literature*, 118:3 (1999), pp. 461–76.
38. Philip C Almond, 'John Mason and His Religion: An Enthusiastic Millenarian in Late Seventeenth-Century England', *The Seventeenth Century*, 24:1 (2009), pp. 156–76; William E Burns, 'London's Barber-Elijah: Thomas Moor and Universal Salvation in the 1690s', *Harvard Theological Review*, 95:3 (2002), pp. 277–90.
39. Bodl., MS Rawlinson D 1152, fols. 62r, 63v, 115r, 116v.
40. Bodl., MS Rawlinson D 1152, fols. 39v, 113v; Bodl., MS Rawlinson D 833, fol. 32.
41. BGE, Ms fr. 605/7a, fol. 4v; Bodl., MS Rawlinson D 1152, fol. 1v; Chetham's, Mun.A.6.14/1, fols. 361–65; Chetham's, Mun.A.6.14/2, fols. 173–90.
42. TNA: PRO, KB 28/22/29.
43. Bodl., MS Rawlinson D 1152, fols. 53r, 54v, 55r, 63r, 95v.

44. Lionel Laborie, *Enlightening Enthusiasm: Prophecy and Religious Experience in Early Eighteenth-Century England* (Manchester, 2015), chapter 5.
45. Chetham's, Mun.A.4.33, fol. 58.
46. Bodl., MS Rawlinson D 1152, fols. 101r, 105r; Schwartz, *French Prophets*, pp. 113–25. A meeting was also held with William Penn in February 1708, see; BGE, Ms fr. 605/7a, fol. 3r.
47. Bodl., MS Rawlinson D 832, fol. 185.
48. Bodl., MS Rawlinson D 1152, fol. 90r; Bodl., MS Rawlinson D 832, fol. 167.
49. Bodl., MS Rawlinson D 1152, fol. 76v; Bodl., MS Rawlinson D 832, fol. 218.
50. Bodl., MS Rawlinson D 1152, fol. 107r; Bodl., MS Rawlinson D 833, fol. 55v.
51. Wilhelm Schmidt-Biggemann, 'Apokalypse Und Millenarismus Im Dreißigjährigen Krieg', in Heinz Schilling and Klaus Bußmann (eds), *1648: Krieg Und Frieden in Europa* (Münster, 1998), vol. 1, pp. 259–63; Bodl., MS Rawlinson D 1152, fol. 89r. On the origins of this prophecy, see Lesley Ann Coote, *Prophecy and Public Affairs in Later Medieval England* (Woodbridge, 2000), pp. 96–98.
52. Sarah Apetrei, *Women, Feminism and Religion in Early Enlightenment England* (Cambridge, 2010), pp. 232–35.
53. Bodl., MS Rawlinson D 1152, fols. 31v, 96r, 116r; Bodl., MS Rawlinson D 833, fols. 54–66.
54. Phyllis Mack, *Visionary Women Ecstatic Prophecy in Seventeenth-Century England* (University of California Press, 1992), p. 234; Douglas Shantz, *Between Sardis and Philadelphia: The Life and World of Pietist Court Preacher Conrad Bröske* (Leiden, 2008), pp. 132–33.
55. Samuel Keimer, *A Brand Pluck'd From the Burning* (London, 1718), p. 80.
56. *The French prophetess turn'd adamite* (London, 1707); Keimer, *Brand Pluck'd*, p. 54.
57. Cheshire Archives and Local Studies, EDC 5/1718/9, EDC 5/1719/2, EDC 5/1720/2; John Lacy, *A Letter From John Lacy, to Thomas Dutton, Being Reasons Why the Former Left His Wife and Took E. Gray a Prophetess to His Bed* (London, 1711); Keimer, *Brand Pluck'd*, pp. 32, 57–58, 124.
58. Bodl., MS Rawlinson D 832, fol. 34v; BGE, Ms fr. 605/7a, fols. 2v, 4r.
59. Keimer, *Brand Pluck'd*, pp. 53, 109–10.
60. Samuel Keimer, *A Search After Religion, Among the Many Modern Pretenders to It* (London, 1718), p.16; Keimer, *Brand Pluck'd*, pp. 38–39, 80, 111; Bodl., MS Rawlinson D 832, fol. 200v; BGE, Ms fr. 605/7a, fol. 5.
61. Sarah Apetrei, 'The "Sweet Singers" of Israel: Prophecy, Antinomianism and Worship in Restoration England', *Reformation and Renaissance Review*, 10:1 (2009), pp. 3–23; *The Tatler*, no. 257 (30 November 1710), p. 2.

62. Bodl., MS Rawlinson D 1153, fol. 337r.
63. François-Maximilien Misson, *A Cry from the Desert* (2nd edn., London, 1707), p. xvii.
64. McDowell, 'Enlightenment Enthusiasms', p. 524.
65. Chetham's, Mun.A.4.33, no. 1, 3–5, 9, 17, 24, 27, 33, 61, 93–94, 182, 190, 196, 295, 321, 340, 359, 389, 436, 439, 444, 491, 494, 496.
66. Keimer, *Brand Pluck'd*, pp. 71, 72, 76; Chetham's, Mun.A.4.33, no. 41, 52, 79, 97, 280, 303, 351, 416, 461, 473–474, 483, 489, 520, 554; Schwartz, *French Prophets*, pp. 248–49.
67. Chetham's, Mun.A.4.33, no. 44, 67, 80, 82–85, 87, 88, 99, 106–107, 305, 350, 387, 415, 452, 499–503, 530; Chetham's, Mun.A.6.14/2, fols. 179–180; Bodl., MS Rawlinson D 1153, fols. 330v, 336r, 342r, 343v-44r, 347v.
68. Bibliothèque du Protestantisme Français, Paris (hereafter BPF), MS 302, fols. 4r-5r; Bodl., MS Rawlinson D 1152, fol. 119r.
69. Bodl., MS Rawlinson D 1152, fols. 112r, 115r; *Esquire Lacy's Reasons Why Doctor Emms was not Raised from the Dead* (London, 1708), reprinted in *Harleian Miscellany* (1810), vol. 11, pp. 64–65.
70. Chetham's, Mun.A.6.14/1, index IV, fol. viii, fols. 343–48. Abraham Whitrow lived in Little Kirby Street in Hatton Garden. His house was opposite the Philadelphians' venue in Baldwin's Gardens. Whitrow may also have been related to the Restoration mystic Joan Whitrowe (fl. 1665–1697), who prophesied against social and economic injustice; see my forthcoming entry in *ODNB*.
71. Bodl., MS Rawlinson D 1152, fol. 123r; Bodl., MS Rawlinson D 1153, fol. 199v.
72. Bodl., MS Rawlinson D 833, fol. 31; BGE, Ms fr. 605/7a, fol. 3r; Chetham's, Mun.A.6.14/1, fols. 431–32.
73. BGE, Ms fr. 605/7a, fol. 3v.
74. Bodl., MS Rawlinson D 1152, fol. 107r; Caleb Gilman, *Veritas exultans, truth exalted and self abased* (London, 1708).
75. Chetham's, Mun.A.4.33, fols. 336–38; Bodl., MS Rawlinson D 1318, fols. 55r-56v.
76. Chetham's, Mun.A.6.14/1, Index IV, fol. viii.
77. Bodl., MS Rawlinson D 1318, fol. 61v.
78. Chetham's, Mun.A.4.33, fols. 341–42.
79. Bodl., MS Rawlinson D 1318, fols. 63v-64v.
80. Bodl., MS Rawlinson D 1318, fols. 65–66; Chetham's, Mun.A.2.114, fols. 179–182.
81. Bodl., MS Rawlinson D 1318, fols. 67r-68v; Apetrei, *Women, Feminism and Religion*, pp. 225–30.
82. Bodl., MS Rawlinson D 832, fols. 78v-79r; Bodl., MS Rawlinson D 833, fols. 33–46.

83. Bodl., MS Rawlinson D 833, fol. 47. Keith was a convinced believer in the Quietist Mme Guyon. Henderson, *Mystics of the North-East*, p. 60; William Munk, *The Roll of the Royal College of Physicians* (London, 1861), vol. 1, p. 344, vol. 2, pp. 18, 21. For Coughen see Ariel Hessayon's discussion in this volume.

84. Bodl., MS Rawlinson D 833, fol. 24.

85. *Plan de la justice de dieu sur la terre, dans ces derniers jours et du relèvement de la chute de l'homme par son péché* (1714); *Quand vous aurez saccagé, vous serez saccagés: car la lumière est apparue dans les ténèbres, pour les détruire* (1714), p. 114.

86. Bodl., MS Rawlinson D 1153, fols. 267r-v, 276r, 330v, 332r, 336r, 342r, 347v; Bodl., MS Rawlinson D 832, fol. 183; Martin Greig, 'Freke, William (1662–1744)', *ODNB*.

87. DWL, MS Walton 1104: I.1, fols. 22r-34v, 40v-52v.

88. Bodl., MS Rawlinson D 1153, fol. 336r; Bodl., MS Rawlinson D 1154, fol. 405r; James Cummins bookseller, New York, MS Ref. 6268 (17 August 1721).

89. Roach composed 'Mariage à la mode, or the Camisar Wedding. A Ballad' after Lacy's adulterous liaison with Gray in 1711; see Bodl., MS Rawlinson D 832, fols. 192–205, printed in Keimer, *Brand Pluck'd*, pp. 59–70.

90. Bodl., MS Rawlinson D 1153, fols. 215r, 267r-v, 334v, 343v-44r.

91. Bodl., MS Rawlinson D 1153, fol. 290r-v.

92. Bodl., MS Rawlinson D 832, fols. 92–93.

93. Bodl., MS Rawlinson D 1318, fols. 52–54; Dutch Royal Library (The Hague), KB, 72 E 14, fol. 5c. The Quaker merchant Benjamin Furly pointed theological resemblances with the radical Pietists Johannes Tennhardt and Johannes Maximilian Daut, see *Eclair de lumière descendant des cieux, pour découvrir, sur la nuit des peuples de la terre, la corruption qui se trouve dans leurs ténèbres; afin de les inciter à la repentance* (Rotterdam, 1711), p. viii.

94. Based on a compilation of data from Roach's diary and papers, the French Prophets' assembly records and diaries and contemporaneous publications.

95. BPF, MS 302, fols. 4r-5r.

CHAPTER 11

Jane Lead's Prophetic Afterlife in the Nineteenth-Century English Atlantic

Philip Lockley

Prophecies die hard in millennial cultures. Visionary and vocal experiences set down by one generation, and received at the time as imminent prophecy, may be recalled and redistributed by later generations enthused by similar eschatological expectations or millennial mentalities. In this way, prophetic figures who attracted followers in one period can experience a prophetic 'afterlife' through the recognition of their written revelations in another.

Some prophetic traditions have undergone periods of prophetic 'silence'—when the perceived voice of God is no longer heard—before resuming.[1] The separatist Pietist tradition of The Community of True Inspiration, better known as the Amana colonies in modern-day Iowa, experienced one such silence between the death of the last of their original *Werkzeuge* (instruments), Johann Friedrich Rock, in 1749 and 'the reawakening'—the emergence of new *Werkzeuge* among surviving congregations in 1817. In this community, the revelations of the founding *Werkzeuge* were picked up and set beside new prophecies in a conscious continuity.[2]

In the case of Jane Lead, the Philadelphian Society formed during her lifetime underwent no equivalent 'reawakening' decades after her death in 1704.[3] Lead nevertheless experienced an extensive prophetic afterlife.

P. Lockley (✉)
Cranmer Hall, Durham University, Durham, UK

© The Editor(s) (if applicable) and The Author(s) 2016   241
A. Hessayon (ed.), *Jane Lead and her Transnational Legacy*,
DOI 10.1057/978-1-137-39614-3_11

Original seventeenth-century printings were carefully preserved, and may be traced in the private libraries of figures with prophetic interests in Britain in the 1790s.[4] German translations of Lead remained influential among radical Pietist traditions in Europe across much the same period, and were probably first taken to America by such groups, which included Johannes Kelpius and his followers, and the *Neu-Teufer*, or German Baptist Brethren.[5] In the nineteenth century, Lead is recognised to have been read by two English-speaking prophetic traditions with a transatlantic reach— namely the Shakers and the Mormons. In the twentieth century, as Chap. 12 in this volume shows, Jane Lead's prophetic afterlife persisted among two distinctive millennial groups in North America—Mary's City of David in Benton Harbor and the Latter Rain movement. Even today, Lead's writings are made available to a global readership through competing committed websites.[6]

Tracing the roots, extent and intellectual basis for a prophetic afterlife is a hazardous historical exercise. Assumptions about influence in the history of ideas –tracings of cause and effect within processes of thought and communication—are notoriously hard to prove positively when a paper trail of reader responses, citations, and explicit references is rarely to hand. Despite the predominance of 'print culture' within the world of popular prophecies, which can allow the historical trajectory of some writings to be traced through the dates, places, and numbered editions of its re-publication, the actual social, intellectual and (pertinent to this discussion) *theological* resonance of the prophecies themselves may remain indecipherable. The subsequent millennial cultures within which past prophets can come to experience an afterlife are not always open about how, when and why they recognised the inspiration of preceding traditions. It can be hard to know whether correspondences in theological ideas across centuries stem from a long-standing direct influence or whether it was interpretative coincidence that led future groups to notice their forerunners.

The cases of the two best-known religious traditions to notice Jane Lead's prophecies in the nineteenth century illustrate these challenges well. The Shakers—or the 'United Society of Believers in Christ's Second Appearance'—originated in a distinctive religious milieu in the North of England only a few decades after the demise of the Philadelphian Society. As 'Shaking Quakers' it is commonly assumed that they inherited much of their early theology and practice from radical Quakers and the 'French Prophets', from whom a link is drawn back to the Philadelphians and so to Lead.[7] Recently, Susan Juster has even termed Ann Lee, the Shaker founder and second messiah, 'the direct heir of Jane Lead'.[8] Yet, neither manuscript nor print evidence for this supposed inheritance is available until the height of Shakerism's presence in the United States in the middle of the nineteenth century. This was the 'era of manifestations' in Shaker history—a time of spiritualistic revivals and ecstatic experiences from the 1830s to the 1850s. In this period, the tradition was especially attentive to forms of prophetic inspiration. Shaker manuscript collections from this time include hand-written copies labelled 'Different Kinds of Inspiration, With Jane Leeds [sic] Own Experience—Between the Years 1676–1701' and 'The Prophecy of Jane Leeds (1676)'.[9] While theories of an unbroken Shaker oral tradition back to Lead continue to be posited, scholars must confront the meagre evidential basis for this scenario. The earliest print edition of Lead's prophecies in Shaker archives was published in 1830 in England.[10] This implies that Lead was really only noticed alongside other claimants to prophetic inspiration when Shakers were specifically seeking to understand the varieties of visionary experience among their second or third generation.

In the case of the Mormons—the Church of Jesus Christ of Latter-day Saints—a uniquely exhaustive research project has recently explored the cultural environment of the tradition's origins between 1820 and 1850, and specifically identified numerous Mormon theological themes in Jane Lead's prophecies—as they appear at least in the same 1830 re-print also in the Shakers' possession.[11] Researchers have identified themes occurring in both Lead's writings and Joseph Smith Jr's theology as general (innocuous, even) as the 'City of Zion', 'New Jerusalem', and 'preparation of the earth and preceding events [to the Second Coming]'.[12] Significant flaws in the methodology of this project leaves its utility for tracking the influence of one prophetic tradition on another severely limited. No account was taken, for instance, as to whether any early Mormons were ever anywhere near the books in question.[13] Nineteenth-century Mormons undoubtedly read Jane Lead, and were struck by the parallels between her visions and their own beliefs. However, the earliest evidence for this occurs in Britain in February 1858. Passages from an 1807 German edition of Lead's *Revelation of Revelations*, encountered in either Britain or Europe, were translated back into English for the Mormon missionary newspaper, *The Millennial Star*.[14] The editor, Samuel Richards, enthused on the way Lead's revelations were 'pointed or expressive of the Latter-day Work', so demonstrating how 'those who are spiritually minded, according to the light and advantages they have, can seek after God and learn of His ways', even before the inspiration of 'the Prophet Joseph'.[15] All further Mormon interest in Jane Lead dates well after this.

Jane Lead enjoyed other prophetic afterlives in the nineteenth-century English Atlantic world beyond these problematic examples. The most extensive programme of reprinting Lead's writings in English was undertaken late in the century by the Glasgow publisher John Thomson, who also reissued works by Boehme, Madam Guyon, and other esoteric traditions to serve a growing contemporary interest in higher thought and mysticism.[16] Thomson secured an international market for his reprints, yet his readership is largely difficult to trace, and leaves, once again, little evidence of either how Lead's prophecies were read or the responses they provoked.

One further afterlife took place among yet another millennial movement: the Southcottians, or the followers of Joanna Southcott. This was arguably the most significant in the transatlantic journey of Jane Lead's English prophetic writings. In the twentieth century this tradition would produce the Michigan-based Mary's City of David, one of the two groups identified as resurrecting interest in Jane Lead in modern America. In their nineteenth-century guises—including during the transfer of their own beliefs and writings to North America—the evolving 'Southcottian' tradition repeatedly found itself either provoking comparisons and associations with Jane Lead among interested outsiders, or appropriating Lead's prophecies for its own purposes.

Southcottian groups lay behind the 1830 edition of Lead's prophecies picked up by the Shakers. Much of the scope, cause and degree of interchange in ideas of this particular prophetic afterlife may be sifted from the printed record and pieced together from scattered sources. Tracing such an afterlife is found to reveal the pliability of past prophecies in the hands of modern millennial cultures—not just ancient traditions. It further shows how even a single prophetic tradition can appropriate earlier revelations in different ways and to different degrees across time and space—spanning both an ocean and a century.

I

Joanna Southcott (1750–1814) was, like Jane Lead, an English female prophet whose religious experiences secured her notice, influence, and adherents beyond the gendered cultural norms of her day. Southcott claimed to receive revelations in dreams and through hearing a divine 'voice' during the 1790s, while living in Exeter (Devon). Southcott published her first book of prophecies in 1801, which invoked the Revelation figure of 'the woman clothed with the sun' and declared the millennial age to be close at hand.[17] Further parallels with Lead's own claims and career are apparent in Southcott's subsequent 14 years as a prophet with a national reputation. Southcott gained the support of a small group of Anglican clerics, and was assisted in publishing an extensive series of prophetic writings. Many of Southcott's recorded 'communications' bear particular comparison in style with Lead's spiritual diary, *A Fountain of Gardens* (written from 1670; published 1696–1701). In both works, apparently everyday events or incidents in an English woman's life and times are revealed—through inspiration—to have a deeper spiritual meaning. In addition, Southcott's theology was strongly anti-Calvinist, and essentially looked towards universal salvation—a position comparable with the theme of Restoration in Lead's own later writings.[18]

Southcott certainly secured a wider readership and audience for her prophecies while alive than Lead did. A conservative estimate of Southcott works in circulation in England during her lifetime is 108,000.[19] A reliable register of convinced 'Southcottians'—that is committed followers 'sealed' as members of her popular movement—by her death in 1814 is over 12,000.[20] Like Lead again, Southcott declared herself a loyal daughter of the Church of England, and was likewise wary of separatist inclinations among her supporters. Eventually, however, Southcott allowed her followers to establish in her name a national chapel network around 1811, often called 'Millennium Chapels', where preaching, hymn-singing, and a form of communion took place.

After Southcott died in December 1814—notoriously expecting to give birth to a messiah called 'Shiloh'—this prior Southcottian embrace of the spatial and devotional forms of popular Protestant Dissent was resumed by many, and maintained for decades. A discernible 'Southcottian tradition' persisted as a variety of English nineteenth-century nonconformity, despite a tendency to division and theological divergence. In due course, branches of Southcottianism adopted the outlook and mission techniques of more mainstream revivalist dissent such as Methodism, and successfully spread to the United States and Canada, as well as Australia, New Zealand and, briefly, South Africa.[21]

Scholarly links between Jane Lead and Joanna Southcott have been drawn before.[22] Most commonly the two are twinned as fellow 'women of revelation' within the English religious culture of the long eighteenth century—a label which denotes not only their corresponding claims to prophetic experience, but also, specifically, their respective evocation of the enigmatic female figure 'clothed with the sun' in Revelation 12.[23] Sylvia Bowerbank has even suggested, in a relatively recent summary of her long-term influence, that 'traces' of Lead's ideas may be found 'in the writings of Joanna Southcott'.[24]

There is in fact no evidence within Southcott's 65 volumes of writings of any direct Lead influence, and certainly no mention of her name. Southcott did not appreciate rivals, and denied reading any prophetic work besides the Bible.[25] Despite—or indeed *because* of—inheriting a significant proportion of her early followers from the incarcerated prophet of the 1790s Richard Brothers (1757–1824), Southcott insisted her adherents recognise her inspiration alone.[26] She eschewed any comparison with other writings or prophets. In the aftermath of Southcott's death, several leading Southcottians further attempted to elevate her inspiration above all others, including successor claimants.[27] Southcott's writings and 'holy mission'—together with the now-assumed 'spiritual' child, Shiloh—came to be endowed with a unique, cosmic significance.

Nevertheless, sifting the evidence of several Southcottians' papers, and the broader publishing context of her career and its aftermath, does reveal that Southcott's efforts to acquire the unalloyed attention of readers and supporters were unsuccessful. The period's expansive culture of prophetic interests won out, and clearly encouraged contemporaries to set Southcott's claims and message beside a notable predecessor: Jane Lead.

The key moment when Lead and Southcott were linked was the final dramatic year of Southcott's life—1814—and the gathering momentum towards the anticipated birth of the Shiloh and its aftermath. Southcott had publically identified herself with the 'woman clothed with the sun' of Revelation 12 for the previous 13 years. Even so, it was the announcement in a work of March 1814 that Southcott would literally fulfil the role of this biblical figure, by bringing forth 'a man-child who was to rule all nations', that appears to have precipitated the comparison in the minds of interested parties.[28] Jane Lead's prophetic writings had notably argued counter to traditional Christian interpretations of the 'woman of Revelation' figure as referring to Mary, and the man-child being Jesus. As Lead's response to a vision in 1676 declared, 'This Woman that is certified of by John in the Revelations hath not had its fulfilling Prophesie to this day, therefore [is] yet to come'.[29] Southcott argued likewise.[30] When, aged 64 and a virgin, Southcott indeed began to show signs of pregnancy, and several respected doctors concurred, the story became a national sensation. From this time on, both Southcott's committed believers and observers with a prior knowledge of Jane Lead's writings noted the connection.

In October 1814, a book entitled *The Holy of Holies Unveiled* was published in London.[31] This 110-page work sought to explain the figures and emblems 'which adorn the Superb Bible for Shiloh'—Southcott's awaited child. However, the book was apparently not directly affiliated to the Southcottian movement, only sympathetic. The title, the author's pseudonym—'Philadelphus'—and much of its subject matter, indicate it was written by someone who considered themselves primarily a follower of Jacob Boehme and Jane Lead.[32] The principal argument of the work nevertheless linked Lead's prophecy to the contemporary figure of Southcott and the messianic child anticipated to be born, and drew attention to further shared themes in their theology.

Philadelphus employed extensive quotes from 'a prophecy from the Diary of the sublime, divinely inspired Mrs Jane Lead' to link Southcott's claim to be the woman of Revelation 12 with Lead's vision of 'the Virgin Woman, who should be impregnated with the most holy seed of God'— the woman 'certified of by John in the Revelations'.[33] This link appeared within a broader discussion of the Boehme-derived theme of the ultimate return of a perfected Adam beside an interpretation of a passage in Genesis 3. This was when God promised, in response to the Fall, that the woman's seed shall one-day 'bruise the serpent's head'. Such a linking of Revelation 12 and Genesis 3 was also a prominent theme in Southcott's own millennial theology: that the Fall would only be overcome by the fulfilment of God's promise to the first woman, and through the specific figure of the woman of Revelation.[34] Philadelphus, in turn, declared:

> [T]his virgin-woman I conceive, to be Eve herself returned; and that she has been manifested for the express purpose of claiming the promise made at the fall, and also to bring forth *the Seed promised to her*, which in my opinion, is no other that the child born of Joanna Southcott, which man-child I am fully persuaded, will have in due time, the same dominion given to it, as was given to Adam in Paradise.[35]

Continuing in the same line of argument, Philadelphus explicitly linked the figure of Eve returned with Southcott: 'Adam has, in the latter part of the sixth chiliad or day, been born of Eve, *who is now called "Joanna"*...'.[36]

He then drew the distinctive Adam and Eve themes together towards the fulfilment of Revelation 20—the realising of the millennial age:

> Therefore I humbly conceive, that the child born of Joanna Southcott, is Adam returned; and that he will prove to be the angel John saw with a great chain, who actually shall command Satan to withdraw from this earth, and will also have power to chain him down to the bottomless pit, and there to remain till the thousand years are expired ... the Millennium.[37]

Little more is known of 'Philadelphus', and it is unclear how influential *The Holy of Holies Unveiled* was among Southcott's close supporters.[38] Even so, it is evident that some were conscious of Lead's past prophecies, and reflected on the resonances with their contemporary prophet's claims. The Revd Thomas Foley, Anglican Rector of Oldswinford, Worcestershire, was one of Southcott's earliest and most prominent supporters.[39] Among his letters prior to Southcott's death survives a hand-written manuscript, marked as an 'extract from Jane Lead's book call'd the fountain of gardens Dec 7 1676'.[40] Lead's particular vision on this date explained the significance of 'a hand all over spread upon me, with an influence of great heat'. This 'heat' was reported 'to fix the life's impregnancy', with a further elaboration on a 'renewing birth', on a coming messiah 'restoring a new world, from which the curse will fly', and details of the work of the spirit in achieving 'the most perfect Restoration'.[41] Foley likely copied this extract from a surviving original edition of *A Fountain of Gardens* from a hundred years before. Only one reprint of Lead's writings appeared in English in Southcott's lifetime: an 1804 edition of *The Revelation of Revelations*, which likely marked the centenary of Lead's death, and did not feature Lead's spiritual diary.[42]

Within two years of Southcott's death, however, passages from *A Fountain of Gardens* were in print: in 1816, *The Wars of David and the Peaceable reign of Solomon* was republished, including 'several extracts' from the diary which, coincidentally or not, were those previously cross-compared with Southcott.[43] No direct link between this edition and the Southcottian movement has been traced.[44] Yet on 6 March 1817, another Southcottian, William Clark, made a hand copy of 'Jane Lead's Prophecy Dec 13, 1676' (a few pages on from the vision Foley had recorded), and included in *The Wars of David*. This was Lead's dramatic experience of 'a bright shine all about my bed', a light that should:

> be as a covering Flame to cloath the Virgin Woman, who should be impregnated with the Birth of the most holy Seed of God. Then queried I, who

this Woman should be? It was said, the Name was known, and written in one,—that was to be of a perfect Heart … This Woman that is certified of by John in the Revelations hath not had its fulfilling Prophesie to this day, therefore yet to come, as it was in Spirit said to me …[45]

Clark annotated his copy of the prophecy, noting it to be a 'confirmation of the Third Book of Wonders'—Southcott's prophetic book which first announced the coming of Shiloh. Two years on from Southcott's death, Clark still hoped that the Shiloh child would somehow return. He wrote further: 'the fulfilment of which will be indeed a wonder of wonders'.[46]

II

During the 1820s, the Southcottian movement remained extensive within England, and began to spread into Scotland and Wales. While several rival figures claimed to be Southcott's successor as prophet, and led their followers in new theological directions, the coming Shiloh himself still haunted the dreams of most Southcottians. The arrival of Shiloh was viewed as being the ultimate vindication of Southcott's prophetic claims: if Shiloh was found among them, the woman clothed with the sun would be seen to have produced her man-child, and the scene in Revelation 12 consequently fulfilled.

Over time, several of the prophetic successors, including John Wroe (1782–1863), a Bradford wool-comber, and Mary Boon, a shoemaker's wife from Devon, attempted to steer their supporters in the North and West Country away from an imminent expectation of a Shiloh messiah.[47] In promoting their own prophecies of the millennium, an earlier Southcottian theology was adapted and altered by these prophets, with some normative interpretations pushed to the sidelines, including that Shiloh would appear as a small child. At the same time, however, a proportion of Southcottians continued to recognise no new prophet after Southcott, and set greatest store by her surviving writings. Among this group, often located in the Midlands, Southcott's prophecies were read and discussed over and over, and their fulfilment looked for in present events, especially the coming of Shiloh.

In 1828, all such Southcottians eagerly expecting Shiloh were confronted with a claimant: John Ward (1781–1837), a London shoemaker and Southcottian convert from 1814, who announced that he was now the Shiloh. Within three years, Ward had persuaded a notable proportion of surviving Southcottians of his messianic status, perhaps around 2,000, mostly from among Southcottians in the Midlands.[48]

Ward's promotional literature and preaching came to feature numerous references to Jane Lead. Indeed, Lead was probably the source of prophecies that Ward referred to most, after Southcott and the Bible, across his messianic career. In 1830, Ward and his followers in Nottingham arranged for a new collection of Lead's writings to be printed, given the title *Divine Revelations and Prophecies.* This was the precise edition eventually found in Shaker and modern Mormon hands. Letters between Ward and his followers indicate that 'Jane Lead's prophesies [*sic*]' were then read aloud in their Birmingham chapel meetings, and volumes of 'Jane Lead's Books' circulated among other interested 'Shilohite' congregations.[49] Ward, therefore, acknowledged Lead's prophecies in a strikingly more open and direct way than earlier Southcottians or sympathisers like Philadelphus. Among Ward's Southcottians, references to Lead were not hidden away in manuscripts, or found in works beyond the boundaries of the movement, but were publicised by the leading figure himself, with his blessing and oversight. Furthermore, Ward and his followers not only recognised the previous links drawn between the Southcottian movement and Lead's prophecies, but now forged new connections.

As the Shiloh, Ward claimed to be not simply a completion of Southcott's prophecies; he was also a fulfilment of the entire Bible and other divine communications. Ward wrote: 'to fulfil the Scriptures, and all other prophecies that have been given to men (who prophesied of the end), ... [God] fixes his standard in one, which is the spiritual man-child brought forth by Joanna Southcott'.[50] 'Let no one say that he bears record of himself', Ward continued, 'but shows that the Scriptures, in union with Joanna's writings, and her writings in union with the Bible, declare plainly, that such a one must arise in this day'.[51] From this insistence that the Scriptures must be 'fulfilled in one man', Ward reached what E.P. Thompson called a 'surrealist solipsism' of believing that 'the true meaning of the Word of God' was himself—that *he*, Ward was the Christ and many other figures in the Bible, including places such as 'Zion'.[52] This latter name he liked so much he adopted it, becoming 'Zion Ward'—a personified fulfilment of a visionary place, as well as being Shiloh.[53] Ward denied the historicity of the Bible, but turned it entirely into an allegory of himself—a plethora of 'types and shadows' pointing only towards his own coming. 'The Scriptures were given by inspiration of God', Ward insisted, 'but from Genesis to Revelation they are not History, but figures of what is to come'.[54]

The logic of Ward's claim 'to fulfil ... all other prophecies that have been given to men' led him to draw attention to the predictions of a range of other prophetic works and figures. In a monthly journal issued in 1831, Ward cited in support of his claims passages from *The Prophetic Messenger* of 1828, sayings of the legendary medieval figure, Robert Nixon, and a recent edition of *Moore's Almanack*.[55] In one edition, Ward further claimed to detect a passage of his own personal history in the 'the sublime prophesies [*sic*] of that highly-inspired woman, Jane Lead, who wrote by inspiration, prophesying and foretelling of this great work, a vast number of years ago'.[56] Ward's journal then reproduced, with his own annotations, Lead's visionary poem beginning 'O England! Hear thy genius loudly call', from the first volume of *A Fountain of Gardens*.[57]

Passages from *A Fountain of Gardens* had featured in the *Divine Revelations and Prophecies* edition of Jane Lead's writings issued the previous year. This collection further reproduced, in a largely idiosyncratic order, passages from *Heavenly Cloud Now Breaking* (1681), *The Wonders of God's Creation manifested* (1695), and *The Wars of David and the Peaceable reign of Solomon* (1700). While the latter work had been reprinted in 1816, including additional parts of *Fountain of Gardens*, there is no evidence that the other works had appeared in English since Lead's lifetime. Ward and his Southcottian followers must therefore have had access to at least some seventeenth-century editions, or manuscript copies passed between generations. It is unclear how directly Ward was involved in the editing exercise which led to *Divine Revelations and Prophecies*, but he certainly approved the initiative. Ward's letters and publications reveal that he had commissioned the printer, H. Wild in Rutland Street, on several previous occasions.[58]

From the first page of *Divine Revelations and Prophecies*, the basis for the earlier associations between Southcott and Lead was reiterated: the text opened with Lead's vision of 13 December 1676, from *A Fountain of Gardens*, of 'a bright shine all about my bed', and 'a covering Flame to cloath the VIRGIN WOMAN, who SHOULD BE IMPREGNATED WITH THE BIRTH OF THE MOST HOLY SEED OF GOD'.[59] These particular lines from the vision, cited by both Philadelphus and William Clark, notably reproduced capitalised words from the 1816 edition, not capitalised in the 1696 original (and added further capitals). This suggests an intention to emphasise particular lines for a contemporary audience.

Elsewhere in the edition it is clear that Ward and his followers wished to draw attention to ideas present in Lead's writings which related to the nature of his own claims to be Shiloh, beyond the existing Southcottian themes that linked Genesis 3 with Revelation 12. Lead's understanding of the 'Virgin Wisdom' or 'Sophia' as a dimension of God is present elsewhere in the edition, including in further passages from *A Fountain of Gardens*.[60] Lead's prophecies looked for the coming of 'another Adam'—a production of Wisdom's own 'Virgin-Nature'—in a more complex reading of the Genesis passage only hinted at in Philadelphus' references to Southcott in *The Holy of Holies Unveiled*.[61] Believing that Wisdom had left Adam and Eve at the time of the Fall, but would return when the Fall was overcome in the millennial age, Lead essentially looked for the 'return of Sophia' in parallel with the return of Christ. Understood as a spirit form, Sophia/Wisdom would imbue humanity with the changes necessary to bring about the millennium. A new Church would form recognising this spirit, producing a new spiritual generation which would realise the New Jerusalem—the symbol of union with God through divine wisdom.

Ward's primary idea was that Shiloh was not a person but a spirit—a spirit always intended to descend on one living individual, who would then impart the knowledge and peace needed to realise the millennium. Ward understood himself to be the first receiver of this particular spirit, and, as its vessel, to have, therefore, become 'Joanna's child'—Shiloh. Ward declared that he was only the first to be changed into a new creation; in time, the spiritual 'man-child' would be channelled among all humanity. Much of this claim and conception of the 'man-child' and Shiloh spirit bore direct comparison with the depiction of Sophia/Wisdom in Lead's prophecies reprinted in *Divine Revelations and Prophecies*. Indeed, Ward's writings reveal him readily appropriating the terms 'Wisdom' and even 'Sophia' to himself, just as he did 'Christ' and 'Zion'. Further references in Lead's writings to a 'three-fold coming of Christ' likewise fitted Ward's malleable conception of himself as Christ come again. By the 1830s, Ward commonly defined his body of 'Shilohite' adherents as the spiritual generation that would realise the New Jerusalem.

III

Zion Ward died in 1837. Few if any committed 'Shilohites' were previously unfamiliar with the Southcottian tradition. This failure to recruit beyond Southcottian circles was not for want of trying: Ward sought to secure as wide a preaching audience and readership as possible, making maximum use of the public and print notoriety and sense of spectacle that his messianic claims provoked in 1830s England.[62]

One non-Southcottian figure intrigued by Ward was James Pierrepont Greaves, a mystic with eclectic interests in spiritual inspiration, including his own.[63] Greaves was a devoted reader of Boehme. He and Ward met in 1834, while the Shiloh was preaching in Yorkshire. The pair held extensive discussions over several months on the nature of spiritual experience. Each probably believed they could convert the other. Greaves essentially believed that 'the Spirit' acted through him when he lived an appropriately ascetic life, and looked to the gradual realisation of the millennial age—a renewing of the world and overcoming of sin—through celibate intentional communities and the creative education of children. Ward, meanwhile, rejected all 'ceremonies' and religious disciplines, insisting on his own essential embodiment of the divine spirit, and primacy as a religious teacher.[64] After achieving no real consensus between their views, Greaves and Ward went their separate ways, persisting in their own circles of devoted supporters.

Ward's encounter with Greaves—and Greaves' eclectic interest in Southcottian inspiration alongside other historic prophetic movements—very likely lay behind the earliest transatlantic journey of Jane Lead's English prophecies. Copies of Lead's writings entered American intellectual circles in the 1840s through Greaves' influence, and specifically in the company of Southcottian works once owned by him. Strikingly, by the early 1850s, traceable Americans were still comparing Lead and Southcott, or noting Lead's similarities to the Southcottian tradition, as an outworking of this original transatlantic journey.

Until his death in 1842, Greaves was the leading figure among English Transcendentalists—a smaller and culturally far less significant group than their New England counterparts led by Ralph Waldo Emerson. The two groups were nonetheless linked through correspondence, reading each other's works, and personal visits. Greaves' community at Ham Common in Surrey was named Alcott House, after A. Bronson Alcott, a leading Boston Transcendentalist.[65]

Bronson Alcott himself visited the Surrey community for several months, just after Greaves had died. At the end of his stay, Alcott was accompanied back to Boston by Charles Lane, Greaves' closest follower. The pair intended to establish a community in New England on an ascetic and mystical model similar to Alcott House.[66] With a library in mind for their community, Alcott and Lane took Greaves' own book collection (left in Lane's trust) and transported a further range of works either received or bought by Alcott while in England. It was probably Alcott himself, once back in the United States in 1843, who declared that the close to a thousand volumes were 'undoubtedly a richer collection of mystical writers than any other library in this country'. The titles of perhaps a fifth of this collection were listed in an edition of *The Dial*—the Transcendentalist journal. Among the works appear 'Tracts, by Jane Lead' and 'Southcott's Tracts'.[67]

The fate of every work in this library cannot be entirely accounted for today: Alcott and Lane's 'Fruitlands' community was dysfunctional, and soon broke up acrimoniously. Alcott retained possession of many books—almost certainly those he purchased or was given. Most of Greaves' remained with Charles Lane, or were handed over to their mutual friend Emerson for safe-keeping. Alcott's books and the titles of those held by Emerson may be traced. Emerson kept 'Southcott's Tracts'—four volumes from 1801 to 1806—as well as an early volume of the Southcottian prophet, John Wroe's communications.[68] Alcott does not appear to have owned the Lead 'Tracts'.[69] This strongly suggests that Lane held on to the latter—an instructive insight, as Charles Lane joined a group of Massachusetts Shakers in 1844.[70] It is, therefore, through a line of succession of Ward, Greaves, and Lane that the broader Shaker movement in America may very well have been introduced to Jane Lead's prophecies.[71]

By 1852, there is alternative evidence that within American Transcendentalist circles interests in the spiritual experiences of Shakers, Lead, and Southcott were intersecting. Maria Macdaniel, a former member of another Transcendentalist community, Brook Farm, wrote from New York to the London-based journalist, and one-time Southcottian, James Smith (1801–1857).[72] During the 1840s, Smith and Macdaniel had both been 'Fourierist' socialists.[73] They were part of a largely forgotten element in early transatlantic socialism that combined spiritual interests with socialist politics and women's rights. In 1852 Macdaniel sent Smith a volume of Shaker writings, assuming Smith would be interested in the Shakers 'as they fully accept the woman as an equal, and treat her as such'.[74] Macdaniel further wished to know Smith's view on the following question:

> What is woman's mission in this age, and more especially has [*sic*] Joanna Southcott and Jane Lead ... given a key to [it], in the purity of the woman crushing the head of the serpent, by living up to the Levitical law, or to the transcendental idea?[75]

While this evidence is fleeting (and the question obscure), it would seem that by 1852, in New York at least, the figures of Lead and Southcott were not only each linked to 'the woman question', in the earliest years of first-wave feminism, but linked together—their theologies in some sense merged by a new culture intrigued by how their prophecies might relate to new political purposes.

The following year, 1853, American Southcottians were themselves encountering Jane Lead, seemingly independently of their past tradition. By this date, John Wroe's distinctive branch of Southcottians had established themselves in the United States through missionary efforts in New York, Providence and Boston.[76] In June 1853, Joseph H. Moses, a Boston convert, wrote to Wroe in Britain confessing to 'being drawn after other messengers', listing the examples of 'Jane Leeds [*sic*], A. McDonald of Scotland' alongside 'considerable different authors'.[77] Moses' missspelling of Lead's name in this re-printed letter is significant, as this matches Shaker manuscripts of this period, but no printed volume.[78] This may imply that Moses came across Lead's prophecies himself, through Massachusetts Shaker circles (nine years after Lane joined them). It is unclear at this juncture how Joseph Moses compared Lead's prophecies with his newly-adopted Southcottianism. However, the distinct theological track followed by John Wroe, while differing markedly from either Southcott's or Ward's ideas, actually offered Moses many new points of comparison.

IV

In the second half of the nineteenth century, both American and British followers of John Wroe—and especially of his successor, James Jezreel— adopted a theology with yet further parallels to Lead's prophecies. Besides comparative views of the 'virgin woman', the child of the woman of Revelation, and conceptions of Shiloh as a descending spirit, 'Wroeite' and 'Jezreelite' Southcottians evolved particular understandings of both bodily life in the millennium and a feminine 'Jerusalem' in the godhead which also correlated strikingly with other Lead beliefs. By 1900, this correlation was increasingly *conscious*, and lay the groundwork for a newly-open appreciation for Lead's prophetic afterlife in the twentieth-century Southcottian tradition.

John Wroe assumed the prophetic leadership of a significant section of Southcottians between 1823 and 1863. During this 40-year ministry— which oversaw the spread of the tradition across the English-speaking world—a substantial evolution in many Southcottians' millennial theology and religious practices took place.[79] During the 1820s, Wroe had persuaded his followers to adopt the Old Testament Laws of Moses and to think of themselves now as 'Israelites'. Behind these directives lay a distinct understanding of both an ancestral identity as Hebrew tribes, and a reading of Revelation where those sealed to enter the millennium were 'the tribes of the children of Israel'. For a period, Wroeite Southcottians probably expected to see the physical New Jerusalem realised in their lifetimes, and adopted various communal practices to foreshadow this moment.[80]

In time, Wroe's prophetic writings indicate a gradual shift in the theological explanation for keeping the Mosaic Law, and developing ideas about the bodily nature of millennial life. In essence, the rigour of keeping the Laws of Moses was conceived as a means of purifying the believer's body, to prepare it for the immortal state of the millennium. A distinctive teaching thus emerged emphasising the attainment of a 'millennial body' prepared for a mysterious transfiguration into immortality at the arrival of the millennium.

A related concept to evolve within Wroe's prophetic theology was 'Jerusalem'. From the late-1830s, Wroe's writings employed this term less as a place name (with a 'new' epithet linked to the book of Revelation), but increasingly referred to 'Jerusalem above' as variously 'the Spirit of God', 'the immortal Bride', and 'the immortal Spirit'.[81] During the 1840s, Wroe's communications discussed 'Jerusalem above' with ever greater frequency. While a female connotation of 'Jerusalem above' may be drawn from the New Testament—as Galatians briefly refers to this being 'the mother of us all'—Wroe's use of the phrase reached beyond this. It characterised 'Jerusalem above' as a divine spirit given to the woman to drive out Satan from the man.[82] Wroe linked this idea to the anticipation of men and women attaining an incorruptible, immortal body:

Jerusalem above ... will cleanse both their bodies and make them like the immortal body of Jesus Christ; but, it must first come to the woman to cleanse her, before she can cleanse the body of the man, to bring him into that everlasting kingdom.[83]

Wroe's several volumes of prophecies make no mention of how these new ideas drew Southcottian beliefs yet closer to prominent themes in Jane Lead's prophetic works. It is possible to speculate on an underlying—unacknowledged—influence of Lead's ideas on Wroe, given the earlier Southcottian links to Lead. However, there is scant evidence to substantiate such speculation. Joseph H. Moses' letter of 1853 is the only reference to Lead in the entire 'Wroeite' corpus up to the prophet's death in 1863.

From 1875, however, a new Southcottian prophet, James Jershom Jezreel (alias James Rowland White), who persuaded many Wroeite-Southcottians in Britain and North America to join his 'New and Latter House of Israel', continued to develop these specific themes of 'Jerusalem above' and the immortality of the body in his own prophecies.[84] And evidence survives from this period indicating that Jane Lead's writings were indeed circulating among Jezreel's followers.

Jezreel's theology was not a major departure from Wroe's later teachings. From its opening pages, Jezreel's printed *Extracts from the Flying Roll* refers to 'Jerusalem above' as 'the female Immortal Spirit', describing this as the spirit which 'withdrew from the mortal woman in the beginning', and would now, as 'the Divine plan' stood ready to be fulfilled, 'hand to man the good wine of the Tree of Life'—so returning humankind to their immortal condition before the Fall.[85] In an ensuing, extensive explanation of the creation and fall, the Adam figure is notably described as 'two spirits male and female in one body', yet at the point of Eve's creation, 'Christ, who is the resurrection, and Jerusalem ... withdrew from Adam, and he slept'.[86] As a consequence, 'the female immortal spirit Jerusalem above' was set to return only at 'the time that man and woman agree to seek for that evil ... to be taken away; – for as they agreed in the fall, so they must agree to seek for the restoration'.[87] Such an agreement and restoration was explicitly linked to the attaining of immortality, or of 'mortal bodies [that] shall not perish'.[88] Elsewhere in *The Flying Roll*, the need to be 'born again of water and the Spirit' was directly linked to being 'born of Jerusalem above'.[89] And those 'being born of the new birth—of water and the Spirit ... suck the breasts of their Mother Jerusalem above—for she feeds them from the tree of life'.[90]

Unlike Wroe and Southcott before him, yet like Zion Ward, Jezreel is reported to have 'approved and recommended to believers in his mission' the reading of Jane Lead—specifically her 'Sixty Propositions to the Philadelphian Church'.[91] A manuscript copy of this work circulated among Jezreelites in the early to mid-1880s.[92] Numerous 'propositions' among Lead's original writings bear striking resemblances to Jezreel's teachings, and elements of Wroe's before him. Proposition 43 declared: 'There may be some at present living who may come to be ... fully and totally redeemed ... having another body put on them'.[93] Subsequent propositions indicated that this 'anointed body' would in some sense come from a process of 'refining work ... searching every part within us, until all be pure and clear', ultimately leading to a people 'whose descent is not to be counted in the genealogy of that creation which is under the Fall; but in another genealogy which is from the Restoration'.[94] In the final propositions, spirits 'purely begotten and born of God' were described as being able to ascend and descend 'to Jerusalem above', so becoming 'members of the firstborn of Jerusalem above, our Mother'.[95]

The extent of circulation of copies of this manuscript within the transatlantic Southcottian movement formed by the late nineteenth century remains unknown. Circulation is likely, however. As Wroe did before him, Jezreel encouraged the spread of the Southcottian tradition in North America, touring the Ohio and Michigan region in person in 1882, when he preached to crowds in a big tent or the open-air. In each location, Jezreel and his supporters hoped to leave a small group of converts to begin a congregation. Links between Jezreel's Kent headquarters in England and the American Midwest were maintained by letter and parcels of printed works for years, even after Jezreel's death in 1885. Explicit notice of Lead's writings made by Jezreel on the English side of the Atlantic would, therefore, have resulted in their attention among American followers. By 1900, Lead's prophecies were an inherited point of reference for many of the American Southcottians who would go on to form the Benton Harbor communities—the Israelite House of David and Mary's City of David—in the ensuing century.

The question remains whether we can reach beyond the comparative theologies and manuscript notice of Jane Lead by Southcottians by 1900, and trace what it was that Jezreel reportedly 'approved and recommended' within them. A few Southcott readers earlier in the century had linked Lead's visions of a 'Virgin Woman' and the promises of Genesis 3 and Revelation 12 with Southcott, and read them as prophecies being fulfilled in her. Ward had likewise promoted Lead's writings as past prophecy realised in himself. Transcendentalists and their associates, viewing Lead and Southcott as comparable female mystics, read them for insights from a divine spirit. And yet Maria Macdaniel's questioning whether Southcott and Lead had 'given a key' to 'woman's mission in this age' implies its own sense of connection between their original revelations and a fulfilment in Macdaniel's present.

A view of how a Jezreelite Southcottian read Jane Lead at the turn of the twentieth century is provided in 1906 by William D. Forsyth, leader of a British branch of post-Jezreel Southcottians called 'the Outcasts of Israel'.[96] Forsyth was responsible for a series of tracts in the early 1900s, among which was a new edition of Lead's *Ascent to the Mount of Vision*.[97] In his introduction to this work (apparently the first English re-print since 1699), Forsyth made the clearest statement yet of how Southcottians had come to view Lead by this date. 'It is evident', Forsyth wrote, 'that the author wrote by the Spirit of divine prophesy [*sic*]: as we see her words run parallel with Israel's [Southcottians'] Faith, Hope, and Standard published before her works came into our possession'.[98] By running 'parallel', Forsyth insisted there had been no cross-fertilising; the correlations resulted from Lead's inspiration being from the same divine source.

Two centuries on from Lead's original visionary experiences, Forsyth now confidently declared that 'God's word' through Lead was surely receiving its realisation in the 'Last Days' she spoke of, and which Jezreel had so recently confirmed. While this can suggest a reading of Lead's prophecies, like earlier Southcottians, as looking for their fulfilment in their prophetic figure, Forsyth actually meant something more. Forsyth reiterated elements of a Jezreel-derived understanding of God as 'Father, Mother and Son'—of God, Christ, and the Mother Jerusalem Wisdom or Sophia.[99] This was a 'perfect truth unfolded of all ages', implying this nature of God had been revealed gradually, from Lead's past prophecies onwards, yet could only come to full light in Jezreel.[100] Jezreel himself was not the fulfilment of Lead's prophecies; it was his prophecies, and those of Wroe and Southcott before him that completed hers. In this way, Jane Lead was not just appropriated by but *incorporated into* the Southcottian tradition's sense of its own prophetic history by the early twentieth century. Jane Lead's inspiration was no longer to be simply recalled and redistributed by Southcottians in the English Atlantic world; it was to be interpreted beside and before that of their own prophets. Jane Lead's prophecies were thus redefined by another millennial culture, not as an afterlife but as prophetic prologue.

NOTES

1. Periods of prophetic 'silence' are also liable to be recognised in the careers of individual prophets believed to have had, then lost, the gift of prophecy, the biblical model for whom is Ezekiel—whose tongue God made to 'cleave to the roof of thy mouth, that thou shalt be dumb' (Ezekiel 3:26).
2. Peter Hoehnle, *Amana People: History of a Religious Community* (Iowa City: Penfield, 2003).

3. The Philadelphians certainly survived Lead's death, and persisted for a decade or more, including the period of the 'French Prophets' in England. This period was not a 'reawakening', however, only a society which continued until its demise. See especially, Lionel Laborie's Chap. 10 in this volume, and his *Religious Enthusiasm in Early Enlightenment England: Camisards, French and English Prophets (1685–1750)* (Manchester: Manchester University Press, 2015).

4. British Library copies of Jane Lead's *A Message to the Philadelphian Society* (1696), *The Signs of the Times* (1699) and *A Fountain of Gardens* (1696) bear the stamp of Philip de Loutherbourg, who, among other claims to fame, was a follower of the 1790s prophet Richard Brothers. Iain McCalman, 'Spectres of Quackery: The Fragile Career of Philippe de Loutherbourg', *Cultural and Social History*, 3:3 (September 2006), pp. 341–54. For an insightful study of related prophecy reading, see Ariel Hessayon, 'Jacob Boehme, Emanuel Swedenborg and their readers', in *The Arms of Morpheus: Essays on Swedenborg and Mysticism*, ed. S. McNeilly (London: The Swedenborg Society, 2007), pp. 17–56.

5. J.F. Sachse, *The German Pietists of Provincial Pennsylvania, 1694–1708* (Philadelphia, 1895), pp. 15, 48; Jeff Bach, *Voices of the Turtledoves: the sacred world of Ephrata* (University Park, PA: Penn State University Press, 2003), p. 43.

6. For instance, <www.janelead.org> and <www.passtheword.org>.

7. Clarke Garrett, *Spirit Possession and Popular Religion* (Baltimore: Johns Hopkins University Press, 1987), pp. 141–47. See also Lionel Laborie's Chap. 10 in this volume.

8. Susan Juster, *Doomsayers: Anglo-American Prophecy in the Age of Revolution* (Philadelphia: University of Pennsylvania Press, 2003), p. 123.

9. The Shaker collection of the Western Reserve Historical Society (WRHS); Manuscripts (Glen Rock, N.J.: Microfilming Corp. of America, 1976), reel 52, Book 6/B39, p. 149; reel 61, Book 7/B203. These copies were made by Rebecca Jackson (1795–1871) and Catherine Van Houten (1817–1896), respectively. A further Shaker transcript of Lead writings survives at University of Kansas, Kenneth Spencer Research Library, MS P182, labelled 'Vision of Jane Lead, March 11, 1676', though the date of transcription is unverified. I am grateful to Ariel Hessayon for drawing this additional source to my attention.

10. This is the copy of Jane Lead, *Divine Revelations and Prophecies. Part the first. First published in London in the year 1700* (Nottingham: H. Wild, 1830) held in the Western Reserve Historical Society Research Library.

11. This produced the Archive of Restoration Culture https://byustudies.byu.edu/PDFLibrary/ArchiveRestorationCulture.pdf [Accessed 7 November 2013]. For the 'cultural biography' of Joseph Smith related to

this project, see Richard Lyman Bushman, *Joseph Smith: rough stone rolling* (New York: Knopf, 2005).

12. https://byustudies.byu.edu/PDFLibrary/ArchiveRestorationCulture. pdf, pp. 1327–31.

13. The copy of Lead's *Divine revelations and prophecies* (1830) held at the Harold B. Lee Library, Brigham Young University, Utah, was only purchased in 1988. I am grateful to Maggie Kopp for her insights into the provenance of this book.

14. 'Extracts from the Revelations of Jane Leade,' *Millennial Star* 20, no. 8 (20 February 1858), pp. 124–25. The original was: Jane Lead, *Offenbarungen der Jane Leade, die letzten Zeiten betreffend: nebst Anmerkungen und einer Lebensberschreibung dieser Englaenderin* (Strasburg: J.H. Silbermann, 1807).

15. 'Extracts from the Revelations of Jane Leade,' *Millennial Star* 20, no. 8 (20 February 1858), pp. 124–25.

16. Between 1884 and 1903 Thomson reprinted at least seven Lead works: *Revelation of Revelations* (1884); *The Heavenly Cloud Now Breaking* (1885); *The Wars of David and the Peaceable Reign of Solomon* (1886); *The Wonders of God's Creation manifested* (1887); *The Signs of the Times* (1891); *The Enochian Walks with God* (1891); *The Laws of Paradise Given Forth by Wisdom to a Translated Spirit* (1903). See also, J. Boehme, *Epistles* (Glasgow: J. Thomson, 1880); M. Guion, *The Mystical Sense of the Sacred Scriptures*, trans., Thomas Watson Duncan (Glasgow: J. Thomson, 1872). Thomson's personal sympathies with these works remains unclear, even if it was an evident commercial specialism: Clegg's Directory listed his business as 'Second-hand, Mystic, Theological, and General'. See, James Clegg (ed.), *The International Directory of Booksellers*, sixth edition (Rochdale: James Clegg, 1903), p. 81.

17. On Southcott's career and theology, see Matthew Niblett, *Prophecy and the Politics of Salvation in Late Georgian England: the Theology and Apocalyptic Vision of Joanna Southcott* (London: I.B. Tauris, 2015).

18. Gordon Allan, 'Joanna Southcott: enacting the woman clothed with the sun' in *The Oxford Handbook of the Reception History of the Bible*, eds. Michael Lieb, Emma Mason, and Jonathan Roberts (Oxford: Oxford University Press, 2011), pp. 635–48. On anti-Calvinism, see especially, Sarah Apetrei, *Women, Feminism and Religion in Early Enlightenment England* (Cambridge: Cambridge University Press, 2010), pp. 172, 278–80; Julie Hirst, *Jane Leade: Biography of a Seventeenth-Century Mystic* (Aldershot: Ashgate, 2005), pp. 115–18.

19. James Hopkins, *A Woman to Deliver Her People: Joanna Southcott and English Millenarianism in an Era of Revolution* (Austin: University of Texas Press, 1982), p. 84.

20. On calculating Southcottian numbers see, Philip Lockley, *Visionary Religion and Radicalism in Early Industrial England: from Southcott to Socialism* (Oxford: Oxford University Press, 2013), pp. 35–36.

21. Philip Lockley, 'Missionaries of the Millennium: Israelite Preachers in the English-speaking World, 1823–1863', *Journal of Religious History*, 37:3 (September 2013), pp. 369–90.

22. Sylvia Bowerbank, 'Lead, Jane (1624–1704)', *ODNB*; J.F.C. Harrison, *The Second Coming: Popular Millenarianism 1780–1850* (London, 1979), pp. 23, 38.

23. Revelation 12:1–6; Juster, *Doomsayers*, 216; Julie Hirst, 'Dreaming of a New Jerusalem: Jane Lead's Visions of Wisdom', *Feminist Theology*, 14 (2006), p. 356.

24. Bowerbank, 'Lead', *ODNB*; see also, Sylvia Bowerbank, 'Southcott, Joanna (1750–1814)', *ODNB*.

25. There is notable new evidence that Southcott was familiar with Richard Brothers' writings before 1801. See especially, Panacea Society Archive, Bedford, PN 222/55, 'Communication given to Joanna Southcott shewing the reason why the Lord chose Richard Brothers' (18 May 1798).

26. On Brothers, see Deborah Madden, *The Paddington Prophet: Richard Brothers's Journey to Jerusalem* (Manchester: Manchester University Press, 2010).

27. On the aftermath of Southcott's death, see especially, Lockley, *Visionary Religion*.

28. Revelation 12:1–5. Joanna Southcott, *The Third Book of Wonders, Announcing the Coming of Shiloh* (London, 1814).

29. Jane Lead, *A Fountain of Gardens* (London, 1697), pp. 468–71.

30. Allan, 'Joanna Southcott', pp. 635–48.

31. 'Philadelphus', *The Holy of Holies Unveiled!!! Or a Full and Divine Explanation of the Deep Theosophic Figures and the Many Scriptural Emblems which adorn the Superb Bible for Shiloh* (London: Dean and Munday, 1814).

32. Towards the end of the work, the title is explicitly linked to Boehme, referring to 'the proud knowledge of those who are let into the Holy of Holies, opened by the Spirit of God, in his chosen instrument, BEHMEN.' Philadelphus, *Holy of Holies Unveiled*, p. 85.

33. Philadelphus, *Holy of Holies Unveiled*, pp. 43–46.

34. Both Genesis 3 and Revelation 12 had long traditions of messianic interpretation in Christian history, and had therefore been liable to linkage before. The distinctive connection made by Southcott—and acknowledged by Philadelphus—was in the identity of the woman, and the form of the messiah.

35. Philadelphus, *Holy of Holies Unveiled*, p. 41.

36. Philadelphus, *Holy of Holies Unveiled*, p. 59. Emphasis in the original.
37. Philadelphus, *Holy of Holies Unveiled*, p. 59.
38. 'Philadelphus' was a relatively common pseudonym, especially in the two preceding centuries. It was notably the name signed by the author of *The State of the Philadelphian Society, or, the grounds of their proceedings consider'd* (London, 1697), which suggests an effort to imply continuity. The early nineteenth-century individual behind the pseudonym nonetheless remains unidentified.
39. On Foley, see Hopkins, *Woman to Deliver*, pp. 88–93.
40. BL, Add. MS 47,798/57.
41. For original, see Lead, *Fountain of Gardens*, pp. 454–57.
42. Jane Lead, *The revelation of revelations: particularly as an essay towards the unsealing, opening, and discovering the seven seals, the seven thunders, and the new Jerusalem state ...* (London: J. Pratt, 1804).
43. Jane Lead, *The Wars of David and the peaceable reign of Solomon symbolizing the times of warfare and refreshment of the saints..: In two treatises ... first published in the year 1700 ... To which is now subjoined Several Extracts ... from the "Fountain of Gardens," by the same author* (London: T. Wood, 1816).
44. Lead, *Wars of David*, iii–iv. The work contains no reference to Southcott. The principal commendation of Lead's work, in the 1816 edition at least, drew on the standing of the eighteenth-century devotional writer, William Law, and his particular endorsement of Lead and Boehme.
45. University of Texas (UT), Harry Ransom Research Center (HRC), Joanna Southcott Collection (JSC), Box 11/1/18. Clark was almost certainly copying from the 1696 original, as his writing reproduces the capitals of the original, and not the 1816 reprint which includes this passage. Lead, *Fountain of Gardens*, pp. 468–71.
46. UT, HRC, JSC, Box 11/1/18.
47. Lockley, *Visionary Religion*, p. 31. In London almost all the traceable Southcottian chapels appear to have had their own local prophet.
48. On Ward, his supporters, and his theology, see Lockley, *Visionary Religion*, pp. 125–42.
49. Zion Ward, *Zion's Works*, ed. C.B. Holinsworth, 16 vols (London, 1899–1904), vol. 14, pp. 66, 75.
50. Zion Ward, *The Vision of Judgment; or, the Return of Joanna from her trance* (London, 1829), p. 4.
51. Ward, *Vision of Judgment*, p. 4.
52. E.P. Thompson, *The Making of the English Working Class*, rev. ed. (Harmondsworth: Penguin, 1968), p. 879.

53. ZW to John Brentnall, 17 June 1829, in Zion Ward, *Letters, Epistles, and Revelations, of Jesus Christ, addressed to the Believers in the Glorious reign of Messiah* (London, 1831), p. 9.
54. PS PN 604, Zion Ward, 'The Creed of the Shilohites' [n.d.], p. 7.
55. Zion Ward, *The Judgment Seat of Christ* (London: C.W. Twort, 1831), pp. 110, 150–53, 180, 201. At least 25 chapbook editions of *Nixon's Original Cheshire Prophecy* or similar volumes were sold across England between 1790 and 1830. Ward would have had little difficulty encountering a copy.
56. Ward, *Judgment Seat of Christ*, pp. 140–41.
57. This poem was also reproduced in Lead, *Wars of David*, (1816), pp. 46–47.
58. Zion Ward, *The Living Oracle; or, the Star of Bethlehem: written in answer to a letter of the Rev. T.P Foley, addressed to Mr T. Pierce of Nottingham* (Nottingham, 1830); Zion Ward, *Zion's Works*, vol. 14, p. 80.
59. Lead, *Divine Revelations and Prophecies*, p. 3.
60. Lead, *Divine Revelations and Prophecies*, p. 30.
61. Lead, *Fountain of Gardens*, vol. 1, p. 79.
62. On Ward's support from the atheist radical, Richard Carlile, see Lockley, *Visionary Religion*, pp. 185–208.
63. J.E.M. Latham, *Search for a New Eden: James Pierrepont Greaves (1777–1842) the Sacred Socialist and his Followers* (London: Associated University Presses, 1999).
64. Ward's and Greaves' respective theologies are briefly discussed in Latham, *Search for a New Eden*, pp. 75–76.
65. Latham, *Search for a New Eden*, pp. 150–67.
66. On the resulting community, see Richard Frances, *Fruitlands: the Alcott family and their search for utopia* (New Haven: Yale University Press, 2010).
67. 'Catalogue of Books', *The Dial*, 3:4 (April 1843), p. 545.
68. Harvard University, Houghton Library, B MS Am 1280.235 'Books of Charles Lane'. Emerson also held volumes of *The Shepherd* journal edited by one-time Southcottian and Wroeite, James Smith—to which Lane contributed.
69. Harvard University, Houghton Library, [*AC85.Al191.Zz] Books from the library of Amos Bronson Alcott.
70. Priscilla J. Brewer, 'Emerson, Lane and the Shakers: A Case of Converging Ideologies', *The New England Quarterly*, 55:2 (June 1982), pp. 270–72.
71. I must acknowledge that Bridget Jacobs has previously speculated on Lane being the conduit for the introduction of Lead's writings to Shakers. I am grateful to the Houghton Library for awarding me the Ralph Waldo

Emerson Fellowship in 2013, which enabled me to test this theory thoroughly—if not conclusively.

72. The letter is reproduced in a biography of Smith: W.A. Smith, '*Shepherd Smith': the story of a mind* (London, 1892), p. 421. On Brook Farm see, Sterling F. Delano, *Brook Farm: the dark side of utopia* (Cambridge MA: Harvard University Press, 2004).

73. On Smith, see Lockley, *Visionary Religion*.

74. Smith, '*Shepherd Smith'*, p. 421.

75. Smith, '*Shepherd Smith'*, p. 420.

76. Lockley, 'Missionaries of the Millennium', pp. 384–85.

77. John Wroe, *Private Communications* (Wakefield, 1853), III.

78. See WRHS MSS Microfilm, reel 52, Book 6/B39, p. 149; reel 61, Book 7/B203.

79. Lockley, 'Missionaries of the Millennium', p. 388.

80. These ideas are discussed further in Philip Lockley, 'Millenarians in the Pennines, 1800–1830: Building and Believing Jerusalem', *Northern History*, 47 (2010), pp. 297–317.

81. John Wroe, *Private Communications* (Wakefield, 1846), vol. II, pp. 1136, 1231, 1248.

82. Galatians 4:26; Wroe, *Private Communications*, II, pp. 1300, 1390.

83. John Wroe, *Private Communications given to John Wroe* (Gravesend, 1853), vol. III, p. 30.

84. On Jezreel see Ruth Windscheffel, *The Jezreelites* (London: I.B. Tauris, forthcoming).

85. James Jershom Jezreel, *Extracts from the Flying Roll* (Chatham, 1878), pp. 4–5.

86. Jezreel, *Flying Roll*, pp. 14–15.

87. Jezreel, *Flying Roll*, p. 24.

88. Jezreel, *Flying Roll*, p. 25.

89. Jezreel, *Flying Roll*, p. 65.

90. Jezreel, *Flying Roll*, p. 84.

91. W.D. Forsyth 'Introduction' in Jane Lead, *Ascent to the mount of vision*, ed. W.D. Forsyth (Littleborough, 1906), p. 3. The 'Sixty Propositions' were originally published within Jane Lead, *A message to the Philadelphian Society whithersoever dispersed over the whole earth. Together with, a call to the several gathered churches among Protestants in this nation of England* (1696).

92. Medway Archives, 06a_DE_SERIES_1001_1200/DE1173 Roll of new members 1882, directory of English members and extracts from *Sixty Propositions to the Philade[l]phia Society* c.1882. Propositions had previously been republished in both *The Wars of David* (1816) and Ward's edition of *Divine Revelations and Prophecies* (1830).

93. Proposition 43 in Lead, *Wars of David* (1816 edition), p. 51.
94. Propositions 44, 45 and 47 in Lead, *Wars of David* (1816 edition), pp. 51–52.
95. Propositions 54, 55 and 58 in Lead, *Wars of David* (1816 edition), p. 53.
96. Sarah Apetrei has recently noted the connection between Jane Lead and the Jezreelites, principally in Forsyth's post-Jezreel tradition, drawing particular attention to the 'feminist' dimension to their interacting theology through Forsyth's 1906 edition. Apetrei, *Women, Feminism and Religion*, pp. 244–8.
97. Forsyth 'Introduction' in Lead, *Ascent*, p. 3.
98. Forsyth 'Introduction' in Lead, *Ascent*, p. 3.
99. Forsyth 'Introduction' in Lead, *Ascent*, pp. 4–5.
100. Forsyth 'Introduction' in Lead, *Ascent*, p. 5.

CHAPTER 12

'A Prophecy Out of the Past': Contrasting Treatments of Jane Lead Among Two North American Twentieth-Century Millenarian Movements: Mary's City of David and the Latter Rain

Bridget M. Jacobs

In 1895, an obscure American religious movement headed by then-jailed 'Prince Michael' Mills printed a version of the Philadelphian Society's 'Sixty Propositions' in its newspaper. An offshoot of the now nearly as obscure Jezreelite movement, Mills' Detroit-based group is noted for converting a young American couple, Benjamin and Mary Purnell, to their faith.[1] Benjamin and Mary became famous in the first half of the twentieth century as the founders of the Israelite House of David, the most successful American Southcottian communal group, best known for its traveling baseball team, jazz bands, amusement park (which was said to have inspired Disneyland), and most visually distinctive to 'Gentile' outsiders, the uncut hair and beards of the Israelite men. Like several other American communal society leaders of the late nineteenth through early twentieth centuries, including his predecessor Mills, Benjamin Purnell

B.M. Jacobs (✉)
University of Louisiana at Lafayette, Lafayette, LA, USA

© The Editor(s) (if applicable) and The Author(s) 2016   267
A. Hessayon (ed.), *Jane Lead and her Transnational Legacy*,
DOI 10.1057/978-1-137-39614-3_12

was accused of running a fraudulent cult and was charged with sexually assaulting women in the group.[2] Although Purnell was never found guilty of rape, rather 'immoral and illegal practices and teachings',[3] the colony was placed into receivership and he died of tuberculosis soon afterwards. Under terms of the receivership and subsequent settlement decree, his widow Mary and her followers were forced to leave the original colony setting up a new colony one block away in 1930. The original colony maintained ownership of its successful tourist enterprises, while Mary's group, the 'City of David', was focused on printing and disseminating Mary's prophetic declarations, which increasingly became infused with Jane Lead's Philadelphian theosophy.

Mary's City of David retained a copy of Mills' 'Sixty Propositions',[4] and included it with the new colony's reprint of Lead's *The Ascent to the Mount of Vision* in 1932, two years after the split. Actually entitled *Jane Lead* on the cover, the inside cover page is titled *The Ascent to the Mount of Vision* and this is typically how it is referred to by colony members in print and in manuscript.[5] It contains the entire *Mount of Vision* and 'Sixty Propositions', as well as extracts from *Signs of the Times*. This version, along with several of Mary's own works which either directly quoted or closely paraphrased Lead's work, was in active print circulation when a Pentecostal version of 'Sixty Propositions' appeared in one of the better known American 'Healing Movement' magazines, *Golden Grain*, in 1949. While the Pentecostal edition did not mirror Mary's City of David's version, it *does* bear striking similarities to earlier Jezreelite versions that had not previously appeared elsewhere in print. Distinctive features include the wrong date (1619) and anonymous authorship, both of which Mary's City of David 'fixed' later, but which earlier Pentecostal publishers (notably those from the contemporaneous Latter Rain movement) did not.

Several scholars, including Sarah Apetrei, Donald Durnbaugh and Nigel Smith have commented on the present-day popular revival of Philadelphian Society texts, which is often centered around 'Sixty Propositions'. Current popular North American reception of this text can be largely traced to these two printed sources circulating in the mid- to late-twentieth century—the more 'faithful' and typographically consistent, yet distinctive Mary's City of David edition, and the progressively more 'edited' version(s) disseminated within the cross-denominational Pentecostal Latter Rain movement. Both appear to trace their print genealogy through earlier Jezreelite renditions, not directly to the 'original' 1697 *Theosophical Transactions* text.

Mary's City of David members believed that 'Sixty Propositions' as well as Lead's other works as they encountered and disseminated them *in print* were divinely inspired, and that they were the chosen caretakers of Jane Lead's printed oracular legacy. Although they made several changes to Mills, once it was committed to print they remained faithful to their revised edition. In addition, 'Sixty Propositions' was just the first of an ever widening canon of Lead works acquired by the group in the 1930s and 1940s, which eventually encompassed most of her extant printed works in English. They were all reproduced for colony use and carefully typed, proofread, and certified by group leaders. Mary Purnell as the co-seventh messenger was the only one in the group who paraphrased or altered Lead's text in any way in her own writings, and once Mary's versions entered print they also remained static.

The Latter Rain movement, which spread within North American Pentecostalism post-World War II, instead privileged the present-day prophetic declarations of its leaders as God's 'rhema' word over the 'logos' or printed scriptural and historical texts. According to Richard Riss's history of the Latter Rain, which emerged as a distinct religious movement in the late 1940s, the gift of prophecy was a 'major distinguishing mark' as compared to the Healing and earlier Pentecostal movements from which the Latter Rain was descended.[6] One of the original Latter Rain elders, James Watt, split from the nascent movement in 1949 in part because it privileged the 'rhema' or oral/spoken words of prophecy over the 'logos' or written/printed Biblical scripture, rather than testing its 'agreement' with the printed text.[7] Consistent with these beliefs, Latter Rain versions of 'Sixty Propositions' feature additional textual changes and omissions beyond those made by the Jezreelites; in one case where the text becomes barely recognizable from the source. Two of the three earlier Latter Rain print versions also added an emergence myth attributed to a well-known Pentecostal healing evangelist, although the actual connection was tenuous at best. In contrast to Mary's City of David where a revised, yet static edition of 'Sixty Propositions' became a centerpiece of its printed theology, contemporary Latter Rain utterances appeared to direct additional editorial changes to the text and/or the contexts in which it appeared, resulting in a dynamically changing text that reflected the movement's equally dynamic, non-print based beliefs. 'Sixty Propositions' was one utterance of many, oral and written, which legitimized the movement as the end-time fulfillment of prophecy. There also seemed to be little interest among Latter Rain writers in reading other Philadelphian Society texts until the very late twentieth century, in contrast to Mary's City of David which systematically acquired as many of Lead's works as possible. However, while the two groups diverged in their treatment of 'Sixty Propositions', both appeared to have co-opted it in support of their similarly embattled movements.

MARY'S CITY OF DAVID: FROM SOUTHCOTTIAN SECT TO MODERN DAY PHILADELPHIAN SOCIETY?

Prior to the 1930 split of the Israelite House of David, only a limited number of Jane Lead's works were known and read by most Southcottian groups through the end of the nineteenth century. These groups recognize a 'third testimony' announcing the imminent return of Christ through a series of seven or eight prophetic 'messengers' in a 'visitation' which began with Joanna Southcott in the early nineteenth century. Most Southcottian groups believe there are (or will be) seven angelic messengers mirroring the seven angels announcing the Apocalypse in the Book of Revelation. The English Panacea Society is the most notable exception: its leader, Mabel Barltrop, renamed herself 'Octavia' to reflect its belief that she was the eighth and final messenger. However, the more typical prophetic line includes Joanna Southcott, Richard Brothers, George Turner and John Wroe, with subsequent groups claiming James Jershom Jezreel (the Jezreelites), Benjamin and Mary Purnell, and/or Octavia.

J.F.C. Harrison implied in his seminal work on eighteenth and nineteenth century English millenarianism, *The Second Coming*, that the Southcottians were influenced by Lead's ideas as subsumed into English millenarian subculture rather than directly through print. However, subsequent scholarship has uncovered little evidence that Lead's printed works were an integral part of early Southcottian print culture. As explored in more detail in Chap. 11 in this volume, while Southcott certainly echoes Lead, she did not directly cite or quote Lead; certainly not to the extent as later found among Mary's City of David, even if Southcott was aware of her or her prophecies as circulating in English millenarian subculture. E.P. Thompson noted that there was a 'revival of interest in Jane Lead' in the late eighteenth century and that William Blake's acquaintance P.J. Loutherbourg—recognizable among Lead scholars as several of the Lead volumes in the British Library bear his inscription—was also a follower of Southcott's predecessor, Richard Brothers.[8] However, since Loutherbourg traveled in several other theosophical circles during this period this bit of circumstantial evidence does not prove that either Brothers or Southcott were avid readers of Lead, nor that Lead's works were included in early Southcottian *print* culture. The only other anecdotal evidence that Southcott might have been aware of Lead's works (notably her spiritual diary, *Fountain of Gardens*) was in Rachel Fox's *Early Dawn of the Great Prophetical Visitation to England*, where she claimed she found one 'extract' from 7 December 1676 as the 'only extraneous matter amid some hundreds of Joanna's Writings' within a 'large box of Joanna Southcott MSS'.[9] However, it is unclear from Fox's text whether Southcott had this in her possession or it was added by other (or later) Southcottian followers, particularly since 'Extracts from the Fountain of Gardens', including this entry, had been appended to both the 1816 edition of Lead's *Wars of David* and John 'Zion' Ward's 1830 Lead compilation, *Divine Revelations and Prophecies*.[10] Fox has conversely stated elsewhere that she found no evidence that Southcott had read Lead.[11]

While John 'Zion' Ward's *Divine Revelations and Prophecies* collection of Lead's works was originally intended to help confirm Ward's legitimacy among Southcottians (it failed miserably),[12] print and manuscript evidence instead shows that Lead was not claimed by Southcottians until the end of the nineteenth and beginning of the twentieth centuries when they began to graft her and/or her works into their prophetic tradition and therefore onto Southcott's prophetic persona. While *Divine Revelations and Prophecies* circulated widely among non-Southcottian circles (most notably among the American Shakers), among Southcottians Lead faded back into obscurity until 'Sixty Propositions' was rediscovered by James Jershom Jezreel and his followers in the late nineteenth century.[13] Benjamin Purnell stated that 'Sixty Propositions ... has been published in the former house, under Jezreel', and one of Jezreel's followers and prospective successors, William Forsyth, similarly claimed that '[Lead's] "Sixty propositions to the Philadelphian Church" ... was all we possessed of the author's works till 1899',[14] which was when the Jezreelites encountered a widely disseminated, but little studied series of cyclostyle reprints of her works by the Scottish 'new life' publisher, John Thomson.

Published between 1885 and 1905, Thomson reproduced at least ten of Lead's works, which were hand copied in cyclostyle from originals held in the British Museum and possibly also in other libraries. During this same period, Thomson also printed conventional movable typeset and bound reprints of works by well-known theosophers with whom Lead is often grouped, including Jacob Boehme and Emmanuel Swedenborg, as well as the lesser-known neo-Swedenborgian Thomas Lake Harris, with whom Thomson was affiliated. However, very few of these more durable, conventional volumes survive, unlike the cheap paperboard cyclostyles which, while still rare, are readily accessible in several academic libraries across North America and England.[15] Occupying a unique place between conventional print and manuscript cultures, the Jane Lead cyclostyle reprints may comprise the most disseminated collection of commercially cyclostyled works extant in world libraries. They appear in major Southcottian collections as well. Three of these cyclostyles added by Panacea Society members are the only Lead-related materials in the expansive Joanna Southcott collection in the University of Texas at Austin, undermining the widely held belief among latter day Southcottians that Joanna Southcott 'referred to', read or cited Lead directly.

William Forsyth's 1906 edition of *Ascent to the Mount of Vision* is derived from the 1905 Thomson cyclostyle version. Foreshadowing Mary's City of David's later attempts to balance devotion to the historic text against their belief that their leaders were jointly the seventh messenger, Forsyth claimed that his edition of *Ascent to the Mount of Vision* 'followed close to the language of the author on this subject as far as possible',[16] while conversely making editorial changes, adding context and commentary, and typographically emphasizing Jezreelite keywords like 'branch' and 'flying roll', thus leveraging the text in support of Jezreel's legitimacy as the sixth messenger. While the Israelite House of David and later Mary's City of David did not acquire Forsyth's edition, they too had the 1905 cyclostyle edition, indicating that the cyclostyle circulated more widely among Jezreelite circles beyond the Forsyth-led group in England.

Aside from the 1895 Michael Mills edition of 'Sixty Propositions' and one or two more of the Thomson cyclostyles, much of Mary's City of David's initial knowledge of Lead also came through several publications of their English Southcottian contemporaries, the Panacea Society, whose works Mary's City of David owned and specifically referred to in their own reclamation of Lead's print works, and which they had in their possession no later than the 1930s. Page references from the Panacea Society's Lead volume, *Early Dawn of the Great Prophetical Visitation to England* indicate that this group in turn took their extracts from the Thomson cyclostyles, not from earlier editions.[17] As noted earlier, Panacea Society members searched for Lead's multi-volume spiritual diary *Fountain of Gardens*— which Thomson did not reprint—and included one entry Rachel Fox claimed she found in a collection of Southcott manuscripts. Fox also included several of the 'Sixty Propositions to the Philadelphian Society, whithersoever dispersed as the Israel of God', which was not included in any of the Thomson cyclostyles but instead closely followed the Mills edition titling and text, possibly indicating a common Jezreelite lineage. Prefiguring Mary's City of David's current position on Lead, Octavia (Mabel Barltrop) and Rachel Fox came very close to claiming Lead as the first messenger, stating that God's end time plan was presented first '(a)s a prophetic whole by Jane Lead' which was then '(s)plit up into the seven prismatic colors' by the subsequent messengers.[18] However, they also stated that 'Ann Lee had a *whole* revelation, so did Jane Lead' before it was 'split up into seven parts',[19] and in an early pre-Panacea Society book *The Mystery of God in Woman*, Fox claimed that Guillaume Postel and St. Theresa of Avila also received the same 'mystery', indicating that this group's leaders did not necessarily believe that Lead was the *only* 'early dawn' of the visitation.[20]

But more importantly in this discussion of how and where Lead's works were circulated, read, and interpreted among Southcottian groups, Mary's City of David had several of the Panacea Society works dealing with Lead in its possession, including the extracts and catalog of Lead's major works in *Early Dawn*, as well as the additional Lead references in *Extracts of the Sacred Roll of Ann Lee's Visitation, Healing for All*, and *How We Built Jerusalem in England's Green and Pleasant Land*.[21] They shared the Panacea Society's belief that '[b]y means of the press, God protects the essential utterances of His prophets, causing them to be revived in later centuries when their witness is required',[22] and that by acquiring and recirculating Lead's texts they were reviving her divine witness. While Lead's works were not consistently part of their print cultures until well after Southcott's death, Southcottian groups, including Mary's City of David and its predecessor, the Israelite House of David, had always placed great emphasis on writing and print, and believed that producing written works was a key signifier of the 'visitation'.[23] According to Ron Taylor, Benjamin's and Mary's corpus of printed works was critical in their ability to gain new converts particularly from the Australian Christian Israelite (Wroeite) Church, which was awaiting the sixth and seventh messengers. Their print works were, according to Taylor, whose ancestors were Australian converts, viewed as the primary sign that they were the seventh messengers (and Jezreel the sixth), not their oral preaching, although both Benjamin and Mary were reportedly charismatic preachers as well.[24] In his biography of Benjamin Purnell, Clare Adkin also found that a 'written message tended to secure the claims of a messenger', which set Purnell apart from Michael Mills who 'overlooked the written message'.[25] It is no wonder that Mary Purnell's new group re-devoted itself to the written word rather than to the famous (yet fading) tourist enterprises that marked the House of David's success. Within this context, Lead's printed works were seen as similar evidence of the 'visitation' brought to its completion within the Purnells' works.

While it is difficult to ascertain exactly how many Lead works Mary's City of David leaders had before or at the time of its split from the House of David, or whether they had acquired any of the Lead-related Panacea Society texts before 1930, there is clear evidence they had at least the Mills 'Sixty Propositions', and one additional Thomson cyclostyle, *The Signs of the Times Forerunning the Kingdom of Christ and Evidencing When it is Come* (no later than 1925), in addition to the previously mentioned 1905 cyclostyle edition of *Mount of Vision*.[26] All three works are included in total or in part in Mary's City of David *Jane Lead* pamphlet in 1932, which is still distributed today as it was originally typeset.[27] The pamphlet closes with 'Sixty Propositions' followed by Benjamin Purnell's pronouncement that while 'little was fulfilled' of 'Sixty Propositions' in the Jezreelite church, the 'greater and almost all, pointed down to this Seventh Church, or Israelite House of David, now having its accomplishment'.[28] Mary's City of David indicated by printing this *after* Benjamin Purnell's death that the new colony under Mary's leadership was the 'Philadelphian church spoken of' by Jane Lead, James Jershom Jezreel, and Benjamin Purnell, as they saw prophesied in 'Sixty Propositions'. While this was presumably written before the colony's split, commentary like, '[t]his Philadelphia church is spoken of as coming out of the wilderness'[29] could just as plausibly have elicited recent memories of Mary and her followers' exile from the original colony, leveraging 'Sixty Propositions' specifically in support of Mary's City of David rather than the more general 'ingathering' at Benton Harbor claimed by both colonies.

While Mary's City of David pamphlet was, when compared to the Forsyth edition, much closer to the source text and free from much commentary or paratext until Benjamin Purnell's closing essay, 'Sixty Propositions' features several textual variants unique to the Mary's City of David edition.[30] First, the date is 'corrected' from 1619—the incorrect date found in Mills—to a much more plausible but still incorrect date, 1699, more than likely extrapolated from *Mount of Vision*. Mary's City of David kept some Mills variants: an obvious one is 'full redemption *through*

Christ' rather than '*by* Christ' in proposition one. However, it added several more references than Mills to the 'ingathering of [the 144,000 of] Israel', and added 'aliens and strangers' to proposition 31. These alterations further amplified Mary's City of David's stance as a small, faithful, yet persecuted group as they saw themselves reflected through 'Sixty Propositions'. They also 'corrected' proposition 14 from 'stem of David' to 'stem of Jesse' which more directly quotes Isaiah 11:1, and made several other minor grammatical and editorial changes which were not necessarily theological or explanatory (see Table 12.1).

Changes like these reflect a belief that while 'Sixty Propositions' was divinely inspired, prior to the subsequent messengers reprinting it for current and prospective followers, they too were divinely inspired to amplify and alter the text.

However, once Mary's City of David's edition of 'Sixty Propositions' was committed to print, the group remained faithful to their revised version of the text, even after they accumulated and based on archival evidence close read an impressive array of other Lead texts in subsequent

Table 12.1 Versions of the 'sixty propositions'

Original 1697 version	1895 Michael Mills	1932 Mary's City of David
Proposition 7: In order to which the *Ark* of the Testimony in Heaven, shall be open'd before the End of this World, and the Living Testimony which is therein contain'd, shall be *Unsealed*	In order to which the Ark of the Testimony in heaven shall be opened before the end of this world, and the living Testimony which is therein contained shall be unsealed [modernized language only]	In order to which, the ark (of God's testimony in heaven shall be opened). Before the end of the world (age) and the living (144,000) testimony which is herein contained be unsealed [parenthetical amplifications added with other wording changes]
Proposition 14: Of the stem of David...	Of the stem of David... [left unchanged from original]	Of the stem of Jesse... [changed to more directly quote Isaiah 11:1]
Proposition 31: Then it will go on to Multiply and Propagate it self Universally; not only to the Number of the *First-born*; but also to the *Remnant of the Seed*: Against which the *Dragon* shall make continual War	Then will it go on to multiply and propagate itself universally, not only to the number of the first born (which is 144,000), but also to the remnant of the seed, against whom the Dragon shall make continual war [modernized language; one parenthetical addition]	Then it will go on to multiply and propagate itself universally, not only as to the number of the firstborn (144,000), but also to the remnant of the seed (aliens), and strangers, against whom the dragon shall make war [added 'aliens' and 'strangers' to amplify text]

years. By Mary's death they had acquired 12 of Lead's works, including several more Thomson cyclostyles, a rare 1804 reprint of *Revelation of Revelations*, and a selection of photostats they requested from the British Museum during the height of German bombing in 1939–41.[31] The group did not print any more of Lead's other works in separate volumes until long after Mary's death in the 1990s, but Mary quoted and paraphrased all of Lead's works they had in their possession frequently in the colony newspaper as well as in her last *Comforter* book, *The Book of Paradise*. Each Lead text was also retyped and bound into books and commonplaces for internal colony use.[32] Mary's 'lieutenant' Francis Thorpe, who assumed leadership over the colony after her death, proofread and certified all the typed Lead texts, and even made corrections in the 1804 *Revelation of Revelations* reprint after the colony acquired a photostat of the original 1683 edition. No other texts or authors read by the colony received this treatment, not even Southcott's or any of the other previous six messengers. It could be argued that if one looks past their non-scholarly, devotional treatment of Lead, Mary and her closest followers were certainly more familiar with her works than most literary or religious scholars of their period or indeed even ours. 'Sixty Propositions'—*as the colony printed it*—became a stable centerpiece of the colony's print culture, as reflected within its later donation of a complete set of archival and print materials to the Communal Society Collection at Hamilton College in upstate New York. Indeed, several copies and editions of 'Sixty Propositions' anchor this collection. In addition, Mary's own printed prophetic utterances—including innumerable direct quotes, paraphrases and allusions from Jane Lead's works—provided documented evidence of both Mary Purnell's *and* Jane Lead's prophetic authority. Aside from the Purnells' own writings, by the end of Mary's life the group's print culture revolved more around Jane Lead than around any of the Southcottian line of messengers.

'A PROPHECY FROM THE PAST': THE LATTER RAIN MOVEMENT'S TRANSFORMATIONS OF 'SIXTY PROPOSITIONS'

In contrast to Mary's City of David, which placed great emphasis on writing and print, and believed that producing written works was a key signifier of the 'visitation', North American Pentecostal movements of the twentieth century valued dynamic oral preaching and communal exercise of the 'gifts of the spirit' more highly, including speaking in tongues, healing, spiritual song and personal prophecy. While the Pentecostal and parallel Healing and Latter Rain movements certainly developed a voluminous print culture, notably in the many magazines and newspapers devoted to its ministers' traveling revivals, print served a different role. Among the Mary's City of David's members, the printed word itself was considered divine (as marked with a dove signifying a word from God). However, print in the Pentecostal and Healing movements was used more often as a vehicle to *proclaim* God's great end-time works but was not usually considered divine in itself. Divine visitations occurred in revivals and in other corporate gatherings, not in print. As a result, print could announce a *sign* of inspiration through the stories told of miraculous healings or prophecy come to pass, but was not itself the divine *signified*. *Voice of Healing*, perhaps the most famous Healing Movement magazine became, according to Pentecostal scholar David Harrell, 'a central advertising bureau for evangelists with proven ministries'.[33] Their ministries 'lived and died with the charisma of the evangelist',[34] not with their print message. Some of the other healing movement magazines, notably *Golden Grain* which was edited by prominent healing evangelist Charles Price, also printed articles that were originally given orally as sermons. *Golden Grain* continued to reprint Price's sermons after his death in 1947 until it ceased publication 10 years later, in addition to printing letters from readers and news about the 'full gospel' revivals continued by his successors, including Evelyn Carvell, a former assistant who also assumed editorship of the magazine.

In the August 1949 issue of *Golden Grain* appeared 'Theological Gleanings from an Unknown Pen of the Seventeenth Century'—an unattributed, un-numbered, and oddly paragraphed version of 'Sixty Propositions'.[35] In addition to transcribed sermons, *Golden Grain* often featured devotional poetry, including work by well-known authors, but not historic texts like this one presented as prophecy. Contextually, it appeared immediately after 'The Gathering Storm', a millenarian sermon that had recently been given in Canada by Lorne Fox, another of the Charles Price traveling ministers. Typical of many other Evangelical and Pentecostal preachers of the period, Fox viewed current world events, particularly World Wars I and II, advances in weapons technology, the ascendency of Soviet-style Communism, and especially the re-establishment of Israel as a nation through a chiliastic lens, predicting that the next world conflict had to be Armageddon. And prefiguring later pronouncements by Latter Rain elders that the healing evangelists of Fox's generation, notably

Price and Smith Wigglesworth, had prophesied the Latter Rain revival,[36] Fox proclaimed:

> Following World War I, God began to speak to humanity again by means of spiritual awakening and revivals all over the world. God raised up the greatest revivalists of the century, among them ... Smith Wigglesworth ..., Dr. Charles S. Price ..., and many others, to carry the full gospel to the nations.[37]

In this context, it would have been very difficult for *Golden Grain* subscribers to read 'Theological Gleanings', i.e., 'Sixty Propositions', as anything but an end-time prophecy in the midst of being fulfilled before their very eyes, from another time when God was also 'speaking to humanity'. And although the text did not come from Price's personal papers as later Latter Rain ministers would claim—editor Evelyn Carvell instead explained at the end of this issue that a 'good sister' in Oakland, CA gave it to her—it is certainly understandable that it would have been attributed to Price given its original Pentecostal print context following Fox's sermon.

The text itself appeared, at least on the surface, unlike any previous printed edition of the text. All other printed versions to this point had been numbered. Indeed, even surviving manuscript versions—notably the ones that Shaker women copied out of the 1830 edition of *Divine Revelations and Prophecies*—were numbered. While one might guess that the *Golden Grain* version might have been derived from the only other North American version in active print circulation during this period, particularly since the close of the opening sentence, 'written 330 years ago'[38] mirrors the Mary's City of David version, close examination of the two versions shows that the body of the text had to have been derived from an earlier or at least different source, since it does not contain any of the unique editorial changes made by Mary's City of David, or even some of the ones from their 1895 Mills source. Instead, it conformed most closely to the 1882 Jezreelite manuscript edition from which Mills was likely also derived. Editorial anomalies like 'abstracted' instead of 'obstructed'[39] are found in the Jezreelite handwritten manuscript, not in other printed editions. Like Mills and the Jezreelite manuscript, 'Theological Gleanings' was anonymous, dated 'A.D. 1619', and similarly subtitled 'to the Philadelphia Society whithersoever dispersed as the Israel of God'.[40] In fact, beyond its paragraphed style and systematic omission of the word 'catholic' (not surprising since this was targeted to a North American

Protestant audience which no longer understood the late seventeenth century meaning of the word), it conformed more closely to Jezreelite and even earlier editions than Mary's City of David's which mirrored the 1697 and 1816 numbered *format* but not necessarily *text*. Another possible factor that might point to the Jezreelites being the primary source was that Evelyn Carvell was closely associated with Myrtle Beall, a Detroit Assemblies of God pastor who had become associated with the Latter Rain during a visit to Vancouver in 1949, and whose church then spread the Canadian Latter Rain revival throughout the United States.[41] Some of the Jezreelites' most successful outreaches in the United States were in the upper Midwest, particularly in Michigan, and not all these Jezreelites later joined with Mills or the Purnells. Did a Jezreelite version of 'Sixty Propositions' circulate among Pentecostal believers in Michigan, and then make its way via Beall's networks to Oakland and then to Carvell? Was Beall or one of her parishioners really the 'good sister' who gave it to Carvell? Since there isn't any archival or print evidence definitively linking 'Theological Gleanings' to Beall it is impossible to do more than conjecture. However, 'Theological Gleanings' so closely matches the Jezreelite manuscript in Strood, Kent (more so than any other printed or manuscript edition found to date),[42] that some sort of Jezreelite origin is not just possible but likely.

One can make an even stronger case that the anonymous 1949 'Theological Gleanings' then became the source for three subsequent Latter Rain versions, appearing in the pamphlets and booklets by founding Latter Rain elder George Hawtin, and two early second generation Latter Rain ministers, Royal Cronquist and Bill Britton, all of whom networked extensively within the wider Pentecostal movement and then the later Charismatic movement of the 1960s and 1970s.[43] The Latter Rain movement, sometimes also called the Latter Rain revival or New Order of the Latter Rain, was a millenarian offshoot of mainstream North American Pentecostalism which began at the Sharon Bible College in North Battleford, Saskatchewan in 1948, and quickly spread across North America through well-established Pentecostal and Healing movement networks. In contrast to classical Pentecostals who 'tarried' in prayer awaiting the manifested gifts of the Holy Spirit, the Latter Rain emphasized receiving spiritual gifts of tongues, personal prophecy, and ministerial offices through the laying on of hands.[44] Taken from Ephesians 4:11, these offices were apostles, prophets (in Latter Rain ecclesiology these two offices have governmental leadership over both the church and the millennial earth), evangelists, pastors and teachers. According to the movement's theology, these offices had been allowed to lapse but were being restored through the last days revival in preparation for the victorious church's millennial reign over earth. The Latter Rain also de-emphasized popular notions of the 'rapture'. They instead believed that this final 'latter rain' of spiritual gifts imparted by anointed spiritual leaders would empower the church to join in perfect unity and facilitate Christ's imminent return. This would occur when the unified 'manifest sons of God' corporately embodied the spirit of Christ, who would then rule and reign over earth—not unlike Lead's Philadelphian ideal. Several Latter Rain leaders also, like Lead, advocated universal reconciliation. Far from achieving unity, the Latter Rain movement caused serious rifts in several major Pentecostal denominations, especially the Pentecostal Assemblies of Canada, the Pentecostal Holiness Church, and the Assemblies of God (USA) which officially denounced the key doctrines of the Latter Rain in 1949. In this context, 'Sixty Propositions' could be viewed as historic and prophetic justification for the embattled movement, particularly as the years passed and it continued to be shunned by mainstream Pentecostal denominations, while key participants exerted their influence on the budding Charismatic movement. There was an ongoing need to legitimize itself as a true 'move of God' to the mainline Pentecostal and Evangelical subcultures in North America from whom it continued to draw converts.[45]

While extant Latter Rain versions of 'Sixty Propositions' are undated, one can estimate that Hawtin's was first, followed by Britton's and Cronquist's, based on the years they were active in ministry as well as on internal textual and contextual evidence. Hawtin's version of 'Sixty Propositions' was republished in his 33 volume *Treasures of Truth* booklet series of the 1980s, which were based on his articles and sermons in *The Page* magazine which began publication in 1961.[46] Royal Cronquist also stated that the 'Anonymous 1619 Prophecy' first 'came into my hands by a stranger when I was only six months old in Christ', which also dates it to approximately 1961.[47] Among these sources it is possible to conjecture that it was circulating in Latter Rain ministerial networks by at least the early 1960s, if not much earlier. J. Preston Eby, who first became connected with the Latter Rain in the early 1950s and who later read and taught on some of Lead's other works including *Revelation of Revelations*, stated that he first learned of Lead through his 'association with brethren in the Latter Rain movement ... Bill Britton, George Hawtin, etc.',[48] which also dates it within this general period, although it was not until much later that 'Sixty Propositions' was attributed to Lead by name in print.

'Sixty Propositions' closes one of Hawtin's treatises entitled, *Here is the Mind That Hath Wisdom,* which is not as overtly apocalyptic as 'The Gathering Storm', but certainly deals with chiliastic themes consistent with Lead's own work three centuries earlier—the restoration of Edenic paradise on earth through devotion to Godly wisdom, the attainment of divine 'sonship' through becoming unified with the Godhead through Christ, and a rejection of all 'worldly' things, including those found in the institutional church, without becoming sectarian.[49] There are some key differences between Hawtin's and Lead's theology, particularly in that Wisdom here is not personified, certainly not female or even close to being a discrete member of the Godhead, but is more generally identified as the (male) mind of the Father and Son. The apocalypse here is gradual, echoing Lead more than the instant 'rapture' popularly associated with North American Evangelicals and Pentecostals: 'Unto this high realm many are now proceeding, and from it the world will be filled with the knowledge and government of the Lord'.[50] Hawtin concludes, 'the following remarkable prophecy, given in the year 1619, forcefully confirms the truths written above',[51] authorizing both his teaching as well as the 'anonymous' prophecy. The implication is, since they both agree, they must be true and hence from God.

Like 'Theological Gleanings' Hawtin's version of the text is unnumbered and paragraphed. Based on comparing idiosyncrasies shared between the two, *Golden Grain* was more than likely Hawtin's source. However, Hawtin's version features modernized grammar and syntax, as well as systematic removal of any reference to 'Philadelphia', 'Philadelphian', or 'Philadelphian Society'. The name 'Jesus' is also omitted, which may reflect 'manifest sons of God' or 'sonship' theology in which Jesus Christ would not return as an individual, but as the Spirit of Christ within an elite group of united 'overcomers'. The 'Philadelphian church' is renamed the 'virgin church',[52] and denominational or sectarian references are deleted or changed. This is especially apparent at the end of the text, which in its earlier forms described the Philadelphian Society as dispersed within existing sects in preparation of the later 'Philadelphian Church' described in most of 'Sixty Propositions'; this meaning is deleted from the Hawtin edition, and 'ought' becomes 'must', implying that the 'virgin church' has already come to fruition within the movement: 'All true waiters of His kingdom in Spirit *must* be numbered among the virgin spirits to whom this message appertains'.[53] Also, in contrast to earlier versions that addressed the Philadelphians in the third person, and assumed both believing and skeptical readers, the second person address, 'Be watchful and quicken *your* pace'[54] targets this specifically to sympathizers of a marginalized movement that by this time had been ostracized by denominational Pentecostals.

Bill Britton's tri-fold pamphlet edition is undated but, based on its apparently being typed on an IBM Selectric auto-justifying typewriter, is probably from the 1970s—prior to widespread use of PCs and laser or ink jet printers.[55] The text closely resembles Hawtin's, although Britton likely also had access to the earlier *Golden Grain* version as one of Hawtin's changes is reverted back to the previous version. The cover fold, entitled 'a prophecy out of the past' (sic), features a hand drawing of a medieval castle, emphasizing the mysterious historicity of the text. Britton includes no other commentary or much paratext, except the tentatively worded conclusion, 'A prophecy reportedly given in the year of 1619, and said to be found among the papers of Dr. Chas. Price'.[56] Britton's treatment produces a text that is vaguely historical, and which may (or may not) have passed through the hands of the famous evangelist.

In contrast, Royal Cronquist, another second generation Latter Rain leader who came out of a branch closely associated with Manifest Sons of God teachings,[57] was anything but tentative in his version of the Charles Price source legend: 'The following prophetic word came by the Spirit anonymously, in the year 1619. It was found in Charles S. Price's papers after his death'.[58] He stated that he took 'the liberty to insert the scriptures, wherever necessary, to validate the two-three witness principal',[59] but the text itself is so heavily edited that it is almost a paraphrase of any earlier printed edition. Cronquist's three editions of the text even diverge greatly from each other, in contrast to Mary's City of David's edition which remained static after the group first committed it to print.[60] Cronquist's three versions of the story, all last edited in the 1990s before his death have some inconsistencies; in the two referring to the 'Anonymous 1619 Prophecy' he claimed to have been 'in Christ' for 35 years but had been studying the text for 25.[61] In the fourth edition of *Epistles of the Kingdom Unto Royal by the Holy Spirit*, perhaps Cronquist's best known text, he called it the '1679 Prophecy' written by 'Scribe-Prophetess' Jane Lead(e)[62]; this corresponds with the advent of the Internet in the mid-to late-1990s when some Latter Rain ministers including Larry Hodges and J. Preston Eby had discovered Lead's connection to the text and 'corrected' the date to 1679, matching the typographical error in the 1816 *Wars of David* edition.[63]

However, this should not necessarily be read as lack of fidelity to the printed text, as it might be viewed from a Mary's City of David perspective demanding a single, 'authentic' printed text, but as Cronquist's greater concern with seeking new, dynamic and deeper understandings of what he described as the 'rhema' or spirit word embedded within subsequent readings of 'Sixty Propositions'.[64] This results in new or different printed words as well as multiple coexisting editions of a single text. He even added dated 'update[s]' to 'Sixty Propositions' from the 'spirit of the Lord', decades after he claimed he first encountered it, emphasizing Latter Rain and Manifest Sons of God tenets he found implicit in the text, and presented similar in format to Lead's printed journal entries:

> Presently, this day of December 29, 1992, there ARE NOT ENOUGH CORRECTLY dedicated and committed, PROPERLY motivated and contending earnestly saints, PRESSING for perfection, believers, in the earth ... who I can QUALIFY for being My Bride-Overcoming-Brethren-Sons ...

> Therefore, in order to fill up the ranks of My Bride-Firstfruits number ..., at the soon coming fullness of the Feast of Trumpets ..., I will have to take out of My Cloud of Witnesses those spirits of just men made perfect ..., causing them to descend ... and receive their glorified bodies, whereby I can complete My Bride-Sons number.[65]

In contrast to Mary's City of David, where the text was edited once, remained stable, and was still recognizable from the original, here we only see echoes of 'Sixty Propositions', reflecting a parallel but male-gendered theology when compared to that of both the Philadelphian Society and of Mary's City of David. The Bride or 'Universal Body of Christ' of Cronquist's text is comprised of sons, and the 'I', the 'Spirit of the Lord Jesus' is also unequivocally male. Even the Wisdom as mind of God in Hawtin's text has disappeared entirely. The text has been transformed through Cronquist's theological lens into a completely new text.

Later Latter Rain ministers, notably Larry and Betty Hodges,[66] attempted to learn something more about Jane Lead as the source of the prophecy, and even acquired some of her other works, although not nearly to the same extent as the Mary's City of David in which 'Sixty Propositions' was just the first of many texts the leadership systematically acquired over several decades in an effort to read more of Lead's prophetic *print* voice.

However, among the earlier Latter Rain leaders who reproduced 'Sixty Propositions', Hawtin, Britton and especially Cronquist, there seemed to be little or no interest in doing more than gleaning and disseminating every bit of insight they could out of this one work, and in adding (or detracting) whatever 'rhema' word they or their readers received through personal meditation, study and reflection. In their hands, 'Sixty Propositions' was not a fixed text by an inspired prophetic author, but an anonymous voice to which they could add their own voices proclaiming the second advent of Christ within a united body of 'Bride-Overcoming-Brethren-Sons'. To a movement which was ostracized yet influential, marginalized yet mainstreamed, the anonymous voice in these three ministers' versions of 'Sixty Propositions' was prophetic agreement 'out of the past'.

NOTES

1. C.E. Adkin, *Brother Benjamin: A History of the Israelite House of David* (Berrien Springs, MI: Andrews University Press, 1990), p. 11.
2. Michael Mills was accused of similar behavior near the turn of the twentieth century and was in jail at the time his group published 'Sixty Propositions'. The Purnells eventually split from the Mills group, founding the 'Israelite House of David' in Benton Harbor in 1903. An examination of the notes and correspondence A.E. Hinds kept for dozens of other American communal groups during this same time period (held in Syracuse University's Oneida Community collection) reveals that many other groups were beset by lawsuits: an indication that these were far from isolated cases and may have been due as much if not more to anti-'cult' suspicions (and the corresponding belief that colonies had fraudulently amassed huge fortunes) during the late nineteenth and early twentieth centuries as it was to any actual or perceived behavior on the part of communal group leaders.
3. Fead quoted in Adkin, *Brother Benjamin*, p. 192.
4. I viewed a reproduction at Mary's City of David, Benton Harbor, MI, in July 2012. The original clipping was donated with other group archives to Mary's City of David collection at Hamilton College, Clinton, New York, which I also visited in July 2012 as part of a Mellon Foundation-funded Central New York Humanities Corridor Visiting Scholar grant.
5. The two surviving colony members (2012) also called it the 'green book', alluding to its grayish green cover. Physically it is little more than a pamphlet.
6. R. Riss, *Latter Rain: The Latter Rain Movement of 1948 and the Mid-Twentieth Century Evangelical Awakening* (Mississauga, ONT: Honeycomb

Visual Productions, 1987), p. 82. Riss's monograph, which was originally his master's thesis, while strongly biased toward the Latter Rain, remains the most complete history of the movement's origins and development to date.

7. J. Watt, 'Regina Highlights' Two are Better than One (2007), http://2rbetter.org (home page), date accessed 20 August 2012. James Watt's early split from the Latter Rain movement mirrors the tension between this movement and the Pentecostal denominations from which it evolved. While twentieth-century Pentecostals placed great value on the 'works of the Spirit' including speaking in tongues, prophetic utterances and healing, theologically these experiences were submitted to and tested against Biblical scripture, even if in practice they often appeared to be on equal if not greater footing. Latter Rain theology explicitly admits these experiences as co-equal to the printed Bible just as the Holy Spirit is considered one with the Trinitarian Godhead. New prophetic 'rhema' utterances are viewed as coming directly from God and therefore are consistent with and carry the same weight as printed Scripture.

8. E.P. Thompson, *Witness Against the Beast: William Blake and the Moral Law* (New York: The New Press, 1993), p. 43.

9. J. Lead, *Early Dawn of the Great Prophetical Visitation to England: Being Extracts from the Works of Jane Lead, Prophetess, 1623–1704* (Bedford: Panacea Society, 1922), p. xv.

10. J. Lead, *Divine Revelations and Prophecies* (Nottingham: H. Wild, 1830).

11. R. Fox, *The Mystery of God in Woman as Revealed in the 16th Century to Guillaume Postel and Consequently to Others* (Bedford: T. Swann, 1920), p. 23.

12. Chapter 11 in this volume discusses the nineteenth-century Southcottian prophet, John 'Zion' Ward, and his edition of *Divine Revelations and Prophecies* in more detail. While this edition of Lead's works circulated among other religious groups, notably among mid-nineteenth-century American Shaker women who copied it into their commonplace books, it did not appear to play a significant role in Lead's print circulation among later Southcottians, including the Jezreelites and the Israelite House of David/Mary's City of David. These late-nineteenth- and early-twentieth-century Southcottian groups had the more broadly circulated turn of the century John Thomson cyclostyle prints of Lead's works discussed below, not the 1830 'Zion' Ward volume.

13. A handwritten manuscript of this text survives in the Medway Local History Centre, Strood, Kent. Other than the paragraphed format and minor editorial changes discussed later in this chapter, this text matches the 1949 *Golden Grain* version almost exactly, and is almost certainly an earlier version of both the Mills and Pentecostal renditions.

14. William Forsyth in J. Lead, *Ascent to the Mount of Vision by J. Lead, 1699* (London: Littleborough, 1906), p. 3.
15. According to WorldCat, at least 33 extant volumes of the Thomson cyclostyle reprints are indexed and held in libraries across North America and Great Britain. More may survive in additional private and non-indexed collections. For example, during my visit to the Mary's City of David in July, 2012, I viewed a non-indexed photocopy that colony trustee Ron Taylor acquired from the Hutterite Studies Center in Canada for the colony's use. Cyclostyle stencil reproduction developed by the Gestetner Corporation was an early precursor of modern duplication methods and was marketed toward small businesses, law firms, churches and organizations as a cheap printing alternative occupying the space between conventional moveable type and hand copying. It was rarely used for commercial mass market printing as Thomson did with the Lead reprint series. While Lewis Carroll's (Charles Dodson's) cyclostyle copies of his correspondence have received more scholarly attention, the Lead cyclostyle series deserves study in its own right as an important chapter in mass print history. Further examination of the Thomson cyclostyles will be included in a book-length study I am now writing on Jane Lead's presence and circulation in eighteenth–twentieth-century English-speaking print cultures. For more history and background on cyclostyle print, see D. Gardey, *Ecrire, calculer, classer: comment une révolution de papier a transformé les sociétés contemporaines (1800–1940)* (Paris: Découverte, 2008); and Gestetner Corporation, *Cyclostyle: The Story of a Little Wheel that Started a Big Revolution* (London: Curwen Press, 1963).
16. William Forsyth in J. Lead, *Ascent to the Mount of Vision* (1906), p. 3.
17. J. Lead, *Early Dawn of the Great Prophetical Visitation to England* (1922). Specific page references in the extracts from Lead's writings (pp. 1–64) are all from the corresponding Thomson cyclostyle editions.
18. Rachel Fox in J. Lead, *Early Dawn of the Great Prophetical Visitation to England* (1922), p. x.
19. A. Lee, *Extracts from the Sacred Roll of Ann Lee's Visitation 1736 to 1784* (Bedford: Swann & Ibbott, 1922), p. i.
20. R. Fox, *The Mystery of God in Woman* (1920).
21. M. Barltrop, *Healing for All: The Story of the Greatest Discovery of any Age* (London: The Panacea Society, 1924); and R. Fox, *How we Built Jerusalem in England's Green and Pleasant Land* (London: Cecil Palmer, 1931).
22. R. Fox, *The Mystery of God in Woman* (1920), p. 22.
23. See Adkin, *Brother Benjamin*, p. 15 for the importance of print to both the Israelite House of David and Mary's City of David, in contrast to Michael Mills who did not leave a significant print legacy. Similar to James Jershom Jezreel, Joanna Southcott, and of course the Purnells themselves, Lead's

voluminous print record is viewed by Mary's City of David as a primary
sign of her prophetic importance in the latter day 'visitation'.
24. R.J. Taylor, Interview with the author, Mary's City of David (Benton
Harbor, MI), 9 July 2012.
25. Adkin, *Brother Benjamin*, p. 13.
26. Research for this section was conducted at the Mary's City of David
collection at Burke Library Special Collections, Hamilton College, Clinton,
New York in July, 2012. It was funded by the Central New York Humanities
Corridor Visiting Scholar grant noted above. All related citations and
references are to archival materials in this collection.
27. J. Lead, *Ascent to the Mount of Vision* (Benton Harbor, MI: Israelite House
of David as Reorganized by Mary Purnell, 1932).
28. Purnell, quoted in Lead, *Ascent*, p. 55.
29. ibid., p. 56.
30. Cross-references in this section are between the 'original' 'Certain
Propositions Extracted out of a Book Entitled, A Message to the
Philadelphian Society, Whithersoever Dispersed Over the Whole Earth',
Theosophical Transactions 2 (1697), pp. 85–90, and the version of 'Sixty
Propositions' found in the 1932 Mary's City of David *Ascent to the Mount
of Vision* pamphlet and more readily accessible to scholars in R.S. Fogarty,
The Righteous Remnant: The House of David (Kent, OH: Kent State UP,
1981), pp. 147–52.
31. During Mary's lifetime, the group acquired the following works: 'Sixty
Propositions', *Mount to the Ascent of Vision, Wonders of God's Creation,
Revelation of Revelations* (1683), *Tree of Faith*, the first volume *of Fountain
of Gardens, Laws of Paradise, Three Messages to the Philadelphian Society,
Enochian Walks with God, Heavenly Cloud Now Breaking, Wars of David*,
and *Signs of the Times*. Mary directly quoted or closely paraphrased all these
works in her own published work, usually unattributed to Lead, from the
mid 1930s until her death in 1952, but especially through the early to mid
1940s.
32. During my visits to the Mary's City of David colony and to Burke Library's
Special Collections at Hamilton College, I was able to locate typescript
copies of all the titles listed above with the exception of *Revelation of
Revelations* and *Mount to the Ascent of Vision*. Since *Mount to the Ascent of
Vision* was readily available in pamphlet form there was likely no need to
additionally keep a typed version for internal use. The 1804 edition of
Revelation of Revelations was probably Mary's personal copy as it featured
marginalia in her own hand alone.
33. D.E. Harrell, *All Things are Possible: The Healing and Charismatic Revivals
in Modern America* (Bloomington, IN: Indiana UP, 1975), p. 56.
34. ibid., p. 4.

35. Anonymous, 'Theological Gleanings from an Unknown Pen of the Seventeenth Century', *Golden Grain* 24:5 (August 1949), pp. 13–17. *The Golden Grain Collection* [CD-ROM] (Baltimore, MD: John Carver Ministries, 2012).

36. See C.D. Weaver, *The Healer-Prophet: William Marrion Branham, A Study of the Prophetic in American Pentecostalism* (Macon, GA: Mercer UP, 2000), p. 44. Latter Rain elder James Watt stated that Price's and Wigglesworth's prophecies specifically referred to the Latter Rain revival as well. See J. Watt, 'Two Concepts of Presbytery—A Historical Analysis, Two are Better than One' (2002), http://2rbetter.org (home page), date accessed 20 August 2012.

37. L. Fox, 'The Gathering Storm', *Golden Grain* 24:5 (August 1949), p. 5.

38. 'Theological Gleanings', p. 13.

39. ibid., p. 13.

40. ibid., p. 13.

41. R. Riss, *Twentieth Century Revival Movements* (1997), pp. 117–18; Riss, *Latter Rain*, pp. 89–93.

42. A handwritten MSS of this text survives in the Jezreelite collection at the Medway Local History Centre, Strood, Kent. Other than the paragraphed format and minor editorial changes discussed here, this MSS matches the 1949 *Golden Grain* version almost exactly, and is almost certainly an earlier version of both the Mills and Pentecostal renditions.

43. George Hawtin was one of the original Latter Rain elders in the North Battleford revival. Bill Britton was an early participant, while Royal Cronquist was a second generation leader coming out of a descendent movement. See, John Robert Stevens's 'The Walk'; Riss, *Latter Rain*, pp. 60–63, 140–43.

44. Riss, *Latter Rain*, pp. 53–97.

45. Riss, *Latter Rain*, p. 144; Riss, *Revival Movements*, pp. 122–23; Harrell, *All Things are Possible*, p. 113.

46. Unfortunately, Hawtin did not indicate which original *The Page* articles his *Treasures of Truth* booklets were based upon, so the only way to determine if and when 'Sixty Propositions' might have appeared in *The Page* would be to visit the Holy Spirit Research Center at Oral Roberts University (the only publicly accessible research library with a complete collection of all its issues).

47. R.D. Cronquist, *Establishing Faith and Unity in the Holy Spirit* (Greenacres, WA: Royal D. Cronquist, 1995), p. 5.

48. J.P. Eby, personal communication (April 2012).

49. G. Hawtin, *Here is the Mind that Hath Wisdom* (North Battleford, Saskatchewan: Geo. R. Hawtin, 1980), pp. 103–06.

50. ibid., p. 103.

51. ibid., p. 103.
52. ibid., p. 104.
53. ibid., p. 106, my emphasis.
54. ibid., p. 106.
55. B. Britton, *A Prophecy out of the Past: A Prophecy Given in 1619* (Springfield, MO: Bill Britton, 197?). The only extant library indexed edition of this tract is held by the Flower Pentecostal Heritage Center, Springfield, MO (www.ifphc.org).
56. Britton, *Prophecy*, p. 5.
57. Cronquist was an 'apostle' in John Robert Stevens' 'The Walk', a California Latter Rain church often labeled a 'cult' which promoted a radical form of Manifest Sons of God (MSOG) theology even when compared to most other Latter Rain adherents. While Cronquist eventually left 'The Walk', he continued to promote MSOG theology until his death in the late 1990s. See Riss, *Latter Rain*, p. 144.
58. R.D. Cronquist, *Establishing Faith and Unity in the Holy Spirit* (1995), p. 31.
59. ibid., p. 31.
60. The three versions of how Cronquist first encountered 'Sixty Propositions' are in *The Human Spirit* (Greenacres, WA: Royal D. Cronquist, 1990); *Establishing Faith and Unity in the Holy Spirit* (1995); *The Epistles of the Kingdom unto Royal by the Holy Spirit* (4th edn. Greenacres, WA: Royal D. Cronquist, 1997).
61. Cronquist, *Establishing Faith and Unity*, p. 32; R.D. Cronquist, *The Human Spirit* (1990), p. 9.
62. R.D. Cronquist, *The Epistles of the Kingdom unto Royal* (1997), pp. 59–60.
63. J. Lead, *The Wars of David, and the Peaceable Reign of Solomon* (London: Thomas Wood, 1816), p. 54. The typographical error was hand corrected in the copy held by Harvard University (available through Google Books), but other copies, including the one held in the Folger Shakespeare Library (Washington, DC), kept the error intact.
64. Cronquist, *Epistles of the Kingdom*, p. 40.
65. ibid., p. 41.
66. See 'The Shofar Letters' at http://www.sigler.org/shofar/. While the late Larry Hodges posted several Jane Lead tracts online starting in the late 1990s, they were (and continue to be) available in booklet form as well upon request.

GENERAL INDEX

Thomas à Kempis, 62
Thomson, John, 244, 261 n. 16,
  271–72
Thomson, Maurice, 21
Thorpe, Francis, 276
Tichborne, Robert the elder, 19
Tichborne, Robert regicide, 19, 21, 29
Toleration Act (1689), 20, 76, 103
Topham, Ann, 224
Totney, Thomas ['TheaurauJohn
  Tany'], 53
Trench, Edmund, 18
Turner, George, 270
Turner, Mary, 224

U
Überfeld, Johann Wilhelm, 191, 200,
  204, 208 n. 19
Universalists, 2, 4, 5, 7, 20, 40, 53,
  56–57, 62, 75, 94, 95, 97, 99,
  100, 189, 190, 193, 194, 196,
  197, 202, 203, 205, 229, 245

V
Vechtmann, George, 210 n. 69
Vere, Mary, 29

W
Wagstaff, George, 2
Waldensians, 78, 141 n. 97
Walthoe, Anne, 230
Walton, Christopher, 3
Walton, Mr [husband of Barbary
  Lead], 48
Walton, Valentine, 25
Waple, Edward, 77, 78
War of Spanish Succession
  (1701–1714), 216
Ward, Ann, 28, 30 n. 8

Ward, Charles, 15, 28
Ward, Edward, 15, 21, 28
Ward [neé Tichborne], Elizabeth, 19, 29
Ward, Francis, 28, 30 n. 8
Ward, Hamond the elder, 15–17, 22,
  23, 28
Ward, Hamond the younger, 15,
  18–19, 21, 23, 27–28, 36–37 n.
  116, 53
Ward, James the elder, 15, 22, 28–29, 48
Ward, James the younger, 28–29
Ward, John [rector of St Michael-at-
  Plea, Norwich], 18
Ward, John [son of Hamond the
  elder], 15, 28
Ward, John ['Zion Ward'], 3, 8,
  249–53, 255, 257, 258, 271, 285
  n. 12
Ward [neé Calthorpe], Mary, 15, 28
Ward, Philip, 15, 21, 28
Ward, Richard (d.1579?), 15
Ward, Richard (b.1610), 15, 28
Ward [neé Skottow], Sarah, 18, 28
Ward, William, 15, 28
Wardley, Jane, 6, 107
Watt, James, 269, 285 n. 7, 288 n. 36
Weigel, Valentin, 146
Weinich, Mr ['Tychius'], 80
Wells, Mrs, 52, 219, 234
Wentworth, Anne, 47–48
Wetstein, Hendrick, 55
Whalley, Edward, 50
Whiston, William, 230
White, James Rowland ['James
  Jershom Jezreel'], 8, 255,
  257–59, 266 n. 96, 267, 268,
  270–74, 278–79
White, Jeremiah, 2, 229
Whitrow, Abraham, 219, 222, 225,
  226, 228, 234
Wigglesworth, Smith, 278
Wild, H., 251

INDEX OF PLACES

© The Editor(s) (if applicable) and The Author(s) 2016
A. Hessayon (ed.), *Jane Lead and her Transnational Legacy*,
DOI 10.1057/978-1-137-39614-3

Made in the USA
Monee, IL
26 July 2021